CLARENCE B. CARSON

Dr. Carson is a native of Alabama. A graduate of Auburn University, he holds the Ph.D. from Vanderbilt University. His field of specialization is American social and intellectual history. He has received two George Washington Honor Medals from Freedom Foundation, and is a lecturer of note on socialist and reformist ideas in America. He is the author of *The Fateful Turn* (1963), *The American Tradition* (1964), *The War on the Poor* (1969), and a frequent contributor to *The Freeman*. His articles also have appeared in *Modern Age*, the *Texas Quarterly*, the *Colorado Quarterly*, and *Spiritual Life*. He is currently Professor of American History at Grove City College in Pennsylvania.

THE FLIGHT FROM
REALITY

OTHER BOOKS BY CLARENCE B. CARSON

The Fateful Turn

The American Tradition

The War on the Poor

THE FLIGHT
FROM REALITY

by

CLARENCE B. CARSON
Professor of American History
Grove City College, Pennsylvania

The Foundation for Economic Education, Inc.
Irvington-on-Hudson, New York   1969

The Publisher

THE FOUNDATION FOR ECONOMIC EDUCATION is an educational champion of private ownership, the free market, the profit and loss system, and limited government. It is nonprofit and nonpolitical. Sample copies of the Foundation's monthly journal, *The Freeman,* as well as a list of books and other publications, are available on request.

Standard Book Number 910614-18-0
Published September, 1969
PRINTED IN THE UNITED STATES OF AMERICA

To
Evelyn

Contents

Preface

OVER THE YEARS, I HAVE HAD OCCASION FROM TIME TO time to talk with individuals and groups about what we may well call "the liberal mind." One reaction that has been given voice often goes something like this: "How could anyone believe in that way? How could they come to think like that?" This work is an attempt to answer these questions, as well as an effort to follow the almost infinite vacillations of "the liberal mind."

It is an inward history of the last hundred years or so, a history of the emergence, development, and coming to fruition of an outlook which may be called "liberalism," reformism, meliorism, or just gradualist socialism. It is, I say, an inward history, not a history of events as we usually encounter them. There are some references to outward events—first and last, a good many of them—, but it is a different order of events, as it were, that occupies the center of the stage. Events of the mind—the attractive setting forth of an idea, the conjunction of two ideas, the formulation of a complex of ideas into an ideology, the mythologizing upon the basis of ideology—have their own occurrence and history. In short, it is the story of how men have come under the sway of that corpus of ideas which has bent them toward efforts to make over America in the image of an ideology. It is the inward account of how diverse ideas from various sources came subtly to be combined, propagated, and generally to be accepted. It is the inward story of that curious subspecies of modern man, the reformist intellectual, and his rise to power and affluence.

That this work has a thesis is obvious from the title. The thesis is that reformist intellectuals have departed from reality at every stage of their movement toward social engineering and social reconstruction, that they were led to believe that such reconstruction was possible because thought was cut loose from its grounding in an underlying reality, because cause and effect were sundered for them, because they turned their eyes from enduring reality to focus upon the transient and changing. In such a frame of mind, they became entranced by utopian visions of a new earth, began to think of themselves as creators, and attempted to make a new reality. By the early twentieth century, they began to draw Americans more generally into the vortex of their conception, and before very long political programs were being introduced in accord with it. The flight from reality has produced the twentieth century government intervention on a vast scale. It is an inward history, but much of ordinary history has been greatly affected by it.

It is my thesis, also, that the current disorders in the United States, the impotence of government to maintain basic law and order, the confusions in foreign policy, and the erosion of values can be attributed to this flight. There must be a fundamental return to reality before order and peace can be restored on any long-term basis.

In a sense, this work is intended as an antidote. Serums are made to counteract deadly poison from that very poison. So, this work recounts the very ideas that have brought us to our present pass. Only so, I suspect, can many of us be purged of these ideas, for they run deep, and most of us have in one way or another, quite often unawares, become infected by them. By bringing them to light, I have hoped to innoculate against them. The medicine is strong, but the infection is deep seated.

The writing of the bulk of this work took place from 1964 through most of 1966. It appeared serially in *The Freeman* during the same period. It has been updated since by the adding of the chapter called "The Return to Reality," most of which has not appeared elsewhere than in this volume.

I would like to thank all who assisted in one way or another in the preparation of the book. In general, I am indebted to those who took the time to write in and offer encouragement and suggestions when it was appearing serially in *The Freeman*. More especially, I am obligated to David C. George and John A. Sparks for their assistance in doing research.

As always, the staff of the Foundation for Economic Education did their work competently and quietly to make smooth the way of troublesome writers. Dr. Paul L. Poirot has overseen the work from its inception as a series of articles to its appearance in book form, has edited it, encouraged its writing, and never lost faith in its possibilities. His decisiveness, promptness, and intelligent restraint makes him editor without peer. Thanks are due, too, to Mrs. Eleanor Orsini for aid in correcting proofs and to Miss Vernelia Crawford for preparing the index. All this was made possible by the founder of the organization, Leonard E. Read, whose integrity and devotion to freedom gives to it its particular character.

My greatest debt is to my wife, Myrtice Sears Carson, who has diligently applied herself to creating peaceful surroundings for my work, has read copy and corrected errors, and has the sound sense of a good wife not to adversely criticize my work.

Finally, this work is dedicated to Evelyn Clare Carson who was born during the time it was being written, but for whose cries it might have been finished sooner, but without whom the doing of it would have been less meaningful.

CLARENCE B. CARSON
Grove City, Pennsylvania
January 1969

BOOK ONE:
The New Reality

1

The Mind of the Reformer

He regarded the world as a flux to be formed by his own mind. —R. R. PALMER

The supreme architect, who begins as a visionary, becomes a fanatic, and ends as a despot. —WALTER LIPPMANN

TWO DEVELOPMENTS STAND OUT ON THE CANVAS OF THE world scene in the twentieth century. Viewers may differ as to whether these two dominate the picture or not, but there should be no denying that they are there. The first is the tremendous surge of reform effort that has been going on in the world for most of this century and that is by now so pervasive that it could be called universal. In the United States hardly a day passes that some reform is not proposed, advanced, revived, or instigated. Speakers scurry about over the country describing the problems and offering the solutions. Newspaper columnists echo the sentiments of speakers or provide them, as the case may be. One day attention may be focused upon the need for reform of the bail system. On another, the system of trial by jury may be up for examination, and proposals may be forthcoming for discarding it. Or again, decaying centers of metropolitan areas may furnish the background for some proposal to use government to renew them.

Nor is the United States alone in being the scene of a prevalent reform bent. Many other countries share the

3

bent with Americans but greatly exceed them in their willingness to radically alter existing institutions to accomplish the reforms. Thus, in predominantly agricultural lands proposals for redistributing the land are favorite remedies for what ails the population. This panacea often has to share the spotlight, however, with plans for rapid industrialization. These economic measures are usually only the most well known of the reforms being undertaken, depending upon the country and what its particular "problems" happen to be. Some countries may be occupied with "crash" programs of school building, others with placating dissident racial or religious groups, others with providing various welfare programs, and so on.

This reform bent is not restrained, however, by national boundaries nor restricted to sovereign states. It has promoted the establishment of institutions in international organizations. For example, the United Nations has associated with it an International Labor Organization, a Food and Agriculture Organization, a World Health Organization, and others. There have been gatherings for regional planning, such as those that were promoted by the Marshall Plan. There is the more general phenomenon of foreign aid, and there are international loan agencies to finance reform programs. Conceiving the matter most broadly, the drive to make over men and societies is in the ascendant today.

The Corrosives of Civilization

The second development cannot be so readily reduced to a phrase for purposes of description. Actually, this development has many faces. One of them, perhaps the most prominent, is disorder. There has been mounting disorder in the world in the twentieth century: disorder in the relations among nations which evinces itself in almost continuous tensions and erupts in sporadic catastrophic violence, disorder in relations among groups which manifests itself in violence between and among groups, disorder in families indicated by broken homes and juvenile delinquency, and disorder of personality manifested in widespread mental illness.

Another face of this development is violence. The volume in the *New Cambridge Modern History* which deals with the twentieth century is called "The Era of Violence." The textbook on the Western world in the twentieth century by Frank P. Chambers has the interesting title, *This Age of Conflict.* Who has paused to consider how many kinds of violence have begun to assume regular forms and have even been institutionalized in this century? A few examples of institutionalized violence may refresh our memories. There are industrial strikes, concentration camps, purges, "nationalization" of property; and even street fights among juveniles have assumed the semiform of "rumbles."

Yet another face of this development is the decline of liberty and the removal of protections from around the individual. In some countries this has occurred rapidly as in communist and fascist revolutions. In others, such as the United States, it has occurred by a process of attrition. The loss of liberty may occur in such an apparently innocuous manner as the zoning of city properties, or it may assume the most drastic proportions of being held in jail without a hearing.

The point, however, is that the circumscription of liberty is a virtually universal phenomena in this century, though there have been some movements to and fro in this matter. Certainly, the one new kind of government to emerge in this century has been totalitarianism. The tendency of governments everywhere has been to adopt some of the

features of totalitarianism, though the exigencies of war
may be the occasion for such adoption.

The composite face this second development wears is the
disintegration of civilization. For what is civilization but
order, peace, settled and regularized relations among men
and groups, and conditions of liberty among individuals?
Disorder, violence, and aggression are the antithesis of
civilization. To the extent that they become pervasive, civilization disintegrates in equal degree. In short, the corro-
sives of civilization have become dominant in many places
on the earth and threaten to become pervasive everywhere.

The pressing question for all of us, of course, is why this
turn of events occurred. Why have there been total wars,
concentration camps, confiscations of property, circum-
scriptions of liberty, institutionalizations of violence in this
century? So far as we know, there were few who expected
any such turn at the outset of the century. The literary
evidence suggests the contrary, for it contains visions of
peace, prosperity, and triumphant civilization in the twentieth century. And those who would be leaders have continued to hold out such visions up to the present, even as
violence mounted and wars became total. Indeed, the
glowing pictures of the future which reformers still paint
have hardly been tarnished by this untoward course of
events.

Yet, it will be my contention that there is and has been
a direct connection between the first and second developments described above. That is, reforms have resulted in
disorder, violence, and the diminution of liberty. To put
it briefly, the attempts to make over society and man have
been made by the undermining of beliefs, the destruction
of institutions, the uprooting of traditions, and the aggressive use of governmental power.

The framework of order and liberty has everywhere been

greatly shaken by this course of events and in many places utterly shattered. A semblance of order has usually been maintained or restored in most places, but it has quite often been at the expense of liberty. To state it another way, the disorder resulting from the undermining of traditional morality and the unraveling of the bonds of social unity has been quelled by governmental power. The result has been the police state which has emerged everywhere in varying degrees in the twentieth century.

The Bent to Reform

Since it will be a part of the burden of the remainder of this work to show the connection between reforms and the disorder of these times, the matter can be left at this point with the assertion that the connection exists. The question can now be stated more directly. Why have men been bent upon reforms and used methods to achieve them which have resulted in varying degrees of disorder and tyranny? Why are men bent upon reforming everything in our time?

This would probably appear to be a silly question to anyone who knows no history before this century. Indeed, the bent to reform goes back at least into the nineteenth century, if not before. Ralph Waldo Emerson asked in 1841: "What is a man born for but to be a Reformer . . .?" Indeed, the bent to reform—the urge to change, to make over, to redo—was well established in the outlook of many considerably before this century got underway.

Even so, it should be made clear that this is not a usual attitude for most people. Quite likely, people have ever been inclined to prefer the well-worn path to the uncharted course, the familiar to the new, the customary to the innovative, and the established to the prospect of reform. So deep-seated is this inclination that peoples have often rebelled against radical change and welcomed the restoration of the old order after a radical attempt at change. At most times and in most places in the past, reforms and reformers have gotten short shrift. Innovation has been much too perilous a game for a profession of innovators to be established. In short, for the reform bent to become acceptable to great bodies of people required a reversal of outlook on a huge and probably unprecedented scale. Insofar as reform depended upon popular approval, a great transformation of outlook had to take place.

The prime movers both of reform and of the changed outlook have been those who may be identified as intellectuals. This brings us to a third development of the nineteenth and twentieth centuries: the vast proportional increase in the number of intellectuals. They could not actually be counted, for the question of who is an intellectual has to be answered by definitions; opinions will differ, and the application of the most precise definition would be exceedingly difficult.

Nonetheless, there should be no doubt that the number and sway of intellectuals has greatly increased, probably in some direct proportion to the triumph of the reformist orientation. They teach school, profess at universities, write speeches, provide the material for the mass media of communication, advise businessmen and politicians, and so pervade societies today. Government leaders are quite often accredited intellectuals, or so one may judge by the number of them (particularly in Latin countries) who effect the title of "Doctor."

It will be my contention, then, that the reorientation of populaces in the direction of continuous reform has been the work of intellectuals. And, it may be incidentally noted at this point, the proposal and fostering of reform quite often provides intellectuals with their work.

It is in order at this point to make some distinctions which will help to focus attention upon the valid historical connections among the above developments. There are reforms and reforms, reformers and reformers, intellectuals and intellectuals. Not all reforms promote disorder; not all reformers have been instrumental in instituting tyranny; not all intellectuals have contributed to the circumscription of liberty. The species involved must be distinguished from the genus.

Four Kinds of Reform

There are at least four levels or kinds of reform. The one that has been most universally appealed to and most generally recognized as beneficial has been *individual reform*. Prophets, preachers, and teachers have ever exhorted their hearers to repent and to reform. They have usually meant that the individual should regroup and integrate the forces within him, that these should be brought to bear upon some worth-while object or end, and that he should act morally and responsibly in the course of his life.

Advocates of this kind of reform differ as to how it may be achieved. Some hold that such inner reform can only be wrought by the Grace of God. Others hold that it can be done by acts of the human will. Idealists usually hold that it is accomplished by focusing upon some worthy ideal. But they all agree that inward reform is possible and desirable. Such reforms and reformers need not detain us for long. They have been with us for as long as there are records, and they have certainly not wrought the contemporary predicament. We need only pause to wish them well, and move on.

The second level may be called *institutional reform*. Such reform is concerned with the changing, creating, or disposing of organizations. Examples of this kind of reform would be the writing and amendment of constitutions, extension or restriction of the suffrage, changes in the modes of the selection of officials, the abolition of trial by jury, the creation of boards and commissions, and so forth.

Since institutions are means to ends, their reform does not necessarily entail movement in any particular direction. Thus, institutions may be reformed so as to create a balance of power in government and enhance liberty. Reform may even give formal recognition to traditional but unestablished institutions. It can be so radical, however, as to disrupt the tenor of political life. And reform can be used to destroy or undermine the institutions which protect liberty and maintain order within society. It all depends upon the methods used and the end that is in view as to the tendency of such reform.

The third kind of reform is much more difficult to name. It should be called *liberal reform,* despite the semantic difficulties involved. Liberal reform is that which removes legal restrictions upon the individual and thus enhances his liberty. There was a great deal of such reform in the eighteenth and nineteenth century in Europe and America. Examples would be the abolition of slavery, the removal of mercantile restrictions upon the economy, the disestablishment of churches, the abolition of primogeniture and entail, and the revocation of class privileges. It was these kinds of reform that gave reform a good name in the nineteenth century and helped to establish the reform bent.

It should be noted, however, that the method of reform is very important even if the end can be universally acclaimed. Thus, the abolition of slavery could be carried out in such a way as to respect the property values involved, or it could be carried out so as to amount to the confiscation of property. The latter was the method used in America; hence, it was accomplished by aggression and accompanied by deep rents in the fabric of society. In general, though, where liberal reform was accomplished by appropriate means it was conducive to order, liberty, and prosperity.

The fourth kind of reform is *ameliorative reform*. This sort of reform involves the use of governmental power to improve people or the conditions of their lives. It is what is ordinarily meant today by social reform, though strictly speaking institutional and liberal reforms are social reforms also. Examples of ameliorative reform can be given that range all the way from a compulsory social security tax to the wholesale confiscation of property. The advocates of such reform are usually called "liberals" in twentieth century America, but they have worn many labels in the world: democratic socialists, social democrats, communists, revolutionary socialists, fascists, and so on.[1]

Method is important, of course, and peoples bearing these names subscribe to a great variety of methods. It is better to have one's purse stolen than to have his life taken. It is better to be put into prison, other things being equal, than to be shot in the back of the neck. It may even be better to have a limited redistribution of wealth accomplished by parliamentary means than to have a dictator proclaim the confiscation of all private property. But all varieties of meliorists appear to share many common objectives in the contemporary world. They want to make over man and society by political means so that they will

---

[1] Technically, Marxist revolutionaries are not reformers. In fact, however, they have not destroyed governmental power, as they were supposed to do, but have seized it. They then use it to effect their ends. That is, they become reformers.

conform to some version they have in mind. Such reforms, when they have been undertaken, have resulted in widespread disorder, suffering, violence, and loss of liberty.

It would take us too far afield from the present inquiry to enter into extensive proofs of the connection between ameliorative reform and the resultant disorder and tyranny. Let us be content, then, with an axiomatic statement of the reasons for the connection. To wit: men live their lives within a framework of customary relations and patterns for achieving their ends and solving their problems. In the absence of positive force, they have worked out and accepted these patterns voluntarily, or they submit to them willingly. Any alteration of these by government involves the use or threat of force, for that is how governments operate. The old order must be replaced by a new order for the reform to be achieved. The result of the forceful effort to do this is disorder.

Theoretically, the new order replaces the old order; in fact, it does not. It is, at best, an uneasy peace maintained by the presence of armies, as it were, for these may be only an augmented police force. Men may adjust to the new *dis*order, resume the course of their lives as best they can, and submit more or less to conditions. In time, they may even forget that the system is maintained by force, or that things could be otherwise. After all, most peoples at most times have lived under varying degrees of oppression. Nonetheless, ameliorative reform introduces violence into life. The force charged with keeping the peace becomes the disturber of the peace. Traditional relationships are disrupted. Liberty is restricted and reduced.

The amount of suffering depends upon the kind and degree of reforms. In communist lands, actual starvation often follows the attempt to make over society. More moderate reforms may only lead to the decline of investment in industry, to the deprivation of those on fixed incomes, to the loss of spontaneity in human relations, to a desultory conformity to the establishment, to the rigidity of conditions, and so on. A considerable literature now exists detailing the consequences of ameliorative reform efforts by governments; anyone not convinced by theoretical proofs should avail himself of it.[2]

Reformist Intellectuals

The blueprints for ameliorative reforms (and revolutions which have eventuated in reform) have been provided by intellectuals. They run the gamut from Saint-Simon to Karl Marx to Eduard Bernstein to Georgy Plekhanov to Karl Kautsky to George Bernard Shaw to Sidney and Beatrice Webb to Eugene Debs to Lester Frank Ward to John Dewey. These, and many others, have made analyses, drawn plans, described utopias, provided visions, and, in short, have supplied the ideological ammunition in the battle for ameliorative reform. There is a sense, then, in which it can be said that intellectuals have caused the reform effort.

Certainly, it would be valid to say that the initiative for such efforts has come from reformist intellectuals under the sway of ideologies. This fact has brought forth from some the conclusion that the attempt to make man and society over results from some inherent trait in *the* intellectual, or that the real villain of the piece is something

---

[2] It is not my contention that all disorder and suffering are caused by governmental intervention or that they would disappear if it did. On the contrary, suffering and disorder—both individual and social—have always existed for human beings and, so far as I know, will continue to do so. My concern is with that portion of suffering and disorder *caused* by planning and executed by collective endeavor.

that may be called *intellectualism*. Undoubtedly, "intellectual" can be defined so as to refer only to those who want to make the world over, and "intellectualism" can be defined as the inherent outlook which promotes such reformism.

This is a dubious use of language. It does not conform to contemporary conventional usage nor does it take into account the etymology of the words. In the current parlance, an intellectual is one who works mainly with ideas. The *American College Dictionary* defines "intellectual" as "appealing to or engaging the intellect . . . , of or pertaining to the intellect . . . , directed or inclined toward things that involve the intellect . . . , possessing or showing intellect or mental capacity, esp. to a high degree. . . ."

Such definitions apply equally as well to those who oppose reform as to those who favor and advance it. It may be that those who work with ideas are more likely to make mistakes in the realm of ideas than those who do not, in something of the same way that those who construct tall buildings are more apt to die from falling than those who stay on the ground. At the same time, those who are at home in the realm of ideas should be least likely to use them wrongly. If that is not the case, the matter requires explanation, not definition.

The question can now be framed which will bring us to the heart of the inquiry. Why have so many modern intellectuals been devoted to ameliorative reform and/or revolution? Why have they (and do they) promote reforms which, when put into effect, result in disorder, violence, and oppression? Is it because they love disorder? Is it because they are violent men by nature? Is it because they despise liberty and long to see oppression introduced? There may be intellectuals of such a character, but most of them certainly are not. Probably, no group of people has ever been so devoted to the ideas of peace, harmony, freedom, and plenty as have modern intellectuals. Their works are replete with references to these words, and contain numerous plans for the realization of the goals that are implicit in them.

There have been explanations from those who perceive that many intellectuals are actually at war with that which they profess to seek. One of these stems from the conspiracy theory of history. According to some versions of this view, intellectuals are "dupes" of the conspirators, notably those in the communist conspiracy, or else they are part of the conspiracy. This view is given a certain plausibility by the existence of a communist conspiracy, and by the attraction which communism has had for intellectuals over the years.

But it must be noted that communism was an idea before any conspiracy existed, that it, too, was a product of intellectuals. Moreover, there have been and are many anticommunist intellectuals who are wedded to melioristic reform. Most reformist ideas have been openly advocated or presented, quite often long before any conspiracy existed. Conspiracies have to do largely with the destruction or seizure of governmental power, though this is sometimes advanced by ideological subversion, which may also be covert. It should be noted, too, that some intellectuals have been taken in, or so they claim, by "front" organizations.

But after everything has been said for this theory, there are too many facts, and too many intellectuals, which it does not account for. Why, for instance, are intellectuals so readily attracted to communism? Since they are supposedly adept at ideas, they ought to be the first to perceive errors in them. Instead, intellectuals are the one group in a country from which the largest contingent sympathetic to communism can be drawn. This must mean that many intellectuals are already committed to the idea of reconstructing the world before they accept any particular ideology, or, to put it another way, that they are prone to ideologies which contain plans for remaking the world. Conspiracies are not causes of ideas, but effects; they may be used to promote particular causes, but they are creations, not creators.

There is another explanation, not quite a formal theory, for accounting for the reformist predilections of intellectuals. It goes something like this: Intellectuals want power and prestige. Reformism offers opportunities for them to achieve these, for they can draw up the plans and to some extent direct the execution of them. To put it baldly, intellectuals do not care how much destruction they wreak so long as they can achieve their own personal power objectives. To anyone who has known or read the works of many reformist intellectuals, this view should be incredible.

Of course, none of us knows the hidden motives of another, but such a view does not square in many instances with what we do know. The theories of most reformists have not been power theories at all. Earlier reformers quite often envisioned a condition in which all political power had been destroyed, when relations among people were free and spontaneous, when the last vestiges of the exploitation of man by man had been removed from human relationships. This thesis can have only limited application at most.

Gulf Between Vision and Reality

This work will be devoted to making a quite different explanation. My thesis will be that the gross disparity between the visions of the intellectuals and the realities which they help to create and perpetuate has resulted from limitations in their conception of reality. They visualize freedom and create oppression. Assuming their good faith and sincerity, this can only mean that they have misconceived the materials with which they are working. Many intellectuals are indeed deluded, but it is no simple delusion such as is imagined when they are described as "duped." It is a delusion rooted deeply in the contemporary outlook, supported by voluminous research, propagated by a prodigious educational effort, and developed by a steadfast attention to an aspect of reality. It has an extensive history and has been developed by some of the best minds of the last century.

The centerpiece of the delusion is the belief that there are no limits to man's creativity. Reality can be endlessly shaped and reshaped to suit the purposes of men. In effect, man has no fixed nature; the universe contains no unalterable laws. Stated so bluntly, many intellectuals might hedge at subscribing to these premises. Yet these are substantially the premises upon which reformist intellectuals have based many of their programs. They have, as R. R. Palmer said of Napoleon Bonaparte in the prefatory quotation to this chapter, "regarded the world as a flux to be formed by . . . [their] own mind[s].

The flight of the intellectuals from reality has not gone entirely unremarked. In the following quotations, each taken from a different contemporary writer, the phenomenon is recognized, though the intellectuals are characterized by different names by each writer. Thus, Thomas Molnar calls them "progressives," but he is talking about the reformist intellectual:

> . . . It [his description] points to the basic attitude of the progressive, his contempt for the structure of life, its given situations and hard data; and it evokes the im-

patience with which he presses for the social, political, economic, international pattern that his ideology dictates him to favor. . . . The envisaged and blurred picture of what would be the opposite of life's actual imperfect conditions has a great fascination for him, and he is apt to denounce as cynics those who call him back from the nowhere-never land to reality.[3]

Eric Voegelin calls the phenomenon "gnosticism," but he, too, is describing the attitude of the reformist intellectual in the following:

. . . In the Gnostic dream world . . . nonrecognition of reality is the first principle. As a consequence, types of action which in the real world would be considered as morally insane because of the real effect which they have will be considered moral in the dream world because they intended an entirely different effect. The gap between intended and real effect will be imputed not to the Gnostic immorality of ignoring the structure of reality but to the immorality of some other person or society that does not behave as it should behave according to the dream conception of cause and effect.[4]

Calling them "liberals," and getting down to specifics, James Burnham says:

. . . The liberal ideologues proceed in a manner long familiar to both religion and psychology: by constructing a new reality of their own, a transcendental world, where the soul may take refuge from the prosaic, unpleasant world of space and time. In that new and better world, the abandonment of a million of one's own countrymen and the capitulation to a band of ferocious terrorists become transformed into what is called "liber-

[3] Thomas Molnar, *The Decline of the Intellectual* (Cleveland: World Publishing Company, A Meridian Book, 1961), p. 132.

[4] Eric Voegelin, *The New Science of Politics* (Chicago: University of Chicago Press, 1952), pp. 169-70.

ation." . . . A crude imperialist grab in the South Seas or the Indian subcontinent becomes a clearing up of the vestiges of colonialism. The failure to retaliate against gross insults and injuries to envoys, citizens and property becomes a proof of maturity and wisdom.[5]

But this view has to be seen to be believed. It must be set forth in its complexity and depth, with an understanding that the quest for truth is not undertaken in a well-lighted room. It is undertaken by men who see only in part, and to the extent that they concentrate their attention upon the most illusory part, to that same extent they may be drawn farther and farther from the object of their search. None of us is immune from this partiality of sight. Thus, it is necessary that we repair to the concrete realities of history, in humility submitting assertions to the test of fact and reason. We must relive, if only in the imagination of the recreation that is history, the sojourn of the reformist intellectual before we can understand him and the delusion into which he has been ensnared.

The reformist intellectual, then, has been caught up in a flight from reality. What is to follow will be largely an account of that flight, told against a background of the central Western tradition of what constitutes reality. The main attention will be focused upon the thought of the American reformist intellectuals, but this will be recounted alongside European intellectual developments, of which the American forms a part.

---

[5] James Burnham, *Suicide of the West* (New York: John Day, 1964), p. 302.

2

Symptoms of the Flight

ANYONE WHO ANNOUNCED TO AN ACADEMIC AUDIENCE
that he was going to do a work on "The Flight from
Reality" might expect that the first questions he would be
asked would go something like the following: "What is
reality?" Or, "What do *you* mean by reality?" That such
questions would almost certainly be asked may be itself
the leading sign of the flight from reality. The questions
are important, of course, and will require answers, but
for the moment that can be deferred to deal with their
implications.

Indications are that few people in academic circles
would consider it strange that the question of what constitutes reality should be raised. In a contemporary work
on the history of Western philosophy—a book which traces
thought from Thales in ancient Greece to Bertrand Russell
in modern Britain—the scholar concludes with these ob-
servations, among others:

> So far we have tried to suggest that, even though
> they are not eternally true, the answers philosophy gives
> are useful and significant in terms of their cultural con-
> text. Now we must point out that, valuable as philoso-
> phy's answers are, they are not as important as the
> *questions* philosophy asks. In fact, we may say that the
> chief function of philosophy is to *ask questions*, rather
> than to answer them. Its function is to rebuff all forms
> of dogmatism and intolerance, to keep before the mind

a sense of possibilities unrealized. . . . Thus the real utility of philosophy lies precisely in what seems to some its futility. Its especial competence lies in its seeming incompetence—in the way in which it discourages too definitive conclusions and too neat solutions.[1]

In short, it appears that philosophy succeeds to just that extent that it fails to answer the questions that it raises. But lest this state of affairs be supposed to be restricted to philosophy, the writer assures us that the matter is otherwise.

> The "incompetence" of philosophy is . . . not a peculiarity of philosophy. None of the sciences has attained an eternal truth. Consider what relativity has done to Newtonian physics. . . . Or consider what the discovery of the non-Euclidian geometries has done to mathematics.[2]

One might suppose, then, that intellectuals, scholars, and teachers would be found in sackcloth and ashes, repenting their impostures upon society or praying for guidance that they might find some truth. Obviously, such is not the case. They make a virtue of the failure to attain truth and belabor those who would proclaim truth as "intolerant" and "presumptuous."

We might expect, at the least, that the clients and patrons of such education would withdraw their support. On the contrary, as is well known, intellectuals, scholars, and teachers have never before enjoyed such influence and affluence as they do today. Billions of dollars are poured into education; students come forth in ever greater numbers to educational institutions; research receives bounti-

---

[1] W. T. Jones, *A History of Western Philosophy* (New York: Harcourt, Brace, 1952), p. 995. Italics mine.

[2] *Ibid.*, p. 997.

ful support from governments and industries, philanthropists and politicians. The failure to attain truth does not appear to inhibit men from "professing" it and students from purchasing whatever it is they have to teach. If the value lies only, or even predominantly, in the quest, one wonders why so many should choose the academic endeavor. Why not, instead, "quest" for a lower golf score? At least there are standards by which improvements in a golf game can be measured.

There is much more to the story of contemporary education, however, as will become clear later. But on the face of it, such attitudes as the above surely constitute symptoms of a flight from reality, both by professors and patrons.

The matter cuts deeper, too. It is true that the study of philosophy has been in somewhat of a decline for a good many years. This would appear to be a realistic response to the bankruptcy of philosophy, understandable and even commendable. Actually, no such interpretation can be allowed. If philosophy is indeed bankrupt, we cannot *know* whether the giving up of the quest for truth by way of philosophy is *realistic* or not. For we do not know what is *real*. The central problem of philosophy is the determination of what is real. If philosophers have not arrived at truth in this regard, it should be obvious that truth cannot be attested in any other area of thought. The possibility of illusion in all matters would be ever present, and no means for separating the illusory from the real would exist. Reason would be of no use, for reason is only as valid as the premises upon which it rests, and the premises must be referable to some reality.

Nor can the scholar take refuge in methods and quests. The man who claims that he is concerned only with imparting a method may be making an honest statement, but he is evading the central question about his labors. How does he know that his method is of any value? The method can only be of use in arriving at truth if it is related to reality in such a way as to discover truth. The employment of a method or an endless quest for the unattainable may have subjective personal value, of course, just as mountain climbing may have, but this can only concern the individual involved, not the public at large.

That philosophers should blithely announce the futility of their quest, that scholars should ignore the consequent absence of underpinnings in their endeavors, that the public should provide support for research that has not been carefully related to some truth, that students should spend years learning methods which may have no applicability to the achievement of their ends, and that hardly anyone in a vast establishment should bother to mention the matter, should certainly be construed as a symptom of the flight from reality. Indeed, the lack of concern about first things that is involved in the state of philosophical thought comes very close to being the flight from reality itself.

But let us stick with symptoms at this point in the study. There are a great many of these. Only a few can be given, and the ones chosen as examples should demonstrate that the flight is widespread, that the intellectuals have succeeded in drawing much of the populace, or at least policy makers, into the web of their illusion. The next two examples will be drawn from economics.

Monetary Manipulation

One of the most pronounced symptoms of the flight in economics is the handling of monetary matters by governments. Specifically, governments virtually everywhere engage in monetary manipulation. They engage in deficit

spending, public works programs to revive sagging economies, issuance of fiat money by banks under their control,
the establishment of minimum wages, and so on. In order to be able to do this, governments make one of the
simplest flights from reality: they cease to make payments
in specie—that is, gold or silver. Following this, their flights
become much more imaginative and complex.

The justifications for monetary manipulation are numerous and ingenious. Money is identified with "purchasing
power," and apologists propose to increase "purchasing
power" by increasing the amount of money in circulation.
Monetary manipulation is used as a method of spurring investment. Consumer spending is promoted by government
expenditures which will place money in the hands of
consumers.

Such practices, and the justifications offered, are founded upon misunderstandings about the nature of money, if
we assume that the apologies are seriously made. Money
is a *medium* of exchange. It is that *through* which an exchange of goods and services is effected. Transfers of
commodities from one owner to another are made by the
use of money. The "purchasing power" resides in the
commodities, however, not in the money. (Money may, of
course, be a commodity itself, as when some precious
metal is used. In this case, it would have "purchasing
power," which would derive from its commodity value.)
The fact that people will turn over goods and services to
others in return for money creates an illusion that money
has "purchasing power."

Governments, presumably operating under the sway of
this illusion, increase the amount of currency in circulation. By so doing, they do not increase the "purchasing
power" of the citizenry. Instead, they reduce the amount of
goods which will be turned over for a given amount of

money, reduce it in proportion to the amount of the monetary increase. Since what money will purchase depends upon the amount of goods and services available, the only way to increase the "purchasing power" of the citizenry is to increase the amount of those goods and services. If the amount of goods are increased and if the amount of currency remains the same, a given amount of money will, in effect, command more goods.

While an increase in the supply of money does not increase "purchasing power," it does have consequences. By increasing the amount of money in circulation, governments confiscate a portion of the value of the money which anyone happens to hold or have due him at the time of the increase. Governments also can and do redistribute this confiscated wealth by spending programs and by other devices. In short, programs which are advanced as stimulants to the economy are, in effect, programs for the redistribution of the wealth.

It is difficult to determine whether inflationary programs are symptoms of a flight from reality by those who advance them or by the general public which accepts them. The United States government has had economic advisers in influential positions for years. These have consistently advanced inflationary policies. They are either ignorant of the consequences of such actions or they are guilty of making surreptitious proposals for the redistribution of the wealth.

Foreign Aid

Another symptom can also be given from the economic sphere. This one has to do with economic assistance given by the United States to other countries since World War II. As is well known, the United States government has spent huge sums of money on foreign aid. This aid has taken many forms: outright grants, technical assistance, "mutual" assistance, loans, and so forth. The aid has been justified on many grounds: the responsibility for aiding allies in postwar reconstruction, the containment of communism, national self-interest, humanitarianism, among others.

Let us restrict our discussion to the economic and humanitarian justifications, however. The humanitarian argument usually goes something like this: There is great suffering in the world, occasioned by hunger, malnutrition, and disease. The United States is a wealthy nation, and it should share its bounty with those in need. The two statements which follow are based mainly on these premises. The first one was made by a representative of the National Council of Churches of Christ in the U.S.A., and on its behalf:

> We believe human life is sacred, being of primary value, so mutual aid is indispensable as it literally makes the difference between life and death for some people, and improves living for millions of others.[3]

The second is from a statement made for the Society of Friends:

> United States policy should be designed to help that part of the human race, about two-thirds of whom are sick or illiterate or politically or economically disadvantaged, develop their God-given potentialities. It means primarily helping others help themselves to do the things they want to do toward our joint community aspirations and ideals. This kind of program must express both a deep, passionate concern for people and a determination that they need not suffer from

---

[3] Waldo Chamberlin, "Statement on Behalf of the National Council of Churches of Christ in the U. S. A.," *United States Foreign Aid*, DeVere E. Pentony, ed. (San Francisco: Howard Chandler, 1960), p. 48.

conditions which are not their fault. We should settle into this task on a long-range basis.[4]

It is understandable and even commendable that men should be concerned with suffering and deprivation in distant lands. Let it be noted, too, that American policy was (and is) *responsible* to some indeterminate degree. This responsibility was not, however, humanitarian; it was economic, though there might well be humanitarian grounds for objecting to the economic policy which fostered suffering. To understand American responsibility for foreign deprivation, it is necessary to know something about how foreign trade is conducted. Presumably, foreigners suffered to some extent because they could not purchase goods which Americans had for sale. They could not purchase these goods because Americans could not (or would not) spend or invest comparable amounts abroad.

We can back into an explanation of this state of affairs by stating the reason for it in this way: Foreign goods were more expensive than their equivalent in American goods. Therefore, Americans bought mainly goods of domestic manufacture. In consequence, foreigners could not buy the needed goods from America.

The solution to this problem should have been rather simple, economically speaking. The people in a foreign land who needed American goods should have devoted themselves to producing those items which could be sold cheaper in America than the ones of domestic origin. This would have provided the wherewithal to purchase American goods. So they might, and probably would, have done if the matter had been left in the economic sphere. It was not. Instead, political interference had made economic so-

---

[4] Edward F. Snyder, "Statement on Behalf of the Friends Committee on National Legislation," in *Ibid.,* pp. 50-51.

lutions virtually impossible. Indeed, such responsibility as Americans bore for the situation could be ascribed to political interference, though it should be kept in mind that countries in which there was suffering often contributed to their condition by domestic political interference.

To be more specific, the main obstacles to international trade in the postwar period, so far as American action affected it, were tariffs and subsidies. Protective tariffs kept foreigners from being able to undersell American products quite often. If some foreign land were able to overcome even this handicap, a clamor would arise from the domestic interest involved for higher tariffs or quotas, or both.

The other great difficulty was that American food products were quite often too high to be sold abroad or to effect a general lowering of food prices in the world. This was directly related to hunger and starvation. American prices were kept high by allotments, parity payments, and other subsidies. It should be kept in mind that foreign governments aggravated the situation by their own subsidies, price supports, minimum wages, and import quotas. Many governments scared away investors by nationalization and confiscation of property, thus creating "underdevelopment" and then clamoring for government-to-government loans to take up the slack.

It should be axiomatic that when political interference has caused a problem, the solution to the problem would be the removal of the political interference. It should be, but it is not today. Instead, the attempt was made to solve problems created by political action by additional political intervention. By and large, governments continued their tariffs, subsidies, regulations, and nationalizations. America granted and loaned money so that other countries could buy goods from America, hire technical assistants, and make capital investments.

The problems that this course of development has created are legion. Foreign countries became dependent upon the United States; the aid was quite often used to bolster corrupt regimes; nations spent huge sums upon prestigious items such as steel mills (though it cost them much more to produce steel than they could have bought it for on the world market) and airlines; and Americans have become busily engaged in interfering in the internal affairs of countries around the world. The debilitating effects of these developments upon the independence and strength of the countries involved need not be dwelt upon here. The economic distortions produced by progressive intervention are manifold.

Much more could be said about these matters, but enough has been said to make the point. Under the guise of humanitarianism and defense, Americans have been drawn into a web of intertwined interventionism. Foreign aid has often forestalled the economic consequences of intervention for foreign countries (such as bolstering the Labor Government in England in the late 1940's), but it could not solve the problems, for it was related to the causes only in the sense that it was like them. Intervening to solve problems caused by intervention can be likened to breaking the other leg of a man who already has one broken leg in order to get him back on his feet. The fact that Americans have been pursuing such policies rather consistently is another symptom of the flight from reality.

Identity of Government with People

Let us take an example now from the area of political theory. The most fruitful field for discovering some flight in the contemporary world would be theories concerning democracy. The myths about democracy are so numerous that to select one is necessarily to neglect a great many

others. Perhaps the central one, however, can be phrased
this way: In a democracy the government *is* the people. A
complete identification exists between the government and
the people. According to this view, government in a democracy manages to catch up, congeal, and utilize the whole
being of a people. More than a hundred years ago, the
American historian, George Bancroft, suggested some such
notion in the following words:

> Thus the opinion which we respect is, indeed, not the
> opinion of one or of a few, but the sagacity of the many.
> It is hard for the pride of cultivated philosophy to put its
> ear to the ground and listen reverently to the voice of
> lowly humanity; yet the people collectively are wiser
> than the most gifted individual, for all his wisdom con-
> stitutes but a part of theirs. . . . It is when the multitude
> give counsel that right purposes find safety; theirs is the
> fixedness that cannot be shaken; theirs is the under-
> standing which exceeds in wisdom; theirs is the heart of
> which the largeness is as the sand on the seashore.[5]

Whatever this passage may mean, it is certainly intended as a justification of democracy. And, so far as it is,
it suggests that a complete identity of people and government occurs. Of course, Bancroft actually assumes such
an identity and is bent upon arguing the superiority of
decisions reached by the people collectively. Our concern,
however, is not with the contention but with the assumption.

All sorts of conclusions are regularly drawn from this
supposed identity of the government with the people. For
example, some say that there is no need to worry about

---

[5] George Bancroft, "The Office of the People in Art, Government and Religion," *Social Theories of Jacksonian Democracy,*
Joseph L. Blau, ed. (New York: Liberal Arts Press, 1954), p.
269.

the public debt. After all, they say, we owe it to ourselves. Others impute morality to government because of its identity with the people. The foreign aid, discussed above, was supported on moral grounds, and this was made to appear logical by assumptions about democracy. Some would hold the American people individually and collectively responsible for the actions of the government in a democracy. It has been alleged, for example, that the American people bore such guilt as there may have been for the dropping of the atomic bomb on Hiroshima. Again, the identification theory tends to validate such an allegation.

Let us set this assumption beside political realities in America, since it is commonly held that the United States is a democracy. Is, or could, such an identification be effected by the political processes now employed? The most common procedure followed by the citizenry to participate in government is by voting. By voting the citizen marks an "X" or pulls a lever beside the name of the candidate for whom he votes. He has chosen one name from among two or more, if the office was contested. If a majority of those voting chose the name, he has helped to select the man who will serve, if the vote was in the general election. If his candidate was not elected, he has participated in the election, but only to a most limited extent in the governmental actions that stem from the man elected.

But, to keep matters simple, let us suppose that his candidate won. Does this mean that there is a complete identity between the voter and the man elected? Hardly. The voter may have known nothing of any of the candidates and have marked his ballot for the one who headed the list. On the other hand, he may have carefully considered the positions of the men on a number of issues and voted for the man who favored a preponderance of those he favored. The voter would not have been unusual, however, if he had voted against the man he disliked by voting for the other candidate. Quite possibly, none of the candidates suited him, but he voted for the one he considered the lesser of the evils.

In any case, so far as the elected official represents the government, so far as voting coincides with participation, no complete identification has been made between the people and the government. By participating in the election, the citizen may have given his tacit approval to the electoral system. By failing to revolt, he may even have given tacit approval to the government. By voting for the candidates of one political party rather than those of another, he may have some effect on general policies to be pursued.

But there is no way to stretch the cloth of the present political process to make a suit that will fit the notion of complete identification between the people and the government. Since no such identification has been vouchsafed, all programs based upon the premise of identity are insecurely based. In fact, they have no real base or foundation. In short, American acceptance, so far as it exists, of the belief, that the public debt poses no problem because we owe it to ourselves, that governments can act morally, that there is a collective responsibility for all government action in a democracy, should be taken as another symptom of the flight from reality.

Government and Birth Control

One other symptom may be noted. There is much professed concern today about what is known as the population explosion. Dire predictions are made about what life will be like if the population increase continues as it has in recent decades. They may be right, but what do they propose to do about it? Most proposals have had to do with birth control. An effort has been made to get the United States government to make available information and perhaps devices for birth control. How much and to what extent governments could or should effect birth control is, of course, highly controversial. But, if government action is taken, it should be noted that governments will be discouraging with one hand what they have been encouraging with the other.

Surely, one of the greatest rational deterrents to having children is the considerable financial responsibility involved. When parents are responsible for feeding, clothing, educating, innoculating, and entertaining their children, they will be most likely to have second thoughts about large families. Modern governments have, however, taken over a considerable part of these activities. Presumably, the same people who favor government propagation of information about birth control would favor an extension of governmental activities in education, in building parks, playgrounds, and zoos, and in providing medical care. They would thus favor relieving parents of responsibilities which they still have. Moreover, tax exemptions for children would seem to promote the bearing of children, if government action affects the matter at all. In short, proposals are made that government facilitate child bearing on the one hand and promote birth control on the other.

No one, to my knowledge, has pointed out these inconsistencies. The fact that they are not generally recognized as inconsistencies is yet another symptom of the flight.

Many other examples could be given of the symptoms of the flight from reality. They could be taken from developments in the arts, in religion, in international relations, in the use of technology, and so on. But perhaps the point has been made. There are widespread indications that programs, policies, studies, and actions are not being checked against any reality. Philosophers proclaim that they cannot determine what is real. Economists sanction programs which bear only a tangential relation to any discernible economic reality. Political theorists concoct relationships that can by no stretch of the imagination be induced from the facts. School building goes on apace and students multiply; yet many professors are in the position of not being able to decide whether education deals with reality or not. These must be signs of a flight from reality.

Now it is not my contention that no system of ideas would support the programs and actions described. On the contrary, it is my belief that there is a vast ideological edifice being used as a launching pad for the flight from reality. My point will be, however, that this launching pad is suspended in mid-air, hanging from a sky hook, as it were. To be more literal, the systems of ideas which are supposed to support the programs are themselves not founded in reality.

The proof of this assertion must be made in connection with a conception of reality, however. Until that is set forth, the above are largely examples of inconsistencies, evidence of a widespread disparity between announced aims and the methods used to arrive at the aims. Inconsistencies are symptoms, not the thing itself. Diagnostically, symptoms tell us something is amiss, in this case that departures have been made from reality. Such a conclusion in the realm of ideas is roughly equivalent to a medical conclusion that the patient is ill. What is wanted, in both cases, is to know what the specific cause of the trouble is. To adjudge the character and content of a flight from reality, it must be viewed from the vantage point of reality.

3

The Nature of Reality

IT IS NOT DIFFICULT FOR MOST OF US TO UNDERSTAND the desire to reform things. On the surface, at least, there is so much that is not the way it should be; or, if that formulation be not acceptable, there is so much that is not the way we would have it be. Many people do not behave in ways that are pleasing to us. They fritter away their time, occupy themselves with amusements that are in reality anesthetics, prefer the dulling to the ennobling experience, act irresponsibly, waste their talents, and fail to devote themselves to the improvement of themselves and others.

Nor does the world appear to be perfectly ordered. Notice how unequally the resources for human living are distributed on the earth. Here is a drought while there is a flood; here is abundance, even surplus, while there is scarcity, even hunger; here the land is fertile while there it is arid. It seems that there is much injustice on this planet. Children who are born of poor parents have not the advantages of those born of rich ones. Men whose land is infertile eke out a bare existence by the sweat of their brow, while those more favorably situated live in the lap of luxury. Men die at an early age before their promise has been fulfilled. There is suffering, deprivation, disease, hunger, malnutrition, disfiguration, malformation of bodies, and so on through all the variants of things to which flesh is heir.

Surely, many will say, things are not as they should be. Why not set them aright? Why not remake man and society more in keeping with our vision of them? Why not introduce those reforms which will most likely lead to an improved world in which to live? More specifically, why not use the power of government to accomplish these ends?

At its deepest, the reform impetus has been animated by such questions and visions as are formulated above. It is understandable, I say, for men to think in this manner, for them to want to pool their power and accomplish such apparently worth-while ends. Some would go so far as to say that it is *natural* for men to think this way. But this last statement should not be accepted. The historical record will not support the view that the urge to reform, in this all-embracing fashion, is natural, unless we believe that most men at most times have been unnatural. The fact is that this reformist view is almost entirely restricted to the last hundred years or so, and probably only became more generally accepted in the last twenty to forty years.

Most men have *not* believed that it was possible to alter, fundamentally, man, society, or the universe, or that it would be desirable to do so if it could be done. True, peoples have dabbled in magic, prayed for supernatural intervention in the course of things, and occasionally used government for ameliorative purposes. But these have had some specific and very limited object, quite different from the objective of remaking everything to accord with human vision.

The major obstacle to unlimited reformism is *reality* itself. Historically, the major obstacle to the rise and triumph of a reformist bent has been the *conceptions* which men had of reality. There is no need to mask the fact that the conceptions which men have had of reality may not have been valid. It should be noted, too, that the special competence of historians of ideas extends only to an account of the ideas which men have held, not to the accuracy, validity, or truth of the ideas. How, then, can a historian do a work which has as its subject, *The Flight from Reality*? Unless he means that many men no longer have any conception of reality, has he not entered the realm of philosophy for the validation of the thesis?

Actually, however, all work proceeds upon some conception of reality, implicit or explicit, just as do all statements which purport to contain truth. The difference in this case is that the issue of what constitutes reality cannot be evaded or simply assumed; it must be articulated in order to validate the thesis.

In setting forth a conception of reality, however, I have no intention of giving one that I have constructed. In fact, I have not constructed one, nor have I felt it desirable to do so. The work has been done already, with many variations and in great detail. There is a great tradition of philosophy to which all those in Western civilization are heirs. A conception of reality is embedded in our language, informs our thought, is elaborated in our institutions, is implicit in our customs, and can be found in books in our libraries. The fact that a new conception of reality has been developed in the last century or so does pose problems of validating the older conception. Even so, I accept as valid some of the central insights of the Western tradition of philosophy and present them as an adequate conception of reality for my purposes.

Histories of philosophy usually devote much of their space to differences in philosophies. This is as it should be. The student needs to know how Plato differs from Aristotle, how Augustine differs from Thomas Aquinas, and how David Hume differs from Thomas Hobbes. These differences are sometimes great, and they are important. The focus upon the differences, however, may result in losing sight of what these and other philosophers have in common.

The Western Tradition

There is a central tradition of Western philosophy, a central insight, quest for, and belief about reality which transcends the differences of such diverse men as Thales, Pythagoras, Plato, Aristotle, Cicero, Augustine, Anselm, Aquinas, Duns Scotus, Descartes, Spinoza, Hobbes, and Kant. They all belong, to a greater or lesser extent, to the major tradition in Western philosophy. The tradition may be called by a variety of names—Platonic-Aristotelian, rationalism, essentialism, realism (in the Medieval sense)— but to be a philosopher in the West has usually meant to belong to it. There have from time to time been dissenters from it such as the Greek sophists and materialists, but from the perspective of a long history these have been but rivulets meandering into deserts where they dried up. (Perhaps the figure is not quite right, for in the recent past there has been a revival of sophistry in relativism and of materialism in mechanistic and atomistic doctrines, but that is a story that can be deferred for later discussion.)

The central insight of the Western tradition of philosophy is that there is an enduring, even an eternal, reality. Indeed, "the real" came to be defined in philosophy as that which is fixed and unchanging. In the main, philosophers have been bent upon making systematic accounts of the universe, of matter, and of life, upon discovering from whence things came and where they were going, upon finding the common denominator which would bring unity out of diversity, upon locating the primal stuff of the universe, and upon describing the cohesive principle that orders reality. The history of philosophy in the West is

THE NATURE OF REALITY   39

traced from the appearance of efforts to do these things.

Permanence is not obviously the most prominent feature of reality. On the contrary, it is quite likely that the untutored eye would discover not unity but diversity, not order but disarray, not system but chaos, not purpose but randomness, not fixity but change. To the senses, each thing is different from every other thing. All things are changing, if not perceptibly, then, over any considerable period of time. Decay sets in rather rapidly for all material things, that is, for all that comes to the senses.

One of the earliest philosophers, Heraclitus, perceived the fluctuating character of all things and proceeded to erect a philosophy around the permanence of flux. A thoroughgoing philosophy of flux, however, tends to disintegrate the very world which men discoursed about long before there was formal philosophy. "If everything is in a state of change, the names which we give them become misleading, for as soon as we label something we seem to give it a 'nature' which is lasting. But if nothing endures, all such labels are a vain and childish attempt to arrest the passage of time, to grasp at fleeting shadows. . . ."[1]

It should be clear, then, that long before the Greek philosophers men had perceived an order in the world, that they had incarnated these conceptions in language which included class names and ways of referring to an ordered reality. Philosophers did not simply create a vision of reality; they worked with one that was already implied in the culture which they had received. Much of philosophy has been concerned with bringing to consciousness that which is implied in language. This is not to say, as some have, that philosophers have been simply playing with words. On the contrary, they have been concerned to delve

---

[1] George Boas, *Rationalism in Greek Philosophy* (Baltimore: The Johns Hopkins Press, 1961), p. 8.

into a reality for which the received words of their culture stand. The mainstream of Western philosophy has been deeply rooted in culture and tradition. It has been to a considerable extent the unraveling of such truth as was bound up in language. (Anyone who holds that his language does not embrace truth, is not descriptive for truth, must first construct a new language by which to convey any truths which he perceives.)

Quite possibly, the philosophical quest arose out of the disparity between the inherited cultural vision of reality and the world brought to men by their senses. What we do know is that the early philosophers focused their attention upon the distinction between appearance and reality. As one writer says, "Whatever else may be said about early Greek philosophy, it is safe to maintain that from its very origins it made a distinction between the world as it appears to man and the world as it really is."[2] The central view for Western philosophy is that of Plato, that there is an underlying reality which is eternal, that change, decay, disorder—the world of appearances—is an illusion insofar as it appears to be that which is real.

Ultimate Reality

The real, then, is that which endures, or is eternal. But what endures? There have been many ways of approaching the answer to this question. It may be noted, too, that an adequate answer accounts for both reality and appearances. There is an answer which antedates philosophy but which has subsequently been embedded in most philosophies. In its monotheistic form, it is the view that God is *the* real, that He is the everlasting, the unchanging, the enduring, the eternal. He is the creator; all things come

---

[2] *Ibid.*, p. 1.

from Him; that which does not have its end and culmination in Him is illusory and unreal. This view was an article of faith long before it was the subject of rational proofs. Efforts at proving it have not succeeded for very long or for very many in changing the fact that it is Faith's answer to the riddle of the universe. Philosophy proceeds discursively; the above view leaps from appearance to reality, not troubling to make the necessary steps.

From a rigorously theistic point of view, metaphysics has usually been concerned with an intermediate realm between the physical world of appearances and the ultimate reality which is God. In short, metaphysics has been the study pursued by those seeking to discover and describe that which gives order, structure, and form to the universe. Metaphysicians have held that the universe is ordered, that reality is structured, that there is a fixity beneath the appearance of flux.

Traditional Western philosophers have held that the underlying reality is made up of *essences*. These essences have been called by a variety of names, and these different names involve some differences of character. But they all refer to permanent features of reality. Essence has been conceived as idea, as form, as potentiality, as law, or as spirit. For some, the essence is that from which all things derive, to others that toward which all things move. Essences may usually be conceived of as *absolutes*, and they serve the role of *principles*.

To pursue metaphysical thought any further would involve us in particular systems. These are complicated and vary considerably from one thinker to another. Undoubtedly, the most fertile systems for Western thought were those set forth by Plato and Aristotle. Some hold that virtually all directions taken by thinkers were at least implied by Plato. It is doubtful that philosophic thought is cumulative in a significant way. There are still thinkers who accept Aristotle or Aquinas as their masters. But over the centuries there was an unfolding and elaboration (though not necessarily progressive) of the premises and assumptions of essentialism which was important.

The search for the permanent resulted in the discovery of an impressive body of laws, the setting forth of conditions within which human life is lived, and an understanding of the structured nature of reality. There were gains and losses of knowledge over the centuries, depending upon the particular focus upon reality, the aptitude of the searchers, and the breadth of the approach. A few of these gains should be set forth as the central insights of Western thought.

An Ordered Universe

Perhaps the central one of these, built upon the premise of an enduring reality, is that there is an order in the universe. At the physical level, much of this order is available to or can be confirmed by experience. There are predictable regularities all around. The seasons of the year follow one another in predictable fashion, and, having completed their cycle, they recur. Seeds taken from a plant reproduce that plant, other things being equal. Animals go through a cycle of life: birth, growth, maturity, death. "Then there are also the regular changes in the positions of the heavenly bodies, beginning with the sun and the moon and after them the planets. The regular sequence . . . of the tides . . . , of eclipses of the sun and moon, were observed at a very early date."[3]

This same sort of regularity or order can be found in other realms, too. The order that has long enamored

---

[3] *Ibid.*, p. 5.

philosophers, since the time of the Pythagoreans, is that in mathematics. H. D. F. Kitto gives an experience of his which must parallel that of early mathematicians, and which awakens a sense of the marvelous character of mathematics:

> . . . It occurred to me to wonder what was the difference between the square of a number and the product of its next-door neighbours. 10 x 10 proved to be 100, and 11 x 9 = 99—one less. It was interesting to find that 6 x 6 and 7 x 5 was just the same, and with growing excitement I discovered, and algebraically proved, the law that this product must always be one less than the square. The next step was to consider the behavior of next-door neighbours but one, and it was with great delight that I disclosed to myself a whole system of numerical behavior. . . . With increasing wonder I worked out the series 10 x 10 = 100; 9 x 11 = 99; 8 x 12 = 96; 7 x 13 = 91 . . . and found that the differences were, successively, 1, 3, 5, 7 . . . the odd-number series.

He draws the conclusion:

> Then I knew how the Pythagoreans felt when they made these same discoveries. . . . Did Heraclitus declare that everything is always changing? Here are things that do not change, entities that are eternal, free from the flesh that corrupts, independent of the imperfect senses, perfectly apprehensible through the mind.[4]

When and as men discovered that these two kinds of orders—the physical and mathematical—were linked together in a reality that could be discovered and described, their sense of wonder and awe sometimes surpassed the bounds of language to capture. There have been many discoveries of this remarkable linkage, but none was more exuberant than Johannes Kepler in reporting them:

---

[4] H. D. F. Kitto, *The Greeks* (Baltimore: Penguin Books, 1951), pp. 191-92.

. . . Having perceived the first glimmer of dawn eighteen months ago, the light of day three months ago, but only a few days ago the plain sun of a most wonderful vision—nothing shall now hold me back. Yes, I give myself up to holy raving. I mockingly defy all mortals with this open confession: I have robbed the golden vessels of the Egyptians to make out of them a tabernacle for my God, far from the frontiers of Egypt. If you forgive me, I shall rejoice. If you are angry, I shall bear it. Behold, I have cast the dice, and I am writing a book either for my contemporaries, or for posterity. It is all the same to me. It may wait a hundred years for a reader, since God has also waited six thousand years for a witness. . . .[5]

One of the considerable joys of the study of history is to visit with those in the past who have lifted the veil to peer from time into eternity, who have experienced the enduring harmony behind the cacophony of passing events, who have renewed in themselves an age-old vision of order.

This vision of order has not been restricted to the physical and mathematical, nor to a union of these, of course. It has been extended to the ethical realm to embrace the relations among men, to human nature, to laws, standards, and principles for living and life.

The Use of Reason

A second insight which went along with this vision of an order in the universe was the view that this order is rational. That is, we can come to a knowledge of this universe by the use of reason. (This does not rule out the possibility that knowledge may come by the more direct mystic experience. But knowledge acquired by the mystic experience is private, not public.) Two methods, with

---

[5] Quoted in Arthur Koestler, *The Sleepwalkers* (New York: Macmillan, 1959), pp. 393-94.

many variations, were developed for using reason to acquire knowledge. One of these is associated with Plato. It is the dialectical method, personified for us by Socrates and called also the Socratic method. The dialectic is used to arrive at clear and consistent ideas. Ideas are opposed against ideas; each statement is examined minutely for inconsistencies; it is held up beside opposing views.

This method assumes that ideas are innate, that the truth is already embedded in the mind and needs only to be called forth. Involved in the calling forth is the clarification which results from the removal of contradictions. This is *a priori* reasoning, for the truth is there before the examination of ideas takes place. *A priori* is also used to refer to deductive reasoning, but it should be noted that deduction is only a method for reasoning to particulars once the universal or principle is known. Since true knowledge to Plato is of ideas—universals, principles, standards —it cannot be arrived at by deduction but rather by the dialectic.

The other method for arriving at truth by reason may be called the Aristotelian. It is the inductive method; in its extended and elaborated form we know it as the scientific method. The procedure is to reason from the particular to the general or universal. Aristotle provided for this method in his metaphysics by maintaining that form is joined to matter in actuality. To put it another way, the particular articulation of matter, such as shape, is given to it by pre-existing form. The forms are eternal, or they derive from or partake of the enduring. It follows, then, that one might gain a knowledge of the universal order by a study of particulars, by the classification of them according to common traits, by the codification of regularities, and by the description of the laws which may be induced from many instances. Of course, the reduction of this method to a simply stated formula did not occur until the modern era.

The Objective Nature of Reality

A third insight is that this rational order in the universe is objective. To put it more deeply, there is a reality which exists independently of human knowledge of it. Reality is something we come to know because it exists, not something which comes into existence when we take cognizance of it. The following, which Boas affirms of Plato, could be said with equal validity of virtually every philosopher in the Western tradition: Plato believed "that the nature of things is whatever it is independently of our knowledge of it. He is far from being a subjectivist in his metaphysics. We discover natures; we do not produce them either by our powers of observation or by our methods of inquiry."[6]

Now, rationalists have usually held that knowledge of objective reality is possible because there is a congruity between mind and reality. The relationship can be simply stated in this way: reality is ultimately rational; man is a rational being; therefore, man can know reality. But the important point here is *objectivity*. The objectivity of the universe makes possible public truth about it, that is, truth which transcends any subjective view about it. Opinions may differ because men are prone to err, but one opinion is not as good as another, nor does the number of men who hold a particular view affect its validity, so long as there is an objective reality to which truth pertains.

Cause and Effect

A fourth insight of the Western tradition of philosophy is that cause and effect operate in the universe and are

---

[6] Boas, *op. cit.*, p. 141.

inseparably linked together. As this insight applies to human action it means this: a given act will have a given effect, other things being equal. That is, if one plants corn, corn stalks will come up, provided the conditions are right, of course. If the corn is not weeded, weeds will choke out the corn and reduce the harvest. In short, there are predictable and even inevitable consequences which follow from any line of behavior.

Given the insights discussed above, the relationship between cause and effect can be rationally explained. There is an order in the universe; it is an order in which effect follows cause; that is the nature of things. Since the universe is objective, the effect of an action is not altered by the intent of the actor. It happened that I set out and cultivated some tomato plants. My intention was to have red or pink tomatoes, but the plants were the kind that produced tomatoes that were yellow when ripe. Hence, the tomatoes were yellow ones. Of course, Everyman acts upon the premise that effect follows cause in simple matters, else he is accounted a fool by his neighbors and will most certainly have to be taken care of by others. But cause and effect are more difficult to discern in complex and subtle matters, and, as we shall see, a great many people have been led away from this insight. The insight has it that effect follows cause regardless of the complexity of the phenomena or the subtlety of the operation.

The Fixed Nature of Things

A fifth insight is that everything has a nature, that this nature is fixed and immutable. Indeed, as I have already suggested, this was the central premise upon which the philosophical quest was based. The quest for the nature of things led to or made possible many of the other insights. The point is repeated here so that the implications may be drawn from it in a particular direction. This work is primarily a social study. Truths about the physical and metaphysical universe are tangential to it and bear upon it only as they have been brought to bear upon it, or as the universe is one, and social relations are an integral part of it. At any rate, the social implications are of greatest concern here, and we will now focus upon them.

Virtually the whole of Western philosophy through the eighteenth century of our era has been essentialist. The quest for and elaboration of the nature of things is writ large in the pages of its history. From our vantage point, this search and quest culminated in the seventeenth and eighteenth centuries, though some of the implications have continued to be drawn out. There have always been social applications which could be and to some extent were made of the resultant knowledge. But never was it done on such a scale and with such effect as in the Ages of Reason and Enlightenment. Thus, it will be appropriate from every angle to focus upon this most recent time for drawing out the social applications of the doctrines about the nature of things.

The Laws of Nature

In this last age of philosophy before ideology began its take-over of thought, social thought proceeded from a conception of the nature of the universe and of man. The fundamental character of the universe, to thinkers of the seventeenth and eighteenth centuries, was its lawfulness. The visible universe was sustained by underlying laws. This was no new insight, but it was given new conclusive proofs by Galileo, Kepler, Leibniz, and Newton. Everywhere thinkers looked, they saw regularity and proportion —the balance of the seasons, the plenitude of life, the variety of scenery, the predictability of the operation of the universe. The planets moved with predictability in their orbits; the earth made its rotation each day, its revolution each year. All things had their seasons, cycles, and natures. Law pervaded reality, and extended outward to touch every relationship and thing.

Man has a nature, these thinkers saw, is participant in a lawful order, has a predetermined place in the scheme of things. There are many ways to look at human nature. The distinguishing feature which has usually been focused upon is the rationality of man. He alone of all creation is a thinker by nature, capable of acting after having taken thought, rather than acting upon instinct; capable of knowing the universe of cause and effect, of law and order, and making calculations in terms of this knowledge; capable of knowing himself and what is appropriate to him. Man also has a discernible physical nature: he is bifurcated, bipedal, mammalian, has a certain form toward which he moves, and when he has arrived at it may be called mature. He is subject to the laws of the universe and of his own nature.

Voltaire put it this way: "It would be very singular that all nature and all the stars should obey eternal laws, and that there should be one little animal five feet tall which, despite these laws, could always act as suited its own caprice."[7] This may be taken to mean, in part, that man is a limited being, limited in that he must act in conformity with physical laws in order to attain his ends, limited by the fact that he is mortal to a relatively short life, limited by his residence in time and place, and so on.

Eighteenth century thinkers were more apt than not to

---

[7] Quoted in Ernst Cassirer, *The Philosophy of the Enlightenment* (Boston: Beacon Press, copyright Princeton University Press, 1951), p. 251.

be optimists; therefore, they were more likely to put emphasis upon possibilities suggested by human nature. The true nature of man was revealed in the mature and fulfilled individual, in the man who had fully developed his powers of reasoning, in the virtuous man who exemplified the virtues of Morality, Justice, and Piety. Above all, human nature was fulfilled and made manifest in a life of order, proportion, and harmony in imitation of the Divine order.[8]

Thinkers saw, too, that there is a natural order for human relations, that there is in the nature of things an implicit social order. They found it by looking into the nature of things. Just as men and the universe have a nature, so do political relations, economic relations, social relations, and so on. Some conceive of human institutions as infinitely variable, of constitutions as arbitrary creations, of laws as products of the imagination. Not so the thinkers of the eighteenth century. Indeed, theirs was no new insight. Aristotle had seen that every government must be either of the nature of a monarchy, an aristocracy, or a democracy. These forms can be combined or mixed, as was done in the case of the American Republic, but no other forms can be made. That is just the way things are.

The Nature of Government

There are natural laws for the relations among men and nations. These laws are antecedent to and take precedence over all of man's attempts to make laws. As Montesquieu declared, "Laws in their broadest sense are the necessary relations which are derived from the nature of things. . . . Before there were any enacted laws, just relations were

---

[8] See Basil Willey, *The Eighteenth Century Background* (New York: Columbia University Press, 1950), pp. 71-73.

possible. To say that there is nothing just or unjust excepting that which positive laws command or forbid is like
saying that before one has drawn a circle, all of its radii
were not equal."[9]

Locke's doctrine of natural rights—the rights to life, liberty, and property—was founded in the nature of man and
the universe. As one writer describes Locke's position:
"There are natural rights of man which existed before all
foundations of social and political organizations; and in
view of these the real function and purpose of the state
consists in admitting such rights into its order and in pre-
serving and guaranteeing them thereby."[10]

The marvel of all this, at least to social thinkers in the
eighteenth century, was that an examination of the nature
of government tended to indicate that it was suited to perform just those functions, and only those functions, which
would maintain life, liberty, and property. That is, if government used force to punish aggressors, a function to
which its nature is suited, then liberty would prevail. Governments need not concern themselves with other interventions, for natural law will operate best and most efficiently
in the absence of government action. Thus, the physiocrats
and Adam Smith showed that economic behavior is governed by laws which derive from human nature and the
nature of the universe, that these laws do not need to be
enforced by governments, and that great harm will result
if governments act in contravention of them. Just so, systems of natural morality were set forth, natural education, and so forth. As these ideas were implemented in
Great Britain, the United States, and elsewhere, freedom
replaced compulsion in numerous activities and the area

---

[9] Quoted in Cassirer, *op. cit.,* p. 243.
[10] *Ibid.,* p. 250.

where voluntary activity had free play was greatly extended.

Man the Discoverer

A sixth, and final, insight of Western thinkers has to do with creativity. In the deepest sense, men do *not* create, according to this tradition. Men can only reproduce, discover, represent, imitate, copy, and report. Reality is not plastic, to be shaped as human beings will. It is absolute, fixed, immutable. Deep sanctions against presumptive efforts at human interference have been embodied in myths, preserved in scriptures, and set forth in treatises. Man is neither god nor demigod, and creativity is in the province of the gods, as pagans would have it, or the province of God.

A jaded and presumptuous generation of men have found this limitation intolerable. The study of history reveals that men who had no thought of creating out of the void, as it were, found great joy in what was possible for them to do. Who would surpass Kepler's exhilaration at *discovering* laws in the universe? Who can write better music than Mozart's *imitation* of the harmony and order that underlies nature? Has there been nobler sculpture than Michelangelo's *representation* of Moses? Thinkers were exuberant, not inhibited, who discovered laws of human relations, and bade men to live in accord with them. The pessimism, malaise of spirit, and joylessness of contemporary would-be creators may be proof enough of the futility of such presumption. In the Western tradition of thought, reality exists; man learns to live in harmony with it or suffers the consequences of his failure.

4

Cutting Loose from Reality

Let us face . . . the bleakness of the modern world: admit that religion and philosophy are projections of the mind, and set about the betterment of man's condition.
— JOHN BOWLE on Auguste Comte

THE BENT OF MEN TO REFORM—TO MAKE OVER MAN AND society in their image—was held in check by traditional philosophy. Philosophy reined in the unbridled imagination just as religion tended to puncture the human ego and divest it of false pride. Above all, rational philosophy imposed a strict discipline upon thought. The philosopher had to keep checking his conceptions and holding them up beside reality; ideas had to bear a demonstrable relation to reality. Reality had objective existence in traditional Western philosophy; its being did not depend upon the human mind.

Men come to know reality by the use of reason. But reason was not conceived as a creation of human ingenuity; it was rather a marvelous faculty given to man that he might guide himself by its use, its possession not an occasion for pride but an indication of the obligation to use it. Indeed, traditionally reason *was* authority, second only to revelation, and some would give it first place. The weight of authority, of reason, of reality, smothered any incipient reformism. It could be argued that philosophy, coupled with religion, usually did the job too well, that philosophers were too sanguine about the possibilities of human improvement, that too low an estimate of human nature was usually held, that the imagination was too severely circumscribed.

This may well have been the case. But if the point needed making, it has been made a thousand times over by now. Moreover, the matter need not detain us in this study. The limits of the imagination and the character of human nature are matters to be determined by reference to reality. They cannot be made by those engaged in a flight from reality, nor are such things simply a matter of striking a nice balance between opposing views. Anyone who believes that a balance between opposing views bears any *necessary* relation to truth or right is already far along on his flight.

My major point is that philosophy disciplined thought and required thinkers continually to refer their ideas to reality. In these circumstances, reality was the main obstacle to reform, as it always is in fact so far as ameliorative reforms by government are concerned, and such reformers as there were had to keep their programs modest or make it clear that they were simply constructing romances.

By focusing upon an enduring reality, philosophers built an imposing amount of knowledge over the centuries. This movement came to its climax, to the present, in the seventeenth and eighteenth centuries. The central insights of this Western tradition of philosophy, to review them, were: (1) there is an order in the universe; (2) this order is rational; (3) reality is objective—that is, exists outside the mind; (4) cause and effect operate in the universe and are inseparably linked together; (5) everything has a nature that is fixed and immutable; and (6) men do not create; instead, they discover, represent, reproduce, copy, and report. So long as these views held sway, the vision of pervasive reform was limited to recognized dreamers and romancers.

A great reversal has taken place. Today, reformist intellectuals have gained the upper hand virtually everywhere, though their tenure in many places is probably precarious. They hold sway, and they press for continuous reform in virtually every area of life. A great many developments preceded this triumph. One of the most essential of these was the cutting loose from reality.

Berkeley, Hume, and Kant

The way was prepared for the departure from reality by accredited philosophers. Figuratively, we might even say that the launching pads were built by philosophers. This is not the same as saying that the men in question were no longer in touch with reality. Indeed, no such judgment is intended, and no critique is to be made of the philosophical speculations which prepared the way for the flight. It is doubtful that philosophers should be blamed for what other men make of their thought. At any rate, even as conceptions of the nature of man and the universe were being clarified and propounded, even as these conceptions were being used to buttress order in society and extend liberty— that is, in the midst of the eighteenth century—some philosophers began to cut the ground from under the conceptions. The most notable of these thinkers were George Berkeley, David Hume, and Immanuel Kant.

Bishop Berkeley undermined the belief in the substantiality of reality. It was a common belief that there are substances such as we denominate wood, glass, iron, and so forth. These substances are called matter, in general terms. By a strict empirical approach, Berkeley demonstrated that we never actually experience any such substances. We see colors, hear sounds, smell odors, taste tastes, and feel hardness or softness. If material substances exist, they cannot be known by the senses. "What Berkeley was concerned to show," says one philosopher, "was that nothing exists independently of minds. He believed that people used the word 'matter' to designate such a supposed independent existent, and he proposed to show that this word, so used, was merely a meaningless noise to which nothing corresponds."[1] He argued that only that which can be known can exist, or that it must be known to exist.

But mind knows only ideas. If matter existed, it could not be known. To affirm something as existing but unknowable involved an unacceptable contradiction to Berkeley. Apparently, he was not really interested in proving that we are wrong in conceiving of substance. Rather, he was concerned to show that it depends for its existence upon our thinking it. As he said, "All the Choir of Heaven and the furniture of earth, in a word all those bodies which compose the mighty frame of the world, have no substance without a mind."[2] The objectivity of reality tended to diminish to the vanishing point when this view was accepted.

David Hume, radical empiricist and philosophical skeptic, challenged, among other things, the conception of necessary causality. Traditionally, effect was said to follow cause of necessity, that is, cause and effect are linked in such a way that they *must* happen in conjunction. One text describes Hume's reasoning in the following way:

---

[1] W. T. Jones, *A History of Western Philosophy* (New York: Harcourt, Brace, 1952), p. 753.

[2] Quoted in *ibid.*, p. 758.

But now Hume asks, how have we arrived at this idea of necessary causality? To what actual experiences or impressions does this idea correspond? The ideas of cause and effect, he replied, are derived from nothing more than our experience of linking two events, one of which immediately precedes the other in time. That which comes first is known as the cause and that which follows is called the effect. . . . Nowhere do I find the *impression* of a *necessary relation* between the two. Where, then, does the idea of causal necessity come from? The answer is that it is based upon psychological habit.[3]

Hume no more disproved the operation of cause and effect than Berkeley disproved the existence of substance, but he did attempt to indicate that the basis of the belief in cause and effect is psychological rather than simply empirical. Moreover, he cast doubt upon the uniformity and regularity of its operation.

It might be well to add that Berkeley and Hume had done little, if any, more than to demonstrate the limits of simple empiricism. By so doing, they were showing the weakness of Locke's psychology and perhaps some of Descartes' assumptions. Since these latter may have been aberrations from the Western tradition, as some philosophers think, the assault might have done nothing more than to turn thought back into the mainstream. It did not, at least for most thinkers. The centuries-long assault upon Aristotle and the Schoolmen had borne fruit: they were discredited. Moreover, the Moderns were too proud of their achievements to repudiate them in the face of philosophical difficulties.

Instead of returning to the mainstream of Western

---

[3] Eugene G. Bewkes, J. Calvin Keene, *et al., The Western Heritage of Faith and Reason* (New York: Harper & Row, 1963), p. 574.

thought, then, most thinkers continued on the journey away from it. The central figure for this further shift was Immanuel Kant. Thought has followed divergent paths since the time of Kant, and most of these directions were made possible, if not tenable, by what he did to philosophy. Kant severed some of the major ties between reason and reality; this operation very nearly killed metaphysics.[4] More specifically, he dealt with the questions which Berkeley and Hume, among others, had raised, that is, the question of validating empirically derived data. Kant believed that scientists were accumulating knowledge, that this was much more certain than Hume's skepticism would allow. Yet he accepted the views that knowledge is mind-dependent and that the senses bring us much less information than they appear to do. It turns out, by Kant's exposition, that the mind is equipped with categories—notably of time and space—which enable it to arrive at knowledge with the help of data.

This is most convenient for the scientist, but, having affirmed the central role of the mind, would Kant not go further and let the mind arrive at truth—via reason—independently of the senses? He would not. Such Pure Reason could not give us certain knowledge. All sorts of conceptions might be arrived at in this manner, but "these are conceptions the possibility of which has no ground to rest upon. For they are not based upon experience and its known laws; and without experience, they are merely arbitrary conjunction of thoughts, which, though containing no internal contradiction, has no claim to objective reality. . . . As far as concerns reality, it is self-evident that we

[4] For an exposition of this development, see Etiene Gilson and Thomas Langan, *Modern Philosophy* (New York: Random House, 1963), pp. 428-35.

cannot cogitate such a possibility . . . without the aid of experience; because *reality is concerned only with sensation,* as the matter of experience, and not with the form of thought, with which we can no doubt indulge in shaping fancies."[5]

Kant went on to maintain that we cannot attain certain knowledge of the soul, of the universe, or of God by the use of Pure Reason. They may exist, but reason does not certify this. Since no direct empirical evidence can be had of them, they cannot be rationally proved or disproved. The proper use of metaphysics, Kant maintained, is to do with it precisely what he had done, to reveal the categories or forms of knowledge, forms which are given such content as they have by experience.

In short, metaphysics seems to be relegated to the role of telling us how we know what we know we know. Even this role for metaphysics is not certain (Kant is baffling and ambiguous, as usual), for he rules that empirical psychology should be separated from metaphysics,[6] and this could conceivably result in an empirical science of how knowledge is attained. This leaves metaphysics with the almost wholly negative role of being used to demonstrate the limits of reason. Kant suggests as much:

> That, as a purely speculative science, it is more useful in preventing error, than in the extension of knowledge, does not detract from its value; on the contrary, the supreme office of censor which it occupies, assures to it the highest authority and importance.[7]

If Kant be accepted, the only further use of metaphysics

---

[5] Immanuel Kant, *Critique of Pure Reason,* J. M. D. Meiklejohn, tr. (New York: Dutton, Everyman's Library, 1934), p. 168. Italics mine.

[6] *Ibid.,* p. 480.

[7] *Ibid.,* p. 481.

would be in the elucidation of Kant's ideas (a not inconsiderable task), since he has already used it fully in the way it can be used. In short, metaphysics could be relegated to the field of history of philosophy. In the main, this is what has happened.

What Kant took away with one hand—the Pure Reason —he returned with the other—Practical Reason. What we cannot know—that is, God, freedom, immortality, moral imperatives, principles, ideals—must be assumed. To accomplish this intellectual feat, Kant resorted to the traditional distinctions between appearance and reality. The phenomenal world, the world accessible to the senses, the only world that can be known, is only an appearance. The real world is unknown and unknowable, as Kant had earlier demonstrated to his satisfaction. Yet it must exist. No, that is not quite right. We must act *as if* it existed.

Kant affirmed the traditional morality, insisted upon the necessity of faith, and proclaimed that man participates in a moral order. Practically, Kant would have it, we do seem to know that there are moral imperatives. There may even be generally accepted beliefs about what many of these are. They can even be "proved" by the Practical Reason, by which Kant means reason operating upon assumptions about what reality must be like in order for appearances to be as we perceive them. Yet this kind of reason operates upon possibilities, not certainties, so far as philosophy is concerned. Kant said as much himself:

> It is just the same as if I sought to find out how freedom itself as causality of a will is possible; for, in so doing, I would leave the philosophical basis of explanation behind, and I have no other. Certainly I could revel in the intelligible world, the world of intelligences, which still remains to me; but although I have a well founded idea of it, still I do not have the least knowl-

edge of it, nor can I ever attain to it by all the exertions of my natural capacity of reason.[8]

This stolid German, this resolute metaphysician, this determined moralist, had left the house of philosophy in ruins: of this there should be no doubt. Let us review the "achievement." Kant had changed the meaning of "objective" from something which exists outside the mind to make it refer to a property of mind itself; he had brought it into the interior world of consciousness.[9] He had taught that mind can only know phenomena. Reason can only deal with reason. Then he declares that phenomena is only appearance, that reality is unknown and unknowable.

Kant did try to put the house together again, or at least to build a shelter to protect the contents. This shelter appears to have been sustained only by the will and intellect of Kant. To put it another way, it was held together by the will to believe. When that was gone, the edifice collapsed. Since Kant could not bequeath to us the will to believe, he left us only the wreckage of philosophy. It is hardly an exaggeration to say that the history of thought since his time has been largely the story of men picking up this or that piece of wreckage and trying to make a philosophy out of it.

The Impact of Philosophy

Several things need to be kept in mind in evaluating the impact of the deterioration of philosophy upon men and societies at large. First, any development in philosophy may wait a long while before it has any general consequences. Men, even most thinkers, tend to operate on the

---

[8] Immanual Kant, *Foundations of the Metaphysics of Morals*, Lewis W. Beck, tr. (New York: Bobbs Merrill, 1959), p. 81.

[9] See Gilson and Langan, *op. cit.*, p. 417.

basis of received ideas, and these may be little altered in the course of a generation. Second, the generality of men do not know what philosophers are thinking and would probably think them demented if they did. Most men accept the reality of an objective universe outside themselves, are conscious of its resistance to their wills, know something of the rules by which one deals with it (at least so far as these rules have bearing upon their immediate tasks), accept cause and effect in the areas to which their immediate decisions reach, and are not apt to be much concerned about how they know what they know. Third, many of the major developments of the nineteenth century continued to rest upon traditional philosophical beliefs and the seventeenth and eighteenth century foundation. Thus, in the political realm the trend was toward constitutionalism, representative government, laissez-faire economy, the establishment of natural rights as civil liberties—all of which were based in earlier thought.

Yet the impact did come. It was felt first in the realm of thought itself, as thinkers diverged in virtually every direction from any unity. One intellectual historian, speaking of nineteenth century thought, says: "In the restless inquiry and searching that have marked men's intellectual pursuits since those days [eighteenth century], it is hard to find any . . . clear picture. Not only did men . . . fail to reach a measure of agreement on fundamentals; even within particular fields it is not easy to trace any simple line of development."[10]

Whatever explanations may be made of this phenomenon, one is central: the loss of the disciplinary role of philosophy. Kant had opened the door to every sort of

---

[10] John H. Randall, Jr., *The Making of the Modern Mind* (Boston: Houghton Mifflin, 1954. rev. ed.), p. 389.

doctrine or idea. It does not matter much that Kant had not intended such a result, or that he had labored mightily to divert men's minds in the direction he wanted them to go. (Let us not attribute too much to Kant. After all, Hume's skeptical work preceded his.) But if reason can deal only with reason, not with reality, why should men bother to test their ideas by reason? If Kant can decide what reality is while asserting that it cannot be finally proved that it is that way, why can't men imagine a reality of their own? After all, some men would not be enamored of Kant's moral universe. If the only knowledge that can be validated is that which comes by way of the senses, why not narrow the search for knowledge to empirical data? If no final proof can be offered for a transcendental realm, why assume that one exists? Why not simply accept the physical world for all there is? These are, indeed, some of the main directions that have been taken since the time of Kant. The flight from reality into melioristic reform was prepared for by these developments in thought. The position ascribed to Auguste Comte, quoted at the beginning of this piece, clearly follows the breakdown of philosophy.

But the concern here is with the cutting loose from reality, not as yet with the flight from it. Developments in philosophy prepared the way for it, but the actual break occurred in specific work by thinkers. There were three major steps in the movement away from a fixed reality.

Abstract Rationalism

The first of these was the appearance of a widespread tendency to *abstract rationalism* among would-be intellectuals or thinkers. Abstract reason is reason cut loose from foundations. Reason must have a referent; it must be about something. Abstract rationalism occurs when someone employs reason without reference to that which is neces-

sary to its valid use. If reason is to lead to any valid conclusions, it must do so in terms of some reality. That is,
it must refer to some metaphysical or physical reality, and,
in the case of social thought, it must be tied to the way
things can and do happen. It should be obvious, then, that
no one intends to reason abstractly, except possibly as an
exercise in logic. There has been no conscious movement
devoted to the use of abstract reason. Rather, its employment can be ascribed to ignorance, or, more kindly, to the
failure to attend to reality.

There have been many varieties of usages of abstract
rationalism. Perhaps the most common occurs when there
is an attempt to apply a rational truth without regard to
the concrete situation or to the temporal manner and
order in which things can and do occur. Rationalists are
most apt to fall into this error. Eighteenth century thinkers and actors, imbued as they were with rationalism, inclined to attend to the nature of things, were prone to this
kind of behavior. Some of the best examples of abstract
rationalism at work occurred during the French Revolution and its aftermath. The French National Assembly issued a decree in August of 1789 which opened with these
words: "The National Assembly hereby completely abolish-
es the feudal system."[11] There follows a lengthy list particularizing what was abolished. The character of many of
these provisions is illustrated by the following example:

> Inasmuch as a national constitution and public liberty
> are of more advantage to the provinces than the privi-
> leges which some of these enjoy, and inasmuch as the
> surrender of such privileges is essential to the intimate
> union of all parts of the realm, it is decreed that all the

---

[11] Eugen Weber, *The Western Tradition* (Boston: D. C. Heath,
1959), p. 504.

peculiar privileges, pecuniary or otherwise, of the provinces, principalities, districts, cantons, cities and com-
munes, are once and for all abolished and are absorbed
into the law common to all Frenchmen.[12]

Presumably, all local prerogatives were abolished by one
stroke of the pen. To fill the vacuum created by the abolition of exceedingly complex and tangled relations, the
Assembly proceeded to issue, a few days later, a general
statement of the new political relationships which should
prevail. The abstractness of some of the principles is
astounding. For example:

The source of sovereignty is essentially in the nation;
no body, no individual can exercise authority that does
not proceed from it in plain terms.[13]

Does this mean that parents shall not exercise authority
over their children until the nation authorizes them to do
so? Possibly not, but who could say? At any rate, catastrophe followed.

It might be supposed that the French leaders had not
taken sufficient care in defining their principles. Even so,
the matter cuts deeper than that. Another example may
reveal the deeper dimensions of the problem of abstract
rationalism. Napoleon sent the following message to his
appointee as king of Westphalia in 1807:

You will find enclosed the constitution of your kingdom. . . . You must faithfully observe it. . . .[14]

Napoleon had caused to be drawn up a constitution for

---

[12] *Ibid.*, p. 506.

[13] *Ibid.*, p. 507.

[14] Quoted in R. R. Palmer with Joel Colton, *A History of the
Modern World* (New York: Alfred A. Knopf, 2nd ed. rev.,
1958), p. 392.

a kingdom and sent it along to be observed. There had been no examination of the concrete situation, nor was there any consultation of the peoples involved. There was a logic behind this action. Human nature is everywhere the same. Natural law is universally applicable. Why not draw up a code for everyone? Though they may not, must not, be obvious to rationalists, there are many reasons why this should not be attempted. In the first place, it is both superfluous and ridiculous to *enact* natural laws. Natural laws operate just the same, and universally, whether they are enacted or not. Moreover, natural laws are of the nature of principles, not of laws passed by legislatures. These principles may *inform* human acts, but acts are particular things, and they must be if they are to be enforced by courts. Second, positive law must be cast in terms of the language, the customs, the institutions, the procedures, even the beliefs, of the peoples involved. If they are not, they will either wreak havoc or be of no effect, or a combination of both. Reason, engaged in constructing programs, must be informed by the concrete situation, else it becomes abstract rationalism.

Of course, there have been many other kinds of abstract rationalism. They cannot be explored in detail here, though some of them crop up in historical exposition elsewhere in this work, but they can at least be named. Abstract rationalism occurs when anyone attempts to maintain that reality is restricted to that which can be known by reason. For example, some have denied the reality of altruism; it is, they say, only a mask under which self-interest is hidden. Self-interest can be rationally explained, so they claim, and there is no need to posit altruism to aid in explanation. Reason has been extended beyond its legitimate function and by so doing it has been made abstract.

Another abuse which may be ascribed to abstract rationalism is the raising of temporary phenomena to the level of universal truths. This results from failing to distinguish between the enduring and the changing. Rationalists are prone to this fallacy. A good example of this is T. R. Malthus' formulation of exact laws of population increase and the increase of the means of subsistence. To wit:

> It may safely be pronounced that the population, when unchecked, goes on doubling itself every twenty-five years, or increases in a geometrical ratio. . . .
> [T]he means of subsistence, under circumstances the most favorable to human industry, could not possibly be made to increase faster than in an arithmetical ratio.[15]

If these "laws" have any other referent than the recent history of England, it does not appear. Perhaps the most common variety of abstract rationalism in intellectual circles is the effort to impose a theoretical system upon reality. This results from what may be a laudable attempt to find the common denominator in a mass of phenomena. Numerous instances of this have occurred in the case of historians applying Marx's class struggle theory to history.

Abstract reason, then, is reason cut loose from reality. Rationalists may have ever been inclined or have tended to extend the use of reason beyond its proper sphere. But this was greatly aggravated from the early nineteenth century on by the state of philosophy. Kant used the Pure Reason to reduce the sphere of reason to a purely formal role. But then he used the Practical Reason to affirm what could not be arrived at by reason. The impact of this was to leave "rationalism" unchecked by reason. This allowed such thinkers as Auguste Comte, and later Karl Marx, to produce and propagate their "rational" systems without being subjected to the traditional philosophical checks.

---

[15] Quoted in Louis L. Snyder, *The Age of Reason* (Princeton: D. Van Nostrand, Anvil Book, 1955), pp. 150-51.

Imagination

A second development in cutting loose from reality occurred by way of the Romantic emphasis upon *imagination*. Romanticism was a conscious movement, more or less, which had its hey-day in Europe in the late eighteenth century and the first half of the nineteenth. Just as most of the paths which modern thought has taken diverge from Kant as their starting point, so romanticism was the spirit or medium in which this thought was developed. There is a vagueness about the thought of Romantics which extended study does little to dispel. Romanticism was a protest, in part, against the Age of Reason, and Romantics tended to exalt the imagination. In consequence, virtually every sort of idea might be advanced and seriously considered.

My purpose, however, is to call attention to a facet of romanticism only, not to make a general description or evaluation of it as a movement. The facet which concerns us has to do with the impetus it gave to the cutting loose from reality. This was mainly by way of the emphasis upon imagination, and its unfettered use.

The philosophical background to this is quite relevant. David Hume, with his radical empiricist approach to knowledge, had shown that we get only bits and pieces—fragments—of information from the senses. Thus, though we have a clear idea of a house, for example, we have never seen a house all at once. We can see part of it at a glance, but to see more we have to shift our perspective; when we do that, we lose sight of the part we saw earlier. Our idea of a house, then, must consist of more than sense impressions; it must have been developed by the imagination. Hume moved the imagination to a central position for philosophical consideration. Berkeley had already maintained that all ideas are mind-dependent. Kant claimed that knowledge is possible because of categories in the mind, went further and moved objectivity into the mind.

We can leave the philosophers at this point, for they were still somewhat disciplined in their speculations. Others were not. They found in these new theories a license to use the imagination at will. More, some returned to faith and idealism after the demise of reason; they felt not only free to use the imagination without stint but a call to do so. The free and extended use of the imagination was the way to the highest truths.

Ralph Waldo Emerson, the American, may be used to stand for those who thought in this way. In his tribute to "The Poet," Emerson gives unstinted praise to the unrestricted use of the imagination:

> The poets are thus liberating gods. . . . An imaginative book renders us much more service at first, by stimulating us through its tropes, than afterward when we arrive at the precise sense of the author. I think nothing is of any value in books excepting the transcendental and extraordinary. If a man is inflamed and carried away by his thought, to that degree that he forgets the authors and the public and heeds only this one dream which holds him like an insanity, let me read his paper, and you may have all the arguments and histories and criticisms. . . . Therefore we love the poet, the inventor, who in any form, whether in an ode or in an action or in looks and behavior, has yielded us a new thought. He unlocks our chains and admits us to a new scene.
>
> The emancipation is dear to all men, and the power to impart it, as it must come from greater depth and scope of thought, is a measure of intellect. Therefore all books of the imagination endure, all which ascend to that truth that the writer sees nature beneath him, and uses it as his exponent. Every verse or sentence possessing this virtue will take care of its own immortality. The

religions of the world are the ejaculations of a few imaginative men.[16]

Romantics, then, were cutting loose from reality by way of the imagination. Man might not yet be a god, though Emerson uses the word to describe the work of the poet, but he was almost certainly a demigod. Perhaps he did not yet create his own reality, but if he did, would he not have reached even greater imaginative heights? In the exaltation of mood, feeling, emotion, what vulgarity it would be to hold the imagination to mundane reality!

Darwinian Evolution

The third movement culminated in the triumph of Darwinian evolution. This marked the definitive break with an enduring reality and an almost exclusive focus upon change. The cynic might observe that the circle of philosophy had been completed. From Heraclitus in Ancient Greece to Charles Darwin in the England of the latter part of the nineteenth century was a long time and a considerable distance, but reality had once again been located in the flux of change. The way had been prepared for Darwin in philosophy. G. W. F. Hegel had located reality in certain ideas at work in history, had made growth and development the center of attention, and had made of the dialectic the process by which historical change took place. Herbert Spencer, the English philosopher, had elaborated a philosophy embracing the evolution of societies. Auguste Comte, the French social planner, had reduced the development of man to three stages. Karl Marx was already busily inverting Hegel to make the class struggle which arises out of the control of the instruments of production the mov-

---

[16] Ralph W. Emerson, "The Poet," *Collected Works of Ralph Waldo Emerson* (New York: Greystone Press, n. d.), p. 137.

ing force in history, rather than ideas. It remained for
Charles Darwin to give scientific sanction to the philosophy
of change.

Actually, Darwin did much more. He brought man into
the stream of evolution, denied the fixity of the species, and
proposed particular theories that would account for change,
or so he hoped. He collected a great deal of material with
which he buttressed his generalizations. Above all, his work
served as a base for the popularizations of evolution.

By that time, the attention of thinkers had been drawn
almost entirely away from trying to discover an enduring
reality. They were no longer looking for the nature of
things. They were no longer describing an enduring order
but rather seeking for the order or sources of changes. The
quest for natural laws, so far as it survived, was turned
toward discovering the laws of growth and development.
Thought had moved from eternity into time, and men
began to locate "reality" in the future. They had cut loose
from reality and embarked on the strange journey into the
unknown and the unknowable—unknowable, at least, until they get there, though it is not at all clear how they
would know when they had arrived.

Even before all this had occurred, however, some men
were becoming increasingly enamored of the visions of the
better world they thought they could create. The imagination could conceive of a better world. Abstract rationalism
could be used to give a "scientific" or "philosophical" gloss
to their visions. They were sufficiently cut loose from reality to believe that they could make a better social world,
and they "set about the betterment of man's condition."

5

The Utopian Vision

. . . I know that society may be formed so as to exist without crime, without poverty, with health greatly improved, with little, if any, misery, and with intelligence and happiness increased an hundredfold; and no obstacle whatsoever intervenes at this moment, except ignorance, to prevent such a state of society from becoming universal.[1]   —ROBERT OWEN, 1816

THE CONNECTION BETWEEN VISIONS OF UTOPIA AND RE-formers may not be apparent to everyone. Utopians are often thought of as quaint characters who lived and wrote sometime in the past, somewhat impractical but harmless fellows. If they were literary figures in their own right, or if they had a pleasing style, excerpts from their works crop up in anthologies of literature, and whole books are sometimes reprinted. But they are not generally credited with having had much to do with what has happened. The matter is quite otherwise, in fact.

Hardly a reform proposal has been made in the twentieth century which did not have antecedents in utopian literature of the nineteenth century or earlier. As one writer points out, in the earlier period "utopists were anticipating the 'welfare state,' the nationalization of industries, 'socialized' medicine and health programs, unemployment in-

---

[1] Quoted in W. H. G. Armitage, *Heavens Below* (London: Routledge and Kegan Paul, 1961), p. 77.

72

surance, old-age pensions, and numerous other such proposals. . . ."[2]

More specifically, one historian points out that Robert Owen, an early nineteenth century utopian, had a considerable impact upon historical development. "Owen . . . was influential in bringing to pass the first labor legislation, the British Factory Acts in 1819. . . . The co-operative buying societies among the poorer folk . . . are also the direct outgrowth of Owen's experiments of New Lanark. He was one of the pioneers of the trade union movement, and laid down the first plans for labor bureaus on the national scale."[3] This writer goes on to give similar examples for many other utopians.

Utopias are articulated visions of a perfect society. They are products of the imagination of their authors, neither existing anywhere at the time they are described nor ever having existed anywhere. They are futuristic in orientation, though there is often an admixture of a return to felicity which man once enjoyed before corruption. Even so, their realization is to come at some future time, or at least that is the implication and hope. Even so, the "role of utopias in social thought . . . is not analogous to that of blueprint to house. Such a misconception makes them of little importance, for as such they have hardly entered the stream of human history at all. Instead, utopias more nearly play the part of the idealized picture of the completed house which precedes the drawing of the blueprint. Utopias are the best societies which their authors can imagine, distant goals toward which their creators would

[2] Glenn Negley and J. Max Patrick, *The Quest for Utopia* (New York: Henry Schuman, 1952), p. 16.

[3] Joyce O. Hertzler, *The History of Utopian Thought* (New York: Macmillan, 1923), p. 282.

have us move, unhampered in their conception by gross obstacles and difficulties."[4]

The Vision and the Means

The construction of a utopia, then, is an elemental flight from reality. The author who does so must, by the nature of his task, withdraw from concrete reality, must envision something which does not exist. Insofar as he neglects to take into account the nature of man and the universe, as most modern utopians have, he is engaged in a full-fledged flight from reality. The role of utopian thought in the development of meliorist reform is this: Utopians provided the vision of the perfect society toward which meliorist reform is supposed to move. Quite often, they also described the means which might be used to achieve utopia and ways of doing things in the perfect society. Utopia is the end; meliorist reform is the means. Utopias have served as the visionary and imaginary flight which has preceded the actual flight.

The fact that twentieth century reformers have usually disavowed any particular utopian hopes must not be permitted to obscure the actual connection. The vagueness of the goals of contemporary reformers are not even to be pitted against any particularized version of utopia. This would tend to discipline reformers to some limited extent, though this may not be the reason for the avoidance of embracing a utopia. Nonetheless, a vague generalized vision of utopia does impel reformers to their exertions.

As I have pointed out elsewhere, this vision is of a utopia that "is altogether pleasant and enticing. It is of a place and time where suffering and privation have been

---

[4] Clarence B. Carson, "Their Young Men Dream No Dreams," *Spiritual Life*, IX (Spring 1963), 32.

banished, where the inhabitants are secure from the ravages of disease and unemployment, where all men have enough of the good things of life . . . , where education and environment have banished the baser things and men have willingly and gladly turned to the finer things of life, where one may speed in a carefree manner down the highway of life with no fear of a collision along the way."[5]

The content for a vision which has become progressively more vague was provided in luxuriant detail by nineteenth century utopians.

Before utopian thought could enter the life stream of that social thought which is believed to have relevance to actuality, a transformation had to take place. Such a transformation had taken place for many of those in intellectual circles by the early nineteenth century. It has already been described as the cutting loose from reality. Uninhibited rationalism became abstract rationalism; the imagination was cut loose from the fetters of reason; men turned their eyes away from the nature of things, from an enduring reality, from metaphysical or eternal realms, to focus their attention upon change and development. In these circumstances, they could not only envision utopias with the utmost freedom but also actually begin to believe in them as possibilities.

Makers of Utopias

The literary genera which we refer to as utopias was not new to the nineteenth century, of course. The name itself adorned a work of Sir Thomas More, a book which was published in the early sixteenth century. But More's book was modeled upon one of much more ancient vintage,

---

[5] *The Fateful Turn* (Irvington-on-Hudson, N. Y.: Foundation for Economic Education, 1963), p. 178.

Plato's *Republic*. It should be noted, though, that Plato's good society differed significantly from most modern utopias. Plato did not envision the transformation of human nature; he took men as they are and proposed to build a good society for them. This would involve, as he saw, a rather rigorous regimentation, and he did not shrink from these implications. Hence, the meaning of Plato's *Republic* for those who prefer liberty (whether he could be numbered among them or not) is clear; it is a cautionary tale, showing the consequences of trying to institute the good society. There were other utopias written in the classical period, but the genera disappeared for the Middle Ages and did not reappear until More's work.

Following More, there were a good many utopian writers from the sixteenth into the eighteenth centuries—what historians are likely to call the early modern period. They include Francis Bacon's *New Atlantis,* Tommaso Campanella's *The City of the Sun,* James Harrington's *Oceana,* Fenelon's *Telemachus,* Andrae Valenti's *Christianopolis,* and Robert Filmer's *Patriarcha.* These utopias have mainly an academic interest. That is, they constitute an historical background for the utopianism which came to inform meliorist reform but they entered into the stream of social thought at the time, little, if at all. They did contain many of the ideas which went into later utopias.

Indeed, More's work contained what can now be recognized as most of the staple ingredients of utopian literature. Utopias almost invariably have two sorts of materials: a critique of conditions contemporary with the work being written, and a vision of the perfect society. More's book has both. Moreover, the good society is pictured as a communistic one. Private property is an evil to be rooted out, a theme which runs the gamut of utopian literature from the sixteenth to the twentieth centuries. More said,

I am persuaded, that till property is taken away there can be no equitable or just distribution of things, nor can the world be happily governed: for as long as that is maintained, the greatest and the far best part of mankind will be still oppressed with a load of cares and anxieties.[6]

The great change that will be wrought by the abolition of property is described:

In all places it is visible, that while people talk of a commonwealth, every man seeks his own wealth; but there, where no man has any property, all men zealously pursue the good of the public: and, indeed, it is no wonder to see men act so differently; for in other commonwealths every man knows that unless he provides for himself, how flourishing soever the commonwealth may be, he must die of hunger; so that he sees the necessity of preferring his own concerns to the public; but in Utopia, where every man has a right to everything, they all know that if care is taken to keep the public stores full, no private man can want anything; for among them there is no unequal distribution, so that no man is poor, none in necessity; and though no man has anything, yet they are all rich; for what can make a man so rich as to lead a serene and cheerful life, free from anxieties. . . .[7]

The chances are good that More was engaging in superb irony throughout much of this work, that at most it is only an exercise of the fancy. In any event, later writers have presented such fancies with deadly, and deadening, seriousness.

Most of the utopian ideas appear to have been suggested during this early period, but we had best not stop to explore them. A considerable change had come over utopian litera-

---

[6] Quoted in Hertzler, *op. cit.*, pp. 132-33.
[7] *Ibid.*, p. 135.

ture by the nineteenth century. Indeed, this century was the century of utopians, par excellence. Many intellectuals turned their attention to describing perfect societies and offering programs for realizing them. There were utopian socialists, communitarians, anarchists, "scientific" socialists, syndicalists, and perfectionists. There was a great deal of enthusiasm for utopian projects, and men began actually to try to put them into effect.

Utopian Communities

The first considerable effort along this line was the communitarian movement. In general, the idea in founding communities was for a group to separate itself from the corrupting influence of the "world" and arrive at perfection in isolation from contaminating influences. There were a great many such communities attempted. Some were religious in orientation, for there was a great deal of religious enthusiasm in the first half of the nineteenth century. Others were secular in origin and aims. But whether religious or secular they were usually communistic, that is, they proposed to labor for the common good and share equally, or according to need, in the goods produced.

America was a popular place to locate such experiments, since they needed physical isolation and considerable tolerance from political authorities. Some of the more famous of the American communities were Brook Farm, New Harmony, North American Phalanx, Amana, Oneida, Nashoba, Fruitlands, Icaria, and the religious communities of the Shakers and Rappites.

Two examples of such communities will suffice. One of the most famous was the one located on the banks of the Wabash river in Indiana; it was called New Harmony. New Harmony was the brain child, and purse child, of Robert Owen, a wealthy Scottish manufacturer. Owen's idea was to found self-sufficient villages. As one writer describes his utopia:

> He saw the world made up of villages, rid of the capitalist and free from that private property which was completely incompatible with social well-being, producing solely for the collective good. . . . Briefly stated, he recommended . . . that colonies of workers should be formed on the co-operative principle. These colonies or villages of co-operation with a population varying from 500 to 2000 souls . . . were to be engaged in both agriculture and manufacturing; they were to be housed in great quadrangles located in the midst of each colony, containing the common dormitories, common kitchen and dining rooms, common schools, library, reading rooms, guest rooms, etc. . . . All were to work at suitable tasks according to their ability. . . .

These villages were to be joined together in a great federation which would replace the old world of the "capitalistic system with its poverty and misery, its injustice and inequality, its falsehood and deception; and all were to be united in brotherly co-operative effort."[8]

In Owen's most ambitious attempt to put his ideas into effect, the community of New Harmony, he was confronted by continual difficulties for the short time that he continued the effort. Splinter groups of dissenters were continually forming and moving off elsewhere. There were complaints about those who ate but did not work. Since decisions were to be made democratically, all work and other activity was frequently stopped for discussions and votes. Some complained that Owen was profiteering from the sale of land, though he sold the land on credit or gave leases for ten thousand years. "Money had been officially abolished but in every lane and alley the Harmonists pri-

---

[8] *Ibid.,* pp. 219-20.

vately traded and bargained and bickered over cash."[9]
"There was trouble over liquor. Prohibition was decreed,
but everywhere people were drunk, supplied by sly boot-
legging members."[10] In short, before its hasty demise New
Harmony had witnessed some of the classic ills accom-
panying efforts to make over men.

The Oneida Community, founded and watched over for
many years by John Humphrey Noyes, carried communal
sharing to what most would probably consider its logical
extreme. To be specific, in this community they practiced
what was called complex marriage. That is, each adult
who was a full-fledged member of the community might
be considered married to every other such adult of the
opposite sex. Noyes was a religious leader, and the strange
beliefs of the community were a part of the religion he
taught. He believed in the possibility of perfection here
and now, and those who had arrived at perfection no
longer lived under the old dispensation. In anticipation of
the Kingdom of Heaven—which was the name bestowed
upon the first establishment begun by Noyes—he wrote:

> When the will of God is done . . . there will be no
> marriage. The marriage supper of the lamb is a feast at
> which every dish is free to every guest. Exclusiveness,
> jealousy, quarreling, have no place there, for the same
> reason as that which forbids the guests at a thanksgiving
> dinner to claim each his separate dish, and quarrel with
> the rest for his rights. In a holy community, there is no
> more reason why sexual intercourse should be restrained
> by law, than why eating and drinking should be. . . .[11]

Though the community lasted for a longer period than

---

[9] Everett Webber, *Escape to Utopia* (New York: Hastings
House, 1959), p. 151.

[10] *Ibid.*, p. 147.

[11] *Ibid.*, pp. 375-76.

most such undertakings, it did eventually break up. One writer points out that young people went away to college and came more and more "to desire the marriage customs of the world where people were allowed to fall in love and not required to cultivate a specious enjoyment at seeing their loved ones bandied through a wide circle of holy hands."[12]

Utopian Socialism

A second, and related, development in utopian thought in the first half of the nineteenth century was the setting forth of what has been called utopian socialism. The theory of modern socialism was developed in this period by those whom Marx scornfully dubbed utopians. They were mostly French, and included Morelly, Babeuf, Saint-Simon, Fourier, Cabet, and Blanc.

Fourier and Cabet developed theories, and attempted to apply them in communities. Fourier's dream may serve as an example of these, though they differed considerably one from another. "In brief, Fourier proposed to eliminate wasteful competition, and oppressive government, by organizing self-sufficient and mainly agricultural units of production."[13] These units he called Phalanstéres. They would, he thought, solve the problems of production, and each person would be guaranteed a basic standard of living. "Along with this expanding production, will go an educational revolution. . . . It will raise mankind to perfection in body and mind. . . . Our present teachers— slaves to abstractions—know how to produce Neros; we

---

[12] *Ibid.*, p. 405.

[13] John Bowle, *Politics and Opinion in the Nineteenth Century* (New York: Oxford University Press, A Galaxy Book, 1964), p. 142.

know how to turn potential Neros into men like Gods."[14]

Mankind was made for perfection and harmony, according to Fourier, not discord and competition. His system would achieve the true end of man. "This economic and educational revolution, by housing the population in self-supporting, autonomous and self-conducted luxury hotels, in which all the occupants would work and play in industrious harmony, would solve the problems of poverty, war, and wickedness."[15] All that he needed to get this plan underway, he believed, was to find a wealthy patron who would finance it, and he waited expectantly through his later years for such a benefactor.

Several important changes in utopian literature occurred in the latter part of the nineteenth century. For one thing, there was apparently a great increase in the number of such works produced. One book lists the better known ones, mainly in English or English translation, for the period 1850-1950. This indicates a great concentration of production of such literature from about 1883 to 1912. Only six works are listed from 1850 to 1883; whereas, there are seventy-four works from 1883 to 1912, seven for 1894 alone.[16]

Another development was the shift from the conception of utopian communities to dreams of world-wide organization. As one account has it, "it was to become rapidly and increasingly apparent that the utopian community was so unrealistic that it could provide no more than a setting for fantasy or satire. Modern utopia must be a state, and indeed it was already beginning to be evident that modern utopia must be the world." By some kind of metamorphosis,

---

[14] *Ibid.*

[15] *Ibid.*, p. 143.

[16] See Negley and Patrick, *op. cit.*, pp. 19-22.

"the economic ideal of utopia, through a kind of economic necessity, becomes the ideal of the world."[17]

A third development was the organization of movements to act not in isolated communities but within societies at large, the attempt to make utopia scientific (as in Comte and Marx), and the development of programs and plans for the realization of the good society, no longer cast in the guise of utopia. In short, men were preparing to achieve utopia in society at large. Steps were being taken to translate utopian visions into reformist measures in the latter part of the nineteenth century.

The Ingredients of Utopia

It may be well, at this point, to sum up and indicate the main strains which went into utopian thought. Utopia was concocted out of a compound of some of man's deepest longings, longings for felicity, harmony, order, peace, security, and repose. Utopian visions have had appeal because they embraced remnants of mythology, relics of religious hopes (quite often transposed), immemorial prejudices, along with notions borrowed from scientific theories. Some of the ingredients of this compound are worth dwelling upon.

One of the strains that has frequently been woven into the fabric of utopia, or at least evoked by it, is the myth of the Golden Age. This myth appears to have had virtually universal appeal, and even extensive and intensive indoctrination in progressivism in contemporary society does not appear to have completely succeeded in exorcising it. The Golden Age myth locates the time of felicity and harmony in the past. The variations on the particular locale range from the recent past to the Garden of Eden.

---

[17] *Ibid.,* pp. 582-83.

At its deepest, the Golden Age myth is of a time before man had lost harmony with nature, or with God. In theological terms, it could refer to the time before man became a moral being, a time before all the travail, tension, and unpalatable choices entailed in being moral. In pagan terms, it could refer to the time when man was simply an animal, guided and living by instinct rather than thought. There have, of course, been many efforts to account for the appeal of the Golden Age myth. Some see it simply as a result of the tendency to romanticize that which lives only in memory, others as the effort to return to the womb, and so forth.

At any rate, elements from the Golden Age myth crop up in much of utopian literature. Utopias quite often have strenuous criticisms of recent social and economic trends, criticisms of everything from the enclosure movement of an earlier time to industrialism in the nineteenth century. It is easy to see that the communitarian ideas owe much to a romanticizing of the medieval manor. Robert Owen even wanted to abolish the plow and return to the spade. "The spade," he said, "wherever there is sufficient soil, opens it to a depth that allows the water to pass freely below the bed of the seed or plant. . . ." Whereas, the plow is a "mere surface implement, and extremely defective in principle."[18] Utopians quite often want to be rid of money—the source of the hated cash nexus—and return to primitive barter and exchange. The appeal of many of their plans is the return of primeval simplicity and felicity.

A second ingredient in utopia, quite often sublimated and transposed in it, is millennialism. Christian eschatology places the Golden Age at the end of time rather than at the beginning (or in addition to placing it at the begin-

---

[18] Quoted in Bowle, *op. cit.*, pp. 148-49.

ning). Whether this Golden Age is to be for eternity in a transcendental Heaven or for a thousand years upon a transformed earth (or that both shall be) has long been a matter for controversy. Of course, utopians have used only the conception of a heaven on earth. For some of them, the Kingdom of God became a kingdom to be made here on earth.

In utopian thought, however, millennialism was divorced largely from its religious content, humanized, and the vision of heaven quite often became the vision of a materialistic earthly paradise. The dictatorship of the proletariat of Marx and Engels does not appear to share much in common with the Kingdom which John saw descending to earth in his vision recorded in the Book of Revelations, but Marx turned more than Hegel upside down (or right side up, as he claimed), and his is indeed an apocalyptic vision of the ushering in of the Golden Age.

In short, millennialism was quite often subsumed into utopian thought, placing the Golden Age in the future, and subtly appealing to deep religious hopes.

By the latter part of the nineteenth century, however, millennialism was being domesticated and secularized as progressivism. Progressivism was a third ingredient of utopianism. This statement needs modifying; progressivism was a late-comer to the scene. Earlier utopias could not have used it. Thus, its major function became a mode for the achievement of utopia. Progressivism, as it is relevant to utopianism, was born out of technological progress by historical inevitability, evolution being the midwife. The flight from reality owes much of its believability both to evolutionary theories and technological progress. These, in turn, made the realization of utopia appear possible. It is not strange that anyone viewing the course of invention and industrial development in the modern era should be struck by the very great possibilities of human ingenuity.

At any rate, Karl Marx and Friedrich Engels described a state of earthly bliss and devised a theory to make its coming historically inevitable. The tools they worked with were technological change, the theory of evolution, and a theory of historical change. By so doing, they associated progress with the realization of utopia, and, for those who have sought utopia by way of reform, unwittingly associated progress with reform—a wholly gratuitous connection, one might add. Reformers in the twentieth century have got maximum mileage out of the supposed connection between reform and progress.

A fourth strain in utopianism is the implied vision of life without tension. To put it another way, though not the way a utopian would describe it, utopia is a land where stasis or absolute stability has been achieved. This does not appear to be compatible with progressivism, any more than progressivism is compatible with a Golden Age in the past. But these are logical objections to nonlogical flights of fancy. Consistency is a requirement of dialectical reason, and it must be remembered that Kant had already cut the ground from under such reason.

In the real world, one may believe that change, development, even progress, are the products of tension. But in utopia one can have the products of capital without capitalism, the products of invention without the incentives to invention, the advantages of freedom without the corollary disadvantages of responsibility, and so on. Why raise difficult questions about the mode of progress without tensions, without frustrations, without incentives? At any rate, utopia will be a land without tensions, without that which produces crime, war, and other disorders. There will be no jealousy, no selfishness, no competition, and no abrasiveness in relationships.

Perhaps this is an overstatement of the case. Some utopians did envisage the continued presence of some dissidents. Let us take a look at what one utopian—Chauncey Thomas in *The Crystal Button*—proposed to do with such people. They are to be kept in hospitals, of course. Why hospitals? Because they are morally deranged. The explanation continues:

"Morally deranged?"

"Yes, I believe you used to apply the term 'prison' to the institution used for the confinement of moral patients."

"They are convicts, then? But why are these associated with your hospitals?"

"Why not? They constitute a part, though happily a small part of the patients that come under the same management and treatment. We simply treat them as persons who are morally deformed or ailing."[19]

Judging by this insight into what utopia will be like, we may be nearer to it than some have thought!

A fifth ingredient of utopia has usually been environmentalism. This has provided utopians with an explanation of sorts for the imperfections which they readily observed and vigorously denounced. If man is perfect or perfectible, if there is no ingrained obstacle within him that would prevent the perfect society, why, one might ask, does perfection not prevail? One historian explains the utopian view, particularly the utopian socialist view, in the following manner:

One and all believed that with proper environment man would be actually perfect. He was naturally good, but existing environment with its overwhelming imperfections and maladjustments destined him to evil and woe.[20]

[19] Quoted in Negley and Patrick, *op. cit.*, pp. 88-89.
[20] Hertzler, *op. cit.*, p. 222.

The correction of the environment, and the education of men, would remove these obstacles to perfection. The Rubicon for such explanations, of course, is how to make an account of why things have not always been perfect.

A heady strain in much of nineteenth century utopian thought, particularly that of socialists, was anarchism. Marx proclaimed that the state would wither away. Marx was in a line extending from Godwin and Proudhon through Kropotkin and Sorel. Those utopian socialists who abominated the state and governments apparently arrived at their position through some such reasoning, or unreasoning, as this: Private property is the root of all social evil, and its existence the cause of man's "fall." (Rousseau thought as much.) Private property, it has been claimed, sets one man against another, leads men to pursue their own interest to the harm of others, promotes selfishness, and so on. The state, as they saw it, was the prime bulwark of property. The vast paraphernalia of government—the courts, the police, the bulk of laws—had to do with the protection of property. Abolish property, and government would lose its reason for being. Or, as revolutionary anarchists were apt to believe, abolish government and things would revert to their natural, and perfect, condition. As one writer says:

> A strong line of thinking thus became absolutely hostile to the State; it considered this most important of all political phenomena either as infinitely elastic and compressible (J. S. Mill), altogether dispensable (Marx and Engels), or the supreme obstacle to total happiness.[21]

The flight from political reality has had horrible consequences in our century. Anarchists did not succeed in

---

[21] Molnar, *op. cit.*, p. 73.

abolishing the state, but they did turn thought away from the very practical problems of how to contain the state. Eventually, most socialists reconciled themselves to the state, used it to their ends, but it tended to become the uninhibited state of totalitarianism. It is worth pointing out that some contemporary libertarians have similar views toward government to those of nineteenth century utopians. Socialists saw the state as the bulwark of property; these libertarians witness the state as violator of liberty and property at the hands of social reformers. Both fail to realize that government is an *instrument,* not a cause, of men's behavior and beliefs.

There were many other strains in utopian thought. Equality and distributive justice were prominent in many utopias. However, in the nineteenth century some thinkers expected utopias to be controlled by scientific elites. Such arrangements have been called technocracies. Scientism crops up quite often in these visions of the future. Rationalism and education were linked by thinkers as assumption and method for arriving at utopia. The above comprise the major assumptions and beliefs of utopians.

The Urge to Reform

Utopia, then, contained the vision of earthly bliss which has drawn us into the crucible of melioristic reform.

It must be made clear, though, that there is a great gulf between Robert Owen's utopian vision of a world without poverty and President Johnson's War on Poverty. To most of his contemporaries, even as for us, Owen was an impractical visionary, one to be taken advantage of by cynical joiners of his communities or to be avoided by more upstanding people. President Johnson, on the other hand, would certainly be reckoned to be a "practical" politician. But the difference between Owen and Johnson is not in the vision they hold forth; it is in the means to be employed. The gulf has been bridged. What was once clearly visionary is now being pursued with all the instruments of power of centralized states, is even the stock in trade of the most corrupt politicians. We are no nearer to utopia in our day, I think, but we are cheek by jowl with a whole panorama of compulsive devices that are billed as instruments for ushering in utopia (though the word itself is not employed).

Most of the remainder of this story will have to do with how the gulf was bridged. It was a tremendous undertaking. It must be kept in mind that thus far we have pursued mainly the development of some ideas among some intellectuals. Though utopian novels were becoming more popular in the late nineteenth century, as indicated by sales, utopian thought had even then hardly entered the mainstream of political thought. Apparently, it was as clear to most of our ancestors as it may be to some of us that utopian visions are flights from reality. Intellectuals had not yet come into the circle of power, certainly not utopistic intellectuals. The position of these people, and their kind, in the nineteenth century is described by one writer:

> These people belonged to no great disciplined order; they are backed by no European authority. . . . When they rebel, they become outcasts and refugees, as were Marx and Lenin, appealing away from the bourgeoisie to which they belong to the masses without.[22]

In short, such people were largely loners and outcasts. We must trace them in their move to the seats of power. Such a movement has been made, and it is rather clear

---

[22] Bowle, *op. cit.*, p. 29.

that such intellectuals would be in line for a Freedom Medal from some President today.

It is not practical, however, to follow the movement from utopia to reform, from visionary to presidential adviser, from lonely dreamer to practical politician, on an international scale. The perspective will now be shifted to the national scale, to the United States, so that the story can be told of how one nation was drawn into the web of those engaged in a flight from reality.

6

An American Dream

No man any more has any care for the morrow, either for himself or his children, for the nation guarantees the nurture, education, and comfortable maintenance of every citizen from the cradle to the grave.[1]

—EDWARD BELLAMY, 1888

THE ATTRACTION OF AMELIORATIVE REFORM IS THE PROM-ise of a better world in which to live. There may be some exceptions to this rule, notably for those who find in reformist activity the means of exercising power over people. But for the generality of people, improvement, not power, has been the lure. They have been drawn into the labyrinth of reform programs by visions of what the world would be like when the reformers had instituted their reforms. Utopian visions have been the magnets pulling peoples into the orbits of reformers.

Yet, so far as we know, most people have rejected and do reject the possibility of utopia. "Utopian" is a term of derision for describing impractical dreamers. The more practical minded perceive the fallacies in the utopian blueprint. Those with keener imaginations foresee the emptiness of utopia, even if it were possible. Man was

---

[1] Edward Bellamy, *Looking Backward—2000-1887* (Boston: Houghton Mifflin, 1888), p. 90.

meant to strive, some will say; contentment is for cows. Even so, it may be that the argument against utopia that has the broadest appeal is the manifest impossibility of achieving it. In short, man and the universe are not so constructed as to make utopia possible.

But the reformist bent has triumphed in America, and in many other places, in our day. And ameliorative reform has as its implicit goal the achievement of utopia. How can this state of affairs have come about? How can men have rejected utopia and embraced reforms which have as their end the achievement of utopia?

From Reality to Utopia

Two developments made such a contradiction appear not to be one. First, there was the cutting loose and flight from reality. This did not make utopia appear possible to most sane people, but it did help to render programs and plans drawn from utopian visions apparently feasible. Second, a particularization of utopia took place, and social reformers advanced what appeared to be limited programs which they hoped would move them to their ultimate goal. At the same time, though, that the means were particularized in specific programs, the goal was generalized into such hazy rhetorical phrases as peace, prosperity, and progress. Thus, a reversal of the utopian mode occurred as the attempts were made to actualize utopia. In utopian literature, the goal—the good society—is often pictured in luxuriant detail; while the means to the arrival at this goal are not usually specified. Note that the utopian could thus avoid the odium that would be associated with the coercion and revolution by which his goal has to be pursued, and the reformer could avoid the disrepute attached to utopianism.

It is hazardous, however, to follow a general analysis of

these developments any further. These generalizations do not do full justice to the complexity of the phenomena. Moreover, the above formulations may be interpreted as implying that utopians and reformers have intentionally played down or remained silent about certain facets of their programs. This may not have been the case. On the contrary, utopians did not envision the force and violence which would accompany efforts to arrive at their goals. By a similar myopia, reformers need not know that they are utopians. It must be kept clear that intellectuals have not only drawn others into an illusory mental realm; they are quite often victims of the same delusions. This was made possible by the flight from reality. But the point at hand is that the impetus to the flight from reality which has eventuated in the triumph of melioristic reform was provided by utopian visions, though these have long since receded beyond the horizon from whence today they emit the colors that are identified by believers as peace, prosperity, and progress.

Those advancing the flight from reality had great difficulty in launching America. The fact has not been sufficiently appreciated. When writers note that Americans did not rush to adopt ameliorative reforms as avidly as Europeans, the matter is often treated as the "social lag" of Americans. Americans "lagged" more than fifty years behind Germans in providing certain kinds of "insurance" programs for workers. Americans "lagged" many years behind England in providing old-age pensions, and some several years in empowering labor unions. Contrariwise, France is far ahead of the United States in rent controls (and in housing shortages), and England is much further along the road to completely socialized medicine.

The matter can and should be described in quite different terms. Americans held out against the lure of utopia, the promises of reformers, the blandishments of revolutionaries much longer than many Europeans. Reform, when it came to America, was more moderate and mild than in most European countries, and did not so drastically alter the existing situation. Still, it has come, and the gradualness of the movement has obscured for many Americans the import of it.

There were tremendous obstacles to the triumph of reformism in America. The institutions, traditions, habits, and beliefs of Americans ran counter to the outlook and practices associated with ameliorative reform. But, the casual observer might object, on these grounds reformism should have come much more readily to America than to Europe. No country was more deeply locked in age-old ways than Russia. The British tradition was hoary with age before America was an adolescent. Surely, America was more flexible than bureaucrat-ridden France, the American more amenable to reform than the Slavic peasant. Besides, the governments in America were generally more responsive to the populace than in Europe.

The greatest weakness in these objections is a misunderstanding of how reformism has been advanced, and by whom. If the "people" had originated and advanced ameliorative reform, it should have come very early to America. Traditions and customs in America were not so firmly fixed as in many countries. On the other hand, popular government was much better provided for in America than in most countries. To blame governmental intervention and security programs upon democracy, however, is to confuse effect with cause. Undoubtedly, there are now many people who have vested interests in certain governmental programs, and there are many others who have accepted the notion that their prosperity is due to the efforts of politicians. But these are effects, not causes, though they do contribute to the continued feasibility of politicians advancing ameliorative reform. Reforms were and are advanced by *intellectuals* (and their satraps among the bureaucracy). In any country where there was a moderately enlightened electorate, it has taken many years of vigorous activity to get a majority for reforms of any great dimensions. The experience of reformers in England and America should give ample evidence for this statement.[2]

Drastic social reforms were introduced most readily in Russia, Germany, and Italy. It was the work of intellectuals, or pseudo-intellectuals. These were countries without a lengthy experience in popular governments, but countries within which tradition was strong. But the intellectuals were—as they have tended to be increasingly everywhere—disaffected from the tradition. Not only was tradition without effective spokesmen quite often, but also the populace was inexperienced in defending it.

In America, things were quite different. The United States Constitution had been formed by the leading thinkers in America. Much of the political tradition had taken shape in the historical memory of much of the populace. The traditions had been freely formed, for the most part, and had the support of intellectuals for most of the nineteenth century. Americans revered their institutions, took pride in them, were accustomed to thinking of them as the best in the world.

---

[2] There is, of course, a demonstrable corollary between universal suffrage and the triumph of reformism in many countries. And reformers have been eager proponents of universal suffrage. The significance of this is not far to seek: the illiterate, unpropertied, and politically inexperienced succumb more readily than does a limited electorate to the promises of reformers.

Equally important as an obstacle to reform was the character of American institutions. The United States Constitution—and probably most state constitutions—is a conservative document. That is, the government which it provides for makes change difficult to accomplish. For a bill to become law it must be passed by a majority of the House of Representatives, a majority of the Senate, and signed by the President. Even then, it may be nullified by the courts as being unconstitutional. The Constitution can, of course, be amended, but amendments must be approved by conventions or legislatures in three-fourths of the states to become a part of the Constitution. Yet there can be no legitimate occasion for violent revolution on majoritarian grounds, for the Constitution can and has been amended, and laws can be and have been passed. (It should be noted here that reformers have managed to advance their unconstitutional programs in the twentieth century without getting the Constitution amended. How they have done this will be taken up later.)

The Constitution was the bedrock of political reality to Americans for most of their history, too. There was good reason for this belief. It was written and approved by men deeply immersed in historical experience and accustomed to attending to the enduring nature of things. It is often alleged that the endurance of the Constitution can be ascribed to its elasticity. The fact that it has lasted so long might better be attributed to its foundation in enduring realities, in realities about the nature and purpose of government, about the nature of man, about the dangers of concentrated power, and about the importance of limited action. The principles derived from these realities· were the bases of the checks and balances instituted. These latter were mighty buttresses to liberty just as they were formidable obstacles to reform.

A Multiplicity of Dreams

It was with some trepidation that I decided to call this chapter "An American Dream." It is mainly about a utopian vision, and utopia was not *the* American dream. Indeed, there was *no* American dream, and this becomes apparent when the situation is viewed historically. There were many American dreams. From the earliest colonial days the diversity and multiplicity of American dreams are obvious. The Puritan leaders in New England had one kind of vision, the settlers of Virginia another. The society envisioned by Quakers in Pennsylvania was different from that of those who planted North Carolina. The dream of Roger Williams in Rhode Island differed dramatically from that of the Lords Calvert for Maryland.

Nor when a united body had been wrought out of these diverse elements did the multiplicity of dreams disappear. The American agreement, as I have pointed out elsewhere, was an agreement to disagree. American unity was not fashioned by the crushing of diversity but by providing a framework in which each man could have his own vision, dream his own dream, make his own way. If a man had visions of utopia, and some did, he was free to pursue it alone or in the company of others, so long as the others joined him voluntarily and could leave when they were ready. The American way was the voluntary way. It was, in essence, individualistic.

Still, there were dreams shared by a sufficient number of Americans that they could be called American dreams. One of the earliest and deepest of these was the desire of men to practice their religious beliefs freely. For most, this was not yet a vision of religious liberty when the earliest settlements in English America were made. The Pilgrims only wanted a place to practice their own version of Christianity; so it was, too, with that larger group of people known as Puritans. They drove out dissenters from among them, proclaiming that those who disagreed with them were free—free to go! Even the enlarged view of religious freedom in Maryland after 1649 encompassed only those who subscribed to certain tenets of religious orthodoxy. Some of the Anglican colonies—notably Virginia—permitted no other religious practices. But by the time of the American revolt from England many Americans had come to accept a new vision, a vision of a land in which each man might freely choose and practice his religion without let or hindrance. Within a few decades, this had become the established practice throughout America.

There was another shared dream, too. It is aptly described in a phrase used by Dumas Malone and Basil Rauch as the title of a textbook for American history. Americans hoped to create an *Empire for Liberty*.[3] The word "empire" had not been loaded with pejorative connotations at the time of the founding of the Republic. It was still a descriptive word. It meant the presence of diverse peoples—diverse in origin, in religion, in language, and so on—under one system of government and one flag. The dream of an empire for liberty in America, then, was the dream of many peoples united by a single constitution, one which protected them in their diversity and provided for individual liberty. This was the American political dream, and it came very close to realization in the course of the nineteenth century.

Many individuals shared a dream, too, each for himself. The essence of the vision is captured in the phrase, *personal independence*. Americans used more earthy phrases to describe the vision: "to be one's own man," "to be beholden to no man," "to be free, white, and twenty-one." The

---

[3] New York: Appleton-Century-Crofts, 1960, 2 volumes.

articulation of this vision ranged from Thomas Jefferson's prized yeoman farmer to Horatio Alger's youth who made good in the big city. The dream was realized (and still is) by many Americans, though not all went from bobbin boy to industrial magnate as did Andrew Carnegie or from obscurity to great influence as did Dwight L. Moody. But affluence and influence were the further reaches of the dream, for it could be both modestly envisioned and fulfilled. For most, it involved such things as a home of one's own, a shop or store with a dependable clientele, a farm free of debt, and so on through the variation of goals which free men may set for themselves.

These were not visions of utopia, nor of euphoria. They involved hard work, careful husbandry, continued striving, and perchance the faith that if one had shown himself a worthy steward of his possessions, there would await him at the end of life the inimitable praise, "Well done . . . ," promised in religious teachings. The utopian dream is the opposite of the American dreams. It is a vision of earthly bliss, not of struggle and accomplishment. It is a collective vision, not an individualistic one. The vision is one for society, and everyone in society must be drawn into it, whether he will or no. It is monolithic; diversity must yield to uniformity and conformity for it to be realized (if it could be). Utopians have, of course, pictured release and "freedom" for individuals in their utopias, but such evidence as we have from attempts to create utopias indicates that no importance need be attached to these claims.

"The Dream" Emerges

In the course of time, though, American dreams have begun to be subsumed into An American Dream. Even in our day, individuals still dream and work for the fulfillment of their dreams—with considerable success as measured by the homes, farms, vacation cottages, and businesses that they own. But The Dream is swallowing up the dreams, as property is circumscribed by restrictions, as taxes increase at all levels, as government guarantees of security replace individual provisions for security, as inflation destroys the utility of money as a means of saving, and as people are bombarded on every hand by products of thought carried on at the level of social units rather than individuals. In short, a transformation has taken place in the type of dreams that are approved by society, and a long term effort has gone on to draw men into the mental context of a single dream or vision.

In political terms, the Dream has had a variety of names: the Square Deal, the New Freedom, the New Deal, the Fair Deal, the New Frontier, and, most recently, the Great Society. In the latter two phrases the character of the Dream is made manifest with greater clarity: it is a collective vision to be arrived at collectively by the use of government to reconstruct men and society.

The terms may be new, but the Dream is an old one. It is a utopian vision for America. The struggle to implant the vision in the minds of Americans has been a long one (and will require considerable verbiage in the telling of it), for the vision was set forth in a manner that began to appeal to some Americans in the last years of the nineteenth century. Utopian novels poured forth in great number and variety from about 1885 to 1912. As one book points out, "the 1890's in the United States [w]as the most productive single period in the history of utopian thought."[4] Some of the more important utopias, mainly by American writers, were: Ignatius Donnelly, *Caesar's Column* (1890); William Morris, *News from Nowhere* (1890);

---

[4] Negley and Patrick, *The Quest for Utopia,* p. 138.

Thomas Chauncey, *The Crystal Button* (1891); Ignatius Donnelly, *The Golden Bottle* (1892); William D. Howells, *A Traveler from Altruria* (1894); H. G. Wells, *The Time Machine* (1895); and Edward Bellamy, *Equality* (1897).[5]

"Looking Backward"

One book, however, may have been more important than all the others combined in awakening the vision in America. It certainly gave great impetus to the production of utopias by its success. This was Edward Bellamy's *Looking Backward,* published in 1888. By 1890 the book had sold 200,000 copies, and was in that year selling at the rate of 10,000 every week.[6] It is, even today, available in an inexpensive paperback edition. Within two years after the publication of the book, 162 clubs located in 27 states were holding meetings. They were called Nationalist clubs. Bellamy did not use the word socialist to describe his obviously socialist system, and his early followers took a more neutral word also. A magazine, called *The Nationalist,* was founded by friends of Bellamy to spread the ideas. The book had an impact upon such well-known figures as William Dean Howells, Mark Twain, and Thorstein Veblen. The Populist Party was influenced by Bellamy, for an observer at the Convention in 1892 declared that Bellamy's readers "were the brains of the convention. They were college professors, editors, artists, and authors. . . ."[7] Bellamy was friendly with all sorts of reformers and intimate with some of the professed socialists. Henry Demarest Lloyd wrote him in 1896, "The movement we are in *is*

---

[5] See *ibid.,* pp. 19-20.

[6] Daniel Aaron, *Men of Good Hope* (New York: Oxford University Press, 1951), p. 104.

[7] Quoted in *ibid.,* p. 130.

International Socialism. . . . Why not recognize it and say so!"[8] Bellamy, however, made socialism palatable as a dream to many people without calling it by that name.

What was there about this book that occasioned its great impact? An examination of *Looking Backward* is in order. It is a novel, a romance, a fantasy. It is set in the city of Boston in the year 2000. It has its hero (Julian West) and its heroine (Edith Leete) who give the story its "love" interest. The very clever device for unfolding the story is that the hero was mesmerized in 1887 and slept unbeknownst to anyone until 2000. This device allows the reader to identify with West as he encounters the surprising changes that have occurred during his long sleep. Boston has been transformed. His first view of the city convinces him of this:

> At my feet lay a great city. Miles of broad streets, shaded by trees and lined with fine buildings, for the most part not in continuous blocks but set in larger or smaller inclosures, stretched in every direction. Every quarter contained large open squares filled with trees, among which statues glistened and fountains flashed in the late afternoon sun. Public buildings of a colossal size and an architectural grandeur unparalleled in my day raised their stately piles on every side. Surely I had never seen this city nor one comparable to it before.[9]

It was Boston all right; the familiar pattern of the Charles River assured him of that. But it was a New City he beheld, located on a New Earth. In short order he was to learn that not only had the change occurred in Boston but also throughout the United States. Beyond that, Europe had been transformed as well, and the rest of the world

---

[8] Quoted in *ibid.*, p. 132.

[9] Bellamy, *op. cit.*, p. 38.

was in the process of a similar change. Utopia had been achieved.

In this New Age, war has been banished from the face of the earth; universal peace reigns supreme. There is no longer any crime to speak of, only something called atavism—vestigial remains of the criminal mind from another era—which produces occasional antisocial acts. There is no longer any corruption or demagoguery in politics—in fact, there is very little politics. There are no labor problems, nor any other class or group problems. All destructive activities have been banished, and a vast surge of constructiveness and creativeness has emerged. As Dr. Leete, the interlocutor of the story, describes the situation:

> "It has been an era of unexampled intellectual splendor. Probably humanity never before passed through a moral and material evolution, at once so vast in its scope and brief in its time of accomplishment, as that from the old order to the new in the early part of this century. When men came to realize the greatness of the felicity which had befallen them, and that the change through which they had passed was not merely an improvement in details of their condition, but the rise of the race to a new plane of existence with an illimitable vista of progress, their minds were affected in all their faculties with a stimulus, of which the outburst of the mediaeval renaissance offers a suggestion but faint indeed. There ensued an era of mechanical invention, scientific discovery, art, musical and literary productiveness to which no previous age of the world offers anything comparable."[10]

What had wrought all these marvelous changes? It all came about very simply, or so Bellamy would have us believe. All private production of goods and provision of services was taken over by the government. The economy was

---

[10] *Ibid.*, p. 161.

rationally organized—i. e., planned, money abolished, income equalized, production scientifically planned, competition eliminated, and men bountifully supplied with goods and services. Labor was provided by an industrial army, to which every male was subject from 21 to 45. The industrial forces were organized in great guilds, and the President of the country chosen from these. Professionals had their own organizations.

One might suppose that this drastic alteration in ways of doing things had been accomplished by revolution. Not at all; instead, it came about by peaceful evolution. Let Dr. Leete describe the process:

> "Early in the last century the evolution was completed by the final consolidation of the entire capital of the nation. The industry and commerce of the country, ceasing to be conducted by a set of irresponsible corporations and syndicates of private persons at their caprice and for their profit, were intrusted to a single syndicate representing the people, to be conducted in the common interest for the common profit. The nation, that is to say, organized as the one great business corporation in which all other corporations were absorbed; it became the one capitalist in place of all other capitalists, the sole employer, the final monopoly in which all previous and lesser monopolies were swallowed up, a monopoly in the profits and economies of which all citizens shared. The epoch of trusts had ended in The Great Trust. In a word, the people of the United States concluded to assume the conduct of their own business, just as one hundred odd years before they had assumed the conduct of their own government, organizing now for industrial purposes on precisely the same grounds that they had then organized for political purposes."[11]

In the accomplishment of this, " 'there was absolutely

----

[11] *Ibid.*, p. 56.

no violence. The change had been long foreseen. Public
opinion had become fully ripe for it, and the whole mass
of the people was behind it.' "[12] Neither violence, discord,
nor compulsion ushered in the new age, nor characterized
relationships within it. Instead, as Dr. Leete explains to
Julian West:

> "If I were to give you in one sentence, a key to what
> may seem the mysteries of our civilization . . . , I should
> say that it is the fact that the solidarity of the race and
> the brotherhood of man . . . are . . . ties as real and
> vital as physical fraternity."[13]

Julian West poses the obvious question at an earlier
point in the book:

> "Human nature itself must have changed very much,"
> I said.
> "Not at all," was Dr. Leete's reply, "but the conditions
> of human life have changed, and with them the motives
> of human action."[14]

A minister takes up the explanation:

> ". . . Soon was fully revealed, what the divines and
> philosophers of the old world never would have believed,
> that human nature in its essential qualities is good, not
> bad, that men by their natural intention and structure
> are generous, not selfish, pitiful [full of pity], not cruel,
> sympathetic, not arrogant, godlike in aspirations, in-
> stinct with divinest impulses and self-sacrifice, images
> of God indeed, not the travesties upon Him they had
> seemed. The constant pressure, through numberless gen-
> erations, of conditions of life which might have per-
> verted angels, had not been able to essentially alter the

---

[12] *Ibid.,* p. 57.

[13] *Ibid.,* p. 137.

[14] *Ibid.,* pp. 60-61.

natural nobility of the stock, and these conditions once removed, like a bent tree, it had sprung back to its normal uprightness."[15]

The mode of the transition from the old to the new society is vague and inexplicit. Unlike Khrushchev—and Marx before him—Bellamy believed that it was possible to make omelets without breaking eggs. But no such vagueness attends the descriptions of the good society which has emerged in 2000 A.D. It is described in loving detail. Julian West visits the department stores from which goods are obtained, and the distribution system from central warehouses is amply described. The system of state issued credit which replaces money is pictured minutely. How men are got to perform the various services for society are spelled out in intricate detail.

Blueprint for Tomorrow

It does not require a great deal of imagination, either, to see that many things which Bellamy envisioned have begun to emerge in many tendencies of our day—if one ignores the compulsion, the thrust to power of politicians, the unpleasantness, and the dreary uniformity of state produced things, that is, if one removes the utopian elements. Bellamy made it clear, in a letter appended to *Looking Backward,* that he intended the book as predicting things to come:

> *Looking Backward,* although in form a fanciful romance, is intended, in all seriousness, as a forecast, in accordance with the principles of evolution, of the next stage in the industrial and social development of humanity, especially in this country. . . .[16]

---

[15] *Ibid.,* pp. 287-88.
[16] *Ibid.,* p. 334.

A few examples of some "forecasts" will reveal Bellamy's prescience. Saving is no longer a virtue in this socialist heaven. Dr. Leete explains why this is so:

"The nation is rich, and does not wish the people to deprive themselves of any good thing. In your day, men were bound to lay up goods and money against coming failure of support and for their children. This necessity made parsimony a virtue. But now it would have no such laudable object, and having lost its utility, it has ceased to be regarded as a virtue."[17]

The explanations that are currently offered for the phenomenon differ somewhat from this, but saving is no longer generally recognized as a virtue among us. Nor in the good society pictured for us is there any longer any connection between amount of work and rewards for it. Dr. Leete is again the narrator:

"Desert is a moral question, and the amount of the product a material quantity. It would be an extraordinary sort of logic which should try to determine a moral question by a material standard. . . . All men who do their best, do the same. A man's endowments, however godlike, merely fix the measure of his duty."[18]

In short, each person receives the same income, regardless of his contribution. Greater ability only denotes greater responsibility to contribute to the general well-being. We have developed a variety of devices, notably the progressive income tax, for achieving this ideal.

Many similar examples are given. There is no longer anything which could be called charity. Each person receives an income by virtue of his being a person, and this income is conceived of as his by right. Any surplus is spent on public works, "pleasures in which all share,

---

[17] *Ibid.*, pp. 89-90.   [18] *Ibid.*, p. 94.

upon public halls and buildings, art galleries, bridges, statuary, means of transit, and the conveniences of our cities, great musical and theatrical exhibitions, and in providing on a vast scale for the recreations of the people.' "[19] (It could be that John Kenneth Galbraith's recommendations for spending on the "public sector" were not as original as has been supposed.) Children are no longer dependent upon parents for their livelihood, and the only family bonds are affectional. State governments have disappeared, and such power as remains has been centralized in Washington. World peace is maintained by " 'a loose form of federal union of world-wide extent. An international council regulates the mutual intercourse and commerce of the members of the union, and their joint policy toward the more backward races, which are gradually being educated up to civilized institutions.' "[20]

Of course, Bellamy was not forecasting; he was dreaming. He was dreaming a dream which evoked or reinforced a vision which had already begun to take shape in the minds of many reformist intellectuals. He made socialism so vague as to how it was to be achieved and so bright as to the future it would bring that many began to lose

---

[19] *Ibid.*, p. 243.

[20] *Ibid.*, p. 140. Bellamy provided something else, too, a distorted version of history in the latter part of the nineteenth century, which many a history textbook still carries. Note this description of competition. " 'The next of the great wastes was that from competition. The field of industry was a battlefield as wide as the world, in which the workers wasted, in assailing one another, energies which, if expended in concerted effort . . . would have enriched all. As for mercy or quarter in this warfare, there was absolutely no suggestion of it. To deliberately enter a field of business and destroy the enterprises of those who had occupied it previously . . . was an achievement which never failed to command popular admiration. Nor is there any stretch of fancy in comparing this . . . with actual warfare.' " *Ibid.*, pp. 230-31.

their misgivings about it. Above all, he domesticated and "Americanized" socialism and contributed greatly to sowing the seeds which have produced a plant that comes nearer and nearer to being An American Dream. Democrats in convention can now regularly evoke unabashedly many of the attributes of Bellamy's utopia as recent accomplishments or things to come in the future. They can do this, just as Bellamy could, without reference to the compulsion, intervention, loss of vitality in human relations, power in the hands of politicians, spreading delinquency, international disorder, and terror and violence let loose in the world. In short, many people have now flown far enough from reality that they no longer distinguish between utopian fancies and the realities of the world in which they live.

This did not come about overnight, however. Some intellectuals, artists, politicians, and unwary readers may have taken up Bellamy's dream as their own in the 1890's, but most Americans did not. The indications are that a great preponderance of Americans who thought about it in those years would have agreed with Andrew Carnegie, who wrote in 1889:

> . . . To those who propose to substitute Communism for . . . Individualism the answer, therefore, is: The race has tried that. All progress from that barbarous day to the present time has resulted from its displacement. . . . It necessitates the changing of human nature itself. . . . We might as well urge the destruction of the highest existing type of man because he failed to reach our ideal as to favor the destruction of Individualism, Private Property, the Law of Accumulation of Wealth, and the Law of Competition; for these are the highest results of human experience. . . .[21]

---

[21] Andrew Carnegie, "Wealth," *Democracy and the Gospel of Wealth*, Gail Kennedy, ed. (Boston: D. C. Heath, 1949), p. 3.

At any rate, American voters turned back populism at the polls, rejected Bryan and his more moderate reformism, turned down the Socialist Party in election after election, and would accept only bits and pieces of reformism for many years.

Before Americans would be drawn into the orbit of the vision, their eyes had to be drawn away from viewing human nature, laws in the universe, absolutes and principles, and the record of history. A new outlook had to precede the general acceptance of the dream. The flight from reality had to be extended.

7

The Pragmatic Sanction of Flux

. . . A pragmatist turns his back resolutely and once for all upon a lot of inveterate habits dear to professional philosophers. He turns away from abstraction and insufficiency, from verbal solution, from bad a priori reasons, from fixed principles, closed systems, and pretended absolutes and origins. He turns towards . . . facts, towards action and towards power.

—WILLIAM JAMES, 1907

Instead of a closed universe, science now presents us with one infinite in space and time, having no limits here or there, at this end, so to speak, or at that, and as infinitely complex in internal structure as it is infinite in extent. Hence it is also an open world. . . . And change rather than fixity is now a measure of "reality" or energy of being; change is omnipresent.

—JOHN DEWEY, 1920

How DIFFICULT IT WAS TO LAUNCH THE BULK OF AMERIcans on the flight from reality! What obstacles were met with in the efforts to turn Americans into the path of melioristic reform! Only a reformer of some years back can really appreciate the immense energy and ingenuity that went into providing a new outlook for Americans and getting them to accept it. Utopian visions appealed to some, but there was still the difficulty of convincing people that these dreams could be turned into reality. Philosophical thought could be cut loose from its moorings in reality, but the generality of men, probably even intellectuals, did not know about it. European ideologies proliferated, but Americans, when and if they heard of them, tended to reject them. No great violence will be done to the reality to describe it figuratively. Hence, Americans clung tenaciously to constitutionalism, to private property, to free enterprise, to the individual way, and to the belief in an order in the universe.

The tasks of those who advanced reformist ideas in the late years of the nineteenth century and the early years of this century were manifold. They had to overcome the inertia which blocks the acceptance of any innovation. They had not only to implant a new version of reality but also to convince many people that they had based their lives upon an illusion rather than upon reality. Moreover, they had to counter the intellectual trends of the times. In our day, we are accustomed to the bulk of professors, teachers, preachers, journalists, and so on being favorable to reform. It was not so in the period under consideration. Colleges, schools, religious denominations, and publications had not yet been won to the melioristic view.

The Trend Toward Naturalism

Indeed, the leading trend in social thought in the latter part of the nineteenth century was diametrically opposed to meliorism. This trend has been called by several names —naturalism, social Darwinism, rugged individualism, among others. Naturalism may be a better generic name for a whole range of thought at the time, embracing the arts and sciences as well as social thought. Social Darwinism may be understood as naturalistic thought in its relation to society. One historian says that the cosmology of the naturalists "was compounded out of the nebular hypothesis of Kant and Laplace, the uniformitarian geology of Lyell, and the organic evolution of Darwin. It assumed universal change under natural law."[1] Social Darwinism, on the other hand, is usually applied to the particular social application of evolutionary ideas by Herbert Spencer and his American disciple, William Graham Sumner. Since this particular usage is common, it may be appropriate to discuss the naturalistic view first, and social Darwinism as a variant of it.

In essence, naturalism was an account of reality in natural terms. That is, the earth, man, life, inanimate matter, and the universe were viewed as the result of natural processes. As evolutionists, naturalists turned away from any enduring reality and focused upon change. But they took with them an interest in natural law from the older outlook. The major impetus of scientists for several centuries had been the quest for natural law. Naturalists were full to overflowing with the scientific (or scientistic) animus, and they continued the search for laws. But a most important change had occurred in the conception of natural law. To earlier thinkers, indeed to virtually the whole tradition of Western thought, natural law had been something fixed in the universe. It was that enduring order in the universe as it is known to man. To naturalists, natural law was the law by which changes occurred, the law, or laws, of evolutionary development.

Natural law was active rather than fixed or passive. It was felt through *forces* at work in the universe. Naturalists gave their attention either to discovering and expounding the stages of development or to describing the forces which produced the changes. In short, they were greatly concerned with what was *determining* the course and direction of changes that had been and (presumably) were

---

[1] Stow Persons, *American Minds: A History of Ideas* (New York: Holt, 1958), p. 222.

occurring. Naturalists were determinists, then; they pictured man's actions as products of forces within or without him but, whichever, beyond his control.

These interpretations amounted to a radical transformation of the significance of natural law. Natural law as order-in-the-universe has ever been a liberating concept. It has served as the basis for limiting governments, for freeing economies, as foundation for positive law, as the basis of government by law, and as the substructure for peaceful relations among nations and peoples. But natural laws as forces are tyrannical, though not necessarily arbitrarily so. That is, natural laws then become active rather than passive, subject to change rather than enduring, founts of change rather than bases for rational order. Naturalism pervades the thinking of Karl Marx, Charles Darwin, Emile Zola, William Graham Sumner, John W. Draper, Frederick Jackson Turner, Theodore Dreiser, and many other writers and thinkers.

The point that concerns us here is the opposition of such an outlook to reform. If change occurs as a result of forces, if the course and direction of change is determined by processes beyond the power of man to alter, if social changes are the product of such processes, reform is impossible. Human intervention in the process is virtually impossible, and, were it possible to any extent, it would be undesirable, for it would only deter the beneficent course of evolution—or so the more optimistic naturalists thought.

William Graham Sumner

The social view of the significance of evolution that was most congenial to the prevailing American way, and to many Americans, was that of William Graham Sumner. His views, as I have suggested, are often cited as the epitome of social Darwinism. Sumner was a thoroughgoing Darwinian, naturalistic in emphasis, and his works are replete with references to "forces" at work upon and within society. Yet the views which he set forth appeared to be in keeping with American institutions and basic beliefs. For example, in defending a higher stage of civilization, he said:

> It sets free individual energy, and while the social bond gains in scope and variety, it also gains in elasticity, for the solidarity of the group is broken up and the individual may work out his own ends by his own means. . . .[2]

He defends private property, and praises virtues which are undeniably those admired by many Americans of his day. Thus,

> The only two things which really tell on the welfare of man on earth are hard work and self-denial (in technical language, labor and capital), and these tell most when they are brought to bear directly upon the effort to earn an honest living, to accumulate capital, and to bring up a family to be industrious and self-denying in their turn.[3]

Moreover, he conceived that sociology would provide facts and theories which would support the American system. It could answer one of the most important questions, he thought. "Shall we, in our general social policy, pursue the effort to realize more completely that constitutional liberty for which we have been struggling throughout modern history . . .?"[4]

---

[2] William G. Sumner, "Sociology," *American Thought: Civil War to World War I*, Perry Miller, ed. (New York: Rinehart, 1954), p. 81.

[3] *Ibid.*, p. 87.

[4] *Ibid.*, p. 91.

Most important for the matter under consideration, Sumner held an uncompromising position to the effect that melioristic reform was practically impossible. Of utopians and socialists, he said: "These persons, vexed with the intricacies of social problems and revolting against the facts of the social order, take upon themselves the task of inventing a new and better world. They brush away all which troubles us men and create a world free from annoying limitations and conditions—in their imagination."[5] Why can't men simply conceive a world of the sort they want and then set out to build it? Sumner offers many reasons —human nature, the nature of the world, natural law— but the primary one was of a different order. This was the argument from the evolution of society.

Specifically, society had reached an industrial stage of development. Sumner conceived society as an organism, and industrial society-as-organism was highly and complexly organized. To talk of altering this organization and instituting another by taking thought was utter folly. Men do not control it;

> It controls us all because we are all in it. It creates the conditions of our existence, sets the limits of our social activity, regulates the bonds of our social relations, determines our conceptions of good and evil, suggests our life-philosophy, molds our inherited political institutions, and reforms the oldest and toughest customs, like marriage and property.

In short, "the industrial organization" exercises an "all-pervading control over human life. . . ."[6] He offers a technological explanation of how this all-pervading organization came about. "The great inventions both make the in-

---

[5] *Ibid.*, p. 73.
[6] William G. Sumner, "The Absurd Effort to Make the World Over," in *ibid.*, p. 94.

tension of the organization possible and make it inevitable, with all its consequences, whatever they may be."[7] The only thing that men can constructively do is this: "We have to make up our minds to it, adjust ourselves to it, and sit down and live with it."[8]

The perils of the sociological mode of thought are great; Sumner's premises had led him to a strange conclusion. In the first essay cited, originally published in 1881, he had boldly asserted that sociological knowledge would expose the tyranny of reformism and demonstrate the blessings of liberty. Yet, in the second essay cited, published in 1894, he was opposing reform by proclaiming that all of us are caught in the web of the social organization, and he did so in words and phrases that would have been worthy of Karl Marx. Sumner's thought is confused and contradictory. Much that he wrote has an individualistic tenor, but he was committed by his mode of the search for truth to the study of thought in terms of society. His confusion was further complicated by the use of analogies drawn from the biological thought of Darwin, thought concerned rightly with organisms, but which could not be appropriately transferred to the consideration of society. Natural law had been moved into the historical stream to become force. Thus, Sumner's conclusion derives from the premises he was using, but it was hardly propitious for human freedom. His assumptions had induced myopia—the myopia which perceives society-as-organism and natural-law-as-force—and he was opposing flights from reality by arguments drawn from a distorted view of reality.

Be that as it may, the evolutionary premises had been used to erect an apparently formidable argument against reformism. The Darwinian modes of progress—competi-

---

[7] *Ibid.*, p. 95.   [8] *Ibid.*

tion for available resources, struggle for life, survival of the fittest, natural law interpreted as force—and the prevailing trends ran counter to reform. If one rejected these, he was hardly nearer to a position which made reformism intellectually feasible, for the traditional view of reality was an even more formidable obstacle to such reformist visions than social Darwinism.

But could the evolutionary ideas not be turned to the advantage of meliorism? They could be, and were. Moreover, those who turned the arguments could appear to be on the side of the angels—that is, in favor of freedom, in favor of the amelioration of circumstances, in favor of humanity. The chances are good that reformers did not generally see this clearly at the time, but social Darwinism made an excellent target, and the repudiation of this pseudo-philosophy could bring down with it much of the traditional philosophy which it had subsumed. At any rate, something like this did occur.

Before examining these latter developments, however, it is in order to show how the evolutionary obstacle to reform was overturned. Social Darwinism carried with it a heavy freight of assumptions about continuous change, stages of development in civilization, and organicism. Who could say what the next stage of development would be like? Something that was impossible at one stage could become highly probable, even inevitable, at the next stage. Sumner admitted as much in his discussion of private property. He believed that the development of protections to private property had been a great advance. However, it "may give way at a future time to some other institution which will grow up by imperceptible stages out of the efforts of men to contend successfully with existing evils. . . ."[9]

---

[9] Sumner, "Sociology," *ibid*, p. 82.

Lester Frank Ward

Lester Frank Ward, a contemporary of Sumner, a sociologist and meliorist, proclaimed that a new stage in evolution had been emerging for millennia, and he believed that it was ready to be brought to fruition. The new stage was the "advent with man of the thinking, knowing, foreseeing, calculating, designing, inventing and constructing faculty, which is wanting in lower creatures. . . ." It repealed "the law of nature and enacted in its stead the psychologic law, or law of mind."[10] He held that men could now take over the direction of social development, and that they could shape it to human ends. His work was a call to men to take up their rightful place in the universe and bring nature and natural law to heel:

> . . . When nature comes to be regarded as passive and man as active . . . , when human action is recognised as the most important of all forms of action, and when the power of the human intellect over vital, psychic and social phenomena is practically conceded, then, and then only, can man justly claim to have risen out of the animal and fully to have entered the human stage of development.[11]

Ward retained the evolutionary frame, the focus upon society, the progressive tendency of naturalism, but he turned the argument against the possibility of reform and opened the way for the advance of meliorism. He drew attention away from the enduring features of man and the universe even more emphatically than Sumner

---

[10] Quoted in Henry S. Commager, *The American Mind* (New Haven: Yale University Press, 1954), p. 206.

[11] Lester F. Ward, "Mind as a Social Factor," *American Ideas*, Gerald N. Grob and Robert N. Beck, eds., II (New York: Free Press of Glencoe, 1963), 129.

had done. The alternatives which he offered can be put this way: either men in society are controlled and determined by natural laws of social development or they are free to alter and control the development of society.

It should be emphasized that the analyses made by both Sumner and Ward are gross. Ward had no more proved that any particular melioristic reform was possible than had Sumner proved that it was impossible. Both of them were at least three removes from the relevant reality. In the first place, the arguments are conducted at too general and abstract a level. One is reminded of Zeno's paradox which purports to prove that there can be no change. The problem lies in the premises upon which the argument is based, not in reality. Second, both arguments rely upon a most dubious extension of evolutionary ideas. Third, both thinkers conceived society organically rather than viewing the matter from the point of view of individuals. Moreover, both appear to have been confused, or at least confusing, about the nature of natural law.

Even so, Ward had opened the way to reformist efforts within the contemporary outlook. Other reformers took advantage of the opening to press through the defenses and advance their reforms.

Developing a New Philosophy of Pragmatism

But reformers needed more than the vision which utopia provided and the theoretical possibility of reform. They needed a philosophy to replace older views and one which would buttress meliorism. Such a philosophy was provided by *pragmatism*. Pragmatism offered refutations of traditional philosophy by proclaiming its irrelevance, was futuristic in its orientation, and made boundless reconstruction the aim and purpose of thought. Most important, it made meliorism intellectually respectable, a necessary step to draw in the bulk of the intellectuals, and it made it possible for thinkers to advance reform without avowing any particular ideology.

Pragmatism stands for an approved method and attitude today. Not only are intellectuals proud to be known as pragmatists, but they bestow what they conceive to be one of the highest accolades upon politicians by describing them as pragmatic. The word has long since passed into the vernacular, and many people use it without any clear conception of its meaning. It is sometimes employed as if it were a synonym of practical, and it is adopted as a mode of thought by those who have given little or no thought to philosophy.

The word was given philosophical currency by Charles Sanders Peirce, a rather obscure American thinker of the latter part of the nineteenth century. But it was popularized by William James. When this had occurred, Peirce abandoned the word, "pragmatism," for a new formulation, "pragmaticism."[12] John Dewey, who was the most prolific writer of this school of thought, called his variant of pragmatism, "instrumentalism." This left James as the only major exponent of pragmatism who used that name for his philosophy. There were important differences, particularly between Peirce and the other two, but these do not concern the basic meaning of pragmatism. Each of them contributed to its development. As one writer says, "It suffices . . . to say that if Peirce may be regarded as the Socrates of pragmatism, and James as its Plato, Dewey is certainly its Aristotle."[13] This may be taken to imply,

---

[12] See Charles S. Peirce, "What Pragmatism Is," *Philosophy in the Twentieth Century,* William Barrett, ed., I (New York: Random House, 1962), 138-40.

[13] Henry D Aiken, "Introduction," *ibid.,* p. 49.

also, that pragmatists claimed to be constructing a new philosophy as important for the future ages as the ancient philosophy had been for those from that time.

Peirce "framed the theory that a *conception,* that is, the rational purport of a word or other expression, lies exclusively in its conceivable bearing upon the conduct of life; so that, since obviously nothing that might not result from experiment can have any direct bearing upon conduct, if one can define accurately all the conceivable experimental phenomena which the affirmation or denial of a concept could imply, one will have therein a complete definition of the concept, and *there is absolutely nothing more in it.*"[14] This was what he meant by pragmatism. With his gift for simplification and clarity, James defined pragmatism in the following way:

> To attain perfect clearness in our thoughts of an object, then, we need only consider what conceivable effects of a practical kind the object may involve—what sensations we are to expect from it, and what reactions we must prepare. Our conception of these effects, whether immediate or remote, is then for us the whole of our conception of the object, so far as that conception has positive significance at all.[15]

Dewey defined the same concept *instrumentally:*

> *If* ideas, meanings, conceptions, notions, theories, systems are instrumental to an active reorganization of the given environment, to a removal of some specific trouble and perplexity, then the test of their validity and value lies in accomplishing this work. If they succeed

---

[14] Peirce, *op. cit.,* p. 138.

[15] William James, "What Pragmatism Means," *Pragmatism and American Culture,* Gail Kennedy, ed. (Boston: D. C. Heath, 1950), p. 13.

in their office, they are reliable, sound, valid, good, true.[16]

How radical pragmatism was (and is) may not appear from these definitions. There is an ambiguity in these formulations of the method. Conceivably, it might be a method for discovering truth, finding principles, uncovering laws that are in the universe. One might proceed from "effects" to their causes, and from thence to the order which makes for regularity of the operation of cause and effect. If this were what is involved, pragmatism would be only a particular formulation of the inductive method of reasoning. It must be made clear, however, that pragmatism was not intended by its proponents to be fitted into any traditional mode of thought, that it was not intended as a means for finding truth, order, or regularity, that it was founded upon a counter view of reality.

Pragmatists were not concerned to discover any fixity or absolutes, nor were they building upon traditional philosophy. On the contrary, a part of the work of all three men under consideration was devoted to refuting (and denouncing) absolutes, fixities, and traditions. Peirce declared that pragmatism "will serve to show that almost every proposition of ontological metaphysics is either meaningless gibberish . . . or else is downright absurd. . . ."[17] In making expositions of his philosophy, James alternated between repudiations of rationalism, idealism, objectivity, and metaphysics and affirmations of pragmatism. Of the belief in the Absolute, he said, "it clashes with other truths of mine. . . . It happens to be associated with a kind of logic of which I am the enemy; I find that it entangles me in

---

[16] John Dewey, *Reconstruction in Philosophy* (New York: Henry Holt, 1920), p. 156.

[17] Peirce, *op. cit.*, p. 144.

metaphysical paradoxes. . . ." Therefore, "I personally just give up the Absolute."[18] Dewey points out that in the older philosophy truth and falsity "are thought of as fixed, ready-made static properties of things themselves. . . . Such a notion lies at the back of the head of everyone who has, in however an indirect way, been a recipient of the ancient and medieval tradition. This view is radically challenged by the pragmatic conception of truth, and the impossibility of reconciliation or compromise is . . . the cause of the shock occasioned by the newer theory."[19]

The Relativism of Pragmatism

Truth is not something pre-existing to be discovered, according to the pragmatists; it is brought within the evolutionary frame of the continually changing. It is not fixed, but changing; not pre-existent, but evolving; not discovered, but made. Peirce says that the *summum bonum* consists "in that process of evolution whereby the existent comes more and more to embody those generals which were just now said to be *destined*. . . ."[20] James says, "The truth of an idea is not a stagnant property inherent in it. Truth *happens* to an idea. It *becomes* true, is *made* true by events."[21] Elsewhere, he makes clear the relationship of this notion to the concept of evolution: "When the whole universe seems only to be making itself valid and to be still incomplete (else why its ceaseless changing?) why, of all things, should knowing be exempt? Why should it

---

[18] James, *op. cit.*, p. 22.

[19] Dewey, *op. cit.*, pp. 158-59.

[20] Peirce, *op. cit.*, p. 149.

[21] William James, "Pragmatism's Conception of Truth," *Philosophy in the Twentieth Century*, I, 194.

not be making itself valid like everything else?"[22] John Dewey says "that there is change going on all the time, that there is movement within each thing in seeming repose; and that since the process is veiled from perception the way to know it is to bring the thing into novel circumstances until change becomes evident. In short, the thing which is to be accepted and paid heed to is not what is originally given but that which emerges. . . ."[23]

To the pragmatists, then, the universe was open. Reality was not something given, something to be discovered, something with fixed feature; it was open, alterable, and changing. For Peirce, according to one interpreter, "laws, like habits, are 'emergent' principles which characterize only certain limited phases of the evolutionary process. In this sense, laws themselves are mutable. . . . There is, however, no universal law of development. . . . The universe as a whole is fundamentally open-ended. . . ."[24] According to Dewey, fixity, where it apparently existed, was not something to be observed, recorded, and admired. "Rather, the experimental method tries to break down apparent fixities and to induce changes. The form that remains unchanged to sense, the form of seed or tree, is regarded not as the key to knowledge of the thing, but as a wall, an obstruction to be broken down."[25] What were once conceived as enduring realities Dewey would have us view as temporary obstacles.

Pragmatists agreed with one another that theirs was primarily a method. In terms of the above elucidation, it should be clear that it was a method for operating in a

---

[22] William James, "A World of Pure Experience," *ibid.*, p. 235.

[23] Dewey, *op. cit.*, p. 114.

[24] Aiken, *op. cit.*, p. 62

[25] Dewey, *op. cit.*, p. 113.

world of flux and change. Change and development do not adequately describe the world view of these pragmatists. The universe must also be described as in a state of flux, for there is no necessary direction to its development. Men located in a world where things are forever fluctuating may be likened to someone embarked on a voyage into perpetually uncharted seas. There would be great need, in these circumstances, for something by which to steer. Peirce, James, and Dewey proposed that pragmatism should be that guide.

They accepted a method, then, to replace the knowledge they had repudiated. The model for that method, or so they believed, was the scientific method. Someone has observed that pragmatism is not so much a philosophy as a way of doing without a philosophy. With equal justice, it should be observed that pragmatism is not so much a method for acquiring knowledge as a means of operating in lieu of knowledge and certainty. At any rate, pragmatism resulted from the efforts of the founders to render the scientific method, as they understood it, into a philosophy. These men were conscious that this latter was what they were doing. Peirce declared that after the "gibberish" of metaphysics had been swept away, "what will remain of philosophy will be a series of problems capable of investigation by the observational methods of the true sciences. . . ."[26]

Confusion of the Scientific Method with Technology

It should be made clear, though, that the scientific method James and Dewey, at least, had in mind was not the method as it received its classic formulation in the seventeenth century. That was a method designed for and aimed at *discovering* and *describing* the laws in the uni-

---

[26] Peirce, *op. cit.*, p. 144.

verse—what is today vestigially referred to as "pure" science. Rather, the conceptions of the pragmatists were based on the technological applications of science. The scientist, as technologist, is concerned with ways to reshape, reform, and reorder natural things. Such technologists have had (and are having) remarkable successes. It has been stated so often that it is now a cliché—but it will bear repeating in this context—that these technological achievements rest upon prior achievements in "basic" science. The meaning is, or should be, that technologists achieve their effects because of a knowledge of underlying laws which preceded their labors. Their work rests upon a foundation of laws, regularities, and established connections.

This is precisely the point which James and Dewey, particularly Dewey, missed. They apparently thought that the technologist was doing what he appeared to be doing—experimenting at random until he came up with something, then going on to other modifications and experiments. Dewey conceived of the scientist not as discoverer but as innovator. Scientific knowledge is obtained, he declared, by the "deliberate institution of a definite and specified course of change. *The* method of physical inquiry is to introduce some change in order to see what other change ensues; the correlation between these changes . . . constitutes the definite and desired object of knowledge."[27] He made clear that he thought that there was only one valid scientific method, and it was the method used both in laboratories and in industries. "Moreover, there is no

---

[27] John Dewey, "The Quest for Certainty," *The Golden Age of American Philosophy,* Charles Frankel, ed. (New York: George Braziller, 1960), p. 414.

difference in logical principle between the method of science and the method pursued in technologies."[28]

At any rate, James and Dewey took what they thought was the scientific method from the limited arena of applied science and gave it universal application as *the* method. They attempted to make experimentation into a way of life. Ideas and concepts were conceived, in this context, as a scientist was believed to conceive of hypotheses, that is, as instruments of change. As James put it,

> *Theories thus become instruments, not answers to enigmas, in which we can rest.* We don't lie back upon them, we move forward, and, on occasion, make nature over again by their aid.[29]

Dewey spells out the implications of this belief:

> . . . Here it is enough to note that notions, theories, systems . . . must be regarded as hypotheses. They are to be accepted as bases of actions which test them, not as finalities. . . . They are tools. As in the case of all tools, their value resides not in themselves but in their capacity to work shown in the consequences of their use.[30]

As tools, then, ideas are relative to the uses to which they are put. If the point does not emerge, it must be stated: pragmatists are relativists.

Pragmatism and Reform

The importance of pragmatism for social reform was made abundantly clear in the numerous works of John Dewey. The indications are that Charles Sanders Peirce was interested in technical philosophy rather than reform.

---

[28] *Ibid.*, pp. 414-15.
[29] James, "What Pragmatism Means," *op. cit.*, p. 15.
[30] Dewey, *Reconstruction in Philosophy*, p. 145.

William James was more concerned with the psychology of belief than with social reform. It was left to Dewey, then, to apply pragmatism to ameliorative reform. He is best known as an educational reformer, but he was much concerned with all sorts of reform. He may well have been the central figure in the promotion of reformism in America.

Dewey openly advocated that philosophy should be re-oriented so as to perform a social function, that is, to make over men and society. Too long, he thought, philosophers had pretended to have some special method for arriving at truth, to be concerned with Reality beyond reality. The time had come for philosophy to come out in the open and get on with the task it had been covertly performing all along. "Philosophy which surrenders its somewhat barren monopoly of dealings with Ultimate and Absolute Reality will find a compensation in enlightening the moral forces which move mankind and in contributing to the aspiration of men to attain to a more ordered and intelligent happiness."[31] More bluntly, and in the form of rhetorical questions, he proclaimed what he conceived to be the real end of philosophy:

> . . . But would not the elimination of these traditional problems permit philosophy to devote itself to a more fruitful and more needed task? Would it not encourage philosophy to face the great social and moral defects and troubles from which humanity suffers, to concentrate its attention upon clearing up the causes and exact nature of these evils and upon developing a clear idea of better social possibilities; in short upon projecting an idea or ideal which . . . would be used as a method of understanding and rectifying social ills?[32]

[31] *Ibid.*, pp. 26-27.
[32] *Ibid.*, p. 124.

Despite the appearance of caution in formulating the ideas, there should be no doubt that Dewey thought philosophy should perform a melioristic function.

In sum, then, the pragmatists had denigrated and repudiated traditional philosophy. They held forth the vision of a universe in a continuous state of flux. Such order as existed would have to be wrought by man, and no order would be final or complete. Man's task was to reshape and remake himself and his environment. There were no pre-existing rules—no fixed principles, no enduring laws, no underlying order—to guide or restrain him in his endeavor. Traditionalists had been wrong in believing that there were static natural laws; naturalists had been wrong in thinking there were forces-as-laws governing development. Pragmatists affirmed a radical new freedom—the freedom to reshape reality according to how they would have it be. The method for operating in this flux was to be pragmatism, the method of continual experimentation in moving toward their indefinite goals.

A philosophy had been formed to buttress and promote melioristic reform.

One other point needs to be made. It has often been claimed that reformism is alien to America. There is a sense in which this is true. That is, it is alien to the system of constitutionalism developed in America, and to the beliefs by which it was buttressed. But it was not alien in the sense of being foisted upon Americans by foreigners. Instead, the reformist bent was established by citizens of America, in the main. This is most important to understanding the nature of reformism in America. Insofar as it was pragmatic, it was not specifically socialism nor communism. Pragmatists do not define goals in such rigid fashion as this. Of course, the reforms have been socialistic in tendency, but this can be ascribed to the utopian visions which reformers imbibed, which were socialistic, rather than to a consciously worked out program to achieve socialism. Of course, other assumptions, to be taken up later, bent the reformer toward socialism. But the pragmatist, *qua* pragmatist, just continues to experiment, not toward a final goal but toward the general goal of growth and improvement which is never to end.

8

The Deactivation of History

Today . . . one rarely finds a historical student who would venture to recommend statesmen, warriors, and moralists to place any confidence whatsoever in historical analogies and warnings, for the supposed analogies usually prove illusive on inspection, and the warnings, impertinent. . . . Our situation is so novel that it would seem as if political and military precedents of even a century ago could have no possible value.

—JAMES HARVEY ROBINSON, 1912

The newer history . . . holds that few situations in a very remote past will allow of being used as data to test the validity or desirability of measures proposed for present or future application. It regards civilization as a great organic complex and contends that, as the general cultural setting of events in the past was so vastly different from the present situation, past events can furnish only a very doubtful and unreliable criterion for judging of the wisdom of present policies.

—HARRY ELMER BARNES, 1925

MANY OBSTACLES BARRED THE WAY OF THOSE WHO WERE attempting to institute melioristic reforms. The most formidable obstacle was reality itself. As a matter of fact, since reality has not demonstrably changed, it still is an insurmountable obstacle to the success of many kinds of reforms. However, reformers have been able to *attempt* many of their innovations. This means that they have been able to alter generally held conceptions of reality.

This was accomplished by embarking upon an extended flight from reality.

Thus far, the story of the advance of reformist ideas has been told within a framework of an enduring reality, and the departure of reformist conceptions from it. In order for large-scale attempts to make over man and society to appear feasible, men had to cease to believe in an underlying structured and ordered reality. Many intellectuals made this step in their thought. It does not follow, of course, that the reason why they ceased to believe in an ordered reality was so that reforms could be instituted. On the contrary, many who contributed to this development in thought were not apparently interested in extensive reforms. Many nineteenth century thinkers who had ceased to believe in a metaphysical reality which endures did not, on the other hand, believe consciously directed reform to be possible.

Nonetheless, by dispensing with the metaphysical framework, they set the stage for reform. If man has a nature, if all things have a nature, if there is an underlying order which endures, it follows that there are great limits to the kinds of change that can be made. These conceptions are, however, metaphysical in character regardless of how obvious and demonstrable they may appear to some people who have not been trained in metaphysics. The metaphysical underpinnings of these conceptions were swept away by David Hume and Immanuel Kant, or, to be more precise, these philosophers held that they could not be directly validated by reason and sensual evidence. The house of philosophy collapsed in the early nineteenth century, and thinkers went off in every direction, erecting ideologies out of the bits and pieces that remained from the wreckage of philosophy.

Reason cut loose from reality, and the imagination freed

from the discipline of philosophy were used to draw up plans for new heavens on new earths. Even Americans began to feel the attraction of utopia by the latter part of the nineteenth century. When the enduring was cut away, time and change were all that was left. New pseudo philosophies—Hegelianism, Marxism, Darwinism—arose to offer accounts for changes in time. These were oriented, however, to the discovery and exposition of the laws of change and were not favorable to consciously initiated reforms. Pragmatists offered a way out of this dilemma by setting forth a radical new freedom, freedom from any underlying laws. John Dewey readily wrenched this pseudo philosophy into the orbit of reformism, calling his variant of the philosophy Instrumentalism.

Some of the ground must be retraveled at this point, however. By moving all of reality into time, thinkers did not remove the conceptual obstacles to the triumph of reformism. They only succeeded in making reality the subject matter of history. The traditional role of history was inspirational and cautionary. Men studied history to be inspired by examples of noble actions, to enrich their limited experience by that of others, to draw sustenance for their lives from the lives of others. There was a negative side to this study of history, too: one could find there indications of the limits of what should be attempted, be reminded of the consequences of precipitate action, discover anew what was beyond his power to alter, be chastened by the records of the failure of others. In short, history has usually played a conservative role in society. It was a major obstacle to reform, as men customarily thought of it and utilized it.

Some reformists, who were also historians, realized this. James Harvey Robinson, writing in the early twentieth century, declared: "History has been regularly invoked, to substantiate the claims of the conservative, but has hitherto usually been neglected by the radical. . . . It is his weapon by right, and he should wrest it from the hand of the conservative."[1] In short, Robinson, as a would-be reformer, perceived that history must be reconstructed in order to make it an instrument of reform. The older history must be deactivated; it must be replaced by a "new history."

Traditional Use of History

Before describing how this deactivation and "instrumentation" of history took place, however, some examples of the traditional use of history are in order. In an earlier America, history was conceived of as a depository of experience which might be examined for guidance in the affairs of men. Nowhere is this usage better exemplified than in the debates over the adoption of the Constitution. In some of the state conventions there were veritable outpourings of historical erudition to buttress one position or another.

Americans were fearful at this time of entrusting overmuch power to governments. They found numerous instances in history of the working out of the dangers that they feared. For example, those attending the Massachusetts convention were treated to the following discourse on the matter:

> Dr. Willard entered largely into the field of ancient history, and deduced therefrom arguments to prove that where power has been trusted to men, whether in great or small bodies, they had always abused it, and that thus republics had soon degenerated into aristocracies. He instanced Sparta, Athens, and Rome. The Amphictyonic

---

[1] James H. Robinson, *The New History* (New York: Macmillan, 1912), p. 252.

league, he said, resembled the Confederation of the United States; while thus united, they defeated Xerxes, but were subdued by the gold of Philip. . . .[2]

A Mr. Nason in the same convention points out the dangers of a standing army:

A standing army! Was it not with this that Caesar passed the *Rubicon,* and laid prostrate the liberties of his country? By this have seven-eighths of the once free nations of the globe been brought into bondage! Time would fail me, were I to attempt to recapitulate the havoc made in the world by standing armies.[3]

A Major Kingsley cites even more specific historical references, as he argues for better control by the people over their government:

Let us look into ancient history. The Romans, after a war, thought themselves safe in a government of ten men, called the *decemviri;* these ten men were invested with all power and were chosen for three years. By their arts and designs, they secured their second election; but, finding, from the manner in which they had exercised their power, they were not able to secure their third election, they declared themselves masters of Rome, impoverished the city, and deprived the people of their rights.[4]

The Virginia convention was the scene of even more vigorous debate founded in historical allusions than was that of Massachusetts. James Madison was one of the most learned of these debaters. In the following citations, he is arguing from history that loose confederations are not adequate to the exigencies of government:

---

[2] Elliot's *Debates,* Bk. I, vol. 2, p. 68.

[3] *Ibid.,* p. 136.

[4] *Ibid.,* p. 62.

> The Amphictyonic league resembled our Confederation in its nominal powers. . . . But, though its powers were more considerable in many respects than those of our present system, yet it had the same radical defect.
>
> The Achaean league, though better constructed than the Amphictyonic, . . . was continually agitated with domestic dissensions, and driven to the necessity of calling in foreign aid; this, also, eventuated in the demolition of their confederacy. . . .
>
> The Germanic system is neither adequate to the external defence nor internal felicity of the people. . . .[5]

By historical references, Edmund Randolph argues for the desirability of union:

> If you wish to know the extent of such a scene, look at the history of England and Scotland before the union; you will see their borderers continually committing depredations and cruelties of the most calamitous and deplorable nature, on one another. . . .[6]

The manner in which they were employing history was not left in doubt. They were reaching back into history for lessons appropriate to actions they were considering. John Marshall makes this clear in the following passage:

> We may derive from Holland lessons very beneficial to ourselves. Happy that country which can avail itself of the misfortunes of others—which can gain knowledge from that source without fatal experience![7]

James Madison adds:

> We may be warned by their example, and shun their fate, by removing the causes which produced their misfortunes.[8]

---

[5] *Ibid.*, vol. 3, pp. 129-31.

[6] *Ibid.*, p. 75

[7] *Ibid.*, p. 225.

[8] *Ibid.*, p. 311.

Common Sense and Philosophy

The didactic use of history rests upon both a common sense and a philosophical foundation. At the common sense level, it is only an extension of everyday practice. If we slip and fall on an icy street, we proceed with caution on icy streets thereafter, realizing that the same thing can happen again. By analogy, we reason that a street is not even necessary to recurrence, that it can happen anywhere on ice. Written history—that is, what is ordinarily thought of as history—is the formalized memory of a people, the record of their experience. History is the public memory of a people, and may serve in more general affairs in much the way that an individual's memories of experience serve him—i. e., as a compendium of dangers to be avoided, a depository of successful methods, a storehouse of what the world is like and how one may operate within it.

At the philosophical level, the didactic use of history was based upon the existence of an underlying order. It assumes that events, in essence, can recur and that the reason for this is an order in which a given cause will produce a given effect. To return to the example used above, a man walking requires traction to proceed. When he loses traction, his forward motion will continue him downward to the earth, and since he will usually try to brake himself, he will usually fall backward. The occurrence of such events can be stated as laws; they recur and are even predictable.

In the same fashion, there are larger developments that can be expected to recur under certain circumstances. For example, if political power is concentrated, and not strictly limited, tyranny may be expected to result. The explanation is to be found in the nature of man. The didactic use of history rests, then, upon the view that beneath the sur-

face upon which changes occur there is a substratum
which endures. This enduring substratum—this metaphysical realm—makes it possible for men to discover from the
study of history what is apt to happen when a particular
course is followed.

In everyday affairs, men have continued to recur to and
use their experience very much as they always have. One
suspects that even the most determined reformist intellectual wears his rubbers, or puts snow tires on his automobile, when he ventures out upon icy streets. He knows, as
do we all, that "history" repeats itself many times over.
But at the level of large and complex matters, history has
been deactivated, the past has been cut off, and men have
been disjoined from the common fund of experience. A
new history has emerged which is not a useful record of
experience but a herald of the future and an instrument
for rebuilding society.

Defaming the Past

One of the culminating steps in the deactivation of history was the defamation of the older history. Just as the
older philosophy had been defamed, just as the older education, religion, and economics would be defamed, just so
history would be denigrated. The work of undermining
the older history was mainly the work of historians. Many
contributed, but three men who mounted the assault in the
first half of the twentieth century will provide us with
sufficient illustrative material. These men were: James
Harvey Robinson, Harry Elmer Barnes, and Charles A.
Beard.

Robinson launched the attack upon the older history first.
His position is made clear in the following:

It is true that it has long been held that certain lessons could be derived from the past. . . . But there is a

growing suspicion . . . that this type of usefulness is purely illusory. The present writer is anxious to avoid any risk of being regarded as an advocate of these supposed advantages of historical study. Their value rests on the assumption that conditions remain sufficiently uniform to give precedents a perpetual value, while, as a matter of fact, conditions . . . are so rapidly altering that for the most part it would be dangerous indeed to attempt to apply past experience to the solution of current problems.[9]

Writing some years later, Barnes much more vehemently denounced the reliance upon past experience. He declared that "the past has no direct lesson for the present in the way of analogies and forecasts." He goes on to cast doubt upon the "wisdom of the Fathers," that is, the wisdom of leaders in past times. "The fact that every civilization prior to our own has ended up in a hopeless wreck should be fairly proof of the frailty of patristic wisdom in all ages of men." In short, "we are grotesquely wrong in assuming that there has been any great amount of true wisdom in the past. . . ."[10] But even if there had been wisdom in the past, he pointed out, it would not be relevant to contemporary problems. Conditions have changed.

Therefore, in our efforts to solve contemporary problems on the basis of the "wisdom of the past," we are somewhat more absurd in our attitude and conduct than the animal trainer who would strap his pet anthropoid in the seat of an aeroplane on the ground of his prior mastery of the technique of the tricycle. Not even a Texas Methodist Kleagle would think of taking his car to Moses, Joshua, Luther or George Washington to have the carburetor adjusted or the valves ground, yet we as-

---

[9] Robinson, *op. cit.,* pp. 17-18.

[10] Harry E. Barnes, *The New History and the Social Studies* (New York: The Century Co., 1925), p. 588.

sure ourselves and our fellow men that we ought to continue to attempt to solve our contemporary problems of
society, economics, politics and conduct on the basis of
methods, attitudes and information which in many
cases far antedate Moses.[11]

It is not necessary to disentangle all the ideas which
Barnes mistakenly or dubiously associated and confused.
The point is that he denied the relevance of historical lessons to the present, and, in the same passages, rejected
all that may have been learned in the past.

Charles A. Beard, a somewhat more disciplined thinker
than Barnes, denied that cause and effect can be isolated
in history. He maintained that no group of complications
can "be isolated from surrounding and preceding complications. Even 'simple' events are complex when examined
closely. 'George Washington accepted the command of the
American troops.' What 'caused' that action?"[12] He goes on
to conclude that it is impossible to draw a conclusion with
certainty about the answer to the question he poses. In
so complex a matter as the American Revolution, he continues, the attempt to assign causes is futile.

To apply the physical analogy of "cause and effect"
we should be compelled to think of the American Revolution as an entity, like a ball, set in motion by impact
of other entities. The latter are the "causes" and the
motion of the ball is the "effect." The impossibility of
making such analogy conform to the recorded facts of
the Revolution is apparent to anybody who employs historical knowledge in the effort. We know that thousands
of events took place in time, and that thousands of per-

---

[11] *Ibid*, p. 589.

[12] Charles A. Beard, *The Discussion of Human Affairs* (New
York: Macmillan, 1936), p. 90.

sonalities were engaged in them, but we cannot find chains of causes and effects in them.[13]

However obtusely he had done so, Beard had put his finger on the nerve that goes to the center of the didactic use of history. If it is impossible to discover cause and effect, it is not possible to know what action produced what results. Without this information there is little to be learned from the past. Beard's examples do not prove his case; instead, they show that it is possible to pose questions in such a way that no answers can be found for them. In the first example, he asked what George Washington's motives were. He was quite right in pointing out that we cannot discover the answer to this question with any certainty. He was wrong, however, if he supposed that the answer to the question would matter if it could be known. The effects of actions, once they have taken place, are not altered by motives. Suppose he had asked another sort of question, a "simple" one involving George Washington. For example, Continental troops were so disposed on Long Island that they could have been cut off by General Howe. Why did this occur? Washington had issued an order that they be situated in this manner. He had *caused* them to be so disposed. If the army had been captured, Washington could have been held responsible. If this had happened, there would have been instruction in it for future military commanders.

The case of the "cause(s)" of the "American Revolution," as Beard poses the problem, is even more instructive. It leads us toward an understanding of the position from which historians denied the relevance of the past for the present. Beard started with a dubious assumption, i. e., that there was some occurrence which could properly be

---

[13] *Ibid.*, p. 91.

called the "American Revolution." This is highly doubtful. At best, this phrase is a *convenient designation* for a considerable number of events and developments—e.g., the break from England, the war, the drawing of constitutions, the making of reforms, and so forth. Moreover, the question as posed may embrace motives, purposes, incentives, desires, accidents, influences, decisions, reasons, as well as cause and effect relationships, in its answer. "American Revolution," when used as a phrase to designate a large number of developments, is a fictional device, not a reality. The real question involving causation concerning a convenient designation should concern who invented it. To treat it as something that actually occurred, to ask what caused it to occur, is bound to lead to confusion. To fail to distinguish among all that an historian might offer as explanation—to lump everything together as "causes"— compounds the confusion. The question of causation is important for the didactic use of history as it concerns the results of human action. Beard had posed no question that brought the problem into focus.

Historicism

Actually, then, the arguments were irrelevant to the positions taken. Beard had not disproved the existence of cause and effect relationships. Barnes had not shown that there was nothing to be learned from the past, nor that men in the past had no wisdom. Robinson had not shown that past experience is irrelevant in present circumstances. They, along with others, did succeed in discrediting didactic history, but what did the work was not the validity of their direct arguments against it but their assumptions. These men were historicists, and if one accepts the historicist position, he must, logically, reject the relevance of the past to action in the future.

In essence, historicism has been defined—or described—in the following way by one historian: "The subject matter of history is human life in its totality and multiplicity. It is the historian's aim to portray the bewildering, unsystematic variety of historical forms . . . in their unique, living expressions and in the process of continuous growth and transformation." In brief, "the special quality of history does not consist in the statement of general laws or principles, but in the grasp, so far as possible, of the infinite variety of particular historical forms immersed in the passage of time."[14]

Historicism was developed by German historians in the nineteenth century; it stemmed from Herder and was shaped by von Ranke, Dilthey, and Meinecke. It arose as a protest against the scientific emphasis of eighteenth century thought and partook of the romantic concentration upon the concrete and the unique.[15] It was, in its inception, a definition of the limits and extent of their craft by historians. They were saying something such as this: Each event when viewed as a whole is unique. That is how we propose to view every happening, occurrence, and development. Perchance, there may be common features to them, there may be laws and principles, but this is not our concern as historians.

Well and good, one might say, let other disciplines explore reality from their vantage points and discover such laws and principles as there are. But there was a catch. In the course of the nineteenth century, all of reality was being thrust into the domain of history by thinkers, by Hegel, by Marx, by the Darwinians. Everything was con-

---

[14] Hans Meyerhoff, ed., *The Philosophy of History in Our Time* (Garden City: Doubleday, an Anchor Book, 1959), p. 10.
[15] See *ibid.*, pp. 9-18.

ceived of as changing, and the historicists themselves were among the first to claim every aspect of life as grist for their mills. This brought them into conflict with the various "scientific" schools (Hegelian, Marxian, Darwinian), for these sought for and expounded "laws" of historical change. On the whole, in the West, the historicists appear to have won.

In the main, however, it was an empty victory. Most of the ideas that were denied entrance at the front door by historicists came in at the back by way of assumptions. Thus, scientism, progressivism, determinism, and a host of other isms have pervaded historical work in the twentieth century. Historicism is particularly vulnerable to determinism, and the historicist has no vantage point from which to resist the intellectual currents of his day. This is so because historicism is ineluctably relativistic. Each event is unique; each happening must be understood in terms of the context within which it occurs. To put it another way, everything is *relative* to its context. Rigorous historicists (some of whom were romantic individualists) have tried to avoid the implicit determinism in this view by insisting upon the uniqueness and individuality of each thing. But most historians are not troubled by such philosophical scruples; thus, they allow the implicit assumption of determinism free play in their work.

The main point, however, is that historicism makes history useless so far as instruction for future action is concerned. Regardless of how luxurious the detail with which events are described—or because of it in part—these events contain no lessons. They are unique, self-contained, or, in the case of the way in which most practitioners handle them, prelude to the future. Future happenings will be unique also, perhaps shaped, even determined, by the past, but unlike anything in it. The relativism in historicism can be utilized to reach yet another conclusion—that *the past is unknowable*. This is roughly the conclusion which Charles A. Beard had reached by the mid-1930's.[16] The reasoning follows this line. Both men and events are conditioned by the context within which they occur, are relative to their "times." If this is so, it follows that the historian writes from his own unique position and can never be certain that he is making truthful statements about the past. It is much more likely that he is revealing much more about himself and his times than he is about the past. The idea was already current that each generation rewrites history in its own image, and Beard's position reinforced it.

The thought may well arise at this point, why bother with history, anyhow? It appears to be useless, meaningless, and in any case, probably unknowable. Some historians have indeed drawn such a conclusion. But the most vigorous defamers of the older history quite often had new uses in mind. They were what may be called historicist-progressives. From historicism they took the idea that history does not repeat itself, that ideas and events are relative to the context within which they occur, and that it is the business of the historian to reconstruct the whole of the past, in all its luxurious detail. From progressivism came their idea that all of later history is a product of earlier history—that the past is prologue. If one could delineate all the trends at any present moment, they thought, he could discern the shape of the future. This was a watered down version of the various historical determinisms of the nineteenth century.

---

[16] His most famous statement of it is in "Written History as an Act of Faith," *American Historical Review*, XXXIX (January, 1934) 219-29.

Instrumenting History

Historicist-progressives turned to the conscious use of history to reform man and society. This was the purpose of James Harvey Robinson's New History. He declared, "We must develop historical-mindedness upon a far more generous scale than hitherto, for this will add a still-deficient element in our intellectual equipment and will promote rational progress as nothing else can do. *The present has hitherto been the willing victim of the past; the time has come when it should turn on the past and exploit it in the interests of advance.*"[17] The historian should come forward and direct the reforms, it appears:

> As for accomplishing the great reforms that demand our united efforts—the abolition of poverty and disease and war, and the promotion of happy and rational lives —the task would seem hopeless enough were it not for the considerations which have been recalled above. . . . The reformer who appeals to the future is a recent upstart. . . . But it is clear enough today that the conscious reformer who appeals to the future is the final product of a progressive order of things. . . . We are only just coming to realize that we can cooperate with and direct this innate force of change. . . .[18]

Even as long ago as 1912 the villain of the piece—conservatism—had been identified. "At last, perhaps, the long-disputed sin against the Holy Ghost has been found; it may be the refusal to cooperate with the vital principle of betterment. History would seem, in short, to condemn the principle of conservatism as a hopeless and wicked anachronism."[19]

Harry Elmer Barnes accepted the "value of historical

---

[17] Robinson, *op. cit.,* p. 24. Emphasis added.

[18] *Ibid.,* pp. 263-65.

[19] *Ibid.,* p. 265.

knowledge as an aid in improving the present and in planning for the future. . . ." He declared that the "chief way in which history can be an aid to the future is by revealing those elements in our civilization which are unquestionably primitive, anachronistic and obstructive and by making clear those forces and factors in our culture which have been most potent . . . in removing these primitive barriers to more rapid progress."[20] The ubiquitous John Dewey can be quoted to the same effect: "Intelligent understanding of past history is to some extent a lever for moving the present into a certain kind of future."[21]

History was not only deactivated, then, but also reactivated. The older history was defamed and cast aside, but a New History was conceived to take its place. History ceased to be a record of man's experience from the past, rooted in an enduring reality, and was given a new role of being an instrument of reform in the present and for the future. This New History was (and is) presentistic and futuristic. The past is consciously and intentionally viewed from the present perspective and in terms of future goals. The emphasis is upon trends and forces at work in history, and upon the changing cultural setting within which men live and events take place.

History was rewritten to the above formulas. The *modus operandus* was something such as this. The historian combed whatever history he happened to be studying for currents and trends leading up to the present situation or which could be expected to culminate in the not too distant future. Quite often, such history was written with a particular idea, goal, or ideal in mind. A favorite goal for

---

[20] Barnes, *op. cit.,* p. 16.

[21] John Dewey, "Historical Judgments," in Meyerhoff, *op. cit.,* p. 172.

American history has been democracy. A historian writing from this angle is apt to discover "seeds of democracy" in Puritan New England, "limited democracy" in the constitutional period, "Jeffersonian democracy" in the time of the badly misunderstood Jefferson, and "Jacksonian democracy" a little later.

Of course, the Jacksonians only witnessed the Advent of Democracy, as any reader of such histories knows. A great struggle had yet to take place. Children and women labored long hours in inhospitable factories. The enfranchisement of the adult population was only well underway. In the latter part of the nineteenth century, the "plutocrats" almost succeeded in wrenching the control of the government out of the hands of "the people." But, in the early twentieth century, "the people" wrested control away from the usurpers, and turned it over to progressive reformers. From that time on, with some set-backs, the advance of "democracy" has been upward and onward. The work is not finished, of course, as one historian points out in the peroration to his text:

> High though our standard of living is, it reveals glaring inequalities. Vigorous efforts should be made to narrow the gap between the rich few and the poor many. A better life must be assured our millions of sub-standard tenant farmers, sharecroppers, migratory fruit-and-vegetable workers, and day laborers, both Negro and white. Millions of our people enjoy less than a decent standard of living, and consequently fall victim to illness, crime, and other misfortunes resulting from a low income. A high standard of democracy and a high standard of decency go hand in hand.[22]

He has, of course, already described trends which,

---

[22] Thomas A. Bailey, *The American Pageant* (Boston: Heath, 1961, 2nd edition), p. 970.

when they culminate, should deal rather effectively with these problems.

It should be noted that the historicist-progressive historian need not come out in the open as an advocate of reforms, as the above quoted historian does. He can, and usually does, accomplish his advocacy in more subtle ways. The story that he tells is usually oriented toward reforms. The trends he discovers make the reforms virtually inevitable. He can describe the surrounding circumstances in such a way (the handling of the Great Depression is a good example) that the reforms are made to appear unavoidable and entirely desirable. All of this he can do while maintaining a stance of "objectivity." All that he has been doing, he may protest, is to describe what happened, to show the context within which it happened, and to sort out the trends which led up to the happening. Actually, many historians of this stripe take no particular pains to hide their melioristic bias. The ones quoted above were hardly doing so. It is a handy stance to have around, however, when some historian arises to oppose reform.

It should be noted, too, that "lessons" have crept back into the New History. They usually have to do with the temporary triumph of the "forces of reaction." Perhaps the most commonly repeated "lesson" is the one to be learned from the failure of the United States to join the League of Nations. Many historians attribute failure of the League to the absence of American support. If America had joined, they say, things would have been different. Look at all the horrors that ensued. The hardly concealed "lesson" was that the United States should join the United Nations and should stay with it and support it at all cost. Notice that this is not a lesson to be learned from history at all. It is a preachment written into history. No one knows what might have happened had the United States joined the

League of Nations. It is pure supposition that the course of events would have been much altered. It is not a lesson drawn from what men did and what the consequences were; it is a lesson drawn from what men *might* have done and what *might* have been the result had they done so.

As the above indicates, history has been cut loose from reality. The only reality with which history can properly deal is in the past. When historians cut loose from reality, and to the extent that they did, they cut all of us off from much of our experience. They opened the way to reform efforts unchastened by experience. They turned history into an instrument for remaking man and society. They wrenched history out of its path of reliance on the concrete experience of the past and attempted to root it in their own subjective longings.

9

The New Reality

[T]he characteristic mood of our own age [is] that the historical condition determines the human situation. Man's existence is history; or "life and reality are history, and history alone," as Croce said. —HANS MEYERHOFF, 1959

From the perspective of the post-Second World War era, the work of the generation of the 1890's can be viewed as a "first attempt" at accommodation to a "new conception of reality." . . . In this process of concession and adaptation, the "activity of human consciousness" for the first time became of paramount importance. —H. STUART HUGHES, 1958

We invoked what we believed to be the three constitutive facts in the consciousness of Western man: knowledge of death, knowledge of freedom, knowledge of society. . . . The third revelation came to us through living in an industrial society. . . . It is the constitutive element in modern man's consciousness. —KARL POLANYI, 1944

IT HAS BEEN SAID THAT MAN IS INCURABLY RELIGIOUS. It may be said with equal validity that man is incurably metaphysical in his thought processes. The flight from reality of intellectuals commenced with the cutting loose of ideas from their foundations in an underlying order. This was an attempt to slough off metaphysics, for metaphysics is the philosophical study which treats of the underlying order. In the course of time, it became (and still is) commonplace in intellectual circles to denounce conceptions—any that happened not to be considered worthy

153

of consideration—as being "metaphysical." In short, meta-physics was laughed out of court; scorn and abuse were heaped upon this mode of thought.

Pragmatists boldly proclaimed a philosophy that was supposed to be shorn of metaphysical assumptions. They proposed to operate upon a basis of continuous experimentation to find successful methods within an ever shifting context. Rigorous adherence to pragmatism, however, would result in some surprises for pragmatists. They would begin to discover that there are regularities, that actions essentially the same will result in predictable consequences.

In brief, if the pragmatists adhered strictly to their method, they would begin to acquire knowledge. If they probed a bit deeper, they would discover that there are laws which account for these regularities and predictabilities. At the point that they discovered and believed in laws and principles they would return most likely to a truly metaphysical outlook.

In general, this has not happened. It certainly has not happened among ameliorative reformers, and these generally like to think of themselves as pragmatic. The reason is not far to seek. At the time of the setting forth of pragmatism, thinkers were already coming under the sway of a "new reality." This new reality was based upon assumptions which served in lieu of and could be used in somewhat the same manner as metaphysics. This is not to say that the conceptions were indeed metaphysical. There is no need to corrupt the language by so denominating them. Rather, they served in this capacity; they rested upon conceptions of an underlying order. Explanations were made in terms of this "order." Pragmatism became largely a philosophy to justify the expediency of men operating on the basis of the "new reality."

Though the conceptions drawn from this new reality are

used metaphysically, the fact is not generally recognized. Moreover, they are not subjected to rational examination. The decline of philosophy and the growth of irrationalism have made this state of affairs possible. Even ideologies in America have not usually been explicit. In consequence, assumptions have to be deduced from casually thrown phrases and the fag ends of ideas which one encounters. Still, the conceptions are there.

Three Basic Constituents

There are three basic constituents of the "new reality." They are: *change, society,* and *psyche.* These are not separate realities but interrelated parts of a single reality. Historically, each of them, as a metaphysic-like entity, can be traced back to its origins in nineteenth century European thought. Change was "reafied" in the thought of Hegel, Marx, Spencer, and Darwin. Society was "thingified" by a line of thinkers that includes Burke, Comte, Marx, and Mosca. Psyche began to assume its modern proportions for Schopenhauer, Nietzsche, Freud, Adler, and Jung. These ideas were picked up and extended by such Americans as Frederick Jackson Turner, James Harvey Robinson, William Graham Sumner, Charles A. Beard, Lester Frank Ward, John Dewey, William James, Thorstein Veblen, and Oliver Wendell Holmes, Jr.

The story of this transmigration of ideas—of Americans traveling to Europe, of their becoming enamored particularly with German thought, of the visits of European scholars in America, of the founding of schools in America based upon European ideas—is much too extended and complex even to be summarized here. Suffice it to say that such events occurred, and that American thinkers frequently followed paths very similar to their European counterparts. As a result of this interchange, American intellectuals embraced and expounded a "new reality."

Three sorts of explanations can be made from the vantage point of this new reality: historical, sociological, and psychological. Three specialized intellectual "disciplines" were developed in the nineteenth and twentieth centuries to make these explanations: history, sociology, and psychology.

Of course, history was not new to the nineteenth century. It had been consciously written since the time of Herodotus in ancient Greece, and had in fact been written and told long before that. Students had studied and learned it through the ages—but not as a separate "discipline." Prior to sometime in the nineteenth century, students learned history as a kind of bonus from the study of literature or "grammar," and men read and wrote it as the spirit moved them to do so. There was no distinct profession which had history in its keeping or was responsible for it. In the course of the nineteenth century, the study and writing of history was specialized and professionalized. And, as we have seen, in the early twentieth century the older history was defamed and a New History advanced. History was cut loose from its foundation in an enduring order and turned into an instrument for reshaping the society for the future.

There was no problem of remaking sociology. There had been no such study or discipline for traditional scholarship. It was only developed after some thinkers began to believe in the reality of society. Its founding is usually ascribed to Auguste Comte, but it can be traced through a host of thinkers in its development. At any rate, sociology became the "discipline" to deal with society.

Psychology was a traditional study; it was a branch of philosophy historically. It has already been noted that the house of philosophy fell apart in the wake of the labors of

Hume and Kant. Even so, psychology had to be wrested from the hands of philosophers who tried to cling to it before it could be "independent." The assault was upon introspective psychology (which was, in turn, innate psychology), and the effort was to make psychology scientific, or so its proponents claimed. The New Psychology was shaped by Wilhelm Wundt, Sigmund Freud, William James, John B. Watson, and others. Many different schools of psychology emerged, but they all shared a common faith in the New Psychology.

The initial effort, then, was to make history, sociology, and psychology separate intellectual disciplines, to get them recognized as a part of the curriculum of education, and, usually, to get them recognized as sciences in their own right. But in the twentieth century there has been a considerable movement to "integrate" these studies. Those who want this have probably had their greatest success in the public schools, where, in some instances, they have been merged into social studies courses. But where they have retained some separation, as is usual, a great deal of "integration" has taken place. For example, sociological and psychological explanations now pervade much of the writing of history. There is a kind of inherent logic to this movement to merge these studies. If they could be joined, a New Philosophy might emerge to deal with the "new reality." Actually, of course, this New Philosophy has already emerged and is used to make explanations of developments. Such explanations are, of course, historical, sociological, and psychological.

All Learning Affected

It may be objected at this point that history, sociology, and psychology do not deal with the whole of reality for contemporary intellectuals, even if they are supposed to deal with part of it. There are, after all, a great many other studies and approaches to learning. The above named do not even include all of the "social sciences." What of economics, of political science, of anthropology? It is in order to point out that these have been historicized, sociologized, and psychologized, if one may employ somewhat facetiously a barbarized language. Note that this is precisely what Thorstein Veblen did to economics. My impression is that European economists regularly write in a way that we would call sociological. The critic may observe that the economic tail often wags the sociological dog in practice. This is only a surface observation, however, for economics is first permeated with sociological assumptions. Economic determinism, for example, is a sociological or psychological, not an economic, idea. As for political science, it is usually filled to overflowing with the above ideas. Anthropology is largely the result of the application of historical, sociological, and psychological methods to the study of primitive societies.

That group of studies known as the humanities may be disposed of quickly. Language has come to be thought of increasingly as an "instrument of communication." Literature is not only arranged chronologically but quite often taught historically. Philosophy, deprived of its content (except the *history* of philosophy and a few esoteric subjects such as ethics and esthetics) has tended to wither on the vine. My main point, however, is that the humanities—or rather, those who teach and speak for them—do not speak authoritatively of any reality other than the historical, sociological, and psychological.

But surely, it may be argued, contemporary thinkers believe that the material realm, that realm with which the sciences are supposed to deal, is real. It is frequently asserted, by those who disagree with them, that reformist intellectuals are materialists. Nothing can be more readily demonstrated than their perpetual concern with material things, with better housing, with better diets, with higher standards of living, and so on. Yet these things are not real, in the sense we have been employing the word, to reformists. The natural world has no enduring form which would make it real. It is something brute, to be made over according to human will. The sciences are instruments to this end.

Actually, the sciences have not been subdued as yet to this new conception of reality. The specialization that has occurred there plus the complex techniques now employed, make them largely *terra incognita* to nonscientists. The "social sciences" were born out of a desire to make the study of social phenomena scientific. Pragmatism was a more general application of an abstracted scientific method. The respect for the Sciences (personified) has continued, but there has been much talk of bringing them under control. But the sciences, too, have been largely severed from their philosophical roots; and since they are restricted to the world of nature, they pose no real threat to the "new reality." If and when reformist intellectuals achieve social controls, they are, of course, in control of scientists, too.

The sciences have played a dual role within the framework of the "new reality." In the first place, they are instruments for reshaping the physical environment to the needs and purposes of man. Second, they provided the method which was to be used for reshaping society and man. Lester Frank Ward, the American catalyst for so many of these ideas, stated the matter bluntly:

> . . . We saw in the last chapter that most individual achievement has been due to invention and scientific

discovery in the domain of the physical forces. The parallel consists in the fact that social achievement consists in invention and discovery in the domain of the social forces. . . .

If we carefully analyze an invention we shall find that it consists first in recognizing a property or force and secondly in making material adjustments calculated to cause that property or force to act in the manner desired by the inventor. . . .

Now the desires and wants of men constitute the forces of society, complicated, as they are in the higher stages, by the directive agent in all its manifold aspects. *Social invention consists in making such adjustments as will induce men to act in the manner most advantageous to society.*[1]

The Deactivation of the Sciences

The story of the deactivation and instrumentation of the sciences deserves a separate chapter, or book. It was one of the most momentous developments of the modern era. Unfortunately, it must be reduced here to a few sentences. The sciences were once conceived as a method for getting truth about the universe, truth which provided a key to the purpose of God for man.[2] So conceived and employed, they provided much information about an underlying order in the universe. Techniques were instruments, within this framework, for the discovery of truth.

But in the course of the nineteenth century, intellectuals (and everybody else, I suspect) began to confuse science with technology. When science came to be identified with

[1] Lester F. Ward, *Pure Sociology* (New York: Macmillan, 1909, 2nd edition), pp. 568-69. Italics mine.

[2] See Edwin A. Burtt, *The Metaphysical Foundations of Modern Physical Science* (Garden City: Doubleday, an Anchor Book, 1954), *passim.*

technology, it had been "instrumented"; its truths became important as they were renderable into techniques. By the middle of the twentieth century, there was much voiced concern about the need for a revival of "pure" research. The justification was that this would lead to the discovery of laws which would, in turn, be renderable into techniques for technological purposes. In short, the sciences had become the handmaidens of technology.

The point of this discussion needs to be spelled out so that misunderstanding will be avoided, if that is possible. Nothing said is intended to disparage technology or to deny the connection between the sciences and technology. (Benjamin Franklin felicitously demonstrated the connection between science and technology around 200 years ago. He reasoned that lightning is electricity. He performed his famous kite experiment to prove his hypothesis. Since lightning is electricity, since electricity is a natural phenomenon, it behaves in predictable ways. In consequence of these conclusions, he made the technological application—i.e., invented the lightning rod.) My point is that when the scientist became identified with technology, he ceased largely to speak authoritatively about the nature of the universe and, instead, provided means for manipulating things within it. He ceased to provide information about an enduring reality, or rather, he no longer made available information which was understood in this way. The treatment of reality was left to the proponents of the "new reality."

Not only were the sciences "instrumented," then, but also they provided the method by which social reform was to be undertaken. Lester Frank Ward was enamored of the analogy between the social and the physical, and he treated the analogy as if it were a one-to-one relationship. "The sociologist," he said, "who really believes there is such a science has a right to claim that all the social forces may be utilized as the physical ones have been. He classes those who maintain the contrary along with those who once believed that the thunders were only engines of destruction, the winds powers of evil, and the gases demoniacal spirits."[3]

Ward's is the underlying preconception of contemporary ameliorative reform. It should be noted that several strange equations were made: science with technology, the physical with the social, things with people. Ward saw nothing untoward, at that point, in recommending that people be manipulated according to the prescriptions of sociologists in the same manner as physical scientists prescribe the manipulation of things. Neither has many another reformer.

The Personification of History

Before examining further the import of the "new reality," however, it is in order to give some demonstrations to substantiate the assertion that these conceptions of change society, and psyche are used in a metaphysic-like manner What does it mean to treat change as if it were real? It means to treat it as if it were an entity, a being with properties, attributes, and characteristics. Actually, this has frequently been done with change by personifying (thingifying, reafying, anthropomorphicizing) it as History.

Let us take a simple and not very significant example first. One often hears some such statement as this: History will decide whether so and so was a great President or not This is palpable nonsense. There is no such being as History to render any such decision. It may be objected that

[3] Lester F. Ward, *Dynamic Sociology*, I (New York: D. Appleton and Co., 1920, 2 volumes), 43.

I am taking a figure of speech literally, that those who make such statements really mean that historians will decide whether or not someone was a great man. If this latter were indeed the meaning to be attached to the initial statement, it would make sense, but it would be in error. Historians do not assemble in a great parliament to render the final verdict upon the characters of the past (for which oversight we should all be grateful). If they were to do so, they would only be playing at being gods. Those who have insufficient knowledge about such matters may suppose that historians come to a consensus about important figures of the past. This is not really the case. Vigorous controversies still go on about figures in the most distant past. In short, there is no reality which conforms to the view that History reaches final decisions.

But there is much reason to suspect that this usage is derived from a much more serious personifying of history. The usage to which I refer is the treatment of history as force or as a vehicle for a number of forces. The conception involved is that the past shapes the future, that the past contains trends, movements, developmental directions which act as forces upon the present and the future. These forces are thought of as acting ineluctably and inevitably to bring about certain developments.

The most famous of such theses was that of Karl Marx and Friedrich Engels, but the idea informs all reformist thought in the contemporary era. Progressivism is deeply imbued with the idea of history as a progressive force. It becomes apparent in such notions as the following: you can't turn back the clock; the latest is the best; it is necessary to adjust to changing times. Such words and phrases as the following, when they are used to refer to ideas, draw their sustenance from this view of history: reactionary, backlash, neanderthal, anachronistic, and so on.

Sir Isaiah Berlin says, "The notion that history obeys laws, whether natural or supernatural, that every event o human life is an element in a necessary pattern has deep metaphysical origins."[4] The matter goes deeper than this however. When history is dealt with as a being, it has it self become metaphysic-like. It has been made into a con stituent part of underlying reality. If anyone objects that the word "history" is only being employed as a metaphor he should be ready to explain why we can't turn back the clock then. Surely, no metaphor would prevent it, or could cause all that has occurred. Whether History only stand for the forces or is itself the force is largely irrelevant The forces themselves are treated by those who think in this way as metaphysic-like beings.

Is Society Real?

The second ingredient of the "new reality" is society The belief in the reality of society was a precondition to the development of sociology, no doubt, and a continuing assumption of those who pursue the study. At any rate that is the way it was and generally has been. But before going further with this analysis some distinctions should be made. There *are* social phenomena. Such phenomena include institutions, customs, traditions, folkways, habits behavior patterns, and so on. Moreover, it may be descrip tively useful to refer to those who share a preponderanc of these as living in a society.

The development with which I wish to deal hinges philosophically, upon whether society is a phenomenon o a noumenon. Or, somewhat more familiar language may be used in describing the basis upon which a distinction

---

[4] Isaiah Berlin, *Historical Inevitability* (London: Oxford University Press, 1954), p. 13.

might be made: Is society an appearance or is it real? Is the word "society" a convenient designation for certain phenomena or does it refer to a real being in its own right? Do social phenomena stem from society or do they stem from people? Are individuals real or are they products (extensions) of society?

The above questions may make the development to be described clearer than it would otherwise be. My point is that thinkers began to treat society as if it were real. This does not mean that they explicitly treated it as a being distinct from those who were supposed to compose it. Lester Frank Ward said, "Society is simply a compound organism whose acts exhibit the resultant of all the individual forces which its members exert." Yet he went on to say, "These acts, whether individual or collective, obey fixed laws. Objectively viewed, society is a natural object, presenting a variety of complicated movements produced by a particular class of natural forces."[5] But, one may ask, whence come these laws? Do they come from individuals? Strictly speaking, this would have to mean that individuals create laws. This could not be, for such would not be laws.

Actually, Ward's confusion arose from the contradictory premises upon which he was operating. On the one hand, he treated society as if it were real, spoke of social laws and forces, and worked to develop a sociology that would describe these laws of society.[6] On the other, he wanted men to take over the direction of society and control the forces to desirable ends. For example, "The social forces only need to be investigated as the rest have been, in order to discover ways in which their utility can be demonstrated.

---

[5] Ward, *Dynamic Sociology*, I, 35.
[6] See *ibid.*, pp. 1-2.

Here is a vast field of true scientific exploitation as ye
untracked. . . . To just what extent the present evil ten
dencies of society may be turned to good, under the man
agement of truly enlightened legislation, it is impossibl
to predict."[7] What does social force refer to, if not to men'
And if they are forces acting upon men, how can men
act upon and direct them?

Ward's thought lies athwart the path of two differen
modes of thought—the deterministic and melioristic—a
the point of divergence. It was filled with the conclusion
of nineteenth century deterministic thought—the talk o
forces, progressive laws, social evolution—which wer
the intellectual currency of the time. He suggested the ide
that mentality had evolved to the point that men coul
consciously guide further evolution. But his position wa
philosophically vague and internally contradictory.[8] Thes
contradictions have gone into reformist thought, for ex
planations have continued to be made in terms of socia
forces; whereas, reformers have exhorted their followers t
conscious reformist efforts. Ward was the fount of thi
confusion.

Society was real to Ward, as it was to John Dewey, an
as it has been to a host of other reformers. They speak o
society as if it had a distinct being and use the wor
"social" as derived from it in this sense. The followin
usages by Ward, taken from the second volume of *Dynami*

---

[7] *Ibid.,* p. 43.

[8] Note his embroilment in the contradictions. "Althoug
every act must in strict science be recognized as the resultar
of all the forces, internal and external, acting upon the agen
still it remains true that achievement is the work of individua
thus acting. . . ." (Ward, *Pure Sociology,* p. 41.) With about a
much sense, one may say: The spokes only turn when th
wheel turns; still it is the spokes turning.

Sociology, will illustrate the point. He refers to "social forces" (p. 161), "social progress" (p. 161), "social advancement" (p. 163), "the life of a society" (p. 163), "state of society" (p. 165), "protection of society" (p. 214), "social growth" (p. 224), "will of *society*" (p. 230), "servant of society" (p. 242), "Society, possessed for the first time of a completely integrated consciousness" (p. 249), "agencies of society" (p. 250), "duty of society" (p. 251), "duties of society toward itself" (p. 467), "how to bring society to consciousness" (p. 467), "members of society" (p. 544), "superficiality of society" (p. 552), "the exclusive work of society" (p. 571), "the welfare of society" (p. 583), "responsible solely to society" (p. 589), "better for society" (p. 591) "society" as having "burden on its shoulders" (p. 595), and a "sphere prescribed by society" (p. 617). If phraseology be accepted as a good indication of underlying assumptions, and it should be, there should be no doubt that Lester Frank Ward believed in the reality of society.

John Dewey followed a similar pattern in his language. The following instances are taken from his *Problems of Men.*[9] He refers to "socially necessary" (p. 32), "social control" (p. 35), "members of our society" (p. 37), "socially helpful" (p. 49), "social forces" (p. 52), "society" as "deprived of what they might contribute" (p. 61), "the interests and activities of a society" (p. 62), "social enterprise" (p. 76), "social pressure" (p. 85), "social breakdown" (p. 90), "social authority" (p. 94), "socially justified" (p. 101), "benefit to society" (p. 102), "social vacuum" (p. 104), "society . . . itself" (p. 131), "social power" (p. 132), "social knowledge" (p. 179), "social materials" (p. 180) "society" as "suffering" (p. 182), and "socially authorized" (p. 185). These are, of course, meta-

---

[9] New York: Philosophical Library, 1946.

physic-like usages. Such usage derives most of its meaning from the conception of society as an organism, which became common after the presentation of Darwinian evolution.

The Emphasis on Feelings

The third ingredient in the "new reality" was the psyche. More specifically, it was psychic phenomena thingified, made into positive active forces. Lester Frank Ward referred constantly to social forces. One may well wonder where these forces come from. They are operative in society, according to him, but they do not come from society. Instead, they arise from within men. Ward put it this way: "The motive of all action is feeling. All great movements in history are preceded and accompanied by strong feelings."[10] Again, "Feeling alone can drive on the social train, whether for weal or woe."[11] Moreover, "Egoism is the feeling which demands for self an increase of enjoyment and diminution of discomfort. Altruism is . . . a kind of feeling which results from the contemplation of suffering in others. . . ."[12]

Ward indicates in the following that feeling is his fundamental conception:

The root-idea to which I will here confine myself is the true supremacy which must be accorded in any just system of philosophy to the *feelings* as the real *end* toward which all efforts designed to secure the advancement of society must be directed. Although it is upon the intellect that we can alone rely to secure such a control of the social forces as shall successfully harmonize them with human advantage, it is feeling that

[10] Ward, *Dynamic Sociology*, I, 11.
[11] *Ibid.*, p. 12.
[12] *Ibid.*, p. 14.

must be alone consulted in determining what constitutes such advantage. Every true system must regard intellect as the means and feeling as the end of all its operations. . . .

The practical work which sociology demands is, when reduced to its lowest terms, *the organization of feeling.* The human body is a reservoir of feeling which, when wholly unobstructed, is all pleasurable.[13]

The concentration upon the psychological has led in many directions in the twentieth century. Some have followed Ward's lead in emphasizing the primacy of feeling. Need and desire have been virtually deified as realities by some writers. Others have focused upon motive as the most important area for knowledge and in terms of which to make explanations. Professional psychoanalysts have focused attention upon removing the obstructions to free expression and action. The arts and education fell under the spell of "self-expression." Many people came to believe that intention was more important than action.

Taken together, change, society, and the psyche provided a new conception of reality. The psyche provided the impetus, or force, society the framework within which and upon which the force was exerted, and history the plane upon which movement took place. This attributes greater clarity to these ideas than they have, however. By the early twentieth century, American thinkers were sloughing off the framework of natural (or social) law within which Ward cast his thought. They continued to use concepts, such as environmentalism, drawn from this framework but quite often without avowing it. The theoretical framework became much vaguer than it had been, even though this might not appear possible.

Most American reformist intellectuals have adopted a

---

[13] *Ibid.,* pp. 67-68.

pragmatic stance, disavowed conscious theory, and ostensibly acted in terms of each situation as it arose. They have not really done this, and it is doubtful whether anyone could. They have, instead, acted on the basis of assumptions and ideologies. Both of these are founded, insofar as they *are* founded, in the "new reality." Men who have no theory, metaphysics, or principles, generally act upon the basis of the fag ends of those they pick up unawares.

Constantly Changing Reality

The most important feature of this new reality is that it is constantly changing. Change is embedded in it as one of its constituents. The other constituents change, too. Few things can be more readily demonstrated than that social structures are greatly altered during the passage of time. As for the psyche, it is the root or origin of important changes, according to the above formulation. It is a force for change. There was an article of faith that reformers brought to the new conception of reality, namely, that it is *changeable*. The point of Ward's work was to establish the proposition that social change can be consciously directed, that it can be *planned*.

He asserted it over and over again, from a great variety of angles. He called the conscious planning of social action meliorism. "Now, meliorism," Ward said, "is a dynamic principle. It implies the improvement of the social condition through cold calculation. . . . It is not content merely to alleviate present suffering, it aims to create conditions under which no suffering can exist. It is ready even to sacrifice temporary enjoyment for greater future enjoyment— the pleasure of a few for that of the mass."[14] He proposed

---

[14] *Ibid.*, II, 468.

that this should be accomplished by legislation. "Legislation (I use the term in its most general sense) is nothing else but social invention. It is an effort so to control the forces of a state as to secure the greatest benefits to its people."[15] He admits that governments have usually made a mess in most of their interventions in society. But this has been occasioned, he declares, by the ignorance of those who made the laws heretofore. The science of sociology will change all this.

> Before progressive legislation can become a success, every legislature must become, as it were, a polytechnic school, a laboratory of philosophical research into the laws of society and of human nature. No legislator is qualified to propose or vote on measures designed to affect the destinies of millions of social units until he masters all that is known of the science of society. Every true legislator must be a sociologist. . . .[16]

The means by which the changes in society should be brought about, according to Ward, were social invention and collectivization. Social invention will be devoted to discovering ways of exercising social pressure by legislation for the good of society. "Social invention consists in making such adjustments as will induce men to act in the manner most advantageous to society."[17] He did not hold with prohibitions and punishments as a rule. These things restrict the liberty of some of the people. "But the contention is that only the most obdurate offenders require to have their liberty restricted, since they, too, have wants, and the social inventor should devise means by which such

---

[15] *Ibid.*, I, 36.

[16] *Ibid.*, p. 37.

[17] Ward, *Pure Sociology*, p. 569.

wants shall be spontaneously satisfied through wholly innocuous or even socially beneficial action."[18]

These actions were to be taken by the collective will
of the populace (whatever such ideas may mean). The
great collective problem, Ward thought, was of the proper
distribution of goods. "This is an exclusively social problem and can only be solved by social action. It is to-day the
most important of all social problems, because its complete
solution would accomplish nothing less than the abolition
of poverty and want from society."[19]

The "new reality," then, was the metaphysic-like foundation for social reform. It was, to speak metaphorically, the
space station built by intellectuals on their flight from
reality from which to launch their reformist experiments
upon the earth.

----

18 *Ibid.*, p. 570.
19 *Ibid.*, p. 571.

10

The New Creativity

THE TWENTIETH CENTURY ABOUNDS IN PARADOXES. NOT
the least of these is the disparity between technological
developments on the one hand and developments in arts,
politics, and social arrangements on the other. No other
century in history can match what has already taken place
in the twentieth in technological inventions, improvements,
and devices. It staggers the imagination to survey what
has been wrought in the last hundred years, to extend the
survey back into the previous century a few years. Some
will not consider all the innovations unqualified blessings,
but everyone must marvel at what has been provided: elec-

173

tric lights, automobiles, mechanical refrigerators, phonographs, airplanes, radio, television, typewriters, calculators,
and so on through an ever-increasing list of contrivances.
It has not been many years since a hospital was usually a
way station to the funeral parlor. A revolution—to use
the word dubiously—has occurred in the last generation
in medicine. Scientific developments have taken place
which have rendered the doings of scientists into something beyond the ken of outsiders. Technological progress
has gone forward at an unparalleled pace.

Political and Artistic Deterioration

By contrast, there has been a decided retrogression in
the arts and literature. The techniques for purveying the
arts and literature have kept pace with technological developments elsewhere. For example, the invention of recording and of phonographs has made possible the reproduc-
tion of musical programs in the home with great fidelity to
the original playing. But the quality of music composed in
this century is generally far inferior to that of the preceding
century. It is true that audiences will now tolerate a selection from a twentieth century composer—from Stravinsky,
Bartok, Ives, or Copland—if it is surrounded in the program by pieces composed in earlier centuries.

Contemporary painting and painters apparently flourish,
but the art of careful drawing and painting is largely kept
alive by commercial requirements. The novel has degen-
erated into barely disguised biographical accounts of the
doings of bohemians, or into thinly coated historical recreations. Contemporary poetry consists of jingles on the one
hand and jumbles of words without form or rhyme or
reason on the other. If the case of architecture is somewhat better, it can probably be attributed mainly to the
taste of those who pay the bills, not to those who purvey

the services. Such exceptions as occur to the above generalizations only serve to highlight the general condition.

The usual objections to the above critique need to be dealt with, at least summarily. It can be objected that the evaluation of the arts and literature is a matter of taste. This amounts, however, to saying that there are no standards by which to judge the arts. The belief, and the practices that follow from it, that there are no standards is just another instance, as well as a cause, of the deterioration in the arts. Another frequent objection to the above critique goes something like this: Every age and time has its mediocre and inferior artists. In the course of time, these are forgotten, and only the giants remain. Such is undoubtedly the case, but it is largely irrelevant as a refutation of the above contention.

My point is not simply that the twentieth century has no musical master of the caliber of Beethoven, or that not every writer has reached the heights of Mozart; it is rather that the composers rated as first-rate are inferior to first-rate composers of earlier centuries, that the second-rate are inferior to the second-rate ones, and that the caliber of music being produced does not measure up to past standards. I read somewhere that a composer had a scholarship for a year, I think it was, in which he composed a violin concerto. Mozart composed five concertos for the violin between April and December of 1775. If it be objected that Mozart was a genius, one should still note that like geniuses are missing from among us. In short, there is no evidence of progress in the arts commensurate with that in the sciences and technology.

Political and social developments are not quite so difficult to evaluate, nor the positions taken quite so controversial as those about the arts. The evidence for positions taken is more readily assembled and more nearly apparent.

The indications of political deterioration in this century are abundant and conclusive. In the political realm, the tendency almost everywhere in the world has been toward totalitarianism, dictatorship, arbitrary government, the police state, the rounding up and imprisoning of political dissidents, the overthrow of older orders, and political experimentation and manipulation. The belief in and observance of lawful modes of operation by agents of governments has fallen below what it was generally in the seventeenth century. (There are, of course, countries in which this is not yet the case.) Socially, the breakup of the authority of the family evinces itself in divorce rates and juvenile delinquency.

Many would object to the particulars of the above formulations, but there is widespread agreement that there is great disparity between developments in science and those elsewhere. In academic circles the disparity is acknowledged backhandedly by some such analysis as this: The humanities and social sciences need to catch up with the physical sciences and technology. Knowledge about human beings has not kept pace, it is alleged, with that about things.

Such a way of putting it almost completely obscures the roots of the untoward political and artistic developments. It puts the best possible face on what has occurred and allows the very men and ideas which have wrought the consequences to go free of responsibility for them. Historically, politics and the arts were not *behind* technology in the application of ideas drawn from science. If anything, the reverse was the case. The artistic, political, and social implications of modern science were being generally pointed out and applied by the eighteenth century. (It will be remembered that modern science emerged in the seventeenth century.) By contrast, the technological implications are still unfolding, and this is largely a nineteenth and twentieth century development.

It does not follow, of course, that the social studies and humanities are *ahead* of technology now. They are neither ahead nor behind. What has happened cannot be fitted into a nice progressivist formulation at all. Politics and the arts have been cut off from reality; the proponents and developers of them have been engaged in a flight from reality. By contrast, technology is still rooted in its scientific foundations, and practicing scientists appear to be closer to reality than do other intellectuals. If technology should follow the path of the social studies and the humanities it would be cut loose from its foundations in laws and might be expected, subsequently, to degenerate.

Creature or Creator?

The key to understanding what has happened in the humanities and social studies (and from them to the arts and to politics) is the new conception of creativity. The way has been partially prepared thus far in this study for understanding the New Creativity, but before pointing out the connections to it of positions already established it may be well to examine the idea of creativity from an historical point of view.

So far as I can tell, the use of creativity to refer to something that man does or can do is a recent innovation. Certainly, this usage has no foundation in the main Western tradition of thought. Traditionally, creation was what God did when he brought the universe into being, or, following the account in Genesis, gave the universe its form and brought beings into existence. One unabridged dictionary gives this as its first meaning of the word "creation." To wit: "The act of creating from nothing; the act of causing to exist; and especially, the act of bringing this world into existence." On the other hand, the *American College Dictionary* drops this particular meaning to third position, and deals with it as a special phrase. It says, "*the Creation*, the original bringing into existence of the universe by the Deity." The most absolute view of creativity imaginable was held by St. Augustine concerning God's creation of the world. He held that it was created *ex nihilo*, out of nothing.

> How, O God, didst Thou make heaven and earth? Truly, neither in the heaven nor in the earth didst Thou make heaven and earth; nor in the air, nor in the waters, since these also belong to the heaven and the earth; nor in the whole world didst Thou make the whole world; because there was no place wherein it could be made before it was made, that it might be; nor didst Thou hold anything in Thy hand wherewith to make heaven and earth. . . .[1]

There were differences among philosophers, of course, as to the extent and character of the Creation. Aristotle did not even believe that the universe had been created; it has always existed, he thought. Probably a more usual view was that the universe was created, but that this consisted of giving it form and order. Be that as it may, what man does was not conceived of as creativity. Plato and Aristotle conceived of the artist as imitating reality. For example, Aristotle said: "Tragedy, then, [by which he meant a tragic drama] is an imitation of an action. . . ."[2] They did not necessarily, or particularly, mean a literal imitation of things as they appear to the sight.

Traditionally, the arts have been imitative of an underlying order. They have evoked ideals, caught the essence of man, or of a man, captured and set forth that which

---

[1] Quoted in W. T. Jones, *A History of Western Philosophy* (New York: Harcourt, Brace and Co., 1952), p. 354.

[2] *Ibid.*, p. 250.

the most sensitive perceive in a thing. In short, the artists, too, labored in a metaphysical framework. They did not create; they imitated, but this was by no means a lowly task. Few things could be more worthy of doing than to make visible by painting and sculpture, to make audible by music, to communicate by drama and poetry, or to cast in concrete form by architecture the underlying order in the universe and the ideals of justice, honor, truth, beauty, and piety by which men should live. That the artist did not create these was no reproach; it was enough that he should convey them. In this context, if the artist were to create, he would be committing a fraud, for he would be deceiving men as to the nature of the underlying reality.

Nor were other kinds of activity conceived of as being creativity. Social thinkers were not supposed to be creating social and political relationships, but rather discovering them and setting them forth. Morality was behavior in accord with the order in the universe and/or Divine injunction. Notice the language in which the work of authors and inventors is described in the United States Constitution in the phrase which empowers Congress "to promote the Progress of Science and useful Arts, by securing for limited Times to Authors and Inventors the exclusive Right to their respective Writings and Discoveries." Even the inventor was apparently thought of as a discoverer.

Something New

But a change has occurred. Nowadays, all sorts of undertakings are described as being creative. There are courses in creative writing in colleges. There are books on creative thinking, researches into the sources of creativity, articles on creative group thinking, and public expressions of concern about how to foster creativity. Invention, discovery, innovation, artistic endeavor, and social thought are now conceived of as being creative. The following definitions and examples of usage indicate the scope of the word as it is now employed. One writer approves this definition heartily: "Creativity is the imaginatively gifted recombination of known elements into something new."[3] Another writer says:

> My definition, then, of the creative process is that it is the emergence in action of a novel relational product, growing out of the uniqueness of the individual on the one hand, and the materials, events, people, or circumstances of his life on the other.[4]

He points out that his definition embraces all sorts of activities:

> Creativity is not, in my judgment, restricted to some particular content. I am assuming that there is no fundamental difference in the creative process as it is evidenced in painting a picture, composing a symphony, devising new instruments of killing, developing a scientific theory, discovering new procedures in human relationships, or creating new formings of one's own personality as in psycho-therapy.[5]

Dictionaries have come to include these new meanings of creativity. The *American College Dictionary* offers as one definition of "create": "to evolve from one's own thought or imagination." Another defines "creation" as "anything produced or caused to exist, in mechanics, science, or art; especially an unusual product of the mind; as the master *creations* of art."

---

[3] Harold F. Harding, "The Need for a More Creative Trend in American Education," *A Source Book for Creative Thinking*, Sidney J. Parnes and Harold F. Harding, eds. (New York: Scribner's, 1962), p. 5.

[4] Carl R. Rogers, "Toward a Theory of Creativity," in *ibid.*, p. 65.

[5] *Ibid.*

It could be objected that this is all a matter of semantics, that the word has come to have an additional meaning, that at most there is some ambiguity in such usages. But the loose use of language is not something to be taken lightly, even if this were all that is involved. We think and express ourselves in words. We may not be conscious of the connotations and overtones of language; these nevertheless influence our thinking and color what we say for those who hear or read it.

But what is involved here is not simply a matter of semantics. A new conception of creativity has been developed. Many have come to think of man as a creator. Invention, discovery, innovation, and origination have come to be thought of as creation. The framework within which this occurred has already been set forth. It included the cutting loose from reality, the sloughing off of the past by denying repetition in history, and the positing of a new reality—a reality consisting of change, society, and psyche. The impetus to social creativity was provided by the visions of utopia that could be created, and a new pseudo philosophy—pragmatism—provided a substitute philosophy which allowed free play to the imagination.

Organs of the New Creativity

Several lines of thought converged to buttress the new conception of creativity. Romanticism was the first of these outlooks to appear. Romantics exalted the imagination, the will, desire, feeling, and subjective experience. They tended to withdraw inward to discover that which was most important to them. Romantics tended to exalt literary and artistic activity, to see in it a means of contact with the Divine, or, depending upon the thinker, a divine activity itself. The poet, or other artist, was thought of as having a particularly high calling, for he could transcend the limits of ordinary experience by intuitions and grasp things of the greatest importance. The artist, at least, became a kind of demigod to many thinkers.

A second strain in the New Creativity came from what can be called evolutionism. If it is proper to speak of revolutions in thought, then it is no exaggeration to say that the theory of organic evolution was the basis for a profound intellectual revolution. All sorts of hypotheses were spawned in the wake of the spread of this idea. If accepted in all its implications, Darwinian evolution fundamentally altered conceptions of creativity. Christians had generally believed, prior to the latter part of the nineteenth century, that Creation was a completed act of God. But now some thinkers began to conceive of creativity as an ongoing process, something that had occurred in time and might be expected to continue in time.

The crucial point for creativity as it is being considered here, was whether or not man could actually participate in this evolutionary creativity. Social Darwinists, such as Herbert Spencer and William Graham Sumner, held that he could not. The course of evolution was determined by "forces." Perhaps the most influential philosophical theory that man participates in evolution is the theory of Creative Evolution. It was set forth in 1907 by Henri Bergson, a French philosopher. Bergson held that evolution cannot be explained by the operation of mechanical forces. There are moments of "spontaneous originality in nature, and especially in certain activities and experiences of mankind. The work of a great poet or painter clearly cannot be explained by merely mechanical forces. . . . This kind of activity . . . , resulting in something new is typical of creative evolution."[6]

---

[6] *Encyclopaedia Britannica,* VI (1955), 652.

There has been a variety of applications of the notion that man participates in evolution creatively. The most important, from the point of view of this study, is the one known as reform Darwinism, a doctrine advanced particularly by Lester Frank Ward. Ward held that by social invention man could direct and control the course of social evolution. That is, he could create instruments for doing this, and, indeed, had been doing so for ages. Man participates in evolution by developing means for cooperating with the process of evolution. The idea would seem to be this: one may by study discern the evolutionary trends. He can then work with them to bring about desired ends. Ward thought he discerned a rising social consciousness in his day, that the time when society would take over the direction of affairs collectively was at hand, and that the acquisition of knowledge would be for the purpose of fostering this development. He said, "If it can be shown that society is actually moving toward any ideal, the ultimate substantial realization of that ideal is as good as proved. The proofs of such a movement in society to-day are abundant."[7]

A third stream to enter the New Creativity has been called scientism. No one has advanced a doctrine or ideology by that name; it is a derogatory term applied to the practice of indiscriminately extending the ideas or methods of science. More specifically, the development to which I allude should probably be called technologism, though the language is already sufficiently barbarized by "isms" without adding another. At any rate, there is a view of creativity drawn largely from technology. Many people have been swept off their feet, as it were, by developments in technology. They have been so awed by the achievements

---

[7] Lester F. Ward, "Sociocracy," *American Thought*, Perry Miller, ed. (New York: Rinehart, 1954), p. 117.

in this area that they have thought there was a major clue for all areas of human activity in technology. There may be, but the development to which I refer was based upon a misunderstanding of technology. As we have seen in an earlier chapter, John Dewey confused science with technology, failed to take into account the fact that technologists apply previously *discovered* laws, deduced methods from the behavior of technologists, and proposed to apply these to all human thought and activity. Essentially, he thought that the inventor created, and that this kind of activity could be endlessly extended.

Existentialism Promoted: Kierkegaard and Nietzsche

The fourth support for the new conception of creativity came from existentialism. Actually, this philosophy did not get much fame, or notoriety, until after World War II with the writings of Jean Paul Sartre and Albert Camus. But the origins of the ideas are traced back into the nineteenth century, primarily to Sören Kierkegaard and Friedrich Nietzsche. Thus, some of the ideas can be said to have buttressed the New Creativity, though the philosophy was not yet known by its current name. Nietzsche's impact, at least, was considerable in artistic circles in the early twentieth century. For example, H. L. Mencken was an early American devotee of Nietzsche.

There are several schools of existentialism, but they generally share several premises with one another. The basic one, the one from which the name comes, is that existence *precedes* essence. Existentialists see man, or perhaps men, as creatures existing in space and time. The most important fact in the world, to them, is existence. They are not interested in, indeed are opposed to, essences, or the search for essences. They want to confront experience in all its richness, not in some abstraction from it. To really be is to act, for in acting one's existence is filled out and extended. Existentialists run the gamut from rugged individualists to Christians to Marxists. But whatever their tendency, they are concerned with the here and now, with the given existence, with acting upon it and coming more fully to be.

Nietzsche provided the most drastic foundation for human creativity. God is dead, said Nietzsche, and he had a profound conception of the significance of what he was saying. He was proclaiming, too, that the past was dead, that the foundations of Western civilization were gone, that man's views must be drastically reoriented. As one writer puts it:

> For when God is at last dead for man, when the last gleam of light is extinguished and only the impenetrable darkness of a universe that exists for no purpose surrounds us, then at last man knows that he is alone in a world where *he has to create his own values*.[8]

It meant something more too; it meant that men created their gods. God existed for Nietzsche, only so long as men sustained their belief in Him. This was an exact reversal of the traditional view, the view that God created man and sustained him by His Providence. There are implicit conclusions that must logically follow: namely, that man is higher than the gods, for he has created them; that man is the lord of creation, for he is the highest being; that if creation could occur, it would probably be by man. Nietzsche talked of a Superman, the unusual man (or men) who would rise above morality, go beyond good and evil to become the new master.

[8] Quoted in William Barrett, "Introduction," *Philosophy in the Twentieth Century*, III, William Barrett and Henry D. Aiken, eds. (New York: Random House, 1962), 148. Italics mine.

Before God!—Now however this God hath died! Ye higher men, this God was your greatest danger.

Only since he lay in the grave have ye again arisen. Now only cometh the great noontide, now only doth the higher man become—master![9]

Not all the exponents of the New Creativity were as sensational in their advocacy as was Nietzsche, of course. But even the pedestrian John Dewey talked about a theory of art which has its foundation in the new view. Dewey discusses essentialism as a way of seeing things. He does not, however, believe that there are any essences which subsist in a metaphysical realm. The habit of looking to essences is merely something created and maintained by artists:

If we are now aware of essential meanings, it is mainly because artists in all the various arts have extracted and expressed them in vivid and salient subject-matter of perception. The forms or Ideas which Plato thought were models and patterns of existing things actually had their source in Greek art, so that his treatment of artists is a supreme instance of intellectual ingratitude.[10]

It turns out, then, according to Dewey, that the foundations of Western philosophy were planted by artists in the mind of Plato. Philosophy, it appears, was really created by dramatists.

A New Creativity has emerged then, a radical view of man's capabilities, a changed conception of art and social affairs. Those who hold these views see man as a creator. The roots of the creativity are in the psyche, in the subconscious; in short, creativity arises from the irrational

---

[9] Quoted in Richard H. Powers, ed., *Readings in European Civilization* (Cambridge: Houghton Mifflin, 1961), p. 505.

[10] John Dewey, *Art as Experience* (New York: Minton, Balch & Co., 1934), p. 294.

depths of the mind. Great value is placed upon innovation, change, originality, experiment, all of which are
supposed to result in new creations.

Perhaps the strangest of contradictions in a paradoxical
age is that between the avowed evaluation of man and
the men one confronts in imaginative literature. On the
one hand, man is held in the highest esteem, supposed to
be capable of doing great things, viewed as entrustable
with great power, held to be innately good, and life is presented in the ethos of the time as a potentially highly en-
joyable affair. On the other hand, novels and stories are
more apt than not to show the gradual degradation of a
man in the course of his life, the disintegration of his personality, the emptiness of the things he does, and so on.
This story is told over and over again in modern fiction.

These contradictions, and others alluded to earlier, can
be explained largely in terms of the New Creativity. The
attempt to locate creativity in the subconscious has resulted in irrational artistic productions. That which is
dredged up from the irrational is irrational; that which is
undisciplined in its production is undisciplined. It is at
least plausible that the contents of the subconscious are
subconscious for good and sufficient reason, that the subconscious is the garbage pail of the mind, and that one
may no more look for the clue to life or for sustenance
for healthy living there than in actual garbage pails. That
which comes to us *directly* from these depths poisons life.
The evidence for such a conclusion now exists in great
profusion.

The attempt to create something out of nothing, or to
draw from the junk yard of the psyche, results in noise
instead of music, chaos rather than order in painting, dis-
figurement rather than form in sculpture, the denigration
of man rather than his exaltation in literature, the death

of art rather than life. Social invention aimed at creation based on the inchoate "needs" and "desires" of people has resulted in arbitrary government, the loss of liberty, the tendency of governments to become total in character, the disruption of economies, social dislocation, and inharmonious relationships among people.

Materializing the Mirage

The explanations for these developments is now before us. Thinkers and artists have cut themselves off from their experience, posited or accepted a "new reality," and believed it was possible for them actually to create something. They calculate or act in terms of time, society, and beliefs or feelings of men, all of which are subject to change. They ignore the underlying and enduring realities: the laws in the universe, the principles of human action, the essentials of artistic or economic production, human nature, and the conditions of liberty.

If man could indeed create, there would be no theoretical reason why governments could not issue fiat money and prevent inflation at the same time, why everything could not be controlled and directed by governments and the liberties of the people increased, why a world government of law could not be established without putting up with the inconvenience of having laws founded upon an enduring order, why the United States (or the Soviet Union) could not intervene in the affairs of other countries without subtracting from their independence, why taxes could not be lowered and government services increased without any untoward effects, why governments could not confiscate private property and still get private investors from other lands to pour money into their industries, why the prices of those things that go into the production of goods could not be fixed and have retail prices remain flexible, why writers could not create a vision of order which would inform their writings without believing in any such real order, why painters could not picture beauty and order without discipline, why children could not be made good by surrounding them with pleasant objects without any support from the belief in and knowledge of a moral order in the universe, why the economy could not be collectivized and individualism retained, and so on through what could be a much longer list of the fads, foibles, and dangerous doctrines of an era.

It is not strange that literary critics should be fascinated with ambiguities today. Men who lack a firm grip on the nature of man and the universe must surely be overcome with the failure of that which was intended and promised to materialize. There is an explanation for all of this. The notion that man can create realities out of irrational longing is not itself founded in reality. All attempts to act upon such premises must needs be abortive.

There is an explanation, too, for the otherwise strange and incomprehensible doings of reformers in this century. They have largely lost touch with reality. They have imagined themselves as gods or demigods who could create a reality out of their dream of it. It turns out that they were only men. It is small wonder that those who feel deepest should turn upon man, then, and describe him as so contemptible.

BOOK TWO:

The Domestication of Socialism

11

The Domestication of Socialism

The ship of reform will gather most headway from the association of certain very moderate practical proposals with the issue of a deliberate, persistent, and far more radical challenge to popular political prejudices and errors. It will be sufficient . . . in case they occupy some sort of family relation to plans of the same kind with which American public opinion is already more or less familiar. —HERBERT CROLY, 1909

Our social revolution must be consummated with a minimum of shock to our delicate industrial, political, and social machinery. . . . Our social reconstruction must be effected during business hours. It must be accompanied by preliminary plans, specifications, and estimates of cost. It must be gradual and quiet, though rapid. —WALTER E. WEYL, 1912

And yet, as Oscar Wilde said, no map of the world is worth a glance that hasn't Utopia on it. Our business is not to lay aside the dream, but to make it plausible. We have to aim at visions of the possible by subjecting fancy to criticism. . . . For modern civilization . . . calls for a dream that suffuses the actual with a sense of the possible.
—WALTER LIPPMANN, 1914

BY THE EARLY TWENTIETH CENTURY THE STAGE WAS SET for the entry of reformism into the stream of American political life. The intellectual ground had been thoroughly prepared for such a move. The flight from reality had proceeded far enough that many men could begin to take seriously visions which their counterparts in other times would have readily recognized as impractical fancies. But the in-

tellectual position from which such recognition would occur had largely been cut away. The disciplinary role of
philosophy had been lost, in the main, with the break from
metaphysics, the downgrading of reason, and the attempt
to root philosophy in empirical data. The vision of utopia
provided a destination for man in the future. For many
thinkers, time had been cut loose from its framework in
eternity, cause disjoined from effect, man severed from his
past experience, and a widening gulf separated thought
from the wisdom of the past. A new pseudo philosophy—
pragmatism—had been set forth to provide a method of
operation into a future which was to be wholly different
from the past. A new conception of reality had emerged
to replace the old, a "reality" made up of change, society,
and psyche. A new conception of creativity held out the
promise that man could and did create his own reality.

These developments had implications for all of life, but,
above all, they made ameliorative reform appear to be
possible and provided the intellectual framework for the
concerted and persistent efforts of reformers to make over
man and society with the power of the state. The notion
that society can be so reconstructed is called meliorism.
But there is more to the matter than that. The belief that
society, and men, can be reconstructed does not, of itself,
imply any particular direction that should be taken in accomplishing this transformation. Yet anyone familiar with
melioristic efforts in this century should be able to see
that there has been one direction to reform. Meliorism and
reform have not been neutral concepts; they have been
loaded with ideas which have bent the thoughts of the
men who held them in a particular direction. Reform has
been informed by ideology.

Indeed, one ideology has dominated reformist thought in
this century. That ideology should be known by its generic

name, socialism, though a variety of names are frequently
employed. There have been attempts to restrict the meaning of socialism to the description of those programs for
public (i.e., governmental) ownership of the means of production and distribution of goods. For example, the *American College Dictionary* defines socialism as "a theory or
system of social organization which advocates the vesting
of the ownership and control of the means of production,
capital, land, etc. in the community as a whole." But such
a definition is far too restrictive. It sacrifices accuracy for
precision and hampers rather than enables in the identification of actual socialists. It conforms neither to the etymology of the word nor to the origin of the ideas nor to
the facts of socialist advocacy.

More accurately, then, socialism should be used to describe the doctrines of those who, according to the *Encyclopaedia Britannica,* "were seeking a complete transformation of the economic and moral basis of society by the
substitution of the social for individual control and of
social for individualistic forces in the organization of life
and work." Richard T. Ely claimed that socialism is "a
principle which regulates social and economic life according to the needs of society as a whole. . . ."[1] This gets
much closer to the heart of the matter. Socialists conceive
of society as an organism, as a being in and of itself, capable of acting to bring about certain ends. The aim of the
socialists is to bring about the control by society of the
economic and social life, and their claim is that this will
result in greatly improved well-being for all. The key word
is *control*. There are, and have been, dogmatic socialists
who insist that this must be effected by the vesting of

---

[1] Richard T. Ely, *Socialism* (New York: Thomas Y. Crowell,
1894), p. 5.

ownership in the "public." But many others have professed not to care who holds the title to property so long as society has the control of it.

Evolution or Revolution?

The only distinction among socialists which has much empirical content is that between *evolutionary* and *revolutionary* socialism. And this is a distinction as to the *means* to be employed, not as to the *ends* to be achieved. Virtually all socialists, at least the earlier ones, have been aware that socialism would bring about a revolution in the lives of the people who adopted it. Some have thought, however, that this change could be brought about gradually, that it would not have to be achieved by violent means. Others have believed that a violent takeover would be necessary, and they are known as revolutionary socialists. Those socialists who are known as communists, and who claim discipleship to Karl Marx, have been the most vociferous advocates of revolutionary socialism, though there have been other revolutionary movements. It seems to me, however, that all of modern socialism stems more or less from Karl Marx and Friedrich Engels. At any rate, they advanced most of the notions which later socialists, of all varieties, have advocated.

Socialism acquired a bad reputation early in its career, if it ever had a good one. After the abortive revolutions of 1848, advocates of socialism lived on the fringes of society. The workers of the world did not rush to unite behind them. The dire predictions of Marx did not come about, except in the heated imaginations of such men as accepted his words as a kind of gospel. Socialist parties made very poor showings in elections. Many of the ideas of socialists could be, and were, readily refuted. Electorates in the latter part of the nineteenth century usually rejected socialist programs with great alacrity. This was emphatically so in the United States.

Yet by the 1960's socialist ideas had come to prevail, to a greater or lesser extent, almost everywhere in the world, including the United States. How had this turn of events come about? In two ways mainly (and they correspond to the revolutionary-evolutionary approach): one way may be summarized as the conspiracy-*coup d' etat*-violence method of gaining political power; the other has been by the propagation of ideas by intellectuals and the gradual intrusion of the attendant programs into the political action of communities. The conspiracy-*coup d'etat*-violence approach has generally been used in the East, the other approach in the West.

In the early twentieth century, the flight from reality became, or began to become, very nearly identical with the advancement of socialism. Much of the rest of the story will deal with how socialism was intruded into American political activities. The first step in this process was the domestication of socialism. It must be kept in mind that no avowedly socialist party has ever got more than a small fraction of the vote in the United States. To the extent that socialism has gained sway, then, it has been by the adoption of socialist programs by the older parties and the championing of these reforms by intellectuals and politicians who avoided the socialist label. It will be my task to show that this is precisely what happened.

Most people in the United States, so far as such things can be determined, have never accepted the bizarre formulations of the thought leaders in the nineteenth century of the flight from reality *or* of socialism. It is likely most men would consider Nietzsche's conception of creativity by a Superman as so much nonsense, and Marx's fulminations as the product of a demented mind. At least, they would, and did, until they were acclimated to them in much milder formulations.

Croly, Weyl, and Lippmann

A part of the task of acclimatizing people to these ideas was accomplished by the domestication of socialism, the making of it more palatable by sloughing off the name, by particularizing it, by "moderate" statements of premises, and so on. A goodly number of people undoubtedly contributed to this work. Reform was made to appear much more desirable, even necessary, by the efforts of the muckrakers. Various and sundry theorists had begun to make some impact with their ideas. There is a considerable body of literature which could be categorized as the domestication of socialism in the United States. But for the sake of brevity and unity this account will be largely restricted to three books by three men. They are Herbert Croly's *The Promise of American Life* (1909), Walter E. Weyl's *The New Democracy* (1912), and Walter Lippmann's *Drift and Mastery* (1914). They were all Americans, were believed to have been somewhat influential, founded *The New Republic* as a joint venture, and shared some common presuppositions and aims.

Croly's book was much more influential than the others, by all accounts. It is supposed to have influenced Theodore Roosevelt in the formulation of the New Nationalism and to have been a major seminal work for progressivism. A recent writer has noted:

> Croly's reputation, however, rested on more than his purported impact on Roosevelt. Men whose own thought first took shape during the progressive period have strongly praised the publicist's contribution. Lippmann called his former associate "the first important political philosopher who appeared in America in the twentieth

century"; Alvin Johnson grants Croly "the palm of the leadership in the philosophy of the progressive movement" . . . , while Felix Frankfurter credits him with "the most powerful single contribution to progressive thinking."[2]

Croly's work is both the most lengthy and the most thorough of the three books. It may well be that *The Promise of American Life* should be ranked as the most thorough "Fabian tract" ever written. Weyl's book is much blunter, less polished, and somewhat more to the point. Lippmann had already developed his ponderous style of presenting a combination of urbanities and inanities as if they were profound. He had already developed the ability, too, to roll with the punch, to apparently accept the devastating criticisms of his position, even to joining in with the chorus of the critics, all the while maintaining the substance of his position intact. He was a pragmatist, along with the other two men, and this made it easy for him to pursue his goal by a new path when he found the course he was following blocked.

There is one difficulty in my thesis that these three men were domesticating socialism, and there is no reason why it should not be made explicit. The difficulty is this. In order for them to have been domesticating socialism, they must have been socialists. Yet it was essential to their task that they not be avowed socialists. At any rate, Croly and Weyl were not avowed socialists, and by 1914 Lippmann had abandoned his connection with socialist parties. Thus, there appears to be a problem of proving that they were socialists.

Actually, however, the above overstates the problem. Whether they were socialists or not, these men were ad-

---

[2] Charles Forcey, *The Crossroads of Liberalism* (New York: Oxford University Press, 1961), pp. 5-6.

vancing socialist ideas and programs. Whether they were intending to "domesticate socialism" or not is irrelevant; my point is that the way in which they were presenting the ideas had that effect. It should be made clear that this is not an examination into the motives of these men. There is no concern here with whether they were sincere or not, whether they were surreptitiously advancing a movement or not, or whether they were good or evil men or not. This is not an attempt to judge them; it is an effort to describe what they did.

The point is that Croly, Weyl, and Lippmann were advocating ideas and programs drawn from the socialist ideology, and that they presented them in a light so that they would be least disturbing to the accepted beliefs of Americans. Let us first examine a few quotations which indicate the socialistic tenor of the proposals of these men. The first is from Herbert Croly, and the context from which it comes is a discussion of the necessity of restricting freedom:

> Efficient regulation there must be; and it must be regulation which will strike, not at the symptoms of the evil, but at its roots. The existing concentration of wealth and financial power in the hands of a few irresponsible men is the inevitable outcome of the chaotic individualism of our political and economic organization. . . . The inference which follows may be disagreeable, but it is not to be escaped. In becoming responsible for the subordination of the individual to the demand of a dominant and constructive national purpose, the American state will in effect be making itself responsible for a morally and socially desirable distribution of wealth."[3]

---

[3] Herbert Croly, *The Promise of American Life,* Cushing Strout, intro. (New York: Capricorn Books, 1964), p. 23.

At one point, Croly candidly admits that in certain senses his program is socialistic. He says that it is socialistic "in case socialism cannot be divorced from the use, wherever necessary, of the political organization in all its forms to realize the proposed democratic purpose."[4]

Weyl said, "To-day no democracy is possible in America except a socialized democracy, which conceives of society as a whole and not as a more or less adventitious assemblage of myriads of individuals."[5] Moreover,

> In the socialized democracy towards which we are moving . . . taxes [will] conform more or less to the ability of each to pay; but the engine of taxation . . . will be used to accomplish great social ends, among which will be the more equal distribution of wealth and income. The state will tax to improve education, health, recreation, communication. . . . The government of the nation, in the hands of the people, will establish its unquestioned sovereignty over the industry of the nation, so largely in the hands of individuals.[6]

Walter Lippmann is not easy to pin down, yet the socialist ideas are there. Quite often he obscures them as prediction, as in the following: "Now the time may come, I am inclined to think it is sure to come, when the government will be operating the basic industries, railroads, mines, and so forth. It will be possible then to finance government enterprise out of the profits of its industries, to eliminate interest, and substitute collective saving."[7]

---

[4] *Ibid.*, p. 209.

[5] Walter E. Weyl, *The New Democracy* (New York: Macmillan, 1912), p. 162.

[6] *Ibid.*, pp. 163-64.

[7] Walter Lippmann, *Drift and Mastery,* William E. Leuchtenburg, intro. (Englewood Cliffs, N. J.: Prentice-Hall, A Spectrum Book, 1961), p. 70.

Sometimes, however, he prescribes directly, as in the following call for all-out planning:

> It means that you have to do a great variety of things to industry, invent new ones to do, and keep on doing them. You have to make a survey of the natural resources of the country. On the basis of that survey you must draw up a national plan for their development. You must eliminate waste in mining, you must conserve the forests so that their fertility is not impaired, so that stream flow is regulated, and the waterpower of the country made available.[8]

These quotations, however their authors hedged them about, do indicate that the books in question were informed by socialism. They are, however, among the more radical statements to be found in the books. In the main, the writers stick to the task of domesticating socialism, rather than to setting forth their assumptions. Let us examine now some of the means by which this is done.

Gradualism

First, the authors of these books were devotees of gradualism, and were themselves proposing the next steps in a movement toward what can be discerned as the goal of socialism. In their gradualism, they were following the path of the English Fabians who had been at work some years already. The Fabian Society, named after the Roman general, Fabius, who fought indirectly by harassment rather than directly, was organized in 1884. Sidney Webb, a leading figure in the Society and movement, explained their conclusions this way:

> In the present Socialist movement these two streams are united: advocates of social reconstruction have

---

[8] *Ibid.*, p. 98.

learnt the lesson of Democracy, and know that it is through the slow and gradual turning of the popular mind to new principles that social reorganization bit by bit comes. . . . Socialists . . . realize that important organic changes can only be (1) democratic . . . ; (2) gradual . . . ; (3) not regarded as immoral by the mass of the people . . . ; and (4) in this country at any rate, constitutional and peaceful.[9]

Whether Croly, Weyl, and Lippmann were consciously socialists or not, they were certainly consciously gradualists. Croly makes his gradualism explicit in the following prescription for taking over the railroads (all the while adopting a pose of objectivity about it which relieves him of responsibility for advocating it):

In the existing condition of economic development and of public opinion, the man who believes in the ultimate necessity of government ownership of railroad road-beds and terminals must be content to wait and to watch. The most that he can do for the present is to use any opening which the course of railroad development affords, for the assertion of his ideas; and if he is right, he will gradually be able to work out, in relation to the economic situation of the railroads, some practical method of realizing the ultimate purpose.[10]

He suggests that the end might be achieved by the extension of government credit to the railroads, followed by a "gradual system of appropriation."

Weyl left no doubt about his gradualism either. He declared "that the surest method of progress is to take one step after another. The first step, often uncontested (*be-

---

[9] Sidney Webb, "Socialism, Fusion of Democracy and Co-operation" in J. Salwyn Schapiro, *Movements of Social Dissent in Modern Europe* (Princeton: D. Van Nostrand, 1962), p. 161.

[10] Croly, *op. cit.*, p. 377.

cause it is only one step), leads inevitably to others."[11]
He gives an example of what he means, in connection with
governmental acquisition of rich mineral lands. "If the
nation could approach the owners of these lands with the
sword of a gentle tax in the one hand and the olive branch
of a fair purchase price in the other, there would soon be
no fear of any monopoly of our mineral resources."[12]

Although Lippmann substituted prediction for outright
prescription, he envisioned a gradual transformation in
America. "Private property will melt away; its functions
will be taken over by the salaried men who direct them,
by government commissions, by developing labor unions.
The stockholders deprived of their property rights are
being transformed into money-lenders."[13]

A Façade of Conservatism

The gradual approach to social transformation, these
writers saw, had the advantages of lessening resistance, of
avoiding shock, and of giving the appearance of continuity
within the society. The latter two advantages take on the
added gloss of appearing to be conservative. That is, they
indicate a concern with conserving much within the existing framework while the framework itself is being fundamentally altered. Indeed, one of the least understood of
the methods of Fabian socialism, if the term may be used
generically, is the façade of conservatism which socialists
frequently adopt. On the face of it, conservatism and the
radical alteration of society are at opposite poles of the
political spectrum. Yet gradualists have quite often not

---

[11] Weyl, *op. cit.*, pp. 265-66.

[12] *Ibid.*, p. 266. Apparently, he meant by monopoly the private ownership of mineral resources.

[13] Lippmann, *op. cit.*, p. 49.

only reduced the distance between them, so far as could be readily discerned, but also have managed actually to convince some people that theirs is the conservative position. It turns out upon examination, of course, that what they want to do is to preserve the material achievements of modern civilization while destroying or replacing the spiritual base, knowledge, and arrangements upon which they are built. But then, that is why socialists can be described as on a flight from reality.

One of the best examples of a socialist book which embodied the conservative façade was written not by an American but an Englishman. Graham Wallas was the author, and the book was *The Great Society* (1914), a name which has cropped up lately. There is no difficulty in placing Wallas ideologically; he was one of the original founders of the Fabian Society. Moreover, some slight discussion of the method of the book in the present discussion is in order because Wallas influenced Lippmann when he was at Harvard in 1910 as a visiting lecturer, and dedicated *The Great Society* to Lippmann.

One might suppose from the title of the book that it is utopian, that it is a prescription for something to be achieved in the future. Yet such is not the case. The Great Society already existed (in 1914), according to Wallas, at least in the highly industrialized countries of the West. The Great Society, Wallas said, had resulted from technological innovations. The developments from these had drawn people together in interdependence upon one another, not only nationally but internationally.

But—and this was the problem with which he purported to deal—there were centripetal as well as centrifugal forces within the Great Society. The centripetal forces threatened to dissolve the society. Wallas said, "But even if the forces of cohesion and dissolution remain as evenly balanced as they are now, our prospects are dark enough. The human material of our social machinery will continue to disintegrate just at the points where strength is most urgently required." To support this statement he supplied a catalogue of the evils within society which any socialist might be expected to give. In order to preserve the Great Society he held that a great reorganization would have to occur. In short, he had made it appear that social transformation was necessary for conservative reasons.

This theme crops up in the works under consideration. Writing before Wallas' book appeared, Croly said: "In its deepest aspect . . . the social problem is the problem of preventing such divisions [the divisions supposedly caused by specialization] from dissolving the society into which they enter—of keeping such a highly differentiated society fundamentally sound and whole."[14] Lippmann argued from similar premises for the development of powerful labor unions. He maintained that industrial peace would be a by-product of powerful unions. "You will meet in . . . powerful unions," he said, "what radical labor leaders call conservatism." On the other hand, "it is the weak unions, the unorganized and shifting workers, who talk sabotage and flare up into a hundred little popgun rebellions."[15] The moral is clear: Support the growth of strong unions in order to maintain peace and conserve social stability.

Giving Historical Setting to the Need for Reform

A considerable portion of Croly's work was devoted to fitting the need for reform into the American tradition. A part of his book is historical in character. His position is that there was an implicit promise in American develop-

[14] Croly, *op. cit.*, p. 139.
[15] Lippmann, *op. cit.*, p. 61.

ment over the years, that Americans had developed democratic institutions, that they had developed a national spirit, that they had at one time effected unity among the peoples. However, "the changes which have been taking place in industrial and political and social conditions have all tended to impair the consistency of feeling characteristic of the first phase of American national democracy."[16] That is, according to him, industrialism had produced deep divisions within society. "Grave inequalities of power and deep-lying differences of purpose have developed in relation of the several primary American activities. The millionaire, the 'Boss,' the union laborer, and the lawyer, have all taken advantage of the loose American political organization to promote somewhat unscrupulously their own interests. . . ."[17] This situation was unwholesome, he thought. "But a democracy cannot dispense with the solidarity which it imparted to American life, and in one way or another such solidarity must be restored."[18]

Some clues to the means for the restoration of "solidarity" could be found in American history. Alexander Hamilton had a vision of using the government to advance national well-being. But Hamilton had been antidemocratic, and had promulgated too narrow a program, at least for twentieth century conditions. Thomas Jefferson had contributed to the development of democratic sentiment, but he had been individualistic, not nationalistic. Croly drew his conclusion: "The best that can be said on behalf of this traditional American system of political ideas is that it contained the germ of better things. The combination of Federalism and Republicanism . . . pointed in the direction

---

[16] Croly, *op. cit.*, p. 138.

[17] *Ibid.*

[18] *Ibid.*, p. 139.

of a constructive formula."[19] So too, the Whigs had a national vision, but they were unable fully to articulate it.

Croly was setting the stage with this historical exposition for offering his solution, and at the same time making it appear that he was joining his solution to a course which Americans had been groping toward for a long time. The solution was for Americans to "restore" their lost or threatened unity by the acceptance of a social ideal. They were to find a national purpose, and they were to move toward the fulfillment of that purpose, or "promise," democratically. Thus, Croly was able to associate two ideas—nationalism and democracy—which had good connotations to Americans with his program for social reconstruction. It should be noted that all three writers salted down their social programs with liberal sprinklings of references to "democracy" throughout, a practice which has long since become habitual, if not compulsive, with reformers.

Alterations Proposed

But the attempt to make their programs appear conservative and traditional by these writers should not be over-emphasized. Croly went much further in this regard than did the others. All of them, however, were fairly explicit in pointing out that they were proposing alterations in the American system. Even Croly said,

> The better future which Americans propose to build is nothing if not an idea which must in certain essential respects emancipate them from their past. American history contains much matter for pride and congratulations, and much matter for regret and humiliation. On the whole . . . , it has throughout been made better than it was by the vision of a better future; and the American of to-day and to-morrow must remain true to that tradi-

---

[19] *Ibid.*, p. 51.

tional vision. He must be prepared to sacrifice to that traditional vision even the traditional American ways of realizing it.[20]

Weyl left no doubt about his view of the centerpiece of the American tradition, the Constitution. He said, "Our newer democracy demands, not that the people forever conform to a rigid, hard-changing Constitution, but that the Constitution change to conform to the people. The Constitution of the United States is the political wisdom of a dead America."[21] Lippmann was even more emphatic, and much more general, in his repudiation of tradition. He subscribed to the view "that we should live not for our fatherland but for our children's land."

> To do this men have to substitute purpose for tradition: and that is, I believe, the profoundest change that has ever taken place in human history. We can no longer treat life as something that has trickled down to us. We have to deal with it deliberately, devise its social organization, alter its tools, formulate its method, educate and control it. In endless ways we put intention where custom has reigned.[22]

Necessary Adjustments to Changing Conditions

The major justification for social reconstruction, then, was not that it was in keeping with the American tradition to do so but that it was made necessary by changing conditions. Thus, these writers domesticated socialism by making its measures appear to be necessary adjustments to changed conditions. These men argued that technological developments, new industrial organizations, the develop-

---

[20] *Ibid.*, p. 5.

[21] Weyl, *op. cit.*, p. 13.

[22] Lippmann, *op. cit.*, p. 147.

ment of a nation-wide market, the appearance of class divisions, the existence of poverty, made necessary the alteration of political action to deal with these changes. Perhaps the other two would have agreed wholeheartedly with Weyl, when he said, "It is ideas, born of conditions, which rule the world."[23] Indeed, Lippmann took the position that many of the changes were already occurring which were reconstructing America, whether it would or not. Croly emphasized the method of the reformer as one in which he grasped the tendencies and reinforced them.

These positions indicate a rather mystifying, or illogical, penchant of melioristic reformers in the twentieth century. They vacillate between the poles of economic determinism on the one hand and a radical view of "freedom" which allows them to create at will, on the other. Generally speaking, Croly, Weyl, and Lippmann got maximum use from ideas drawn from contradictory positions. The determinist position allows its holder to claim that he is describing an inevitable evolution, to assume a position as a scholar and possibly a scientist rather than an advocate, to avoid responsibility for his advocacy, and to leave the reader with no choice but to adjust to the predicted course of development. On the other hand, the meliorist position allows its holder to talk of social invention, of imagination, of creativity, of a new way which has been discerned, and to appeal subtly to the reader's desire to join him in being in the forefront of momentous developments. In the real world, these are inconsistencies, but on the flight from reality you can have it both ways.

Finally, the pragmatism of these writers permitted them to offer every sort of reformist idea that has ever been advanced without dogmatically subscribing to any of them.

---

[23] Weyl, *op. cit.*, p. 199.

Some indication of the range of ideas which they subscribed to or advanced should be given. Many of them have since become the assumptions of intellectuals and some goodly number have been put into practice. In general, Croly, Weyl, and Lippmann subscribed to the notion that the problem of production had been largely mastered, that the major task ahead was one of distribution. They spoke confidently of "unearned increments," of "social surpluses," and of the "need" to distribute the wealth more equitably. None of these men, however, was an opponent of bigness in business. They considered trust-busting an anachronistic and destructive undertaking. The problem, as they saw it, was not to break up huge industries but to assure that they were operated in the interest of society. To assure this, they advocated governmental regulation, discriminatory taxation, and outright ownership, if necessary.

These writers used slightly different verbiage to describe their broad programs of reconstruction, but Weyl gives the gist of their recommendations in the following:

> With a government ownership of some industries, with a government regulation of others, with publicity for all (to the extent that publicity is socially desirable), with an enlarged power of the community in industry, and with an increased appropriation by the community of the increasing social surplus and of the growing unearned increment, the progressive socialization of industry will take place. To accomplish these ends the democracy will rely upon the trade-union, the association of consumers, and other industrial agencies. It will, above all, rely upon the state.[24]

Some of the means to these ends are interesting because they have been employed, but they are no longer so openly

---

[24] *Ibid.*, p. 297.

avowed. For example, these writers favored the alteration of the Constitution by interpretation. Croly declared that, on the whole, the Constitution was an admirable document, "and in most respects it should be left to the ordinary process of gradual amendment by legal construction. . . ."[25] Weyl said, "For the time being, the Constitution will probably change, as it has changed during the last century, by process of interpretation. . . . It is possible for them [the Supreme Court] by a few progressive judicial decisions to democratize the Constitution."[26]

In various forms, one or more of these writers proposed socialized medicine, consumer regulation, inheritance taxes, graduated income taxes, state insurance programs, socialized education, executive leadership, centralization of government, excess profits taxes, national planning, and a government guaranteed minimum standard of living. Croly even argued explicitly that government should discriminate in favor of certain groups in order to assure equality. He said, "The national government must step in and discriminate; but it must discriminate, not on behalf of liberty and the special individual, but on behalf of equality and the average man."[27]

In general, though, their particular programs were not dogmatically advocated. They were pragmatic about the particulars. Pragmatism is not, of course, a test of the ultimate end to be achieved; it is a test of the methods to be used. If one method does not work, then another one is tried, and so on. The end remains the same, and inaccessible to pragmatic demonstrations. As Weyl said, "The

---

[25] Croly, *op. cit.*, p. 351.

[26] Weyl, *op. cit.*, p. 317.

[27] Croly, *op. cit.*, p. 190.

democracy [for which one may accurately substitute "socialism"], though compromising in action, must be uncompromising in principle. Though conciliatory towards opponents, it must be constant to its fixed ideals. Though it tack with the wind, it must keep always in sight its general destination."[28]

This was one of the ways, then, by which socialism was domesticated in America.

---

[28] Weyl, *op. cit.*, p. 269.

12

The Democratic Illusion

CUSTOMS DO CHANGE. IT WAS ONCE THE CUSTOM FOR children to read and be told fairy stories, fables, legends, and myths. Young children were taught to believe in Santa Claus (and, in this case, still are), told of the legend of Robin Hood, read stories of fairies who performed work for adults, and led to believe that there was a pot of gold at the end of each rainbow. Generally speaking, such fables are no longer approved by the "experts" on child rearing. The stories have been taken out of the textbooks in the early years of schooling. Parents have been warned against filling their children's minds with illusions. According to the new dispensation, children were to be taught the facts of life from the beginning, and that as prosaically and clinically as possible.

Whatever else might be said for or against this newer viewpoint, it did have a seductive logic about it. Children who had not been provided with illusions would not have to be disillusioned. They should have a progressively firmer grasp upon reality as they grew up, and, as adults, be truly realistic. It has not worked out that way. Today, adults are told fairy stories, fables, legends, and myths, and a large number of them apparently believe them. Many men apparently believe that government is a kind of Santa Claus who can bestow goods for which there is no charge, that in a democracy people may legitimately play Robin Hood by taking from the rich to give to the poor, that we have solved the problems of production and that the good fairies will continue to produce goods when the incentives to production have been removed, and that there is a pot of gold at the end of the rainbow which the politician describes if we will only follow his policies.

There is much more to current illusions, of course, than improper rearing of children, but the question that the above development raises should not be left suspended. The wisdom that is bound up in established customs cannot always be perceived by the naked eye. On the contrary, what may appear illogical upon first examination may have reasons that stem not from abstract logic but from the way people are. Men are given to illusions, probably always have been and will be.

Supplying children with illusions in felicitous stories and myths may have the effect of an innoculation against illusion (following the principle of innoculation of inducing the disease in a mild form). As the child grows up, he sheds the illusions one by one, or in bunches. The legends, stories, and myths may provide him invaluable points of reference for the discernment of reality. He knows, from them, what sort of things belong to the real world and what sort to illusion. Those who do not have some embodied illusions as points of reference may have much greater difficulty in separating illusion from reality, or, to put it another way, may succumb much more readily to the illusory.

At any rate, illusions abound in the twentieth century. They are usually decked out in more sophisticated garb than the above examples would indicate. Men are drawn along on the journey toward the pot of gold at the end of the rainbow by phrases such as "creating a democratic society," "adjustment of monetary supply to demographic tendencies," "transforming the environment to meet human needs," "an equitable distribution of the wealth," "mutual cooperation for the advancement of the general welfare," "increasing the purchasing power of the underprivileged," "rectifying maladjustment induced by technological innovations," "preventing the stagnation of the economy," and "balancing expenditures between the public and private sector." The language is new—out of euphemism by sociology, midwifed by would-be bureaucratic intellectuals —but the illusions are as old as the daydreams of improvident men.

Let us examine one of the current illusions in somewhat more detail, show why it is an illusion, and use the example as a way of reviewing the story of the flight from reality thus far. An illusion which appears to be gaining ground steadily in the United States is that poverty can be abolished. Already, war has been declared upon it, and we are led to expect that the demise of poverty will occur in the not too distant future.

The Problem of Production

From one point of view, the abolition of poverty can be made to appear quite plausible, in this country at least. The argument for it goes something like this: The problem of production has now been solved. America now produces enough goods, or has the means for doing so, so that no one need suffer privation. To support such a contention, evidence can be adduced of the glut of goods now available despite the fact that some factories are not producing at their full capacities. Let us assume that the description is accurate, that there is a glut of goods and the capacity —potential or actual—for producing abundance that will abolish poverty. Even so, the conclusion does not follow.

The fundamental fallacy is in the major premise—that the problem of production has been solved. It has only been solved if the matter is viewed as being static. That is, it has only been solved for today and a few more days, after which it will emerge once more if something is not done. Redistributionist schemes derive such plausibility as they have by abstracting a static picture from the situation as it momentarily exists. It becomes apparent when an actual redistribution is undertaken that the problem of production has not been solved.

Planners will shortly learn, if they did not already know or suspect it, that poverty stems not primarily from unfair distribution but from the unwise choices which men make. The main reasons for poverty, other things being equal, are improvidence, laziness, lack of foresight, slovenliness, the use of capital for consumer goods or goodies, and physical or mental debility. (Of course, governments can and do intervene in ways to contribute to the poverty of individuals.) Most poverty, then, can be attributed to the choices, or failures to choose, which men make. To put it another way, poverty results from the uses men make of their liberty.

There is reason to believe that this has long been apparent to social reformers, for their programs regularly result in the reduction of the choices which men have available to them. To state it bluntly, the attempt to abolish poverty is made by taking away the liberty of people. This can be done crudely or with considerable subtlety. When it has been done crudely, Western Europeans and Americans have usually been horrified at it. Thus, communist measures have repulsed most Westerners rather than attracted them. In the West, then, the removal of liberty has been advanced much more subtly, and the programs for abolishing poverty, or what-not, have been mild initially. The removal of choices takes such forms as increased taxation, inflation, and governmental controls.

But even when choice has been removed, poverty will not be banished. Prosperity, even more than poverty, is the result of innumerable choices of individuals—of decisions, of individual initiative, of saving, of prudent investment, of invention, and so on. When liberty prevails generally, a great many people may contribute to their own and to the prosperity of others. As liberty is reduced, they lose the means, the opportunity, and the incentive for innovation, invention, discovery, and increased productivity. In consequence, poverty is extended to more and more people rather than being abolished.

This is not simply a matter of speculation; there are a goodly number of historical examples for those who prefer experimental evidence. The Russian Bolshevik innovations caused poverty on a titanic scale in the 1920's and 1930's. The programs of the British Labor Party after World War II came near to completely wrecking what still remained of an English economy after decades of increasing intervention. Reports from Communist China indicate that collectivization has wrought devastation in places there. But one need not go so far afield for evidence. Ninety miles from the shores of the United States the scene has been enacted almost before our eyes. The Pearl of the Antilles, once a fertile paradise of productivity, has been transformed in short order into a land of hunger and shortages. There are many other examples throughout history of the failure of men to produce when they are denied the fruits of their labor—at Jamestown, at Plymouth, at New Harmony, and so on.

In the final analysis, poverty cannot be abolished because when men are tolerably free, it is an individual and family matter. It is a result of their habits, customs, indiscipline, and themselves as they are. Any collective approach to the abolition of poverty, as if it were a thing itself, can only temporarily alleviate the condition of some people, if it can do that, at the expense of a general impoverishment. The ultimate importance of liberty does not derive from the fact that free men will produce more bread, but they will, if that is what they want.

The above principles were generally well known among nineteenth century Americans, and among people elsewhere, too. Men who proposed to abolish poverty were considered laughable or dangerous, or both. It is no longer so. The story thus far has dealt with how the way was prepared for contemporary illusions, with how thinkers were cut loose from reality by focusing upon the abstract and ephemeral, with how utopian ideas were spread, with how past experience was defamed and traditional philosophy discredited, with how some thinkers began to conceive of themselves as creators, with how the programs for social transformation were made more palatable by the domestication of them. By the early twentieth century reformist intellectuals were beginning to draw publicists and politicians into the web of their delusion. A considerable number of Americans began to accept some of the milder programs of social reform.

But the programs of ameliorative reformers involved taking away the control which people had of their own affairs. They involved taking away some of the cherished liberties of at least some people. Now it is doubtful if there have ever been people more jealous of their liberties than Americans. It was for this that Americans rebelled against England and effected their independence, so generations of school children had learned. They had learned, too, in the inspiring phrase of Patrick Henry, that liberty was more precious than life. They had carefully limited and restricted their governments so that these might be less likely to become tyrannical. Americans would not lightly have yielded up their liberties, even if they had thought it would have resulted in more bread.

American Democracy

Many things went into making the reduction of liberty acceptable, but none of these could be ranked with the claim that what was being done was democratic. Americans had come, by the early twentieth century, to value what they thought of as democracy. Indeed, they had come to associate it with their system of government and their liberties in such a way that they could not readily perceive how things that were claimed to be democratic could be antithetical to their liberties. Some reformers perceived that the American attachment to democracy could be turned to good account; they need only identify their programs with democracy.

Herbert Croly made this rather clear as early as 1909. He declared that the loyalty of Americans "to the idea of democracy, as they understand it, cannot be questioned. Nothing of any considerable political importance is done or left undone in the United States, unless such action or inaction can be plausibly defended on democratic grounds. . . ."[1] Elsewhere, he points out how this fact can be utilized, saying that "the American people, having achieved democratic institutions, have nothing to do but to turn them to good account. . . . A democratic ideal makes the social problem inevitable and its attempted solution indispensable."[2] In short, he was maintaining that the political instrumentality of democracy should be used to transform man and society.

It is doubtful if anything in the history of Christendom can match the enamorment of Americans with democracy in the twentieth century. They have fought a war to make the world safe for it, written numerous books about it,

---

[1] Croly, *The Promise of American Life,* p. 176.

[2] *Ibid.,* p. 25.

taught courses about it, thingified it, prayed for it, and embraced it as the unquestioned good. Many writers sprinkle the word on their pages as if it were seasoning, politicians justify their programs by it, and educators call upon it as if it were heavy artillery.

What is so strange about it is that the appeal to democracy is founded upon an illusion. It is an illusion born in ambiguity, nourished by a political party, brought to maturity in romantic confusion, and placed in the service of social reform. But before reviewing this history briefly, the character of the illusion should be made clear. The fundamental illusion here is that these United States, either singly as represented by the general government or taken together by including the state governments, are a democracy. The general government of the United States is not a democracy. It is not a democracy historically, etymologically, nor in the sense in which reformers use the word to justify their programs. The root meaning of democracy is rule, or government, by the people. Government, according to the *American College Dictionary*, means, "the authoritative direction and restraint exercised over the actions of men in communities, societies, and states; direction of the affairs of a state, etc.; political rule and administration. . . ." It should be clear that in the United States the people do not govern. They do not make the laws. They do not administer the laws. They do not enforce the laws. These functions are performed by those people in government service. Nothing should be plainer than this.

Some of the confusion about our system of government can be cleared up by reference to the most famous, and repeated, purported description of that system, the phrase extracted from Lincoln's Gettysburg Address. As rhetoric, the phrase—"government of the people, by the people, for the people"—has much to commend it. It is simple, well balanced, and easily remembered. Unfortunately, it has come to have the standing of revealed truth when, in fact, as description, it is part true, part false, and part dubious.

It may be accurate to say that ours is a government *of* the people, that is, that it *derives its powers* from the people, *operates by the consent* of the people, and that those who govern are *chosen or appointed* from among the people. But it is not a government *by* the people. To think that it is, is to confuse the governed with the governors. Men exercise the powers of government; they govern or rule. Those who govern are not the people; no magic of voting, appointment, or delegation can transform them into the people. By constitutions, those who govern in the United States are granted *limited* powers to be exercised for a *limited* time to perform *limited* functions. In theory, the people have unlimited power; they may do whatever mortal men can do. (In practice, however, they are limited by constitutions, and those who govern are charged with seeing that they observe these.) Not so, the governors; they are strictly limited. To believe that the people govern is an illusion; it confuses governors with governed, and opens the floodgates to unlimited power of the governors over the governed. Lincoln's description here was inaccurate. As to whether ours is a government *for* the people, that depends upon how the powers are exercised.

The notion that the United States is a democracy is almost as old as the republic about which the confusion exists. As early as 1835 Alexis de Tocqueville, a Frenchman, published a book in Europe whose title in English translation is *Democracy in America*. Partisans of the Democratic Party were already beginning to refer to our system as democratic. By the latter part of the nineteenth century, the name had stuck, and Americans came to assume that theirs was a democracy.

It was generally understood at the time of the drawing and ratification of the Constitution of 1787 that it did not provide for democracy. The Founders understood that, in classical terms, they were providing for a mixed government. Its various branches were described as monarchical (the executive), aristocratical (Senate and possibly the Supreme Court), and democratical (House of Representatives). They understood very well, of course, that of the offices they were providing for, the President was not to be a monarch, the Senate not to compose an aristocracy, nor the House a democracy. The terminology was drawn from their understanding that there are three forms for the exercise of political power—monarchy, aristocracy, and democracy—and that they were assigning authority and responsibility to bodies derived from each of these forms. The power to be exercised was derived from the people by the representative principle. The resulting government they understood to be a republic.

The Founders neither intended to found a democracy nor did they. There were two main objections to a direct democracy at the time. One was that the country was too extensive for any such mode of the exercise of power. The other objection was much more fundamental and universal in its implications. It was that even if it were territorially practical to have direct democracy, it would not be desirable.

In the debates over ratification in the Massachusetts Convention Moses Ames, who had presumably experienced direct democracy in the town meetings, made the point emphatically. "It has been said that a pure democracy is the best government for a small people who assemble in person. . . . It may be of some use in this argument . . . to consider, that it would be very burdensome, subject to faction and violence; decisions would often be made by surprise, in the precipitancy of passion, by men who either understand nothing or care nothing about the subject. . . . It would be a government not by laws, but by men."[3]

In the government actually founded, the role of the electorate was twofold: to give its *consent* by the choice, either directly or indirectly, of those who were to govern, and to *limit* the actions of those in government by periodic elections.

Jacksonian Democracy

Yet by the Jacksonian period "democratic" was being used by some to describe the American way. The Jacksonians claimed to be lineal descendants of the Jeffersonians, and a good case can be made in justification of the claim. Later historians have written of "Jeffersonian Democracy," though Jefferson called his the Republican Party. Nevertheless, Jefferson did use the term "democracy" to refer to American ways, and it is appropriate to go back to him for an historical examination of the matter in hand.

The belief that the United States is a democracy arose mainly from an ambiguous use of the word "government." If Jefferson, Jackson, and their followers, had consistently thought of government as that which has a monopoly of the use of force in a given jurisdiction, they would not have thought of the United States as a democracy. They understood the political arrangements in this country too well for that. But they thought of government as also embracing the management by an individual of his personal affairs as well. This is often referred to as self-government. The difficulty with such usage is that it introduces am-

---

[3] Elliot's *Debates*, Bk. I, vol. 2, p. 8.

biguities; it blurs the distinction between an individual's control of his affairs and the actions of agents of government—a distinction too important to be ignored. The confusion of these distinct activities set the stage eventually for a vast extension of governmental power at the expense of the individual's control of his affairs.

Of course, neither the Jeffersonians nor the Jacksonians foresaw any such consequences. Indeed, there is great irony here, for both men and their followers were opponents of large governmental establishments and defenders of individual liberty. The Jeffersonian Republican Party drew its following from those concerned to limit the powers of the general government, to delineate the rights of the individual, and to secure the powers of local governments. The Jacksonians were vigorous opponents of governmental intervention in the economy, of the grant of special privileges, and of the use of large governmental powers in the lives of the citizenry.

Jefferson made his position clear on the role of government in his First Inaugural Address. He said that what was needed was "a wise and frugal government which shall restrain men from injuring one another, shall leave them otherwise free to regulate their own pursuits of industry and improvement, and shall not take from the mouth of labor the bread it has earned." Still, he did confuse the issue as between political government and self-government. On one occasion, he wrote: "We of the United States, you know, are constitutionally and conscientiously democrats." He offered this explanation for the claim:

> We think experience has proved it safer, for the mass of individuals composing the society, to reserve to themselves personally the exercise of all rightful powers to which they are competent, and to delegate those to which they are not competent to deputies named, and

removable for unfaithful conduct by themselves immediately.[4]

That he thought of the matter primarily in terms of men managing their own affairs is made clear in the following. He said that Americans had imposed on them "the duty of proving what is the degree of freedom and self-government in which a society may venture to leave its individual members."[5] Moreover, "I have no fear but that the result of our experiment will be that men may be trusted to govern themselves without a master."[6]

The Jacksonians were, if anything, more concerned with limiting government than the Jeffersonians and, at the same time, more fertile in producing confusions about self-government and democracy. In the *Democratic Review,* initiated in 1837, the author declared:

> The best government is that which governs least. No human depositories can, with safety, be trusted with the power of legislation upon the general interests of society so as to operate directly or indirectly on the industry and property of the community.[7]

The same author declared, "This is the fundamental principle of the philosophy of democracy, to furnish a system of administration of justice, and then leave all the business and interests of themselves, to free competition and association; in a word, to the *voluntary principle. . . ."*[8]

---

[4] Edward Dumbauld, ed., *The Political Writings of Thomas Jefferson* (New York: Liberal Arts Press, 1955), pp. 48-49.

[5] *Ibid.,* p. 77.

[6] *Ibid.*

[7] Joseph L. Blau, ed., *Social Theories of Jacksonian Democracy* (New York: Liberal Arts Press, 1954), p. 27.

[8] *Ibid.,* p. 28.

William Leggett, another Jacksonian, enunciated similar principles in the 1830's. "The fundamental principle of all governments," he said, "is the protection of person and property from domestic and foreign enemies. . . ."[9] When it has done that, he thought, men may be expected to look after themselves:

> As a general rule, the prosperity of rational men depends upon themselves. Their talents and their virtues shape their fortunes. They are therefore the best judges of their own affairs and should be permitted to seek their own happiness in their own way, untrammeled by the capricious interference of legislative bungling, so long as they do not violate the equal rights of others nor transgress the general laws for the security of person and property.[10]

He identifies this with democracy by saying that "if government were restricted to the few and simple objects contemplated in the democratic creed, the mere protection of person, life, and property . . . , we should find reason to congratulate ourselves on the change in the improved tone of public morals as well as in the increased prosperity of trade."[11]

Walt Whitman, too, was an apostle of democracy (or of Democracy, for the word had not lost its partisan connotations when he wrote the words below). His views were similar to those above. "*Men* must be 'masters unto themselves,' and not look to presidents and legislative bodies for aid."[12] This being so, that government is best which governs least.

One point, however, must not be forgotten—ought to

---

[9] *Ibid.*, p. 75.
[10] *Ibid.*, p. 76.
[11] *Ibid.*, p. 87.
[12] *Ibid.*, p. 131.

be put before the eyes of the people every day; and that is, although government can do little *positive* good to the people, it may do an *immense deal of harm*. And here is where the beauty of the Democratic principle comes in. Democracy would prevent all this harm. It would have no man's benefit achieved at the expense of his neighbors. . . . While mere politicians, in their narrow minds, are sweating and fuming with their complicated statutes, this one single rule, rationally construed and applied, is enough to form the starting point of all that is necessary in government; *to make no more laws than those useful for preventing a man or body of men from infringing on the rights of other men.*[13]

The Jacksonians, then, had a theory of democracy, a theory which involved limited government, free trade, a society of equals before the law, and each man pursuing his own interests limited only by the equal rights of others. In this way, the energies of each man would be released to make the most for himself and contribute the greatest amount to the general well-being. They perceived that from the diverse activities of men a near miraculous harmony of achievement emerged. They surrounded their idea of democracy with a romantic aura, and some men sang praises to it. The author in the *Democratic Review* broke forth in what amounts to a lyrical litany to democracy:

We feel safe under the banner of the democratic principle, which is borne onward by an unseen hand of Providence, to lead our race toward the high destinies of which every human soul contains the God-implanted germ; and of the advent of which—certain, however distant—a dim prophetic presentiment has existed, in one form or another, among all nations in all ages.[14]

It is quite probable that it was some such conception of

---

[13] *Ibid.*, p. 132.
[14] *Ibid.*, p. 30.

the American system as this that Lincoln had in mind when he drew the fateful phrase for the Gettysburg Address. And, in this sense—conceiving the people as individuals, and government primarily as self-government—it may have been descriptively apt to refer to the system as a government of, by, and for the people. It is not difficult to understand, either, how many Americans could come to value democracy so highly. As I have pointed out, however, the conception was flawed by ambiguity. There was no clear distinction between government as force and "government" as a man's management of his own affairs.

Indeed, the Jeffersonians and Jacksonians did not see the need for making such a distinction. What is correctly called government was only an extension of the principle of a man's control of his affairs to a different arena, when the government was popularly based. They were majoritarians; they thought that when government derived its power from a broad general consent that the liberties of the individual would be most secure. The effort to extend the suffrage was thought of as part and parcel of an attempt to be rid of special privileges, governmental favors, and the use of government for special interests.

In historical perspective, their case was an impressive one. Governments had ever and anon been used for the advancement of the few at the expense of the many. Men of wealth and station had used government to consolidate their positions, to confer titles and hereditary positions upon them, and to grant them exclusive franchises and monopolies. Could the poor not see that their hope lay in limiting government, in *laissez faire*, in allowing each man to receive as his efforts and ability merited? Could those of the middling sort not perceive that their advantage lay with a free and open economy?

For the moment, in the mid-nineteenth century, they

could. There were as yet no widespread theories about using the government positively to benefit the less well off. No grandiose plans for redistributing the wealth had yet been spread to bemuse and enamor the ne'er-do-wells. In the last decades of the nineteenth century, however, the situation was changing. Social theorists, utopians, reformers, communitarians, populists, anarchists, socialists, and others were spreading their ideas. The programs ranged from Henry George's proposal to confiscate all rent, to the Populist idea of partial government ownership of the means of production, to Daniel De Leon's full-fledged Marxist socialism. The siren song that all sang, however, was that the government (as force) should be used for the benefit of the general populace, at the expense of the few. The hoary practices of discrimination by government were to be reversed; the have-nots were at last to be made the beneficiaries of government.

The "New Democracy"

Clearly, however, American institutions, traditions, and beliefs ran counter to any such usage. American democracy stood for limited government, for equality of all (including the rich) before the law, for each man to seek his own good in his own way, and for each to receive the rewards of his own labor. Perhaps a revolutionary socialist would conclude that democracy would have to go, then. After all, some were concluding that socialism would have to be ushered in by an elite. However, evolutionary socialists—Fabians, gradualists—proposed to turn the materials at hand to their ends. Democracy was a concept too deeply ingrained in American thought, as Herbert Croly indicated, to be ignored. It must be somehow subsumed into the new vision; it must be "instrumented" for new social ends.

But for this to be done the conception of democracy would have to be transformed; the old democracy would have to be displaced by a New Democracy. This was the burden of Walter Weyl's book, *The New Democracy,* examined in the last chapter in another connection. He made no secret of the fact that this was what he was about. He referred to the "so-called individualistic democracy of Jefferson and Jackson," and declared that whatever its merits had been at the time it was now obsolete. "The force of our individualistic democracy might suffice to supplant one economic despot by another, but it could not prevent economic despotism."[15] What he meant was that when each man got the rewards of his efforts, some got much more than others. In consequence, "to-day no democracy is possible except a socialized democracy."[16] The reason for this, he claimed, was that the "individualistic point of view halts social development at every point. Why should the childless man pay in taxes for the education of other people's children? . . . To the individualist taxation above what is absolutely necessary for the individual's welfare is an aggression upon his rights and a circumscription of his powers."[17]

This conception of democracy would have to be changed:

In the socialized democracy towards which we are moving all these conceptions will fall to the ground. It will be sought to make taxes conform more or less to the ability of each to pay; but the engine of taxation, like all other social engines, will be used to accomplish great social ends, among which will be the more equal distribution of wealth and income. The state will tax to improve education, health, recreation, communica-

---

[15] Weyl, *The New Democracy,* pp. 161-62.
[16] *Ibid.,* p. 162.
[17] *Ibid.,* p. 163.

tion . . . , and from these taxes no social group will be immune because it fails to benefit in proportion to cost. The government of the nation, in the hands of the people, will establish its unquestioned sovereignty over the industry of the nation, so largely in the hands of individuals.[18]

The "people," however, had generally been less than enthusiastic at that time about such thorough-going "democracy." To change popular opinion, Weyl believed it would be necessary to undertake an immense educational program. People must be led to

recognize that we have the social wealth to cure our social evils—and that until we have turned that social wealth against poverty, crime, vice, disease, incapacity, and ignorance, we have not begun to attain democracy. We must change our attitude towards government, towards business, towards reform, towards philanthropy, towards all the facts immediately or remotely affecting our industrial and political life.[19]

Such an "educational" program was, of course, undertaken, and the story of it will be told later.

But the important point here is this: The ambiguity of the earlier conception of democracy was dissolved into an illusion. Democracy was transformed into a political conception. The government (as force) was to undertake the myriad functions being prescribed. What had formerly been done by the people (individually) was now to be done for them by the government. But that would not be democratic. The people collectively could not even perform the simpler offices of limited government. To understand this it is only necessary to imagine all Americans gathered to welcome a foreign ambassador or directing a military un-

[18] *Ibid.*, pp. 163-64.
[19] *Ibid.*, p. 273.

dertaking. No, an electorate could not even direct the simplest of activities; for that it had to choose representatives, and these had to appoint agents. These agents were not the people, a fact well understood earlier, and they had to be checked else they would become despotic. For that, elections would serve, or so they hoped.

Now, however, governments were to undertake vastly complex activities, activities whose complexities eluded the understanding of all except a few. Governments were to plan economies, control economic activities, attempt to effect distributive "justice," enter into every facet of the lives of people. If this could be done, it certainly could not be done by the "people." All constructive activity requires organization. If more than one person is involved, hierarchical organization becomes necessary. Authority and responsibility must be located in a single head, and if the undertaking involves a great many people, there must be a "chain of command." Insofar as the American political system provides for such organization, it is not democratic (it is monarchic and aristocratic, a fact well understood by the Founders); insofar as it is democratic, it does not encompass such organization and activity.

In short, the reformers could not effect their programs by democratic means. They could, however, change the conception of democracy into a conception of ends and use undemocratic means to the end. The story of how they did this needs to be told, also.

13

The "Democratic" Elite

THERE HAVE BEEN STRANGE AND INCONSISTENT DEVELOP-
ments in the movement toward what is billed as democracy in twentieth century America. The phrase that all
men are equal has been a rallying cry of professed democrats. They have proclaimed their shock at the existence
of distinctions, discrimination, and hierarchies. Leveling
has been much in favor among them.

Yet these democrats appear to have developed myopia
where certain kinds of distinctions are concerned. This is
most pronounced where the presidency of the United States
is concerned. For example, following the assassination of
President Kennedy, and the subsequent events in Dallas,
various columnists announced in shocked tones that there
was no Federal law providing for the punishment of assas-
sins or murderers of a President. Such cases fall under
state law. This, the commentators declared, was hardly
the way things should be. The matter should be corrected
by making assaults upon the President a Federal crime.

Closely related to this is the employment of an extensive
Secret Service to guard the President. Millions of dollars
are spent annually to this end, and the amount has been
recently greatly increased. Lengthy lists of potential as-
sassins have been compiled, and a concerted effort is being
made to make the list as complete as possible. The men

assigned to guard the President are expected to serve as human shields of his body if the occasion warrants such action.

It is not my purpose here to make any evaluation or judgment of such actions. They may or may not be justified. However, it would be difficult to do so from a "democratic" or equalitarian standpoint. If all men are equal, what would justify giving more protection to one man than another? Why should a guard place himself between the President and an assassin's bullet? Is it a more heinous crime to kill a President than it is to kill anyone else? If not, why should it be made a Federal crime to do so? In short, the attention and care lavished upon the President is hardly in keeping with the democratic ethos.

Here is another anomaly. Supreme Court decisions are made in the name of democracy and hailed as being "democratic." For example, the famous decision of Brown *v.* Board of Education of Topeka, *et al.* was preceded by the following argument, among others, by lawyers for the appellants (who were seeking a decision for integration of the schools in question):

> The importance to our American democracy of the substantive question can hardly be overstated. The question is whether a nation founded on the proposition that "all men are created equal" is honoring its commitments to grant "due process of law" and "the equal protection of the laws" to all within its borders when it, or one of its constituent states, confers or denies benefits on the basis of color or race.[1]

Mr. Chief Justice Warren, who gave the opinion for a unanimous court, declared: "Compulsory school attendance laws and the great expenditures for education both

---

[1] Quoted in Benjamin M. Ziegler, ed., *Desegregation and the Supreme Court* (Boston: D. C. Heath, 1958), p. 68.

demonstrate our recognition of the importance of education to our democratic society."[2]

Again, it is not my purpose to evaluate the decision in
question. My concern is with the use of the words "democracy" and "democratic" in connection with it. No branch
of the general government is so remote from popular control as is the judiciary. It is the least "democratic" of all
the branches. The members of the courts are appointed by
the President, by and with the advice and consent of the
Senate. They have life tenure in their offices, and can
only be removed from office by actions taken in both houses
of Congress. The special function of the courts is to maintain a government of laws, and it was thought by the
Founders that they would be more likely to do so if they
were not subjected to popular pressures.

Federal court decisions, by their nature, are authori-
tarian and autocratic. That is, they are supposed to be
made on the basis of the authority of the Constitution and
precedent. They are autocratic in that ordinarily the members of the courts are not answerable to anyone for the
decisions that they make. Their powers are not absolute,
but they are as near to it as any granted under the Constitution. On the face of it, "democracy" is not a word one
would associate with the Supreme Court.

A third strange development should be described also.
As America has moved closer and closer to what is supposed to be democracy, the tendency has been for more
and more power to be concentrated in the central government. Local and state governments have yielded up, or had
taken from them, many of their governmental functions.
In like manner, individuals and voluntary groups have
lost exclusive control of many of their affairs as the gen-

---

[2] *Ibid.*, p. 78.

eral government has undertaken to regulate and control them. It is not immediately clear why such a course of development should be styled democratic.

If by democracy is meant government by the people, it would appear that a counter movement would be more nearly democratic. That is, individuals and groups could better control their affairs and govern themselves at the local level. Local governments are surely more sensitive to the wishes of the electorate than are governments far removed from them. State governments might be expected to reflect more accurately the wishes of their inhabitants than would the Federal government.

Ideologizing Democracy

These anomalies can best be cleared up by an understanding that "democracy" is used largely as a word cover for an ideological thrust. Melioristic reformers have been bent upon remaking society along certain lines. They have used the materials at hand to effect their ends. The belief in democracy by Americans was a major constituent element of the materials at hand. A new conception of democracy, however, had to be developed and propagated before it could be used in this way. It had to be wrested from its individualistic context and collectivized. It had to be changed from a means into an end. It had to be instrumented to the purposes of reform.

It is tempting to charge the reformers with the cynical manipulation of a hallowed concept, with the malicious bending of words to their own ends. It is a temptation, however, that should be resisted. To appearances, at least, reformers have quite often been as confused as those they were drawing into their confusion. The intellectuals who provided the theories of reform were on a flight from reality. They were cut loose from methods of analysis and thought which would have enabled them to think clearly. It may be more accurate to think of them as feeling their way to usages of democracy that would accord with their ideological aims than to conceive of them as coldly planning linguistic *coups*.

At any rate, the idea of democracy was confused from the outset in the United States. As I have shown, the Jeffersonians and Jacksonians used "government" in an ambiguous sense in order to conceive of themselves as democrats. Moreover, there were mystical elements in the conception. Jean Jacques Rousseau is usually credited with, or blamed for, intruding mystifying elements into the conception of democracy. He introduced the idea of a general will into thought about the matter. This general will was a kind of pseudo-metaphysical concept. It involved the notion that there is a general will in society, that the aim of a society should be to discover this and for individuals to bring themselves into accord with it.

The general will was not simply the wishes of a majority of the electorate; it was that which all would wish for themselves if they but knew what they willed. No method was ever agreed upon for discerning the general will, but here was a fruitful idea that could be used, with variations, by dictators, majoritarians, technocrats, and assorted democrats. All modern notions of democracy are freighted with mystical and intellectually impenetrable conceptions.

Reformers took over the existing illusions about democracy in America, and added to them. Perhaps the chief illusion taken over is that the United States is a democracy. This illusion has already been explored in some detail, so it needs only summary treatment here. These United States, taken together, are a constitutional federated republic. Those who govern do so on the basis of the representative principle. The people do not actually govern, nor has there ever been any reason for supposing that they do. The power and authority of the courts derive from the Constitution, not from any supposed democratic character of decisions issued by them.

Perhaps the most important illusion added by the reformers is that socialism can be democratically achieved. There is some evidence that many reformers believed this in the early years of the movement in America. In the late nineteenth and early twentieth centuries much of the effort of reformers was devoted to making America more democratic. This was particularly true of those known as populists, but it was only to a lesser degree true of the Progressives. The platform of the Populist Party in 1892 called for, among other things, a secret or Australian ballot, the direct election of Senators, legislation by initiative and referendum, and the limitation of the President to one term in office. The Progressives added to this program. They pressed for a provision for the recall of judges. Also, there had been a movement for a long time for female suffrage. The Progressives took up this clamor as a part of their platform. The Bull Moose Party platform in 1912 called for a national presidential primary.

Some major changes were made in consequence of these efforts. The Seventeenth Amendment, ratified in 1913, provided for the direct election of Senators. The Nineteenth Amendment, ratified in 1920, extended the vote to women. Some local governments and states adopted the initiative and referendum procedures for some matters, and a goodly number of states provided for presidential primaries.

But these populistic devices only partially solved one of the problems of reformers. A wider suffrage did enable them to elect reformers to office—sometimes. Even this was not an unmixed blessing, as reformers were shortly to learn. The electorate sometimes displayed strange tastes.

They preferred an experiment in national prohibition to participation in a League of Nations. They preferred a "return to normalcy" to various and sundry redistributionist schemes. Still, reformers could be more readily elected to office when there was a more inclusive portion of the populace within the electorate. At least, the over-all trends of this century would tend to indicate this.

Nor is the reason far to seek. The more extensive the electorate the more readily can it be swayed by demagoguery. If the propertyless can vote, they are more apt than those who have property to favor assaults upon it. The less the electorate is restricted to those who have demonstrated practical judgment, the more readily will it adopt or favor impractical schemes.

Centralization of Power

Even so, the major obstacle to social reform was not surmounted. The extension of the suffrage and the adoption of populistic devices did not mean that government would be by the people. There were still the governors and the governed. Indeed, most of the populistic devices—such as the initiative and referendum—if they had been adopted, would have made socialistic reforms impractical to carry out, if not impossible. Reformers envisaged a planned, controlled, and directed economy. This required the centralization of power, the concentration of authority, and centralized direction. Democracy would tend to diffuse power, to locate decision-making with the numerous individuals who compose the electorate, and to make extended concerted action in a particular direction exceedingly unlikely.

Moreover, the reconstruction of society is a complicated and delicate undertaking. As Fabians (to use the term generically) have conceived the matter, it is to be done slowly. This would mean with a tenacity and with eyes fixed on distant goals which few men demonstrate. In short, the ordinary run of men cannot direct the government in this undertaking. One writer put the matter succinctly some years ago:

> The task of the government of a democratic society implies a wisdom and understanding of the complicated life of modern societies very far removed from the simple "horse sense" which is sufficient for the running of small and simple democracies. It is clear that a modern state can do its job only with a lot of expert help, expert statesmen, expert administrators. We must nowadays go on and say "expert economists and expert scientists." Perhaps we must go further and say "expert sociologists."[3]

To state it less obliquely, democracy and socialism are antithetical goals. More precisely, democratic means are not suited to the achievement of socialistic ends.

Transforming Means into Ends

Yet the thrust toward the realization of an ideology which should be called socialism has been carried on in the name of democracy. Two things were done to make it possible to avoid confronting this anomaly, to keep the name while working for and accepting the substance of something else. First, *democracy was transformed into an end.* Second, the business of *government was increasingly turned over to an elite.*

It may be regrettable, but there is nothing particularly unusual about means being transformed into ends. People do it regularly, and in numerous instances. A house is a thing to live in, an automobile a conveyance to get one

---

[3] A. D. Lindsay, *The Modern Democratic State* (London: Oxford University Press, 1943), p. 267.

from one place to another, money a means of acquiring goods. Yet men will quite often treat these as ends in and for themselves. There may even be something wholesome and preservative in this tendency. Certainly, a house should become a home—something that has value and meaning beyond its accommodative usefulness. Things need much care and attention, and it may be that if we think of them only as means we will neglect them.

It would hardly be worthy of comment, then, if all that were involved were the transformation of democracy from a means into an end. Any such transformation does, of course, tend to lead away from reality. But the transformation of democracy involved a second remove from reality. As we have seen, the United States was not a democracy. Insofar as some of the means for governing were democratic, they fitted into a larger pattern of diverse means. The form of government could only be conceived of as democratic, descriptively, by abstracting some methods from the context of American government. Thus, the conception of American democracy was, and is, an abstraction. When it was made into an end, the abstraction was thingified.

Some examples will help to clarify this. Voting is a very important practice within the American system of government. In this way, many of those who govern are chosen. They are limited in their exercise of power by the fact that they must stand for election from time to time if they are to continue in office. Not only is government limited in this way, but it receives popular consent for action by this device. Nothing should be clearer than that voting is a *means* for making choices, giving the consent of the electorate, and limiting those in power. But it is often treated as an *end* today. Spot advertisements on radio and television, notices in newspapers, and posters and billboards exhort Americans to vote, though it does not matter for whom they vote. This is to treat voting as if it had meaning in and for itself, as if it were an end, not a means.

The abstraction is taken a step farther when this "democratic" procedure is taken from its governmental context and extended to the action of voluntary groups. The following actually occurred. Someone rose in a faculty meeting and made a motion that each member of the faculty should pay a certain amount into a flower fund, this amount to be withheld from the paychecks. The motion was seconded, and after some little discussion the motion was acted upon favorably by the faculty. The action was later nullified when an alert business manager pointed out that the enforcement of this act would be illegal. In fact, the faculty had assumed governmental powers, the powers of taxation.

But, one might object, the procedure was democratic, was it not? It certainly was, but it was not action in accord with the American system. If the faculty assumed the powers of taxation, there was no limit to the extent of such powers, no constitutional authorization, no independent judiciary, no procedure for investigations and hearings, no veto powers to prevent precipitate action. This was an excellent example of the abstraction of procedures from their whole context.

Actually, though, such pseudo governments do exist in America, and have for some time. Labor unions have been empowered to act as pseudo governments, with powers of taxation and enforcement. Farmers vote restrictions upon themselves and other farmers, and indirectly tax all of us. Indeed, elections abound and are apt to occur at any time or place where two or three are gathered together. Some of these are innocuous enough, but others turn any assemblage into a lobbying group or pseudo-legislative body. It would be highly unusual for anyone to arise when a vote was proposed and challenge the appropriateness of the procedure. Such votes are accepted as if they were justified in and for themselves.

It may be that men have a tendency to turn means into ends, but this development in democracy was not simply the result of some inclination rooted in human nature. It served a purpose. It was promoted and propagated. Reformers articulated a vision of democracy as a goal or an end. Many men contributed, first and last, to this development but none more consistently and vigorously than John Dewey. Note how, in the following, he makes democracy an end and a goal:

> . . . A democracy is more than a form of government; it is primarily a mode of associated living, of conjoint communicated experience. The extension in space of the number of individuals who participate in an interest so that each has to refer his own action to that of others, and to consider the action of others to give point and direction to his own, is equivalent to the breaking down of those barriers of class, race, and national territory which kept men from perceiving the full import of their activity.[4]

More,

> . . . A society which makes provision for participation in its good of all its members on equal terms and which secures flexible readjustment of its institutions through interaction of the different forms of associated life is in so far democratic. Such a society must have a type of education which gives individuals a personal interest in social relationships and control, and the habits of mind which secure social changes without introducing disorder.[5]

---

[4] John Dewey, *Democracy and Education* (New York: Macmillan, 1916), p. 101.

[5] *Ibid.*, p. 115.

In short, democracy is not only an end, but it has an end or aim—social control and social reconstruction.

Emphasis on Equality

In particular, the end of democracy has been most often thought of as equality. That is, democracy has often been defined as equality, and programs for providing equality have been described as democratic. One writer described the phenomenon, with obvious approval, in this way some years ago:

> There is excellent historical and psychological ground for the supposition that democracy, whatever it may mean of fraternity, must at least be an effort to embody equality in action. American modifications made in the democratic form may be interpreted as approach toward or recession from equality. What we have only now been considering in America as expansion of governmental regulation, even up to the creation of what has been called "the service state," has been done primarily in the name of equality of opportunity. From the "Square Deal" of Roosevelt, through the "New Freedom" of Wilson, up to and into the "New Deal"—this has all been an adventure in equalization. In fact, the general bent of American democracy has been the extension of liberty in the name of equality for the sake of solidarity.[6]

One may take issue with his use of "liberty" in connection with these developments, but he has aptly described the animating aim of the programs.

The provision of equality could, and has, become an all embracing goal. When governments are used to do this, they must engage in innumerable activities. Wealth must be more or less redistributed; production and distribution

---

[6] T. V. Smith, *The Democratic Tradition in America* (New York: Farrar and Rinehart, 1941), p. 17.

of goods must be directed; prices must be more or less controlled; individuals and groups must be regulated so as to prevent discrimination, and so on. Such a goal as actual equality, if it could be achieved, could only be reached by the extended and concentrated effort of those who were acting with the force of an all powerful state. It would require the location of such power in the hands of men, and it would have to be centrally directed.

Several things had now been done to "democracy" by these abstracting processes. First, the methods associated with it had been made into ends—voting for the sake of voting, for instance. Second, it had been changed into a substantive goal, more or less divorced from its procedural methods. That is, if "true democracy" is equality, the methods of democracy are surely secondary. Third, the achievement of this goal required extensive and extended social reform. Fourth, the reforms required by "democracy" would be themselves "democratic." It follows, then, that whatever has to be done to achieve the goals is "democratic," however far removed it may be from democratic procedures.

As a writer observed in an earlier quotation, the effort must be directed by experts—by an elite, if you will. The above is the line of reason, or unreason, by which something so uncongenial to democracy as an elite could be justified. But government by an elite was not only uncongenial to democracy; more important, it was also uncongenial to the American way, and to Americans. Americans liked to manage their own affairs, both private and public. The notion of having their affairs managed by experts might not be expected to be too popular. Still, it has come to pass that an elite increasingly governs, and their responsibility to the populace is often quite indirect, if not nonexistent.

The Theory of an Elite

Elitist ideas have been very prominent in European thought for the past century. As one historian says, "The ideal of an elite guiding mankind toward a better life in a new society has played a role" in many social theories. "Marxism had its elite in the Communist Party, and Nietzsche longed for an elite of individualistic supermen."[7]

Perhaps the most extensive theory of an elite set forth was by Vilfredo Pareto in a three-volumned work called *A Tract of General Sociology*. He held that man is fundamentally irrational—or that most men are, that he is governed by "residues" and "derivations"—residues being, roughly, inherited beliefs, and derivatives being particular formulations from these which serve to motivate behavior and attitudes. An elite could govern through its knowledge of the psychology of the masses. "The main business of this elite must be to manipulate residues through controlling their derivations. Here propaganda came into its own, for the residues were irrational and thus the derivations had to appeal to the irrational in man. . . . Thus if meat inspection was desired, the appeal could not be to civic pride but instead to the fear of death through poisoning."[8]

America has had no Pareto. The nearest thing to him was probably Thorstein Veblen. Veblen did set forth a theory, or, in the peculiar argot of progressives, a prediction, of an elite. His elite was made up of industrial technicians, and when it ruled it would be a technocracy. Veblen held that increasingly business was managed and guided by technicians. These had been brought in in the

---

[7] George L. Mosse, *The Culture of Western Europe* (Chicago: Rand McNally, 1961), p. 293.

[8] *Ibid.*, p. 295.

service of what he called "absentee owners," the holders of corporate stock, and so forth. But he expected that in time they would perceive that these owners contributed nothing to production. When they did so, they might be expected to revolt by way of a general strike of technicians and take over the industries. He did not profess to know when it would occur. "But so much seems clear, that the industrial dictatorship of the captain of finance is now held on sufferance of the engineers and is liable at any time to be discontinued at their discretion, as a matter of convenience."[9] When they took over, they would administer the industrial system for the benefit of the general welfare, so Veblen thought, not for the profit motive.

Of course, American reformers did not generally openly advocate government by an elite, or press for the formation of a technocracy. Instead, they acclimated Americans to the idea in a more piecemeal fashion, and talked in terms of more congenial ideas. They spoke of leadership, of experts, of civil service, and of public administration. Americans were, and are, much devoted to things scientific, and it was convincing to appeal for experts and technicians in government affairs. Indeed, in the 1920's, the introduction of such methods in government was often referred to as being businesslike.

The simplest illustration of the application of these ideas to government can be found at the local level of government. The city manager system was a direct outgrowth of the idea of having experts govern. The movement for city manager systems got underway in the early twentieth century, and was part of the general reform movement led by Progressives. The system is well de-

---

[9] Thorstein Veblen, *The Engineers and the Price System* (New York: Viking, 1921), p. 82.

scribed in the following words by an enthusiastic advocate:

> . . . A small council is elected at large and chooses a city manager. It may dismiss him but may not control his acts. The manager appoints the necessary city officers and acts for the city in much the same way that the general manager would for an ordinary corporation. He is responsible only to the councilmanic directors. . . . The amateur administrator, chosen on political grounds, is displaced by the expert brought in from the outside to manage the city. Politics is adjourned. At least this is the hope.[10]

Without perceiving the irony of it, this writer says: "The return to simplicity is hopeful whatever may be its details. The earliest type of city government in the United States was that of a single body. . . . Power and responsibility were concentrated. . . ." In short, "In essentials we are now back where we began. . . ."[11] He did point out in an earlier paragraph, however, that the city manager system might well be oligarchic. But he seemed mainly concerned that this situation would result from lack of public interest. To which one might reply, it is oligarchic, or, more precisely, monarchic, whether the public is interested or not.

City Planning Developed and Extended

A corollary movement was the city planning movement. The aim was centralized control of the development of cities and the drawing up and execution of master plans. One advocate stated the aims in this way:

> In a big way, city planning is the first conscious recognition of the unity of society. It involves a socializing of

---

[10] Lindsay Rogers, "Government by City Managers," *World's Work*, XLIV (September, 1922), 519.
[11] *Ibid.*, p. 524.

art and beauty and the control of the unrestrained license of the individual. It enlarges the power of the State to include the things men own as well as the men themselves, and widens the idea of sovereignty so as to protect the community from him who abuses the rights of property. . . .[12]

These wonders were to be achieved by expert planners:

City planning involves a new vision of the city. It means a city built by experts, by experts in architecture, in landscape gardening, in engineering, and housing; by students of health, sanitation, transportation, water, gas, and electricity supply; by a new type of municipal officials who visualize the complex life of a million people as the builders of an earlier age visualized an individual home.[13]

This vision was, of course, transplanted to the nation as a whole. The idea of governing by an elite of leaders and experts was transferred there also. The President has most often been conceived of as *the* leader. The constitutional role of the President is considerable, but the office has grown mightily in power and prestige in this century. Theodore Roosevelt and Woodrow Wilson contributed to its stature. Theorists have come forward, too, to proclaim the role of leadership inherent in the office.

The following, written in 1921, exemplifies the tenor of such thought:

Thus the President is the one official whose position marks him at the present time as the national leader. Any man, no matter how obscure he may be to-day, will on the morrow of his election to this high office step into the blinding radiance of universal scrutiny.

[12] Frederick C. Howe, "The Remaking of the American City," *Harper's,* CXXVII (July, 1913), 186-87.

[13] *Ibid.,* p. 187.

The writer continues:

The legal functions of the President's office are so eminent that he cannot escape the responsibilities of executive action, however much he may be inclined to avoid them. His constitutional powers alone make him the pivot upon which all the administrative machinery operates. He appoints all the heads of departments and may direct their major policies. His power of appointment to all the greater offices is far-reaching. He can recommend, shape, and veto legislation. . . . In short, he is the most potent constitutional functionary in the world.[14]

Moreover,

All these constitutional powers have been vastly augmented by practice and custom. The President today can do innumerable things that George Washington or Thomas Jefferson would never have dared do even if they had thought of them. The constitutional conception of the President is that of a chief executive, an administrator; custom has added to this conception that of leadership, of initiation.[15]

Already, then, the idea of presidential leadership had taken shape, an idea which has been used to provide a head for the exercise of centralized authority.

Experts Turned Bureaucrats

The President was to be assisted, of course, by numerous scientists, social scientists, experts, and technologists. Charles A. Beard made what well may be the classical argument for the use of technologists in 1930. Arguing in the manner of the historicist, he maintained that condi-

---

[14] Samuel P. Orth, "Presidential Leadership," *Yale Review,* X (April, 1921), 453.

[15] *Ibid.,* pp. 453-54.

tions of life had changed in America. The major source of these changes had been technological innovations. In consequence of these, according to him, governmental functions had been greatly augmented. He declared,

> Under the pressure of new forces, government itself has become an economic and technical business on a large scale. It comes into daily contact with all industries, sciences and arts. As a purchaser of goods . . . , operator of battleships, arsenals, canals and wireless stations . . . , regulator of railways, telegraph lines and other means of transportation and communication, it must command . . . competence equal to that of corporation managers. . . .[16]

Thus, he concluded, "Few indeed are the duties of government in this age which can be discharged with a mere equipment of historic morals and common sense."[17]

The matter is not one for despair, however. "Fortunately, in introducing these bewildering complexities into government, technology has brought with it a procedure helpful in solving the problems it has created: namely, the scientific method. . . . Though undoubtedly limited in its application, the scientific method promises to work a revolution in politics no less significant than that wrought in society at large by mechanics."[18] The mechanics of the scientific method in government would be, of course, experts turned bureaucrats.

We now have the key for solving the problems originally posed in this chapter. Namely, how could the Supreme Court make "democratic" decisions? How could proponents

---

[16] Charles A. Beard, "Government by Technologists," *New Republic*, LXIII (June 18, 1930), 116.

[17] *Ibid.*

[18] *Ibid.*

of democracy and equality promote a privileged position for the President? How could centralized government be advanced in the name of democracy? On the face of it, these are incongruities. An explanation has been made, however, and it remains only to sum it up. Democracy was transformed into an end. As an end, government was to act to realize it. All actions that have as their end the effecting of democracy are then democratic. Thus, however autocratic the exercise of authority by the Supreme Court, if it helps to realize an equality of condition, it is "democratic." The realization of "democracy" requires central direction; hence, a leader. The President is that leader in the United States, and his protection becomes important because of his essential role in bringing about democracy. In this way, too, an elite could become "democratic" because of its necessity to the bringing about of substantive democracy.

More broadly, "democracy" was instrumented for social reform. Indeed, social reform was justified because it was supposed to bring about democracy. Thus, men have yielded up the control of many of their affairs in the name of democracy. Local governments have lost many of their prerogatives in the name of democracy. An ubiquitous bureaucracy makes numerous rules and regulations affecting the lives and liberties of Americans. But it is staffed by a "democratic" elite.

14

Capturing the Hearts of Men

. . . And Christianity, by the lips of all its teachers, ought with all its emphasis to say to society: "Your present industrial system, which fosters these enormous inequalities, which permits a few to heap up most of the gains . . . needs important changes to make it the instrument of righteousness."
—WASHINGTON GLADDEN, 1886

I take this as my thesis: Christianity is primarily concerned with this world, and it is the mission of Christianity to bring to pass here a kingdom of righteousness and to rescue from the evil one and redeem all our social relations.
. . . The mission of the Church is to redeem the world, and to make peace with it only on its unconditional surrender to Christian.
—RICHARD T. ELY, 1889

. . . Church and State are alike but partial organizations of humanity for special ends. Together they serve what is greater than either: humanity. Their common aim is to transform humanity into the kingdom of God.
—WALTER RAUSCHENBUSCH, 1907

MELIORIST REFORM IN AMERICA HAS USUALLY BEEN advanced with religious zeal. It has quite often been forwarded as a moral crusade. The political conventions of Populists and Progressives had something of the atmosphere of revival meetings. Reform programs have frequently been enveloped in a sentimental gloss of morality which frightens the timid away from challenging them and permits their instigators to adopt postures of not-to-be-questioned rectitude. Reformers have pictured themselves (and undoubtedly thought of themselves) as champions of the poor, the downtrodden, the dispossessed, the underdog, the meek, and the maltreated. They have proclaimed their cause as just and have assumed that their motives were pure. Above all, they have identified their reformist mission with the mission of Christianity, have sanctified their reforms by this identification, and have drawn many people into their effort by an appeal to Christian charity.

Religion has been "instrumented" for the purpose of social reform and reconstruction. The pressure of organized religion has been brought to bear increasingly upon governments to use their political power to reconstruct society. Churches and churchmen have supported the unionization of labor, the forced redistribution of wealth, coerced integration, and a host of particular programs for rebuilding society along the lines of the socialist vision. The task here is to describe summarily how this transformation of religion came about, to tell how social concern developed among some clergymen, how a new theology was constructed to justify social reconstruction, and how the organized churches were drawn into this effort. In short, it is the story of how many in the churches and many religious institutions came under the sway of and became subservient to reformist ideology. To turn it around, it is the story of how the moral zeal of religion was brought to bear upon social reconstruction, advancing by emotion things that could hardly have been advanced by reason.

The Christian Revelation

It is the story, in the main, of the social gospel movement. But before telling it, some explanation of the nature of what was involved in it is in order. There is a tension created by the Christian revelation. On this point, all students of the life and teachings of Christ may agree. Believers have ever found themselves and their ways insufficient when held up beside the account of these as found in the Bible. Men are not as they should be. They are, in the traditional language, condemned, lost, tried, found wanting, and convicted. As the Apostle Paul, the foremost interpreter of the meaning of the revelation, said: "For there is no distinction; since all have sinned and fall short of the glory of God." There is, then, a gulf between what men are and what they should be.

Nowhere does this gulf stand out in relief more clearly than in the Sermon on the Mount. Since this message was frequently central in the thought of the preachers of the social gospel, it will be helpful to quote a few passages to demonstrate its character.

> You have heard that it was said, "An eye for an eye and a tooth for a tooth." But I say to you, Do not resist one who is evil. But if any one strikes you on the right cheek, turn to him the other also; and if any one would sue you and take your coat, let him have your cloak as well; and if any one force you to go one mile, go with him two miles. Give to him who begs from you, and do not refuse him who would borrow from you.
>
> You have heard that it was said, "You shall love your neighbor and hate your enemy." But I say to you, Love your enemies and pray for those who persecute you, so that you may be sons of your Father who is in heaven; for he makes his sun rise on the evil and on the good, and sends rain on the just and the unjust. For if you love those who love you, what reward have you? Do not even the tax collectors do the same? And if you salute only your brethren, what more are you doing than others? Do not even the Gentiles do the same? You, therefore, must be perfect, as your heavenly Father is perfect.[1]

---

[1] Matthew 5:38-48, RSV.

There is much more of a similar character, but the above passages may serve as examples. There could hardly be a more vivid contrast between what men ordinarily accept as sufficient for virtuous and just behavior and what is required by Christianity. This gap, nay, this yawning gulf, between what men are and what they should be has produced great tensions in those who would be Christians. Some men have attempted by extraordinary moral heroism to bridge the gulf. In early times, there were hermits who went apart from the world, denied the demands of the flesh, persecuted their own bodies, and in this way attempted to live spiritually at the expense, to some extent, of the physical. Still others went into monasteries and nunneries to escape somewhat the baleful lure of the world and the flesh. Throughout the ages, there have been those who have tried to attain to perfection by way of self-abnegation in one form or another.

Fundamentally, though, Christians have usually agreed that Jesus Christ bridged the gulf between man and God with his Sacrifice, that what is impossible for man can be accomplished, and has been, by the Grace of God. A way was provided for the resolution of the tension, though this is not supposed to have relieved those who are Christians from the acceptance of the norms for behavior revealed in Scriptures and from ordering their lives according to them.

It must be made clear that the norms proclaimed by Jesus are a Revelation. They are not such as men might discover by studying the nature of the universe, the nature of man, and the nature of society. This is no natural morality. Men do not naturally go an extra mile when they have been compelled to go one. Indeed, they naturally resist compulsion in the first place. They do not naturally add their cloaks to the penalty when they have been sued for their coats. It is difficult to imagine anything less natural than to turn the other cheek when one has been struck. Nor is there an order in the universe that automatically and of necessity rewards these norms of behavior. Those who prosper in this world do not always give to beggars and lend to those who would borrow from them. On the contrary, those who prosper have ordinarily managed their affairs much more circumspectly and less generously. It is not economical to run one's affairs according to these norms.

It does not appear that social order could be maintained without resisting evil. All orderly societies, so far as I know, have rested on some rough approximation of justice as consisting of an eye for an eye. This would appear to be the natural mode of dispensing justice. It is not clear how social order could be maintained except in this way. In the nature of things, society cannot dispense justice by awarding freezers to those who have stolen refrigerators. The assault upon property would not only be legalized but rewarded as well. It is so unlikely as to be impossible for anyone to arrive at such norms for behavior by a natural study and the use of human reason. Thus, these norms constitute a Revelation.

Several points need to be made clear about the character of the content of the Revelation. First, there is *no* implied condemnation of natural law, the natural order, or positive law. Jesus made it clear in the Sermon on the Mount (Matthew 5:17) that this was no part of his intention. He said, "Think not that I have come to abolish the law and the prophets; I have come not to abolish them but to fulfil them." Nor in what followed did he condemn the laws as they had been handed down and established. For example, he said (Matthew 5:27-28): "You have heard that it was said, 'You shall not commit adultery.' But I say to you that every one who looks at a woman lustfully has already committed adultery with her in his heart." This was not a call for social reconstruction. There was, in the saying, no claim that the law against adultery was not as it should have been. Certainly, no one could logically interpret the passage to say that it would be all right now to commit adultery. His commandments are *more than*, not *instead of*.

Jesus was revealing the norms in terms of which actions may be virtuous, not in human terms but in God's. There is no virtue, he was saying, in obedience to the law. Any sensible person would do this to avoid the penalties attached to it. (The same would go for natural law or conformity to the order in the universe.) Men do conceive of such actions as virtuous quite often, but this is from their perspective as men and limitations as men.

Second, these commandments can only apply to individuals and voluntary groups. They have to do with actions that are virtuous. They are virtuous because they are not compelled, because there are no earthly or natural sanctions for them, because no earthly rewards nor penalties necessarily attend them, because they are freely done. If these norms were made a part of the order that men or natural law enforce, they would lose their virtuous character. Then even the Gentiles (that is, non-Christians) would usually obey them, for it would be expedient to do so.

Third, these norms are of such character that they cannot effectively be made a part of the order of positive law in society. Attempts to do so can only produce disorder and chaos. To see this, one need only imagine a law requ ꞉ ꞁꞅ that if someone seeks your coat you must give him your cloak also. The penalty for not doing so might appropriately be a fine of 10,000 dollars or ten years in prison, or both. Can there be laws against lustful glances, compelling the turning of the other cheek, requiring that one love his enemies, and so forth? If not, these norms cannot be made a part of the social order.

The Revelation is of another realm than that of natural law, of an order in the universe, or of positive law. It is a revelation of God, of the realm of the spirit, of the arena of love, of that which is unbounded by expediency or the narrow and limited views of men while they sojourn on earth. It does not condemn nor deny the efficacy of the order that is established for men on this earth. It does not bid them erect an order that is in keeping with the Revelation. Instead, it proclaims the norms in terms of which human behavior stands condemned, in terms of which man stands in need of Grace, in terms of which individuals may gauge their acts.

The Social Gospel

The social gospel inverts the Gospel. It turns Divine norms into norms for human society. It turns the condemnation of individuals into a condemnation of the social order and converts the impetus of Christianity into pressure for social reconstruction and revolution. The holy tension between what a man is and what he should be is transformed into a temporal tension between the present society and the one that should exist.

The social gospel movement was, and is, a headlong flight from reality. In the first place, it was a flight in that it used the impetus of religion to buttress the general flight involved in melioristic reform efforts. Secondly, it was a flight from the religious base upon which it rested. To be more specific, it transformed the highest spiritual goals into a quest for material improvement.

The central doctrine of the social gospellers has been that the Kingdom is to come on earth. One of their favorite scriptual quotations has been the one commanding Christians to seek first the Kingdom of Heaven. They pray for and propose to work for the coming of the Kingdom. Yet their efforts have been devoted, in the main, to the amelioration of the material conditions of life. They have favored shorter work weeks, higher pay, a more equal distribution of the wealth, various and sundry governmental programs for the abolition of poverty, and so forth. Indeed, they maintain that by ameliorating the conditions of life—by social regeneration—they will provide the foundations for the spiritualization of life. A paraphrase of their rendition of the scriptural injunction should read something like this: Seek ye first material well-being and the Kingdom of Heaven will be added unto you.

In the third place, theirs is a flight from the higher morality upon which their admonitions are based. Their call for social reconstruction is in considerable part a call for the use of governmental power to produce their ends. Insofar as they succeeded, they would remove the moral character from the acts that they approve. They would make it compulsory to do what otherwise might be done willingly. If it is a requirement of law that the cloak be given as well, no virtue would attach to the giving of the cloak. Even the "Gentiles" would do it, for it would be expedient to do so.

Moreover, the reconstruction of society in terms of the Revelation, if it could be done, would remove the opportunity for performing moral acts. Only those who have property may give generously of it; only those who have money may lend it to all would-be borrowers; only those who have choice as to the disposal of their time and energies may go the second mile. The social planning, the assault upon property, the confiscation of savings involved in the social reconstruction advocated by the social gospellers would remove the opportunity for acts of charity. Indeed, if "social justice," as many of them have defined it, prevailed, there would be no occasion for charity. More succinctly, there would be no morality. Life would be reduced to expedient calculations in terms of rewards and punishments established by positive law.

Fourthly, they have been using the religious motif to advance the politicalizing of all life. It is not necessary to imagine the consequences, in this case. They are already occurring. Religion is being driven out of public affairs, by court decision, even as the power of government is being used to achieve ends which are proclaimed as religious and moral. To see this, one need only recall the school prayer decisions and the integration decisions of the courts. However illogical this may appear, to those who do not wear ideological blinders, it follows logically from the use of governmental power to achieve supposedly spiritual ends. When this is done, the political modes are advanced at the expense of religious ones, and independent religion cannot survive the politicalizing of life. Compulsion can only be advanced at the expense of independence, and religious activities cannot be exempted from this rule.

How, then, could so many ministers and religious leaders have been drawn into the social gospel movement? How could so many church organizations have been drawn into the effort? How could so many churchgoers have come to believe that it is the business of the church to support and advance governmental ameliorative programs? In a general way, these questions have already been answered in earlier articles. The breakdown of philosophy, the spread of irrationalism, the loss of a firm grip upon physical and metaphysical reality, the development of utopian notions, the vision of man's being able to create conditions to his liking set the stage for the flight in religion.

One point needs to be made emphatically: The social gospel never has been an intellectually respectable doctrine, any more than has the generality of meliorist and revolutionary ideas. Its proponents did not proceed by a careful analysis of Scriptures. They were under the sway of a philosophical monism which bent them toward the confusion of all things. The spiritual and the material, the moral and the legal, the eternal and the temporal were fused in such a way as to obliterate all necessary distinctions.[2] Their theology has always been vague, their grasp of economics exceedingly insecure, and their understanding of politics virtually nonexistent.

The Preachers

The social gospel movement got underway in the latter part of the nineteenth century. The big names in its development were Washington Gladden, Richard T. Ely, W. D. P. Bliss, George D. Herron, and Walter Rauschenbusch. These shared with and drew from the ideas of such men as Henry George, Edward Bellamy, and Henry Demarest Lloyd, who are not so closely identified with the movement in religion. But there were many others who participated in and contributed to this development in the latter part of the nineteenth century. In the preface to what has become the standard work on the movement, the author points out that "many have assumed that social Christianity was the accomplishment of a handful of clergymen who at the opening of the twentieth century challenged religious conservatism by the proclamation of the social content of their faith. Study of an extensive and varied literature indicates,

---

[2] See, for example, the discussion of this in James Dombrowski, *The Early Days of Christian Socialism in America* (New York: Columbia University Press, 1936), pp. 14-15.

however, not only that the social gospel originated in the early years of the gilded age but also that its prophets were legion and their message an integral part of the broad sweep of social and humanitarian efforts. . . ."[3] The spreaders of the social gospel were not careful thinkers. Generally, they had picked up a variety of socialist, progressivist, and meliorist assumptions, accepting them as valid without subjecting them to analysis or test against Scripture or economic and political reality.

To challenge the philosophical soundness of the social gospel is not to question the sincerity of its preachers. There is no reason to doubt that many of them were passionately devoted to their cause, that they were absolutely convinced of the rightness of what they said, and that they meant well quite often. They saw suffering and hardship and believed that those who attributed it to an unjust order were correct. They saw or read of hunger and disease and thought that this was related to institutional arrangements. There was poverty in the midst of a land in which some had great wealth. They assumed that the remedy for this lay in some sort of redistribution. Their concern for others made them particularly susceptible to utopian visions and socialist dreams.

The social gospellers captured the hearts of men by their descriptions of suffering and hardship. Washington Gladden accepted Henry George's thesis that poverty was increasing as industrial progress took place. Note his characterization of conditions among those in deep poverty:

> . . . Below these still, there is another large class of the really poor, of those whose earnings are small, whose

---

[3] Charles H. Hopkins, *The Rise of the Social Gospel in American Protestantism,* 1865-1915 (New Haven: Yale University Press, 1940), p. vi.

life is comfortless, who have nothing laid by, who are often coming to want. . . . This class of the very poor—those who are just on the borders of pauperism or fairly over the borders—is rapidly growing. Wealth is increasing very fast; poverty, even pauperism, is increasing still more rapidly.[4]

Walter Rauschenbusch introduced the element of pathos in his descriptions:

The fear of losing his job is the workman's chief incentive to work. Our entire industrial life, for employer and employee, is a reign of fear. The average workingman's family is only a few weeks removed from destitution. The dread of want is always over them, and that is worse than brief times of actual want. . . .

While a workman is in his prime, he is always in danger of losing his job. When he gets older, he is almost certain to lose it. The pace is so rapid that only supple limbs can keep up. Once out of a job, it is hard for an elderly man to get another. Men shave clean to conceal gray hairs.[5]

Not only were conditions bad, according to social gospellers, but they were getting worse. A somber tone of impending crisis characterizes much of their writings. Gladden declared:

Such, then, is the state of industrial society at the present time. The hundreds of thousands of unemployed laborers, vainly asking for work; the rapid increase of pauperism . . . ; the sudden and alarming growth of the more violent types of socialism, are ominous signs of the times.[6]

---

[4] Washington Gladden, *Applied Christianity* (Boston: Houghton Mifflin, 1886), pp. 10-11.

[5] Walter Rauschenbusch, *Christianity and the Social Crisis* (New York: Macmillan, 1907), pp. 235-36.

[6] Gladden, *op. cit.*, p. 161.

Rauschenbusch pointed out that while there had been hardship involved in the development of industry in America, this was mitigated somewhat by the availability of cheap land (the frontier thesis), but this was now a thing of the past and trouble lay ahead. He put it this way:

> But there is nothing in the nature of our country that will permanently exempt us from the social misery created by the industrial revolution elsewhere. . . . The influences which formerly protected us and gave us a certain immunity from social misery are losing their force. We are now running the rapids faster than any other nation. We do everything more strenuously and recklessly than others. . . . If we are once headed toward a social catastrophe, we shall get there ahead of scheduled time.[7]

The preachers of the social gospel attributed the cause of suffering and hardship to the existing order. The crisis was approaching because of the hardening of the lines of the order. The existing social order was so made up and bent by those who benefited from it that it would bring America to revolution and destruction if something were not done about it. While Gladden was more moderate in his indictment of the established order than later advocates of the social gospel were to be, he did believe that the system led to the difficulties. Though he disavowed the complete socialist prescription, he thought they were right when they pointed to certain tendencies and ascribed them to the system:

> The tendency of wages to sink to starvation point, the tendency of the workmen's share of the national wealth to grow constantly smaller, the tendency of commercial crises and depressions to become more frequent and disastrous . . .—all these are, as I believe, the natural

---

[7] Rauschenbusch, *op. cit.*, p. 219.

issues of an industrial system whose sole motive power is self-interest, and whose sole regulative principle is competition.[8]

George D. Herron was less restrained but saying essentially the same thing in his indictment:

> The inevitable result of the system of wages and competition will be to increase social inequalities; to increase the wealth of the few and the poverty of many. . . . The present industrial system could not exist were it not for the fact that great multitudes of the unemployed have been brought to this country systematically and purposely, for the sake of reducing wages and producing a state of poverty.[9]

As Herron said elsewhere, "The economic system denies the right of the sincerest and most sympathetic to keep their hands out of the blood of their brothers."[10]

Rauschenbusch's indictment was no less severe:

> If it were proposed to invent some social system in which covetousness would be deliberately fostered and intensified in human nature, what system could be devised which would excel our own for this purpose? Competitive commerce exalts selfishness to the dignity of a moral principle. It pits men against one another in a gladiatorial game in which there is no mercy and in which ninety per cent of the combatants finally strew the arena.[11]

The villain of the piece, depending upon the inner urge of the moment, was capitalism, private property (they dif-

---

[8] Gladden, *op. cit.*, pp. 69-70.

[9] Quoted in Dombrowski, *op. cit.*, pp. 187-88.

[10] George D. Herron, *Between Caesar and Jesus* (New York: Crowell, 1899), pp. 24-25.

[11] Rauschenbusch, *op. cit.*, p. 265.

fered as to the extent of the condemnation of this), the profit motive, competition, monopoly, and all of the assorted demons of socialist analysis. The anticapitalistic mentality, as Ludwig von Mises has called it, flowered luxuriantly among the social gospellers. It is difficult to recognize the businessman in the following allusions, or illusions, of Edward A. Ross, a sociologist with a religious emphasis:

> Today the sacrifice of life incidental to quick success rarely calls for the actual spilling of blood. How decent are the pale slayings of the quack, the adulterer, and the purveyor of polluted water, compared with the red slayings of the vulgar bandit or assassin! Even if there is blood-letting, the long range, tentacular nature of modern homicide eliminates all personal collision. What an abyss between the knife-play of brawlers and the law-defying neglect to fence dangerous machinery in a mill, or to furnish cars with safety couplers![12]

Yet the difference between businessmen and common criminals, we gather, is in the magnitude of the offense of the former.

One other indictment of capitalists will serve to illustrate the character of these generally. Rauschenbusch said:

> When men of vigorous character and intellectual ability obey the laws of Capitalism, and strive for the prizes it holds out to them, they win power and great wealth, but they are placed in an essentially false relation to their fellow-men, the Christian virtues of their family stock are undermined, their natural powers of leadership are crippled, and the greater their success in amassing wealth under capitalistic methods, the greater

---

[12] Ray A. Billington, *et al.*, eds., *The Making of American Democracy, II* (New York: Holt, Rinehart and Winston, 1962, rev. ed.), 35-36.

is the tragedy of their lives from a Christian point of view.[13]

The "New Theology"

The condemnation and rejection of the existing order was, of course, prelude to the calling for a new order. Advocates of the social gospel were all bent upon social reconstruction, in one degree or another. Some were avowed socialists, some unavowed, and others were to appearances less radical in their aims. But they appealed to Christianity as the justification for making over or modifying the social order. The theory was not particularly complicated. Most of the early proponents of the social gospel held that society is an organism. Individual men are products, more or less, of the environment. In order to save men, then, it is necessary to redeem the society by reconstructing it along Christian lines. When this work of reconstruction had been accomplished, the Kingdom would have come. Those who were engaged in the task of rebuilding society were working for the coming of the Kingdom. Existing society was criticized from the scriptural vantage point of strictures such as those found in the Sermon on the Mount. The new order would incorporate these into the social structure.

There should be no doubt that this bringing of the Kingdom, as they understood it, involved radical social reconstruction for the preachers of the social gospel. Walter Rauschenbusch has usually been accorded the position of theologian of the social gospel. In his book, *A Theology for the Social Gospel*, he declared:

Since love is the supreme law of Christ, the Kingdom of God implies a progressive reign of love in human af-

---

[13] Walter Rauschenbusch, *Christianizing the Social Order* (New York: Macmillan, 1912), p. 315.

fairs. We can see its advance wherever the free will of love supersedes the use of force and legal coercion as a regulative of the social order. This involves the redemption of society from political autocracies and economic oligarchies; the substitution of redemptive for vindictive penology; the abolition of constraint through hunger as part of the industrial system. . . . The highest expression of love is the free surrender of what is truly our own, life, property, and rights. A much lower but perhaps more decisive expression of love is the surrender of any opportunity to exploit men. No social group or organization can claim to be clearly within the Kingdom of God which drains others for its own ease, and resists the effort to abate this fundamental evil. This involves the redemption of society from private property in the natural resources of the earth. . . .[14]

The above passage gives the flavor of the bombast, but the tangle of gratuitous assumptions and accusations may obscure the message. He has stated the aim somewhat more succinctly elsewhere. The vision which he would see fulfilled has "the purpose and hope of founding on earth the Reign of God among men. Faith in the Kingdom of God commits us, not to an attitude of patient resignation, not to a policy of tinkering and palliatives, but to a revolutionary mission, constructive in purpose but fearless in spirit, and lasting till organized wrong has ceased."[15]

Reign of love there might be, according to the vision, but it was to be preceded by a reign of men. The advocates of the social gospel were also advocates of greatly increased governmental activity. Even Washington Gladden, who expressed some doubts as to the coercive route to moral redemption, favored an extended and extensive role for government. He observed:

---

[14] Quoted in Gerald N. Grob and Robert N. Beck, eds., *American Ideas*, II (New York: Free Press of Glencoe, 1963), 217.

[15] Rauschenbusch, *Christianizing the Social Order*, p. 324.

> The limits of governmental interference are likely to be greatly enlarged in the immediate future. . . . It may become the duty of the state to reform its taxation, so that its burdens shall rest less heavily upon the lower classes; to repress monopolies of all sorts; to prevent and punish gambling; to regulate or control the railroads and telegraphs; to limit the ownership of land; to modify the laws of inheritance; and possibly to levy a progressive income tax. . . .[16]

Those who came somewhat later, however, had no qualms about using the power of the state to usher in the Kingdom.[17] Richard T. Ely declared that it is "as truly a religious work to pass good laws, as it is to preach sermons; as holy a work to lead a crusade against filth, vice, and disease in slums of cities, and to seek the abolition of the disgraceful tenement-houses of American cities, as it is to send missionaries to the heathen."[18] He approved of what he called coercive philanthropy. "Coercive philanthropy is philanthropy of governments, either local, state, or national. The exercise of philanthropy is coming to an increasing extent to be regarded as the duty of government."[19] George D. Herron called for the thoroughgoing use of the state for religious purposes.

> Government has a right to existence and authority for no other end than that for which God sent his only begotten Son into the world. It is the vocation of the

---

[16] Gladden, *op. cit.*, pp. 100-01.

[17] Several decades later, Reinhold Niebuhr argued that collectives may act immorally to attain "social justice," since they are by nature immoral. See *Moral Man and Immoral Society* (New York: Scribner's, 1932), *passim.*

[18] Richard T. Ely, *Social Aspects of Christianity* (New York: Crowell, 1889), p. 73.

[19] *Ibid.*, p. 92.

states, as the social organ, to so control property, so administer the production and distribution of economic goods, as to give to every man the fruit of his labor, and protect the laborer from the irresponsible tyranny of the passion of wealth.[20]

Rauschenbusch declared that "embodying a moral conviction in law is the last stage of moral propaganda. Laws do not create moral convictions; they merely recognize and enforce them."[21] In practice, of course, devotees of the social gospel have usually supported the whole panorama of reform programs.

However strange these doctrines may seem, there is good reason for exploring them. They have had a tremendous impact upon America. In the course of time they began to be taken up and spread by churches and organizations within them. In the latter part of the nineteenth century, the social gospel movement was restricted to a relatively small number of ministers, sympathetic reformers, founders of small magazines, and radical organizations. But by 1912 Walter Rauschenbusch could rejoice that the social gospel was catching on.[22] There were many signs of this. As early as 1887 the Episcopalians set up a Church Association for the Advancement of the Interests of Labor. In 1901 the Congregationalists provided for a labor committee. The Presbyterian Church established a department of church and labor in 1903. In 1908 the Methodist Episcopal Church came out for organized labor.[23] The Federal Council of the Churches of Christ in America, organized in

---

[20] Quoted in Howard H. Quint, *et al.,* eds., *Main Problems in American History,* II (Homewood, Illinois: Dorsey, 1964), 67.

[21] Rauschenbusch, *Christianity and the Social Crisis,* p. 363.

[22] Rauschenbusch, *Christianizing the Social Order,* ch. II.

[23] See Harold U. Faulkner, *The Quest for Social Justice,* 1898-1914 (New York: Macmillan, 1931), pp. 219-22.

1908, adopted a reformist creed from the beginning. Among the things for which it stood were:

> For equal rights and complete justice for all men in all stations of life. . . .
> For a living wage as a minimum in every industry, and for the highest wage that each industry can afford.
> For the most equitable division of the products of industry that can ultimately be devised. . . .
> For the abatement of poverty.[24]

Many changes were being wrought under the religious impetus. Rauschenbusch pointed out that the "Young Men's Christian Association used to stand for religious individualism. The mere mention of 'sociology' once excited ridicule. Today the association has developed a splendid machinery for constructive social service. . . ."[25] The missionary effort was being changed by the new ideas. The emphasis was beginning to shift toward social service, medical missionaries, and so forth. In due time, more and more ministers came under the sway of the social gospel, and church organizations began to wield their influence both for general and for particular social reforms.

Of course, as these ideas were adopted by the old established churches, they were usually given more ambiguous wording and less radical formulation. After all, many of the founders and advocates of the social gospel were socialists. George D. Herron was dedicated to what has been called Christian socialism. Anyone conversant with socialist doctrines will be able to discover them in more or less pure form in Rauschenbusch's work. There is a definite gradualist slant to the writings of Gladden. The "re-

---

[24] Quoted in Rauschenbusch, *Christianizing the Social Order*, pp. 14-15.
[25] *Ibid.*, pp. 17-18.

spectable" churches did not accept such doctrines in the blunter formulations of them. Yet to the extent, and it has been considerable, that the churches, their ministers and spokesmen, have adopted these doctrines and advocated the programs based on them, to that extent have they been drawn into the effort to bring about socialism in America. For these doctrines depend for their justification upon the rhetoric of socialism; they are meaningful within the intellectual framework of socialist doctrines; the particular programs have long been devices for gradually moving toward socialism.

Men's hearts have been captured by the inversion of the Gospel, and they have been drawn into the orbit of reformism by doctrines ideologically derived from socialism but phrased in the language of religious concern. This was another step in the domestication of socialism in America.

15

Remaking the Minds of Men

In the third place, the administrator . . . will realize that public education is essentially education of the public: directly, through teachers and students in the school; indirectly, through communicating to others his own ideals and standards, inspiring others with the enthusiasm of himself and his staff for the function of intelligence and character in the transformation of society. —JOHN DEWEY, 1937

A new public mind is to be created. How? Only by creating tens of millions of new individual minds and welding them into a new social mind. Old stereotypes must be broken up and new "climates of opinion" formed in the neighborhoods of America. But that is the task of the building of a science of society for the schools. —HAROLD RUGG, 1933

. . . The young should receive careful training in mutual undertakings, in organizational work, and in social planning so that they may form the desired habits and dispositions.
                                        —GEORGE S. COUNTS, 1952

NOTHING IS SO UNLIKELY AS THAT THE ESTABLISHED institutions in a society should be used to transform and reconstruct society. After all, the institutions derive their reason for being and support from the existing order, if they are not anachronisms. They exist to perpetuate and serve that order. In a word, they are conservative. Certainly, this has almost always been true of such fundamental institutions as the home, the church, and the school. The home has traditionally been the place where the

275

child has been civilized, has been taught rudimentary manners, has been taught how to get along with others, has been nurtured and trained in manners and morality. This training derives largely from the experience of the parents, what they have been taught, and what understanding they have of the world in which they live. The school has been the place for the teaching of the accumulated knowledge from the past, and the church has been the rock which served to anchor man in the enduring as he tended to adapt himself to the winds of change. These are conservative functions, for by them the experience, heritage, knowledge, and Revelation are passed from one generation to another.

Yet, in this century, a concerted attempt has been made to undermine and/or direct these institutions to the ends of social reconstruction. Religion, as has been shown, was drawn into the stream of social reform by the social gospel. Parents have yielded much of their responsibility for the upbringing of their children to various social agencies, notably the schools. And, whether they have or not, the authority which they formerly wielded has been restricted by new doctrines on child rearing, by the assaults upon custom and tradition, by the loss of confidence in the wisdom embedded in the heritage, and by the wedge that has been driven between the old and the young by the "peer group" orientation and conformity. The parents most affected by these changes probably fall into two categories (with some overlapping): the "best educated"—that is, those who have spent the most years in school—and those who are glad enough to avail themselves of the irresponsibility that is involved.

That some people should revel in their irresponsibility requires no explanation—though why they should be encouraged to do so does. But that those who should be best educated are inept in appropriating and using their heritage is a matter warranting careful consideration. This consideration brings us to the subject of this chapter: the undermining of education, the transformation of the schools, and the instrumentation of education for melioristic reform.

There are few possibilities more remote than that the schools should be made into instruments of reform. It required great ingenuity and imagination to bring it off—a concerted effort over an extended period of time by men dedicated to the task. The reason for such difficulties is not far to seek. Schools have for their task the education of children. Education has, at least historically, been concerned with conveying knowledge; or, at any rate, it has been associated with the acquisition of knowledge. Such knowledge consists of the skills, methods, and information which has been learned in times past. To put it another way, knowledge is of what is and what has been. There is no knowledge, in particulars, of what will be in the future, though much may be deduced from a knowledge of the universe and what has happened as to what can and cannot be in the future, but even this is only knowledge of what is and has happened.

But the educational reformers proposed to use schooling as preparation for building a different society for the future. That is, they were futuristic, oriented to what would be rather than to what was and had happened. In short, they proposed to use the schools as breeding grounds for social change rather than for education. Theirs was, and is, a flight from the reality of knowledge upon which education is supposedly based. Insofar as such education is focused upon the future, it is usually an uninhibited exercise of the imagination. Insofar as it is an attempt to implant some ideological version of what the future should be like, it is nothing but propaganda. Insofar as it is concerned with rooting out traditional ideas and beliefs, it is brainwashing. Insofar as schooling has been turned from imbuing with knowledge to social reconstruction, it has been turned from a solid task to sentimental hopes and vague visions of the future. (But, it may be objected, education is to prepare one for living in the future. So it is. It is *for* the future [or the extended present], but it is *of* the past and what now is. If there is aught of value to be learned, in school or elsewhere, it has to be of the past and what is.)

There is general agreement that education has been transformed in America in the twentieth century. Those who have described it, however, have focused upon different things. Some have emphasized the great increase in numbers in the schools and the larger proportion of the young who have stayed in school much longer. Indeed, it is a cliché of the educationists that this accounts mainly for the changes in content and method. It is alleged that education was formerly aristocratic in emphasis and that in the twentieth century it was adjusted to the generality of the young. Some emphasize the impact of new developments in education and the attempts to make it scientific. Others focus upon leaders, movements, and associations.

This account will focus upon three major developments in education: (1) the undermining of education, (2) the reorientation of schooling and its instrumentation to social reform, and (3) the centralizing of control over education. Attention will be centered on the educational reformers, their aims and accomplishments. It should be clear that this results in only a partial account of what has happened in education. The reformers have quite often been thwarted in their aims by determined classroom teachers, by resisting administrators, and by the tendency of people to continue established methods. Still, the reformers have succeeded, much more than they have been inclined to admit, in transforming the schools.

Progressive Education

The main impetus to educational reform and the central tendency of it came from the Progressive Education movement. The chief proponent, and later patron saint, of Progressive Education was John Dewey. As early as 1897 he declared that "education is the fundamental method of social progress and reform."[1] In *The School and Society* (1899), "the school is cast as a lever of social change . . ., educational theory . . . becomes political theory, and the educator is inevitably cast into the struggle for social reform."[2] He was to follow this with many articles and books on education, and the theme of reform is always there, either in the forefront or as assumption. As has been pointed out before, Dewey was a central figure for reform in general. He had come under the influence of a new conception of reality and was an indefatigable worker in trying to bring this world into conformity with it. Dewey would, and did, put the matter otherwise: he had perceived the underlying direction that things were taking and used his energies to try to persuade men to make the appropriate adjustments and changes so that they might stay in the stream of history. He was a monist, a meliorist, an antitraditionalist, a social analyst, an environmentalist (modified), an equalitarian, a democratist, a historicist—in short, a Progressive.

Dewey was under the sway of a new conception of reali-

---

[1] Quoted in Lawrence A. Cremin, *The Transformation of the School* (New York: Alfred A. Knopf, 1961), p. 100.

[2] *Ibid.,* p. 118.

ty. What was real to him was change, society, and psyche.
His ideas stem from William James, from G. W. F. Hegel,
from Charles Darwin, from Lester Frank Ward, and from
the gradualist revision of Marxism. His conception of
change had the mystical overtones conferred upon it by
Hegelianism, Darwinism, and the reform Darwinists. It
was something produced by such "forces" as industrialization; it was not to be denied, but it could be controlled
and directed by human ingenuity. What was important to
him was society. It was the firm reality in terms of which
one acted, wrought changes, and made improvements. He
wrote much about the individual, about individual freedom,
about the individual child, but the reality within which the
individual moved and had his being was always society.
The psyche was both the obstacle to reform and the means
by which reform was to be brought about.

Dewey was not so much an innovator as a prodigiously
productive amplifier. He was in a stream of American reformers—Henry George, Edward Bellamy, Lester Frank
Ward, Henry Demarest Lloyd, and so forth—which goes
back into the nineteenth century, and which broadened
and became more numerous in the twentieth. Moreover,
many of these conceived of this social function for education. To Lester Frank Ward, according to one historian,
"education was the 'great panacea'—for political as for all
other evils."[3] Albion Small, a disciple of Ward, declared
in the 1890's, "Sociology knows no means for the amelioration or reform of society more radical than those of which
teachers hold the leverage. . . . The teacher who realizes
his social function will not be satisfied with passing children to the next grade. He will read his success only in the

---

[3] Henry S. Commager, *The American Mind* (New Haven:
Yale University Press, 1950), p. 214.

record of men and women who go from the school . . . zealous to do their part in making a better future."[4] In 1911, Charles A. Ellwood wrote that the schools should be used as "the conscious instrument of social reconstruction."[5] A few years later, Ernest R. Groves proclaimed that "society can largely determine individual characteristics, and for its future well-being it needs more and more to demand that the public schools contribute significantly and not incidentally to its pressing needs by a social use of the influence that the schools have over the individual in his sensitive period of immaturity."[6]

Dewey was by no means alone, even at the beginning, but he was a central figure. He went to Columbia University to profess philosophy in 1904, and taught there until his retirement in 1930. Teachers College at Columbia University became the center from which so many of the doctrines of Progressive Education were spread to the rest of the country. Many of the most influential of its spokesmen held forth there: William H. Kilpatrick, Harold Rugg, George S. Counts, and others.[7] One historian, though eager to disclaim any untoward implications, points up the influence of William H. Kilpatrick, a student and disciple of Dewey:

> In all, he taught some 35,000 students from every state in the Union at a time when Teachers College was training a substantial percentage of the articulate leaders of American education. Any competent teacher occupying the senior chair of philosophy of education at

---

[4] Quoted in Cremin, *op. cit.,* p. 99.

[5] Quoted in Edward A. Krug, *The Shaping of the American High School* (New York: Harper & Row, 1964), p. 254.

[6] *Ibid.,* p. 254.

[7] See Augustin G. Rudd, *Bending the Twig* (Chicago: Heritage Foundation, 1957), pp. 235-37.

the College between 1918 and 1938 would have exerted a prodigious influence on educational theory and practice. In the hands of the dedicated, compelling Kilpatrick, the chair became an extraordinary strategic rostrum for the dissemination of a particular version of progressive education. . . .[8]

Others spread the word from rostrums in other universities: Boyd Henry Bode at Ohio State University, Theodore Brameld at the University of Minnesota, and many lesser known names in hundreds of departments and schools of education in American colleges and universities.

Undermining Education

Before the New Education, or New Schooling as it should be called, could be installed, however, the old education had to be discredited and displaced. The discrediting of the old has gone on for many years and at many levels. The deepest level of attack was the philosophical, and at this level it was an attack upon the possibility of knowledge. Throughout a long career John Dewey carried on a running attack upon absolutes—that is, upon all claims to truth, to established knowledge, to any fixity in the universe. Dewey was a relativist, as have most of the Progressives been. The following are examples of Dewey's own avowal of relativity:

> Reference to place and time in what has just been said should make it clear that this view of the office of philosophy has no commerce with the notion that the problems of philosophy are "eternal." On the contrary, it holds that such a view is obstructive. . . .
> This movement is charged with promotion of "relativism" in a sense in which the latter is identified with lack of standards. . . . It is true that the movement in

---

[8] Cremin, *op. cit.*, p. 220.

question holds since the problems and issues of philosophy are not eternal they should link up with urgencies that impose themselves at times and in places.[9]

Dewey was, of course, a master of answering criticism by misconstruing the objections to his philosophy. Surely no one was taking him to task for dealing with contemporary issues, or denying that what interests men may change from time to time. The question was rather of whether or not there are enduring principles and laws in terms of which questions may be settled. Dewey did not believe that there are. He affirmed his relativism in what was for him a rare lack of ambiguity, in the following words:

> In the second place, liberalism is committed to the idea of historic relativity. It knows that the content of the individual and freedom change with time; that this is as true of social change as it is of individual development from infancy to maturity. The positive counterpart of opposition to doctrinal absolutism is experimentalism. The connection between historic relativity and experimental method is intrinsic. Time signifies change. The significance of individuality with respect to social policies alters with change of the conditions in which individuals live.[10]

In short, everything is continually changing.

Other Progressives attacked the belief in established truth and proclaimed their relativism. Note the disdain which William H. Kilpatrick had for those who believe in truth:

> When people have interests they wish to hold undisturbed, they fall naturally into this older Platonic logic and, as if they had some private access to absolute truth

---

[9] John Dewey, *Problems of Men* (New York: Philosophical Library, 1946), p. 12.

[10] *Ibid.*, pp. 136-37.

which establishes beyond question the positions they wish to uphold, call all new ideas . . . *subvertive* and *pervertive*. These people in their hearts reject freedom of speech and freedom of study because they themselves already have "the truth" and these freedoms might if followed "subvert" their "truth."[11]

Boyd Henry Bode asks us

. . . to consider the nature of an educational system which centers on the cultivation of intelligence, rather than submission to authority. Such a system recognizes no absolute or final truths, since these always represent authority in one form or another, and since they impose arbitrary limits on social progress and the continuous enrichment of experience.[12]

The relativism of the Progressives is a crucial point for their educational theories. If there is no truth, it is appropriate to inquire what education is about. Why should children be sent to school? Why should there be a huge educational establishment? The Progressives had answers to these questions which satisfied them, but their answers will be told at the proper place below. The point here is that the relativistic position served as the point of departure for the undermining of traditional education. If there is no truth, the teacher who lectures to his class is indoctrinating or propagandizing them. If nothing is established, the giving and grading of examinations is a spurious undertaking. If there is nothing enduring, the teaching of subject matter is surely a waste of time.

The assault upon education was not usually carried on in so blunt a fashion; had it been, it is doubtful that it

---

[11] William H. Kilpatrick, ed., *The Teacher and Society* (New York: D. Appleton-Century, 1937), p. 36.

[12] Joe Park, *Selected Readings in the Philosophy of Education* (New York: Macmillan, 1963), p. 153.

would have been as successful as it was. It was conducted on a more piecemeal basis, until many of the traditional courses and methods had been discredited. The traditional schools were charged with being aristocratic, with perpetuating inequalities and being unsuited to the generality. Educational reformers parodied the idea of mental discipline and held their distortion of it up to scorn. Many of the subjects were virtually useless, they claimed; for example, Latin, higher mathematics, and various other "cultural" courses. (At the beginning of the twentieth century, "culture" did not have its present high standing among "democrats.") Drilling in facts was deplored, along with emphasis upon content itself. The teacher who exercised authority was castigated as an autocrat. In short, they tended to undermine the authority of the teacher, discredit the courses of study, deplore the imparting of information, and assail disciplinary techniques.[13]

The traditional was disparaged and conservatives denounced by Progressives. For example, Dewey declared that the "traditional scheme is, in essence, one of imposition from above and from outside. It imposes adult standards, subject-matter, and methods upon those who are only growing slowly toward maturity.[14] Kilpatrick claimed that there were many conditions hampering the schools from performing their social function. "Most obvious among such hindering conditions stands the common tradition . . . that the work of the school is properly limited to a few simple and formal school subjects, the assigning of lessons in these, and hearing the pupils recite what had been assigned."

---

[13] For examples of such criticisms, see Krug, *op. cit.*, pp. 278-82.

[14] Park, *op. cit.*, p. 135.

In short, "the traditional school was thus a place where lessons were assigned and recited. . . . To each question asked there was always one and only one right answer. Subject-matter was, on this theory, the kind of thing that could be assigned and then required under penalty. If the assignment were not recited precisely as required, the pupil could be held responsible. . . ."[15] Dewey called for the "modification of traditional ideals of culture, traditional subjects of study and traditional methods of teaching and discipline. . . ."[16]

Dewey spoke favorably of reason and intelligence, but the traditional modes for training and sharpening these were largely displaced from the schools. One historian points out that the academies, and presumably many of the other types of high schools as well, used to teach, among other things, political economy, ethics, moral philosophy, mental philosophy, mental science, and logic.[17] Undoubtedly, there was much that was open to criticism in the older education, as there is with all human undertakings. But Bernard Iddings Bell makes some informative points about it. "Latin and Greek did teach language *qua* language. There was almost no instruction in English, but young people who learned how to use other languages found themselves surprisingly proficient in the use of their own." Moreover, "the use of symbols and graphs in algebra and geometry and trigonometry and the insistence upon the supremacy of logic in mathematics did make for sound abstract thinking."

He concludes that those "who advocate the new sub-

---

[15] Kilpatrick, *op. cit.,* pp. 26-27.

[16] John Dewey, *Democracy and Education* (New York: Macmillan, 1916), p. 114.

[17] Krug, *op. cit.,* p. 4.

jects seem to suppose that their critics are vexed merely because they are no longer willing to teach the ancient languages or some other particular course sanctioned by tradition. This is not the real source of criticism. The point is that the older schools taught *their students to think* and that the newer schools mostly do not."[18] My larger point, which the above tends to bear out, is that the advocates of Progressive Education were undermining education itself.

This will become clearer by examining what they proposed to substitute for the older education. It should be clear that the Progressives did not believe that there was any body of knowledge to be purveyed in the schools. There was no enduring reality, on their view, to which such a body of knowledge could refer. Nor were they overly enthusiastic about skills and methods, for these, too, would change with changing conditions. Two things might be worthy of study, in the manner in which learning has been conceived traditionally: contemporary conditions and the historical forces and trends at work.

Conditioning the Child for Social Reconstruction

There was a two-fold purpose of education: (1) training the child to adjust to changing conditions, and (2) developing in the student a favorable attitude toward and ways of thought suited to continuous social reconstruction. These two purposes were not separate; rather, they were intertwined. Taken together, virtually all of the recommendations and programs of Progressive Education can be subsumed under them. The programs that are a part of the adjustment motif also fit into a larger pattern.

Education should be child centered, not subject matter

---

[18] Bernard I. Bell, *Crisis in Education* (New York: Whittlesey House, 1949), pp. 48-49.

centered, they said. They were able to evoke with this slogan a great deal of sentimentality which people have come to lavish upon children. Moreover, the rationale for child-centeredness in education had a rather long, if not respected, historical background. It went back to Rousseau, to Froebel, to Pestalozzi, and came down through E. L. Thorndike and John Dewey. Fundamentally, it held that children are naturally good, that each of them has his own little personality which unfolds as he grows up (maturation was the scientistic term applied to this), that if he is allowed to develop freely and spontaneously the natural (and good) product will emerge, and that the teacher should be a kind of midwife in the process. These doctrines, like most others, can probably be traced back to Plato.

Dewey and his disciples subsumed the residues of these ideas into their ideology and turned them to the purpose of socializing the child. Child-centered schooling, in this framework, takes the authority away from the teacher for imposing an order upon the experience and from teaching certain things. It vests the determination of this in the children. Many methods were devised for doing this: the discussion method in class, in which each child "expresses" himself; the curving of grades, which places the "standard" in the class rather than with the teacher; social promotion, by which a child is kept with those of his same age regardless of achievement.

The Progressives talked much about the individual child, and many have supposed that this was the central concern. Some may have supposed this was the aim, and adopted it as their own, but the child-centered method does not individualize; it socializes. The facts are these: a child is not a fully developed individual; usually, he does not know what he wants; he has only a very limited number of ideas to express; his will is undisciplined; he does not know what to do in most circumstances. In short, he turns to those around him for guidance and for standards. If the teacher, or an adult, does not direct him, he turns, perhaps gladly and sometimes initially, to the other children. John Dewey knew this. He said:

> The conclusion is that in what are called the new schools, the primary source of social control resides in the very nature of the work done as a social enterprise in which all individuals have an opportunity to contribute and to which all feel a responsibility. Most children are naturally "sociable." A genuine community life has its ground in this natural sociability.[19]

What Dewey was saying was that the new schools would bring the child under the social control of the group because of the natural "sociability" of children. The teacher need not be excluded entirely from the process, of course. As Dewey said:

> . . . When pupils were a class rather than a social group, the teacher necessarily acted largely from the outside, not as a director of processes of exchange in which all had a share. When education is based upon experience and educative experience is seen to be a social process, the situation changes radically. The teacher loses the position of external boss or dictator but takes on that of leader of group activities.[20]

A cheerleader, one supposes, by which the uninformed utterances of children are encouraged and rewarded!

The process would be one, ineluctably, of adjustment of the child to the group. More broadly, however, the group would be adjusting to the contemporary situation, or, at

---

[19] Park, *op. cit.*, p. 143.
[20] *Ibid.*, p. 144.

any rate, shifting to every wind that blew. Children, so un-
taught, would have nothing upon which to base their
actions but what other children did; all would likely follow
the line of least resistance by yielding to whatever pressure was exerted upon them from whatever quarter. They
would know nothing but the momentary, would see no farther than the end of their collective nose, would be, in a
word, conformers and adjusters.

This would fit them for the larger, and ultimate, purpose of Progressive Education—social reconstruction. Children who have little besides their shared ignorance upon
which to base their ideas can be readily drawn into the
orbit of social visionaries. They can be, and have been,
filled with notions of the goodness of people, of how everybody deserves this or that, of how unjust certain things
are, and so on. They would have no clear notion of the
limiting character of the universe, of cause and effect, of
an order which makes things turn out the way they do.
They would have been encouraged to assert their wills
("express" themselves) and have no reason to suppose that
the way they (collectively) think that things ought to be
would not be the way they could be. In short, they would
be admirably fitted out with the pretensions of social reformers.

Changing the Social Order

There can be no valid reason for doubting that the
Progressive Education leaders conceived of social reconstruction as the prime function of schooling. This strain
runs through their writings from the earliest to the latest.
They have differed from time to time as to the bluntness
with which they stated it (it reached its apogee in the
1930's), but it has been a continual refrain. Dewey declared at the outset that "the teacher always is the prophet

of the true God and the usherer in of the true kingdom of God."[21] Many years later he proclaimed the view that "the schools will surely as a matter of fact and not of ideal *share* in the building of the social order of the future. . . . They will of necessity . . . take an active part in determining the social order. . . ."[22]

George S. Counts said, "In the collectivist society now emerging the school should be regarded . . . as an agency for the abolition of all artificial social distinctions and of organizing the energies of the nation for the promotion of the general welfare. . . . Throughout the school program the development of the social order rather than the egoistic impulses should be stressed; and the motive of personal aggrandizement should be subordinated to social ends."[23] Harold Rugg maintained that changes that have occurred necessitate "the scrapping of the formal school and setting up of a thoroughly new one." The reason for this is that "the climates of opinion of American communities, those now dictated by the dominant groups that own and control the economic system, must be made over. . . ."[24]

In order to use the schools in this way, the habits and training of teachers had to be changed, for, above all, it was the teachers who could assure this employment of the schools. Harold Rugg described one aspect of the program in this way:

Summing the matter up, then, I see the necessary strategy of the educator in educational and social recon-

---

[21] Quoted in Cremin, *op. cit.*, p. 100.

[22] Quoted in John H. Snow and Paul W. Shafer, *The Turning of the Tides* (New York: Long House, 1956), p. 30.

[23] *Ibid.*, p. 29.

[24] Quoted in Rudd, *op. cit.*, p. 68.

struction as that of (1) creating intelligent understanding in a large minority of the people, (2) practicing them continually in making group decisions concerning their local and national issues, and (3) having them constantly exert pressure upon legislators and executives in government to carry out their decision.[25]

Goodwin Watson gives these pointers to teachers on how to develop social reform habits:

> . . . When the young student goes to visit the tenements of crowded slum areas, he is working on the first level. . . . When he joins a housing movement or association . . . , he begins *participation*. As he begins to accept committee assignments, he enters the third stage. . . . When he goes out into a community backward in its housing and succeeds in starting some effective action, his development has reached the stage where he can *initiate* on his own responsibility. . . . Activity in aiding unemployed youth, in consumer's co-operatives, inter-racial good will, world peace, public health, parent education, political parties . . . will follow a similar course.[26]

Harold Rugg held that "the teachers should deliberately reach for power and then make the most of their conquest. . . . To the extent that they are permitted to fashion the curriculum and the procedures of the school they will definitely and positively influence the social attitudes, ideals, and behavior of the coming generation."[27]

The character of the social reconstruction which Progressives had in mind should not be left in doubt. Though they may have differed as to the extent to which society

---

[25] Harold Rugg, *American Life and the School Curriculum* (Boston: Ginn, 1936), p. 455.

[26] Kilpatrick, *op. cit.*, p. 315.

[27] Park, *op. cit.*, pp. 187-88.

should be reconstructed and as to how this should be done, they did not differ in believing that it would involve radical change. John Dewey said, "In order to endure under present conditions, liberalism must become radical in the sense that, instead of using social power to ameliorate the evil consequences of the existing system, it shall use power to change the system."[28] An examination of the writings of a goodly number of these men indicates that they favored a direction which is generically known as socialism.

As a matter of fact—and it is a hard and enduring fact —people do not generally want to be made over. They do not want themselves and their society (for a given society is all the people in it) reconstructed according to somebody's blueprint. Certainly, parents do not want their children used as instruments of such reconstruction nor the schools turned into social reform institutes. Parents, insofar as they give such matters thought, want children to be made into adults for the society in which they live. The Progressives faced tremendous obstacles all along the way. Parents wanted the old education, at least in substance; school boards resisted their innovations; teachers persisted in teaching as if they had some knowledge to purvey.

Centralizing Control over Schools

The schools were, however, an attractive target for social reformers from the outset. Many of them were tax supported by the beginning of the twentieth century, and by then or within a few years all of the states compelled attendance. Early in the twentieth century, David Snedden noted that the schools were "the only educational institutions which society, in its collective and conscious capacity, acting thru the state, is able to control." In these, an

---

[28] Dewey, *Problems of Men,* p. 132.

education could be introduced which proceeded "from the broadest possible conception of society reconstructing itself."[29] But this was easier said than done. Schools were usually locally controlled, frequently locally financed, under the keeping and direction of local boards of trustees. These were resistant to the innovations that the Progressives advanced.

To accomplish the ends which they sought, the schools had to be brought under their power and control. The effort to accomplish this was conducted on many fronts, always under such rubrics as "efficiency," "modernization," and "progress." Subtle attacks upon "reactionary" boards, communities, and parents were carried on. Patriotic groups were defamed.[30] More to the point, control of the schools was shifted away from local control. States began to supplement the income of schools, certify teachers, provide normal schools and schools of education, and to specify courses of study. School districts were consolidated, and school buildings located away from many communities. Courses in "education" were required for teachers in the public schools, which usually brought them under the influence of Progressives. Teachers were given tenure, which tended to remove them from the disciplinary power of local communities. Various and sundry slogans and ideas were promulgated to render the resistance of the patrons of the schools of no effect. If parents object to some book being used in the schools, they are accused of "censorship" and "book burning." If they object to what is being taught, they are accused of violating the "academic freedom" of the teachers. That Progressives were frequently aware of

[29] Krug, *op. cit.*, p. 253.

[30] See Dewey, *Problems of Men,* p. 91; Kilpatrick, *op. cit,* pp. 29-37.

precisely what they were doing should be clear from this statement by John Dewey:

> In short, the social significance of academic freedom lies in the fact that without freedom of inquiry and freedom on the part of the teachers and students to explore the forces at work in society and the means by which they may be directed, the habits of intelligent action that are necessary to the orderly development of society cannot be created.[31]

In short, academic freedom is necessary so that the schools may be used for social reconstruction. Another device developed by the educationists for protection of themselves from the "vulgar" is a scientistic jargon.

A complete account of how progressivism entered the schools would call attention to the changes in the curriculum, to the submergence of such disciplinary studies as history and geography in something called "social studies," to the introduction of the problem-solving technique (which is an imaginative way to get students to become reformist minded), to the writing of textbooks informed in the new ethos, and so on. But enough has been told to suggest the character of the rest.

The Progressives have not succeeded, of course, in completely undermining education. Many dedicated teachers have persisted in teaching fundamentals, at least in the lower grades. Many administrators and boards of education have limited the extent to which changes were made. Even so, the Progressives succeeded much better than most of them have ever admitted. They have managed to introduce group-consciousness and ideas of adjustment into the very heart of the schooling process. They have convinced many young people that the welfare state is

[31] Dewey, *Problems of Men,* p. 79.

inevitable, that it is democratic to advance social reforms, and that there is little to nothing to be learned from the past. Their effort has resulted in a tendency for the young (in their "peer groups") to be oblivious to adults, for schools to be separated from communities, for children to be ignorant of or contemptuous of their heritage and tradition, and for childhood to be perpetuated beyond its normal years.

Thus have young minds been shaped to strange ends, and thus have Americans proceeded on their flight from reality. To what end? Bernard Iddings Bell summed it up felicitously, if fearfully, some years ago:

> When men or nations get tired of dodging fundamental questions in a multitude of distractions, they turn to a search for something else that will, so they suppose, give them the sense of significance which they know they lack. . . . If they remain adolescent in their approach to life they are frequently tempted to seek meaning for themselves and for their nation in terms of coercive power. They develop a Messianic complex. They seek to live other people's lives for them, ostensibly for the good of those other people but really in the hope of fulfilling themselves.[32]

---

[32] Bell, *op. cit.*, p. 20.

16

From Ideology to Mythology

THE STUDY OF THE HISTORY OF IDEAS HAS PRODUCED some interesting results. Among these is the conclusion that at any given time in a society there is apt to be a prevailing set of ideas. These are not, of course, readily apparent to the superficial observer, not even to the superficial historian. Superficially, it is the disagreements among men, their debates, the points over which they contend that catch the attention. But beneath these there are often broad and fundamental areas of agreement in terms of which discourse takes place and disputed questions are settled, or compromises are worked out.

These broad areas of agreement which constitute the prevailing ideas have been called by a variety of names: *Weltanschauung* (world outlook), frame of reference, basic premises, ethos, underlying philosophy, and so on. Historians can often discern that this ethos (or whatever name it should be called) is reflected and articulated in the arts, literature, politics, religion, morals, and institutions of a people. Periods in history have now quite often been given names which are meant to signify the prevailing ethos at that time: the Age of the Renaissance, the Age of the Baroque, the Age of the Enlightenment, and so on.

Such classifications should be accepted, however, with some reservations. The extent of agreement, even upon fundamental premises, can be easily exaggerated. Neat classifications appeal more to those who have only a passing acquaintance with an "Age" than those who have studied it deeply. Dissent from the prevailing ethos can be uncovered at almost any point in history. There is a tendency, too, to exaggerate the extent of the change from one of these periods to the other. There is a continuity in the basic ideas and beliefs of Western Civilization which cuts across the periods which historians define. Also, there is a relativism implied in many of these accounts of changing world outlooks which should be entertained cautiously. Prevailing ideas do change, to greater or lesser extent, from epoch to epoch, but this does not mean that one set of ideas is as good as another or that truth is relative to the premises of a given age. The results of logical deductions *are* relative to the premises from which they are deduced. Their truth content, however, depends upon the validity of the premises, that is, upon their conformity to reality.

With these reservations in mind, let it be asserted again that at a given time in society there is usually a prevailing ethos. This work has to do with such an ethos. Now, according to the unconventional wisdom of our age—that is, according to the uninhibited imaginations of a goodly number of would-be seers—we live in an Age of Transition. Indeed, it is often held that we have been in the slough of this transition for some time. At best, such a nonclassifying classification is a convenient dodge. It certainly avoids coming to terms with the ethos of our time, with describing it, with classifying it, and with holding it up for examination. Moreover, it is not a classification that can be validated with evidence. True, there can be assembled evidence that changes are occurring. But such evidence exists for all times for which there is any evidence. In short, to call an epoch an age of transition does not distinguish it, or classify it, from any other age.

We may indeed hope that much of the contemporary

ethos may be transitory; it has certainly focused upon the ephemeral. But when the presently prevailing ethos has passed from the scene, its passing will not mark the end of an Age of Transition. For this ethos has a distinctive character. Moreover, it has been with us for a sufficient time to enable us to classify it with confidence. Ours is an AGE OF MELIORISM. The prevailing ethos supports continuous reform with the ostensible aim of improvement.

For seventy or eighty years this ethos has been building. The men whose thought is reckoned to be so influential upon our times have been meliorists: Edward Bellamy, Lester Frank Ward, John Dewey, William James, Thorstein Veblen, Charles A. Beard, Louis D. Brandeis, Woodrow Wilson, Walter Lippmann, Herbert Croly, and so on. The words which connote approval in our society are quite often those conducive to the reform effort: e.g., innovative, inventive, imaginative, progressive, creative, cooperative, flexible, pragmatic, open-minded, and involved. The arts, literature, religion, social thought, and education are permeated with the innovative and reformist spirit. There exists a bountiful literature describing the need for amelioration and containing proposals for collective effort to bring it about.

Ideological Origins

This work, thus far, has been an attempt to describe the historical development of this ethos and its propagation in American society. The story has been traced from the breakdown of philosophy to the birth of ideology to utopianism through the elaboration of a new conception of reality and creativity to some of the ways that meliorism (or socialism) was made attractive to Americans. In the final analysis, Americans generally began to accept the programs and policies of melioristic reform as they began to view things from a new ethos, a new outlook, a new frame of reference, or from a different set of fundamental premises. Men were drawn into this framework in a variety of ways: by being told that it was democratic, that it was an extension of that to which they were already devoted; by an appeal to concern for others; by having the programs of education for the young instrumented to this new way of looking at things which, when accepted, constituted a new frame of reference.

The intellectual sources of this melioristic frame of reference are in various ideologies. Nineteenth century thought has been categorized, at least once, by the phrase, the Age of Ideology. Certainly, ideologies abounded in the nineteenth century. All thought tended toward the formation of ideologies. This tendency was mirrored in the language which came to be used to describe the products of thought. The attachment of the "ism" suffix indicates the ideological tendency of the system of ideas to which it refers. This formation of words became epidemic in the first half of the nineteenth century. As one history book points out, "So far as is known the word 'liberalism' first appeared in the English language in 1819, 'radicalism' in 1820, 'socialism' in 1832, 'conservatism' in 1835. The 1830's first saw 'individualism,' 'constitutionalism,' 'humanitarianism,' and 'monarchism.' 'Nationalism' and 'communism' date from the 1840's. Not until the 1850's did the English-speaking world use the word 'capitalism' . . ."[1] Many others were to follow: "romanticism," "Marxism," "Darwinism," "scientism," and so on. Some of these concepts with the suffix "ism" were not ideologies, properly speaking, but the tendency to attach the "ism" to all con-

---

[1] R. R. Palmer with Joel Colton, *A History of the Modern World* (New York: Alfred A. Knopf, 1958, 2nd edition), p. 431.

cepts and beliefs reflects the ideological propensities of thinkers.

A great variety of ideologies developed in the wake of the breakdown of philosophy in the nineteenth century, and some even began to appear earlier. Rousseau propounded a democratist ideology, Bentham and the utilitarians an economicist ideology, Comte a sociologist (or socialist) ideology, Hegel a statist ideology, Marx a materialistic and historicist ideology, Mill an ideology of liberty, Spencer an evolutionist ideology, George a neophysiocratic ideology, and so on.

Technically, an ideology is a system or complex of ideas which purports to comprehend reality. Actually, modern ideologies have usually been both more limited than this would suggest and much more zealously attached to by their proponents. The makers of ideologies have usually operated in some such fashion as the following. They quest for and think they have found the philosopher's stone, a magic key that will unlock the mysteries of the universe. It is some abstraction from the whole of reality. For Rousseau it was the general will, for Comte the stages of the development of the mind, for Hegel the conflict of ideas, for Marx the class struggle, for Spencer it was the evolutionary process, for Mill something called liberty, for George the unearned increment on land, for Bentham social utility, and so on. With the philosopher's stone in hand, the ideologue proceeds to spin out—to reason abstractly— an account of how things got the way they are, what is wrong with the way things are, and what is to be done about them, if anything.

The ideological version of reality is at considerable variance with existent reality. This is understandable, for the ideologue has not only proceeded by reducing it to abstractions—which are always less than and different from the reality to which they refer—but also hung all his abstractions upon some central abstractions. If he concludes, as he seems invariably to do, that things should be brought into accord with his ideological version of them, he becomes a reformer. Indeed, all that does not accord with his version is irrational (and those who oppose it, anti-intellectual), for he has reached his conclusions logically, that is, by abstract reason. It is as if an inventor should construct an automaton on the basis of his analysis of actual men and then proclaim that all men should be like his mechanical figure. Utopias are just such parodies of the possibilities of reality, and are no more desirable than men would be if turned into mechanical contraptions.

The ideologue tends to fanaticism. Whatever it is that he thinks will set things aright—that is, bring them into accord with his mental picture of them—becomes for him a fixed idea. This fixed idea may be democracy, equality, the triumph of the proletariat, the coming of the kingdom, the single tax, the realization of an idea for society, or whatever his panacea happens to be. Come the proletarian revolution, one will say, and the good society will be ushered in. Employ creatively his abstraction, the "state," another will hold, and a great and productive social unity will emerge. Extend democratic participation into every area of life, and life will be glorious. Abolish property, abolish government, single tax the land, redistribute the wealth, maintain racial solidarity, organize interest groups, form a world government, develop an all embracing commitment to the nation, use government to make men free, and so on through the almost endless number of enthusiasms which have animated those under the sway of some ideology or other. The totalitarianisms they create when they try to put these ideas into effect stem from the total commitment to an abstraction in the first place.

Meliorism has drawn such intellectual substance as it has had in America from these nineteenth century ideas. It drew sustenance from democratism, from egalitarianism, from nationalism, from utopian socialism, from Darwinism, from Marxism, and from statism. But the attempt to reconstruct society has not usually been advanced by the avowal of an explicit ideology. After the early years of the twentieth century, American intellectuals began to avoid ideological labels for the most part, even as more and more of them were influenced by ideas drawn from ideologies. Even those who thought of themselves as socialists became less and less definitely aligned with an explicit socialist ideology. There has been considerable talk lately of an end to ideology; a book has been written on that theme. And yet, the pressure toward melioristic reform continues to mount, and the arguments for reform and the direction that it takes is still drawn from ideology.

In general, American reformers, those who have gone by the name of "liberal" for a good many years now, have no consistently explicit ideology. Certainly, the generality of Americans who have come to expect and favor reforms are unaware of holding any ideology. What has happened is that many of the ideological assumptions that propel us toward melioristic reform have become a part of the mental baggage of most people. They have taken on a frame of reference, a way of looking at things, which makes increasing governmental activity seem natural to them.

Myths and Images

How did this come about? In the main, ideology was subsumed into mythology. People pick up the ideology through the myths which they have come to accept. A mythology is a body of myths or legends which purports to account for the way things are. In traditional usage a mythology is a kind of sacred history for a pagan religion. It contains the stories of the doings of the deities, and is a means of inculcating religious teachings. In the common parlance, a myth is a commonly believed view of something that is not true to fact, that will not stand up under careful scrutiny. However, some contemporary scholars use the word in a much more neutral and descriptive manner. The following definition tells what anthropologists are apt to mean when they refer to myths:

> Myths are the instruments by which we continually struggle to make our experience intelligible to ourselves. A myth is a large, controlling image that gives philosophical meaning to the facts of ordinary life; that is, which has organizing value for experience. A mythology is a more or less articulated body of such images, a pantheon. . . . This is not to say that sound myths of general application necessarily support religions; rather that they perform the historical functions of religion—they unify experience in a way that is satisfactory to the whole culture and to the whole personality.[2]

Another writer, thinking along the same lines, defines mythology in this way:

> Briefly stated, what I have in mind are first, the images (imagined scenes or objects) and *imagents* (imagined actions or events) underlying, sustaining, and activating some conceptually represented, developmental philosophy of life, or ideology, individual and social, and second, more particularly, a large assemblage of narratives in prose or poetry, each illustrative of a better or worse course of action, a better or worse state of being,

---

[2] Mark Schorer, "The Necessity of Myth," *Myth and Mythmaking*, Henry A. Murray, ed. (New York: George Braziller, 1960), p. 355.

or a better or worse mode of becoming, for an individual, for a society, or for the world at large.[3]

It is symptomatic of the contemporary state of mind that elaborate and serious studies of mythology should be made, tricked out in the paraphernalia of scholarship. It is one more indicator of the loss of confidence in our culture, for to many such intellectuals all beliefs are inculcated by myths, and all myths stand more or less equal in their sight. The test of an adequate mythology, one gathers, is the extent to which it is psychologically satisfying. Note, too, that such studies tend to justify myths, just as William James justified religion, on psychological grounds. Their truth or falsity is not to be objectively determined; they are useful and appropriate, in general, if they satisfy the individuals in a given society.

Even so, it is these latter usages of "mythology" to which I refer when I say that ideology has been subsumed in mythology. There are some differences, however. It is assumed, in the above, that the stories and legends by which myths were purveyed were imaginary. This is not the case, at least generally, with the twentieth century mythology which propels us toward ameliorative reform. The stories and legends are quite often as accurate factually as modern research can make them. At any rate, the details are factual, or are supposed to be. Their mythical character is most profoundly to be found in the assumptions which are provided from ideology.

This modern mythology, the mythology of meliorism, is purveyed as history. That is, it is what people understand to have happened in the past, though it is most relevant to what is now happening and the trends presently at

---

[3] Henry A. Murray, "The Possible Nature of a 'Mythology' to Come," in *Ibid.*, p. 300.

work. This does not mean that it is only something taught in the schools from history books. On the contrary, it has been purveyed in popular nonfiction, in imaginative literature, in newspapers and magazines. The mythology is evoked in political speeches, in sermons, in newscasts, in lectures, and in all of the ways that people communicate with one another. That is to say, it is a part of the way people see, interpret, and understand (or misunderstand) what is going on.

The American Mythology

The basic mythology concerns American history from about the time of the Civil War to the present. The myths can be found in almost any textbook on the subject. The following is a bareboned summary, hopefully not a parody, of some of the central myths found in such accounts. America was plunged into crisis in the latter part of the nineteenth century. This crisis portended catastrophe if something were not done. The signs of the crisis were all around: industrial depressions, increasing tenant farming, the growth of slums and tenements, periods of unemployment, labor strife, falling industrial wages, falling agricultural prices, the decline of craftsmanship, and generally worsening conditions. The sources of the crisis, according to the mythology, were to be found in profound underlying changes that were taking place. These changes are evoked by such words as industrialization, mechanization, urbanization, and, perhaps, proletarianization. Fundamentally, rapid changes in technology, and the manner of its utilization, were producing vast maladjustments in society.

These changes called for fundamental alterations in attitudes, in social institutions, and in the patterns of behavior of a people. Instead of this having taken place, however, older American patterns had been extended and had ossified. Individualism had become rugged individualism, economic liberty become license to plunder the resources of America for private aggrandizement, the government of the people an instrument for advancing the fortunes of a nascent plutocracy. Vernon Louis Parrington, no mean mythmaker himself, describes the development this way:

> The war . . . had opened to capitalism its first clear view of the Promised Land. The bankers had come into control of the liquid wealth of the nation, and the industrialists had learned to use the machine for production; the time was ripe for exploitation on a scale undreamed-of a generation before. . . .
>
> It was an abundant harvest of those freedoms that America had long been struggling to achieve, and it was making ready ground for later harvests that would be less to its liking. Freedom had become individualism, and individualism had become the inalienable right to pre-empt, to exploit, to squander. . . .
>
> In such fashion the excellent ideal of progress that issued from the social enthusiasms of the Enlightenment was taken in charge by the Gilded Age and transformed into a handmaid of capitalism. Its duties were narrowed to the single end of serving profits and its accomplishments came to be exactly measured by bank clearings. . . .
>
> Having thus thrown the mantle of progress about the Gold Dust twins, the Gilded Age was ready to bring the political forces of America into harmony with the program of pre-emption and exploitation. . . .[4]

In consequence of these things, according to the mythology, the rich were getting richer and the poor were getting poorer. Farmers were oppressed by high and discriminatory

---

[4] Vernon L. Parrington, *The Beginnings of Critical Realism in America: 1860-1920* (New York: Harcourt, Brace & World, 1930, 1958), pp. 8-19.

rail rates, and workers were being exploited by robber barons. The wealth of America was being channeled into the hands of a few beneficiaries of special privilege by both government action and inaction. Farmers were muttering, becoming angry, beginning to organize. Workers were feeling the pinch of deprivation, becoming increasingly discontented, and beginning to organize. These clouds upon the horizon surely portended a coming storm.

The solution to the problem is usually carried implicitly within the mythology. Fundamental adjustments must be made in keeping with the changed condition. The power of the people collectively, that is, government, must be used to tame these forces let loose in the land, to restore balance and harmony, to bring about an adjustment. But, as everyone who is familiar with the mythology knows, the cavalry did not come dashing to the rescue, or, to be literal, the government did not act forcefully to bring about this harmony in the late nineteenth century. True, it did begin to tinker, to prohibit trusts and regulate the railroads ineffectively, to allot a few crumbs of the governmental bounty by way of inflation to the poor and dispossessed. But these were puny efforts beside the massive transformation called for by these forces at work in society.

Things did begin to look up in the early twentieth century, according to the legend. Reformers began to be heard in the land; politicians began to advance some of their programs; even Presidents began to use the language of reform. Local governments, state governments, and even the United States government began to make faltering efforts at more comprehensive reforms. But alas, the effort was short-lived; the advance gave way to retreat once more in the 1920's. Business returned to the saddle once more; the roaring twenties witnessed the last fling of a moribund capitalism. The public was drawn into this

Roman holiday, spending its substance in riotous living or engaging in the speculative boom occurring on the stock market.

The Great Depression

The long expected catastrophe finally came—the Great Depression. As fate would have it, the country was saddled with the last of the rugged individualists, Herbert Hoover, when the day of accounting arrived, and he fiddled with puny ameliorative efforts while Rome burned. The situation went from bad to worse. Arthur Schlesinger, Jr., himself a mythmaker of the first order, describes conditions on the day of the first inauguration of Franklin D. Roosevelt:

> The fog of despair hung over the land. One out of every four American workers lacked a job. Factories that had once darkened the skies with smoke stood ghostly and silent, like extinct volcanoes. Families slept in tar-paper shacks and tinlined caves and scavenged like dogs for food in the city dump. In October the New York City Health Department had reported that over one-fifth of the pupils in public schools were suffering from malnutrition. Thousands of vagabond children were roaming the land, wild boys of the road. Hunger marchers, pinched and bitter, were parading cold streets in New York and Chicago. On the countryside unrest had already flared into violence. . . .[5]

Following Roosevelt's inaugural address, of course, "across the land the fog began to lift."[6]

Whether the fog lifted or not (some think it settled permanently upon Washington), government intervention was certainly undertaken in earnest thereafter. According

---

[5] Arthur M. Scheslinger, Jr., *The Crisis of the Old Order, 1919-1933* (Boston: Houghton Mifflin, 1957), p. 3.

[6] *Ibid.*, p. 8.

to the legend, government took up its proper role in affairs. It began to tame the wayward and destructive forces let loose by industrialization, to bring order out of the economic chaos induced by an economy of private aggrandizement and cutthroat competition, to take sides among the citizenry to rectify the imbalance between labor and management and between agriculture and industry. The United States government undertook planning, regulating, controlling, subsidizing, inflating, harnessing, spending, and taxing with a right good will. Of course, it took some time for those in government to learn just how to manage all these things in the best possible way. Some relics of the depression remained throughout the 1930's, and it was only after the outbreak of the war that full prosperity was finally restored. But the right direction had been taken, so the mythology goes. Government has now mastered most of the economic forces which once wrought such hardship in the land: that is, depression, unemployment (well, not quite!), destructive competition, hoarding (of money), and so on. There remain problems, of course, and the process of reform must go on, but the basically right direction has now been taken. The great progress that has been made in the last thirty years should be attributed to this governmental activity.

Government intervention, then, has produced great and lasting good. One will rarely find a dissenting voice about this in textbooks. On the other hand, it has done little if any demonstrable harm. This summary of the mythology can be closed with a quotation to this effect from one of the most consistent mythologizers of this generation, Senator Joseph Clark of Pennsylvania:

> That nightmare of "federal control" which haunts the dreams of our conservative friends is an hallucination. I cannot think of one example of the "heavy hand of the

federal government reaching out into our private lives" that has actually been restrictive of our personal freedoms or detrimental to our economy. . . .

The federal government has been subsidizing education in this country ever since the Northwest Ordinance of 1784 [sic]. No harm and much good have resulted. The same is true of social security, housing, urban renewal, and government plans for the health care for the aged.[7]

There is enough truth in this account to make it superficially plausible. Men can thrust their experiences into this framework, and it will seem to make sense of them. After all, two generations of publicists and researchers have collected mountains of facts with which to buttress the mythology. In like manner, two generations of interpreters have woven these facts into smooth and plausible accounts of what has been and is happening. Nor is there any reason to suppose that many of them have any doubts about the correctness of their interpretations. For aught we know, the deluders are deluded by their own delusions.

Be that as it may, the above summary is of a full-fledged mythology, believed and accepted by millions of Americans, so far as judgments of such things can be made. This mythology is purveyed as history, consists of what many people think has happened. This history-as-mythology does contain distortions and exaggerations, but it must be kept in mind that it is not a mythology simply because of these. Nor is it rescued from mythology by the number of facts which can be summoned to give it the appearance of validity; these are but grist to its mills. It is a mythology because it stems from a mental construct instead of reality, because it embodies ideologies.

---

[7] In Edward Reed, ed., *Challenges to Democracy: The Next Ten Years* (New York: Frederick A. Praeger, 1963), p. 102.

Origins of Mythology

Let us examine first the myth that the rich were getting richer and the poor poorer in the latter part of the nineteenth century. However the myth arose, it was given a dramatic and effective formulation by Henry George. The idea is captured in the juxtaposition of words in the title of his most famous book, *Progress and Poverty*. The central thesis is presented in the following words:

> And, unpleasant as it may be to admit it, it is at last becoming evident that the enormous increase in productive power which has marked the present century and is still going on with accelerating ratio, has no tendency to extirpate poverty or to lighten the burdens of those compelled to toil. It simply widens the gulf between Dives and Lazarus, and makes the struggle for existence more intense. The march of invention has clothed mankind with powers of which a century ago the boldest imagination could not have dreamed. But in factories where labor-saving machinery has reached its most wonderful development, little children are at work; wherever the new forces are anything like fully utilized, large classes are maintained by charity or live on the verge of recourse to it; amid the greatest accumulations of wealth, men die of starvation, and puny infants suckle dry breasts; while everywhere the greed of gain, the worship of wealth, shows the force of the fear of want. The promised land flies before us like the mirage.[8]

These assertions can be phrased so as to make them into a problem, and it was as a problem that George, along with many other nineteenth century economists and would-be economists, treated them. They constitute a nice "problem" indeed! How can increasing productivity result in more and more poverty, or greater poverty? The problem can be

---

[8] Henry George, *Progress and Poverty* (New York: Schalkenbach Foundation, 1955), p. 8.

dramatized by introducing some statistics, though George could not have been familiar with these. American farmers produced approximately 100,000,000 bushels of wheat in 1850; this had risen to 600,000,000 by 1900. They produced 4,590,000 bales of cotton in 1850, and 10,226,000 in 1900. Corn production increased from 590,000,000 bushels in 1850 to 2,662,000,000 in 1900. This represented a considerable increase in productivity per acre generally, too, for land in cultivation had less than tripled.[9] The value of the annual product of manufacturing increased from approximately $2 billion in 1860 to $13 billion in 1900.[10] This represented great increases in consumer goods. In 1859, men's clothing manufacturers turned out a product worth $73,219,765; in 1899, they made a product worth $276,861,607. The worth of the factory produce for women's clothing was 20 times as great in 1899 as it was in 1859. In 1849, flour and grist mill products were valued at approximately $136 million; in 1899, this had increased to about $560 million.[11] These figures represent increases in goods, rather than inflation. In fact, prices declined generally during the period under consideration. One writer notes that if wholesale prices be indicated by the figure 100 for 1860, they had fallen to 95.7 in 1890, and would decrease somewhat more during the next decade.[12]

It is difficult to see how this greater production and increasing productivity could result in increasing poverty. Of course, population might have increased faster than

[9] Henry B. Parkes, *The United States of America: A History* (New York: Alfred A. Knopf, 1953), p. 435.

[10] *Ibid.*, p. 395.

[11] Walter W. Jennings, *A History of Economic Progress in the United States* (New York: Thomas Y. Crowell, 1926), pp. 430-33.

[12] *Ibid.*, pp. 483-84.

production (shades of Malthus!), though such resulting poverty could hardly have been attributed to the productivity. But it did not. The population of the United States was 23,191,000 in 1850; by 1900 it was 75,994,000. Population had a little more than tripled; production of staple agricultural products had quadrupled, quintupled, and sextupled, while the production of many manufactured products had increased in a much higher ratio than that. Again, these goods might have been shipped out of the country in return for foreign gold, thus shorting Americans of the goods they produced (though surely foreigners would have had a great bounty of goods). But the value of exports only trebled between 1866 and 1900, having fallen drastically during the Civil War.

There is no need, however, to wrestle with phantoms. The poor were not getting poorer generally in America. Such evidence as is available presents quite a different picture. Private production income (all income except that from government sources) increased from about $4 billion in 1859 to $28 billion in 1914, and grew especially fast from 1869 to 1899. Per capita income, in terms of actual money, rose from $134 in 1859 to $185 in 1899. "Considering dollars of constant purchasing power, the increase was from $285 to $488 in the period between 1859 and 1914."[13]

It can be objected that no one receives the income per capita, that this is only an average, and that the increase might have only made the rich richer. This does not appear to have been the case. One historian estimates that the proportion of the income of Americans derived from wages and salaries rose relative to that from rent, interest, and

---

[13] Gilbert C. Fite and Jim E. Reese, *An Economic History of the United States* (Boston: Houghton Mifflin, 1959), pp. 304-05.

so forth.[14] At any rate, "the index of money hourly wages for men in all industries practically doubled between 1860 and 1890. . . . Since the index of commodity prices fell rapidly [that is, commodity prices fell, *not* the index] after 1865, the purchasing power of wages, 'real wages,' often attained a spectacular improvement."[15] Samuel Gompers, head of the American Federation of Labor and one who should have known about such matters, was asked this question in 1900: "You would not agree to the statement sometimes made that the conditions of the working men are growing worse and worse?" His answer, "Oh, that is perfectly absurd."[16]

Where did this absurdity spring from? Some may suppose that it was drawn from earlier developments, drawn, for example, from the "early stages of the Industrial Revolution" in England. This period has long been the whipping boy of reviewers of the horrors of industrialization. Horrors there may have been, but they could hardly have been the product of industrialization generally.

A competent and thorough economic historian, T. S. Ashton, has lately exorcised this demon from the pantheon of historical mythology. He says, "An historian has written of 'the disasters of the industrial revolution.' If by this he means that the years 1760-1830 were darkened by wars and made cheerless by dearth, no objection can be made to the phrase. But if he means that the technical and economic changes were themselves the source of calamity, the opinion is surely perverse." He points out that there were a great many more people to be fed and clothed at

---

[14] Edward C. Kirkland, *Industry Comes of Age* (New York: Holt, Rinehart and Winston, 1961), p. 402.

[15] *Ibid.*

[16] Quoted in *ibid.*

the time. Ireland did not solve this problem and consequently lost much of her population. If England had followed the agricultural pattern of Ireland, he thinks that a like fate would have befallen her. Instead, "she was delivered, not by her rulers, but by those who, seeking no doubt their own narrow ends, had the wit and resource to devise new instruments of production and new methods of administering industry."[17]

The Labor Theory of Value

The roots of the progress-and-poverty notion do not lie in what happened (though the myth was no doubt assisted by interpretations of what happened); they lie rather in ideology. The seeds of the myth were planted, so far as I know, by David Ricardo, with an assist from Thomas Malthus. They were deeply embedded in economics for most of the nineteenth century. Ricardo held that the price of labor must ever and again fall to a level that will maintain workers at a bare subsistence of livelihood. He arrived at this conclusion by a grotesque bit of ideological hocus pocus. According to what is now called classical economics, to which Ricardo subscribed and contributed, commodities have a natural price (or value) and a market price. The natural price is determined by the costs of production. The market price is determined by supply and demand. Under conditions of free competition, the market price will tend always toward the natural price.

Ricardo proceeded to apply this theory to the price of labor; that is, he ideologized by applying an abstraction

---

[17] T. S. Ashton, *The Industrial Revolution, 1760-1830* (New York: Oxford University Press, A Galaxy Book, 1964), pp. 110-11.

about one phenomenon to an analogous one, ignoring the differences. The cost of production applied to labor came out as the cost of maintaining life. "The natural price of labor is that price which is necessary to enable the laborers, one with another, to subsist and to perpetuate their race, without either increase or diminution."[18] The market price of labor will fluctuate, he held, due to the operation of supply and demand. When wages rise above their natural level, he thought, population will increase because more life can be maintained. That is, the supply of labor will increase, thus driving the market price of labor down to the natural price, or even below it, for a time. In short, the price of labor will tend toward the subsistence level. Malthus maintained, of course, that population increase would inevitably outdistance any increases in production. Thus was the "dismal science" loaded down with its freight of notions about continued and widespread poverty.

Later thinkers did not generally accept the demographic theories of the classicists. Moreover, there was a sloughing off of the philosophic dualism, of which natural price and market price were an extension, perhaps unwarranted. What was accepted by revolutionists and reformers was the existence of poverty. But as thinkers began to think in terms solely of a temporal context in which society was the pre-eminent reality, some of them began to attribute this poverty to the social system.

We are now back to the original problem: How can increasing productivity result in continuing poverty? The problem was, of course, ideological, not actual, but ideo-

---

[18] David Ricardo, "Principles of Political Economy," *The Age of Reason*, Louis L. Snyder, ed. (Princeton: D. Van Nostrand, 1955), pp. 153-54.

logues abounded in the nineteenth century.[19] It is not logical, if the demographic theory is not accepted, that the great increase of goods made available by the use of machines should result in the maintenance of the status quo, or worse, in the material well-being of people. Surely, the goods had to be consumed for there to be a market, and this should improve the situation, not make it worse. Something must be fundamentally wrong with the system. There must be hoarding, waste, unjust distribution, and so on.

Marx concocted the theory that it was the consequence of the exploitation of the workers by the bourgeoisie. So great was the exploitation, and so essential was production to capitalism, that capitalists must have periodic wars in order to dispose of or destroy the goods that they produced. Henry George thought that the problem arose fundamentally from land "monopoly," and that the private expropriation of the unearned increment on land led to poverty. Thorstein Veblen thought that some considerable part of the bounty made available by productivity was dissipated in conspicuous consumption by the wealthy. At any rate, men wove ideologies, envisioned cataclysms, and conceived of programs of reconstruction to right the wrongs that were supposed to be in the system.

These ideological constructs alone probably would not have been sufficient to attract many people into reform or revolution. Nor would it be fair to the intellectuals involved to suggest that they were simply led astray by ideology. There was poverty, hardship, suffering, and malnutrition. In the latter part of the nineteenth century many children did work in factories. There were times of unemployment

---

[19] It should be noted that an explanation of the demand for labor was eventually forthcoming that did not entail the dismal conclusions of Ricardo. It was the marginal utility theory.

in industries; monetary wages did sometimes decline; debtors were hard hit by deflation. Some farmers did lose their farms; tenant farming was on the increase in many areas. Poverty has not disappeared in the twentieth century, nor is it likely that it ever will completely. Of course, this does not stem from increased productivity, nor from the system that makes it possible.

The Muckrakers

But the existence of poverty made it possible to embed the ideological preconceptions in mythology, that is, to describe poverty and implicitly attribute it to the system. This has, of course, been done. Muckrakers did it to great effect in the early twentieth century, but this has been done over the years, and is still being done. Instances of poverty and hardship have been told in lurid detail: pinch-faced children going off to work in factories, fathers with hungry families unemployed, men the victim of technological unemployment, the unsavory character of life in the slums. Some of the titles of books suggest the character of the indictment: Jacob Riis, *How the Other Half Lives* (1890); Robert Hunter, *Poverty* (1905); John Spargo, *The Bitter Cry of the Children;* and Edwin Markham, *Children in Bondage.*[20] One example from the stories told in such books should suffice. The one below is from an account of life in the slums in the latter part of the nineteenth century:

> Enough of them everywhere. Suppose we look into one? No.—Cherry Street. Be a little careful please! The hall is dark and you might stumble over the children pitching pennies back there. Not that it would hurt them; kicks and cuffs are their daily diet. They have little else.

---

[20] See Louis Filler, *Crusaders for American Liberalism* (Yellow Springs, Ohio: Antioch Press, 1950), pp. 268-71.

Here where the hall turns and dives into utter darkness
is a step, and another, another. A flight of stairs. You
can feel your way, if you cannot see it. Close? Yes! What
would you have? All the fresh air that ever enters these
stairs comes from the hall-door that is forever slamming,
and from the windows of dark bedrooms that in turn
receive from the stairs their sole supply of the elements
God meant to be free, but man deals out with such
niggardly hand. That was a woman filling her pail by
the hydrant you just bumped against. The sinks are in
the hallway, that all the tenants may have access—and
all be poisoned alike by their summer stenches. . . .
Here is a door. Listen! That short hacking cough, that
tiny, helpless wail—what do they mean? They mean
that the soiled bow of white you saw on the door down-
stairs will have another story to tell—Oh! a sadly familiar story—before the day is at an end. The child is
dying with measles. With half a chance it might have
lived; but it had none. That dark bedroom killed it.[21]

Government Intervention

The origins of these conditions were, of course, "the
system." Riis said, "We know now that there is no way out;
that the 'system' that was the evil offspring of public
neglect and private greed has come to stay, a storm-centre
forever of our civilization."[22] That is, tenements are a fix-
ture; the only hope lay in amelioration. Among the things
that Riis suggested might be done was that the "state may
have to bring down the rents that cause the crowding, by
assuming the right to regulate them as it regulates the
fares on the elevated roads."[23] The circle is completed with
these suggestions: from ideology to mythology to reform.
These stories of conditions are usually told in such a way

---

[21] Jacob A. Riis, *How the Other Half Lives* (New York: Saga-
more Press, 1957), pp. 33-34.
[22] *Ibid.*, p. 2.
[23] *Ibid.*, p. 217.

as to suggest that only by government intervention can the situation be righted. If the wages of the poor are held down to the subsistence level continually, there would be no way for them to get out of the slums and tenements.

Once government intervention got under way on a large scale, the character of the myth began to change. Now articles, stories, monographs, and textbooks began to present bright pictures of life in America. Happy children now play in uncluttered parks; families live in low-rent housing; farmers use bright new equipment; and workers are joyously bargaining collectively. The following are from captions under upbeat pictures and drawings in a recent textbook. They ascribe this fine state of things to government:

> Senior citizens like these in Sun City, Arizona, are helped by their federal social security payments to live comfortably after retirement and to enjoy a variety of pleasure-time activities.

> Federal grants of money assist cities in replacing slums with satisfactory low-rental dwelling units.

> Reciprocal trade agreements with other countries aid in bringing loaded cargo ships to our ports.

> Workmen have gained many benefits and services since the day in 1900 [caption to an unhappy sketch] when this luncheon counter exposed to dust and contamination, was used to provide a hot meal in the center of a machine shop.

> Wheeler Dam, with its eight outdoor generators, is one of many dams built by TVA to assist in flood control and provide cheap hydroelectric power for industries and residents in the Tennessee Valley.

> With TVA's help, Tennessee farmers have learned the importance of fertilizing their soil [something that was once believed to have been taught to the early settlers in America by Indians]. With low-cost fertilizers produced

by TVA plants, the soil has been built up and now yields profitable crops.[24]

There is still poverty, of course, according to the prevailing ethos, but it, too, has changed in character. It is "hard core" poverty, a variety which may be expected to yield ground before political ministrations, but only after an extended war upon it.

The poverty myth is only one of a large number of myths that make up the mythology. Space does not permit going into others in such detail. However, it is important to provide another example or so to demonstrate the process of mythologizing more adequately.

Competitive "Warfare"

One of the most pernicious of myths is the one that equates competition with war. The following may serve as a generic assertion of the myth: "Competition is of the nature of warfare; in warfare the victory is with the strongest. . . ."[25] The roots of this myth are traceable to a variety of ideological formulations: to the Malthusian concept of the pressure of population on the means of subsistence, to the Marxian notion of the class struggle, to the Darwinian idea of the struggle for survival and survival of the fittest, among others. The description of the rise of the bourgeoisie by Marx and Engels encapsulated this notion of competition-as-war in the revolutionary framework of their historicist eschatology; that is, they thrust it into the historical stream so that it could be mythologized as history. They said, "The bourgeoisie finds itself involved in a

[24] Lawrence V. Roth, *et al., Living in Today's World* (River Forest, Illinois: Laidlaw, 1964, 2nd edition), pp. 267-76.
[25] Washington Gladden, *Applied Christianity* (Boston: Houghton Mifflin, 1886), pp. 31-32. His particular reference was to the "conflict" between capital and labor.

constant battle. At first with the aristocracy; later on, with those portions of the bourgeoisie itself, whose interests have become antagonistic to the progress of industry; at all times with the bourgeoisie of foreign countries."[26]

The next step, of course, was to find an actual instance of such conflict. J. P. Morgan and associates and Jim Fisk supplied the instance which became the classic example in books on American history. It occurred in connection with the contest over control of the Albany & Susquehanna Railroad. The following is a summary of the battle that ensued:

> The combat took ever new and fantastic turns. Feeling ran high. To end the deadlock, the Ramsey-Morgan party finally despatched a force of armed men, estimated by the press to be between 150 and 450 in number. . . . At the same time, an equally formidable mixed body of Erie's Bowery toughs and sheriff's deputies departed for battle from Binghamton behind their own engine. Outside of a long tunnel, fifteen miles beyond Binghamton, the enemy locomotives, whistling and tooting their bells wildly, breathing fire and fury, met in head-on collision. . . .
>
> The warriors of both armies had all jumped off as the two steam chariots collided, and yelling defiance had fallen upon each other with clubs, spades, axes and firearms. But the Ramsey-Morgan thugs were the better armed, and the Erie soldiers soon had the worst of it. Retreating as fast as they could, tearing up tracks and destroying trestles, they went back toward Binghamton, where they barricaded themselves anew and called regiments of the National Guard to their rescue.[27]

---

[26] Karl Marx and Frederick Engels, *The Communist Manifesto* in Eugen Weber, ed., *The Western Tradition* (Boston: D. C. Heath, 1959), p. 611.

[27] Matthew Josephson, *The Robber Barons* (New York: Harcourt, Brace, 1934), p. 139.

Such an occurrence is no more a natural consequence of business competition than is rape of relations between the sexes, and probably less common, but it provided excellent propaganda for those under the sway of ideology. Writers with good imaginations could, and did, take facts, surmises, and interpretations about the behavior of businessmen and weave them into a picture of jungle life, red in tooth and claw. Henry Demarest Lloyd, perhaps the earliest of the muckrakers, writing in the latter part of the nineteenth century, declared: "We are still, part, as Emerson says, in the quadruped state. Our industry is a fight of every man for himself. The prize we give the fittest is monopoly of the necessaries of life, and we leave these winners of the powers of life and death to wield them over us by the same 'self-interest' with which they took them from us."[28]

Matthew Josephson probably did the most thorough job of mythologizing competition-as-war in *The Robber Barons*. In this book, businessmen were likened to medieval barons, and the story is told in a framework and with the terminology drawn from medieval warfare. Note the martial language used to describe the actions of western railroad builders in the following:

> Power such as they had foreseen but dimly came to the hands of the *empire-builders*. . . . By *seizing* one valley, or the passageway to it, they brought an adjacent one into their effective *control,* as the *medieval barons* had done of old. . . . Their network of branch lines was spread throughout the Pacific Slope, through the payment of proper *ransoms* by the communities which required such outlets as a matter of *life and death*. But more ingenious, the new *barons* who held the

---

[28] Henry D. Lloyd, *Wealth against Commonwealth*, Charles C. Baldwin, ed. (Washington: National Home Library Foundation, 1936), p. 330.

only overland route to the Pacific connected these lines with water-front facilities, which they, upon a large scale, *wrested* from the coast cities by the threat of extinction.[29]

Similar terminology was used to describe the behavior of the oil men:

> Tomorrow all the population of the Oil Regions . . . might rise against the South Improvement Company ring in a grotesque uproar. . . . But Rockefeller and his comrades had stolen a *long march* on their *opponents;* their *tactics* shaped themselves already as those of the giant industrialists of the future *conquering* the pigmies. *Entrenched* at the "narrows" of the *mighty* river of petroleum they could no more be *dislodged* than those other barons who had formerly planted their strong castles along the banks of the Rhine could be dislodged by unarmed peasants and burghers.[30]

This myth went into the warp and woof of history as many Americans were to understand it. Here is an example of it in a recent textbook.

> Rockefeller flourished in an era of completely free enterprise. So-called piratical practices were employed by "corsairs of finance," and business ethics were distressingly low. Rockefeller, operating "just to the windward of the law," pursued a policy of rule or ruin. . . .
>
> The Standard Oil Company was undeniably heartless, but its rivals were no less so in this age of dog-eat-dog competition. A kind of social-economic Darwinism seemingly prevailed in the jungle world of big business, where, in certain areas, only the fittest survived. . . .[31]

---

[29] Josephson, *op. cit.,* p. 88. Italics mine.

[30] *Ibid.,* p. 120. Italics mine.

[31] Thomas A. Bailey, *The American Pageant* (Boston: D. C. Heath, 1961, 2nd edition), p. 532. For a soberer evaluation of these men and events, see John Chamberlain, *The Enterprising Americans* (New York: Harper & Row, 1961-63), ch. 8.

The myth of competition-as-war has served over the years as the major propellant of government intervention, from antitrust legislation to fair trade laws to inspection acts to a great variety of other regulatory measures. It has even served as the basis of the interpretation of the coming of wars among nations as a result of trade competition. In short, the myth serves to promote reform.

"Privileges" to Business

One other myth will be examined with some little care. The examination of this myth is particularly instructive as to exaggerations and distortions involved in the making and purveying of myths. This myth has to do with the privileged position of business *vis à vis* government, with how businessmen were supposed to have been the beneficiaries of government largess, with how a plutocracy used government for its own ends, particularly in the late years of the nineteenth and the early years of the twentieth centuries. According to Vernon Louis Parrington, America was spread out upon a table like a great barbecue:

> Congress had rich gifts to bestow—in lands, tariffs, subsidies, favors of all sorts; and when influential citizens made their wishes known to the reigning statesmen the sympathetic politicians were quick to turn the government into the fairy godmother the voters wanted it to be.[32]

Lincoln Steffens proclaimed that businessmen corrupted government:

> Another such conceit of our egotism is that which deplores our politics and lauds our business. This is the wail of the typical American citizen. Now, the typical American citizen is the business man. The typical business man is a bad citizen; he is busy. If he is a "big

---

[32] Parrington, *op. cit.*, p. 23.

business man" and very busy, he does not neglect, he is busy with politics. . . . I found him buying boodlers in St. Louis, defending grafters in Minneapolis, originating corruption in Pittsburgh, sharing with bosses in Philadelphia, deploring reform in Chicago, and beating good government with corruption funds in New York. He is a self-righteous fraud, this big business man.[33]

The most common example of this sort of thing cited in histories is the one about government grants and subsidies for the building of the railroads. Now there were land grants from the United States government (and indirectly, or directly, from state governments) made for the building of some railroads, and there were loans made also. However, the extent and character of this has been greatly exaggerated and distorted generally. Some years ago, Colonel Robert S. Henry examined the treatment of these loans and grants in 37 American history textbooks. A few of the books gave an approximately correct description or account of the land granted. But, for example, "eight others show the area granted . . . as anywhere from nearly one-fifth more than it was, up to about four times the correct area. . . . Others make neither arithmetical nor graphic presentation of the area granted, but rely entirely on adjectives. In most of the books, in fact, such adjectives as 'huge,' 'vast,' 'enormous,' 'staggering,' and 'breath-taking' are parts of the treatment of the subject of area. . . ." He points out that less than 8 per cent of the railroad mileage in the United States was built by land grant aid from the United States government. "The fact that more than 92 per cent of all the railroad mileage in the United States was built without the aid of an acre of Federal land grants is nowhere brought out in the texts examined. . . ."

---

[33] Lincoln Steffens, *The Shame of the Cities* (New York: Young People's Missionary Movement, 1904), p. 5.

A similar exaggeration was made in the texts regarding loans. The loans made were to be repaid with interest. Virtually all of the principal was eventually repaid, along with a large sum of interest. "Thirty-four of the thirty-seven texts examined mention the bond aid to these Pacific roads. In one-third of the works, it is not made clear whether the financial assistance referred to was a loan or a gift. Three describe the aid definitely as gifts—which they were not. Twenty-one refer to the transactions as loans, but only four mention the fact that the loans were repaid, while three make the positively erroneous statement that the loans were never repaid."[34]

Such is the fabric of exaggeration, distortion, misstatement, error, and ignorance by which a myth has been bolstered and purveyed. This myth early served as a basis for demands for governmental regulations of the railroads. It may even have added to the appeal of the perpetual socialist agitation in the late nineteenth and early twentieth centuries for government ownership of the roads. It certainly contributed to the "image" of the railroads as villains.

The Growth of Myths

The above are only a sampling of the myths that have been and are given currency. There is the myth of the class struggle read into American history, the myth of the "people" as an originative force, the myth of the connection between increasing government intervention and progress, the myth of the conservative businessman who is opposed to change and progress, the myth of the spontaneous rise

---

[34] Robert S. Henry, "The Railroad Land Grant Legend in American History," *Issues in American Economic History*, Gerald D. Nash, ed. (Boston: D. C. Heath, 1964), pp. 324-25. The article was originally published in 1945.

of labor unions in response to oppression, the myth of the role of the environment in perpetuating poverty, the myth about the United States being a democracy, and so on.

There is even an extensive myth to the effect that older American beliefs were myths: for example, the "myth of the self-made man," the "myth" that the budget should be balanced, the "myth" that saving and frugality are economically useful, and the "myth" that private initiative and free enterprise account for American economic productiveness. In the 1930's, Thurman Arnold published a book called *The Folklore of Capitalism* in which he castigated the beliefs of Americans as articles of faith, superstitions, myths, and folklore. By 1956, the book had been through fourteen printings! Myths have been got up which inhibit the exploration and exposure of the mythology of reform: the myth of the "extreme right," the myth of the Red scare, the myth of McCarthyism, and so on.

In short, an ethos has been developed, spread, and more or less accepted which promotes continuous reform by the use of government power. This mental framework has become the angle from which millions of Americans see things. They have imbibed it by way of a mythology which they have supposed was history. A language was developed, along with the mythology, which has been used to evoke it to promote reform measures. The language consists of such terms and phrases as "labor," "agriculture," "privileged," "underprivileged," "monopoly," "oligopoly," "economic royalist," "robber barons," "profiteers," "hoarders," "black marketeers," "vested interests," "extremists," "unearned increment," "social surplus," "general welfare," "malefactors of great wealth," "absentee ownership," "conspicuous consumption," "right winger," "neanderthals," "sweat shop," "rent-lord," "speculator," "anti-intellectual," "witch hunter," and so on. The terms used change some-

what over the years, depending upon the standing of reform among the American people and what is conceived
to be the immediate danger to the continuation of reconstruction.

Finally, it should be noted that a mythology is much
more difficult to deal with than an ideology, and a much
more effective way to draw people generally under its sway.
An ideology consists of ideas; it can be examined; the
ideas can be refuted if they are false. But when an ideology
has been embedded in a mythology, and this has become
widely accepted, many people will not even know that
their beliefs are rooted in ideologies. They think that what
they believe is simply the way things are, or have been.
That government action can produce prosperity, for instance, will not be thought of as rooted in ideology but as
something that has historically happened. Moreover, it is
much easier to manufacture myths than it is to give a valid
historical account; one needs only to examine such evidence as seems to prove his point, read his view of things
into the account, and make it come out according to the
mythological or ideological version one starts with. There
is also the near certainty that the process of exploding
myths and giving more accurate and valid historical accounts will proceed much more slowly than mythmaking,
be much less dramatic, and probably occur after the object
for which the myth existed has been obtained.

At any rate, a mythology has been formed and spread
in America. The attitudes and beliefs of many Americans
have been shaped in conformity with it. The minds of men
have been remade. It is this mythology that promotes the
continuous reform efforts. It is this that has catapulted us
into the Age of Meliorism.

17

The Origins of Reform Methods

THERE IS NOT, TO MY KNOWLEDGE, ANY THOROUGH HIS-
torical study of the origins of reform methods. References
to this subject are apt to be casual; for example, that
Marx did not tell precisely how a country went about
achieving communism. This absence of careful study is
the more amazing in view of the tremendous amount of
scholarly activity in this century, accelerated by the increasing numbers of students undertaking and completing
doctoral work. Revolutionaries, reformers, and their assorted "isms" have come in for a great deal of study, of
course. But the focus of such studies has usually been
upon ideas and ideologies, their origin, development, and
spread. It is as if ideas, aims, and purposes were all-important but how they were put into effect was of little or
no account. It is likely that historians are reflecting their
materials when they give this emphasis, for reformers
have been concerned mainly with their central ideas, or
obsessions, and with the great results that would occur
once they were put into effect, not deigning to concern
themselves overmuch with the vulgar business of making
them operational.

Yet method is extremely important; for social reformers,
it should be all-important, for their ideas are instruments
for changing the existing state of things. If this could be
done, it would have to be done by the methods adopted
for the purpose, and by methods adapted to the purpose.

The results achieved will be those that follow from the methods used. The consequences of actions are determined by the methods rather than by the intent, purpose, desire, will, wish, hope, or faith of those who act. Dreams, hopes, visions, ideas, purposes, and desires may move a man to act; but, however noble his purpose, however much enthusiasm he brings to the matter, however much thought he may have given to the idea that something ought to be done, his actions will still be only as effective as the methods he adopts for achieving his end.

The Theory in Practice

It may well be that many reformers and revolutionists have believed their aims would be achieved by such things as the inevitable working out of the inherent processes of history, by the victory of some ideology in the contest of ideas, by men of good will when they have in their hands the instruments of government, by the withering away of government, by a politically conscious elite acting for the "people" or the "proletariat," by a return to nature, or by the enfranchisement of whole adult populations. But when revolutionists and reformers have actually come to power, they have come face to face with the problem of method which they had hitherto evaded. That is, how is the sought-after social reconstruction to be brought about? How is an ideology to be turned into actuality? How does one go about, for example, realizing the "principle," "from each according to his ability, to each according to his need"? How can the ability of a man be determined? It cannot be with any exactitude, but if it could, it would only pose a new problem. How can a man be induced to perform according to his ability? If he does not, what is to be done? In general, either the rewards or punishments will have to be increased. But, according to the Marxian formulation, the rewards are not to be apportioned in terms of performance. That means that the punishment will have to be increased, an excellent device for tyranny but not one calculated to get from each according to his ability. The latter part of the famous formulation poses just as great practical difficulties as the first. What are the needs of a person? Who is to determine them? If they could be determined, how would they be met? By what instrumentalities would the goods be gathered and handed out to the needy? What assurance would there be that this would be done "justly"?

Nearer home, note these pronouncements by Theodore Roosevelt in his acceptance speech following his nomination by the Progressive party in 1912. "Our aim is to promote prosperity, and then see to its proper division. . . . We wish to control big business so as to secure among other things good wages for the wageworkers and reasonable prices for the consumers." What are "good wages" for workingmen? What are "reasonable prices" for consumer goods? Even if these questions could be answered, other than in the marketplace, how could government go about securing these ends? Who would decide what are "reasonable" prices? How would he go about administering them? By what instrumentalities would such controls be effected? What institutions are appropriate to such regulation?

In the nineteenth century, reformers and revolutionaries usually talked in the broadest generalities. They favored the expropriation of the expropriators, a single tax upon the unearned increment or social surplus, government ownership of the means of production, or government ownership of public utilities. How would property be taken over? Who would manage it? Who would determine what should be produced? Who would determine what prices should be paid for goods? How would these things be determined? Americans did not usually talk the language of revolution, not if they expected to be elected to office; but they, too, often talked vaguely about how their ends were to be achieved and glowingly about the ends.

This lack of attention to methods has often become apparent when socialists have come to political power. In Soviet Russia, following the Bolshevik seizure of power, chaos reigned, particularly from 1917 to 1921. The communists were rather adept at the destruction of the existing order, at murder, at regicide, at expropriation; but they knew almost nothing about building and producing. Force is, after all, much better suited to destruction than to construction. Moreover, ideologues often have only the foggiest of notions about how the world's work gets done. But the important point here is that the socialists in Russia had not devised methods, if such could be devised, for accomplishing their aims. Almost thirty years later, when the Labor party finally came to power with a full commitment to the "nationalization" of major industries in England, they still had only the vaguest of ideas as to how this could be accomplished.

That is not to say that methods of reform have not been adopted. Even communist revolutions have become somewhat stylized. Fabians, or gradualists, have adopted methods, too, and these have tended to be universalized. In the United States, where the socialist tendency has been gradual, methods have been adopted for each reformist move, and the move has been made by and with the method adopted. This reflects the legalistic approach to socialism. In other words, insofar as reform has been undertaken within the existing framework, and insofar as the existing framework requires government by law, reforms have been given a semblance of lawfulness. This has meant, to some considerable extent, that the methods of reform have been adopted prior to or concurrent with the introduction of the reforms themselves. This was necessary to give the reforms the appearance of legality.

Methods from the Past

The central question is: Where did these methods come from? American reformers have usually claimed that their reforms were new, unique, and innovative, that they were adopted to deal with new and unique conditions. The old, the traditional, the customary, was held to be out of date, no longer appropriate to these modern times. The new reform methods were progressive, as opposed to the outmoded methods to be replaced. There has been much talk of bold, new social planning. Lester Frank Ward and John Dewey wrote confidently about "social invention." The pragmatic approach, according to the lore of the contemporary orthodoxy, is one of continual innovation, testing, and adjustment as to methods.

Such claims are interesting, but the only reality to which they refer is the mythology of reform from which the rhetoric emanates. The methods of the reformers are not new creations; they are usually variations upon methods that have a considerable antiquity. The methods of reform have been obtained by the process of abstraction of older or contemporary methods, the abstraction of them from the context in which they existed, and the application of them to different purposes. Many of them have long histories and have been subjected to a variety of uses. Let us examine some of the sources of reform methods, and in so doing look at some of the methods themselves.

Reform in America, and elsewhere, has proceeded by dealing with the population as if it were divided into classes. To put it another way, reforms have usually been

aimed at, or provided for, people in certain groups; and
these groups are often thought of as composing classes.
For example, it has been common to refer to the business
class, the working class, the professional class, the white
collar class, and so on. In practice, reformers have extended this idea considerably; there are many other classes
or sub-classes: farmers, women, the aged, teen-agers, Negroes, minority groups, and veterans. Americans have always spoken of classes; the word was a part of the English
language which they inherited. It is a word which had
rather precise meaning in the Middle Ages in Europe, and
had rather definite descriptive meaning in many European
countries down to the twentieth century. It referred to divisions within society which were established at law or
were protected by law, to a system in which one was born
into a particular class and might be expected to remain in
that class for the whole of his life. A class system, in
short, is a system in which certain groups are empowered
and/or disabled by legal prescription, and the condition
has usually been hereditary, though it need not be.

Now, in this sense, America has hardly had classes at
all. After the adoption of the Constitution, the only definite
class was that made up of Negro slaves. After the abolition
of slavery, there were no classes in America, though Negroes suffered some disabilities by law, and women may
have, also, in some places. Americans still referred to upper, middle, and lower classes; but these were vague classifications which one might apply according to his predilections. Into the breach came sociologists with their baneful
penchant for "thingifying" abstractions. To be more specific, there came Karl Marx and assorted hosts of socialists
and reformers. Marx concocted a theory of universal history in terms of class struggle. His idea of class was probably drawn from earlier history, but he applied the abstrac-

tion of it to the industrialization going on around him. The bourgeoisie and proletariat were for him classes as rigid as any that had ever existed. This conception, or, rather, misconception, of class was spread by socialists in the latter part of the nineteenth century. Many American intellectuals came to hold this conception also.

According to the rhetoric of reformers, "labor" was sinking into a permanent state of dependence, "farmers" being reduced to the perpetual state of sharecropping, Negroes bound over to a new servility, and small businessmen squeezed out. "Big business" was often the villain of the piece. The point here is that the population was divided into classes. This division provided reformers with one of their methods, the method of using government to disable certain "classes" and to empower others. Anyone familiar with the reforms of the last fifty years or so should recognize the method as it has been employed: regulate and control "business," particularly big business, subsidize farmers, and use the power of government to support labor unionization, for example.

Other general methods of reform were abstracted from the system of government in the United States. One of the most prominent of these abstractions is that of the "democratic process," that is, of voting, majority rule, and representation, and its broad application to all sorts of undertakings. For example, the methods drawn from government have been generally applied to union organization and activity. There are votes as to whether the workers in a craft or plant shall be represented by a union, votes on whether to strike, whether to accept the terms of contracts, and the like. The decision of the majority is usually binding upon all. Representatives of the workers negotiate with companies; and these, too, are chosen by the vote of the workers. These are clearly methods abstracted from the

American governmental framework. This particular method has become a method of reform because the United States government has long since thrown its weight behind these processes, and undertakes to guarantee that they will be faithfully applied. Thus, methods which have an important and legitimate role in government are applied to a supposedly nongovernmental matter.

Federalism, too, has been instrumented to reform purposes. In the American system of government, as conceived, local governments performed most governmental functions, local initiative was essential to political action, and local customs and traditions determined the character of action taken. Some reforms have been undertaken at the local level, but over the years the tendency has been to have them initiated, financed, and administered by the central government. Local governments have been used increasingly as administrative units and as a framework within which to impose and control governmental programs by the central government. An example of this would be the welfare program, that is, the program of old-age assistance, aid to dependent children, and aid to the disabled. Moneys are provided by both the United States government and the state government involved. The program is administered at the county level; but it is administered according to prescriptions laid down by the central government, in the first place, and, within that, according to state law and procedure. Thus, the county is reduced, in this and many other instances, to an administrative unit. The federal system of government becomes an instrument for reformers by reversing the direction of the flow of authority; it becomes one of the methods for reform.

Many of the methods of governmental reform have been abstracted from practices, procedures, and services of voluntary organizations. For example, cases of need and hardship were generally looked after and provided for in the nineteenth century by voluntary charitable organizations. In rural areas and small communities, permanent organizations might not exist; each case would be handled by relatives, neighbors, and churches as it arose. But in cities, more nearly permanent charitable organizations were formed and maintained. Many services provided by such organizations were eventually taken over and provided by governments.

It would make an interesting and informative study to examine into the question of how many services now provided by governments were originated and initially provided by private industry, individuals, and voluntary groups. My guess is that it would include almost all of them. Many roads and bridges were built and operated by private companies in the United States in the first half of the nineteenth century, though they were often chartered monopolies, in keeping with the mercantile mode of operation. Education was generally provided during the same period by voluntary means. Voluntary associations within professions, such as the legal and medical, have maintained standards and "policed" themselves. Industries had inspectors before government provided them. Insurance was a private function long before government got into the business. There were private savings banks before the United States government set up Postal Savings in 1910. Hospitals were built and maintained by physicians, churches, and voluntary organizations. Volunteer fire departments even preceded city fire departments. Housing for the poor was provided by private enterprise long before "public housing" measures were undertaken. Even the tenement, which is surely the model for government-financed housing in large cities, was initially built by private initiative. It was, after all, the apartment house in times when capital, technology, and entrepreneurship had not made the labor of many workers sufficiently remunerative to afford better. The chances are good that "Duncan Hines ate here" before state inspectors did generally, and his is still considered the more important recommendation. In perspective, it looks as if the vaunted "social invention" of reformers has been restricted largely to inventing arguments why government should perform services that were already being performed.

Not only have many of the services now performed by governments been taken over from the individuals and voluntary groups who originated and maintained them, but administrative organization and procedure was taken over, too. Boards of trustees, boards of directors, boards of deacons, committees, and boards of education—the control bodies of private organizations—often have been perpetuated by governments. When a state takes over a private college, for example, it usually continues the same mode of administrative control, having a president or chancellor and whatever its board of control happens to be called. It will, of course, be brought under the sway of the government, in one way or another. The various "authorities" by which governments engage in business activities, as, for example, the Tennessee Valley Authority, will have some figure as head who will likely be called chairman, patterned after the chairman of the board of directors of a private corporation, and a board or commission which itself appears to have been abstracted from corporation organization.

Some methods of doing things have had a long and checkered career. Take, for example, the recording of births, marriages, and deaths. A few hundred years ago such records were kept by churches. In nineteenth century America, following the change in the political position of churches, many families kept such records in the family Bible. Counties took over the function, and began to require that reports be made to them of these affairs, authorizations be got from them in some cases, and certificates began to be issued commonly. The Federal census, authorized as a population count for the purposes of apportionment of electors and representatives among the states, began to collect and contain more and more information about the citizenry. Now, the information which governments collect through these and other devices is being made into an instrument for the advancement of reform by way of governmental planning based upon the projection of figures drawn from the information.

Ancient Practices Revived

A goodly number of the methods of reform are adapted from other eras. An example of this is the use of the power of eminent domain to acquire property for reform uses. The power of eminent domain is the power to take private property for public use by government. Such a power was assumed to be appropriate to government at the time of the adoption of state constitutions and the United States Constitution, for provision was made for its exercise. The theoretical justification then was that it derived from the sovereignty of a government. The idea of sovereignty was carefully formulated in the sixteenth century, was drawn from the powers of the monarch, and served to buttress the thrust of kings to absolute power in the seventeenth and eighteenth centuries. But the powers of the monarch over the land of the realm go back to the feudal system, when the patents or rights to land belonged to and stemmed from the king.

It is somewhat a matter of choice as to whether one traces the power of eminent domain to feudalism or to di-

vine right monarchy. The use of the term "eminent domain" appears to be peculiarly American, but the power
is not. For most of American history, the power was used
only to a limited degree, and some limitations upon it were
embedded in constitutions. However, in recent years it has
tended to be used as an open sesame for governmental appropriation of land for reform purposes. This is particularly glaring in the case of urban renewal projects, but its
use is not restricted to this arena.

Other practices can be traced back to the Middle Ages,
at least. The "just price" is a Medieval conception and
practice which has been used in price controls. Maximum
wages were set by the English government as early as the
fourteenth century, in connection with the Black Death.
The setting aside of lands as forests and parks has its
model in the Medieval "commons" and the king's forests.

The most fecund historical source for commercial regulation and control is mercantilism, which reached its
earlier apogee in the seventeenth and eighteenth centuries.
The protective tariff was the classic mercantile device for
regulating and inhibiting trade among the peoples of various nations. Monarchs also issued patents and charters
which gave to individuals and companies monopolies of
trade. Regulations upon the export of precious metals were
adopted. Monarchs inflated the currency, as governments
have done from time immemorial, largely by reducing the
metal content of coins supposed to have a certain and
fixed value. Practices to promote the "economic self-suffi-
ciency" of nations were used within the mercantile framework. Subsidies and bounties were paid for the production
and manufacture of certain goods. Sumptuary laws were
passed to discourage or prohibit their consumption.

Virtually all of these mercantile practices have been revived within the last century. Modern reformers have made

some alterations in them, however. They are more apt to set minimum wages than maximum wages. They call their "just price" a "fair price." Mercantilist governments usually subsidized the growing of scarce items, while modern reformers tend to subsidize the production of goods in surplus. However, the recently authorized reduction of the silver content in American coins differs not at all from the ancient practice.

Other reform methods have been borrowed from the Europe of more recent times. Many American intellectuals have been, of course, enamored of things European. For some of them, it has been enough recommendation of a practice to declare only that it is what is done in Europe. If European countries have government-financed radio and television stations, it is taken to be a proper way to do things. If European countries subsidize the arts and maintain theaters and concert halls, it is presumed to be an enlightened undertaking. Be that as it may, reformers have learned some of their methods from the Europeans. England undertook to impose an income tax in the first half of the nineteenth century. Imperial Germany set up welfare programs in the latter part of the nineteenth century, and England got into the welfare business just before World War I. Reforms attempted in England are quite often copied by American reformers, without making royalty payments either.

War a Prolific Incubator of Reform Methods

But perhaps the most prolific womb of methods has been war; it has been a veritable incubator of reform methods. Reformers have long been fascinated by the "accomplishments" of a country at war. They have noted the full employment, the rise in wages, the immense production, the rise in farm prices, and, altogether, the aura of prosperity.

There are those who suppose that war does indeed bring prosperity. A considerable myth was propagated by Charles A. Beard and others that the great industrial surge in the latter part of the nineteenth century was a product to a large extent of the Civil War. No one has ever explained how the great waste and destruction of war could produce prosperity, or why construction is the product of destruction. Such history is on a par with a history that would claim that because roosters crow before the sun comes up that their crowing causes the sun to rise. Still, these myths have attracted a large following. Reformers have abstracted methods used in wartime from their context and applied them in peacetime. One history, in dealing with the origins of the New Deal, contains these remarks:

> The power which the federal government could exert over the economy had been amply demonstrated by the War Industries Board and other wartime agencies in 1917 and 1918. Roosevelt and a number of his advisors, including George N. Peek, Hugh Johnson, and Bernard Baruch, seem to have been greatly influenced by their experiences in economic planning during World War I.[1]

This does not begin, however, to tell the impact of war upon reform. Perhaps the most momentous abstraction from war has been the inflationary device. Now inflation—that is, the increase of the amount of currency in circulation—has not been restricted to war. But in the United States the government inflated most extensively during wars until well into the twentieth century, if not to the present. This has been true because those in power have not seen fit—have not thought it politic—to finance the wars by the ordinary route of taxation. They have, instead, employed surreptitious tax measures such as inflation.

---

[1] Gilbert C. Fite and Jim E. Reese, *An Economic History of the United States* (Boston: Houghton Mifflin, 1959), p. 590.

The first time that this measure attracted the attention of reformers to any extent was after the Civil War. The government had issued a large number of greenbacks during the war. It later began to retire them from circulation, which was a responsible fiscal undertaking. Nonetheless, it drew the fire of reformers. A political party called the Greenback party was even organized. This particular movement died out but not the desire to inflate. The silverite movement of the latter part of the century was an extension of the inflation movement. During World War I the government had a much more potent mechanism for inflation—the Federal Reserve Banks. The extensive use of this system to facilitate government financing during World War I was continued afterward, and this system became an important auxiliary of the Treasury and for manipulating the currency supply.

During World War I, the first concerted attempt in American history was made to co-ordinate, regulate, and direct the economy by the government to a definite end. Economic planning was carried out on a large scale. The War Industries Board, under the guidance of Bernard Baruch, was eventually given powers to establish priorities for all types of materials for war use, and to convert old facilities for manufacturing from their former use and to cause new facilities to be brought into being. Baruch had a life-and-death power over manufacturing and could, through the threat of the denial of materials, bring a business into line.

An Advisory Food Committee, with Herbert Hoover as Food Commissioner, was set up. It was soon given great powers over certain kinds of agricultural activities. Food processors had to be licensed by the government. The act granting these powers prohibited the use of foodstuffs for making alcoholic beverages; thus began the "great experiment" in national prohibition. The price of wheat was set by the government, and a corporation was set up to achieve this end. A War Trade Board was authorized and given power to regulate exports and imports. An Emergency Fleet Corporation was organized with power to buy, lease, build, and operate ships. The model for this was the private corporation, but the government was going into business. The first government dam on the Tennessee River was built during and after World War I. A War Labor Board was set up to mediate labor disputes, the first time the government became officially involved in these matters. The government could manipulate wages by the wages it paid in government-owned war plants. "Wilson used this power to make an informal but firm bargain with labor. He undertook to establish the principle of union recognition in government plants and to secure wage increases as rapidly as prices rose. In return, he extracted a no-strike pledge from organized labor in basic industry for the duration of the war."[2]

This experience was abstracted and much of it applied to reformist ends. The crisis motif has been taken from its war context and applied to depression conditions, for instance. Reformers have come to talk about *wars* on poverty, on death, and so forth. But the methods used during World War I have been specifically applied to peacetime uses also. The concentration of powers in the hands of the President, done during war, has now become a common mode of operation by government. The creation of all sorts of boards and commissions has become standard operating procedure. The War Industries Board served as a model, of sorts, for the National Recovery Administra-

---

[2] George H. Mayer and Walter O. Forster, *The United States and the Twentieth Century* (Boston: Houghton Mifflin, 1958), p. 244.

tion. The costs of the agricultural programs in the early New Deal were to be paid by a tax on food processors, a tactic obviously drawn from the method of control during World War I. The National Labor Relations Board was modeled after the War Labor Board. A dam built because of the exigencies of war became the first of a large number to be built upon the Tennessee River by the government. The list is not complete, but it should be suggestive.

The Method Affects the Result

On the face of it, all of this may not appear to matter much. After all, does it make any difference whether reformers are original, in some kind of "creative" sense, or not? Is it not appropriate to use the methods with which one is familiar, or which may be learned from history, for the accomplishment of new ends? Is this not how everyone operates, more or less? Perhaps so, but it must be kept in mind that it is the reformers who have insisted upon the uniqueness of the times and upon the new and experimental character of what they were doing. If it were not new and different, it would not be "progressive." Moreover, if the methods had been tried before, there would be historical evidence as to their efficacy.

As to the validity of the process of abstraction employed in this way, it should be kept in mind that this depends upon the identity of the nature of the things to be dealt with. It may be appropriate to adapt a method used in one undertaking to use in another, if the undertakings are similar in kind. For example, if a corporation is an effective business organization for manufacturing bolts, it is reasonable to suppose that it will be equally efficient in organizing for the manufacture of nuts. The assembly line method for manufacturing buggies may be abstracted from this undertaking and applied to the manufacture of automobiles. But the assembly line cannot be utilized to produce custom-made automobiles. They may be called custom-made, but they will be uniform because products of an assembly line must be, or, rather, they must be if the method is to be effectively used.

We are back now to the original point of departure in this chapter. The methods employed determine the results produced. Aim and purpose have bearing upon the matter only if they have determined the methods to be used. To be more specific, feudal methods produce neofeudalism when they are applied. Mercantile methods produce mercantilism. The reason for this can be readily understood. When government deals with groups within a population as if they were a class, it creates a new class system. In short, if it grants privileges or immunities to some element of the population, empowers or disables it, it has brought into being a class.

When wartime measures are applied to civil purposes, the measures retain their warlike character. War mobilization methods are suited, if to anything, to the augmentation of governmental power for the destruction of an enemy. When these methods are used for civil purposes, if they could be, their character is unaltered. Their use still results in the augmentation of governmental power, and such power remains, in the main, destructive. There is no real enemy—of flesh and blood, with weapons and war plans—that can be designated by the name, "poverty," against which to use this power. There are only people and goods, and such power as is exercised will be exercised against these, not against some abstraction.

This should have been clear when the New Deal's war on poverty was conducted; it was conducted initially by plowing up crops and shooting animals. But then, war is war, and its methods are the methods of destruction. However subtly methods abstracted from war may be applied to the domestic situation, they continue to be wars on person and property: whether they be wars on savings by inflation, wars upon possessions by taxation and confiscation, wars upon human relationships by the prescription of behavior, or wars upon production by way of crop limitations.

Methods abstracted from other kinds of activities are equally inappropriate to reform by the use of governmental power, though they may not always be so devastating in their consequences when applied. The use of force or the threat of force by labor unions is nonetheless a use of compulsion—an assumption of pseudo-governmental powers—regardless of whether the principle of majority rule has been applied or not. When governments provide welfare for the needy, it ceases to be charity, even though the same organization for the provision of the service be adapted from private and charitable societies. The adoption of the forms of business organization by governmental bodies does not result in maintaining responsibility along the lines that it was established in private companies. A government board is just not responsible for what it does in the way that the board of directors of a private corporation is. When the power of eminent domain is joined to presidential power, or to that of somebody under the President, it takes on its old character of absolutism, embedded in the method all along.

We are not to suppose that reformers are aware of the grotesque incongruities that exist between their professed aims and the methods they use. It is unlikely that many of them are aware of the origins of the methods they employ. They have a rhetoric which hides them from such recognition. They talk in terms of bold, new experiments, of breakthroughs and innovation, of pragmatic testing; but theirs are the age-old methods of feudalism, of absolutism, of mercantilism, of war, and of voluntary methods joined to political power. The flight from reality is in the mind; in the real world the results of actions follow from the methods used.

18

The Flight from Economics

. . . In these crises there breaks out an epidemic that, in all earlier epochs, would have seemed an absurdity—the epidemic of over-production. . . . Because there is too much civilization, too much means of subsistence, too much industry, too much commerce. —KARL MARX and FREDERICK ENGELS, 1848

. . . The essence of social progress lies not in the increase of material wealth but in a rise of the margin of consumption.
—SIMON N. PATTEN, 1893

. . . In industry after industry potential output is vastly greater than demand—a condition which grows steadily worse.
—STUART CHASE, 1931

. . . Shall we continue to believe that panics, deflation, and bankruptcy are our only remedy for overproductivity in industry? Or shall we . . . control overcapacity and reconstruct the purchasing power of our people?
—REXFORD G. TUGWELL, 1935

Given a sufficiency of demand, the responding production of goods in the modern economy is almost completely reliable. We have seen . . . why men once had reason to regard the economic system as a meager and perilous thing. And we have seen how these ideas have persisted after the problem of production was conquered. —JOHN K. GALBRAITH, 1958

THE METHODS OF REFORM HAVE BEEN DRAWN FROM A variety of incongruous sources—from war, from business, from charitable organizations, from voluntary societies, from feudal practices, from mercantile policies, among

351

others. The consequences that have followed attempts to use these methods have been determined by the methods. But there is more to the matter of the methods of the reformers than their origin. There have been strange justifications for the use of the methods and peculiar, as well as particular, applications of them.

The particular orientation of most reformers has been materialistic. They have professed concern with the material well-being of people. Their interest and concern has had to do with hunger, deprivation, disease, malnutrition, poverty, poor housing, infestations, and exposure. Such matters fall in the realm of economy. Many of the programs and policies of reformers are aimed at or have to do with things economic. These emphases make economics the central discipline for reformist attention; their programs succeed or fail to the extent that they are more or less economically sound. It would not be too much to say that the vast meliorist reform effort would only be morally, socially, and rationally justified if it were in accord with sound economics.

Uneconomical Programs

On the face of it, many reform programs appear to be uneconomical. Reformers have, at various times, advocated crop restrictions and control upon industrial production, subsidies for products already in "surplus," loans to foreign governments to enable them to buy American goods, give-away programs both domestic and foreign, deficit spending by government in order to produce prosperity, inflation in order to increase "purchasing power," easy money policies to promote spending, the raising of wages by promoting unionization and establishing minimum wages, the establishing of prices above or below market prices, special taxes upon corporations which had become major instruments of production, graduated income taxes which would fall proportionately heaviest upon those with the highest incomes, the governmental provision of income to those who do not produce, and so on. These are not measures of a character that would usually be called economical. Men have not customarily thought it economically sound to spend more than they make, to take from those who produce and give to those who do not, to pay more than the market price for goods and services, to give away their substance.

A deeper look at economics reveals that such actions are, indeed, uneconomical. Economics has to do with scarcity. This character of economics is indicated by the conventional uses of words related to it. For example, one dictionary defines "economical" as "avoiding waste or extravagance; thrifty." It "implies prudent planning in the disposition of resources so as to avoid unnecessary waste. . . ." To "economize" is to "use sparingly or frugally." "Economy" refers to "thrifty management; frugality in the expenditure or consumption of money, materials, etc."

Economics can be defined as the study and exposition of the most effective means for men to maintain and increase the supply of goods and services at their disposal. These goods and services are understood to be scarce; and economics has to do with the frugal management of time, energy, resources, and materials so as to bring about the greatest increase in the supply of the goods and services most desired. An aspect of economics, one with which much of academic and theoretical economics has dealt, is the study and setting forth of answers to the question of what are the best social conditions within which economic behavior may take place. Such a study is known as political economy, but it, too, has been premised upon the existence of scarcity.

With these definitions in mind, it should be clear that the methods of reformers have not been economical. Crop restrictions are means of increasing scarcity rather than diminishing it. Minimum wages, above the market rate, increase the shortage of labor by pricing it out of use (cause unemployment). Price supports for goods make them unavailable to those who cannot afford them at that price, thus increasing *their* scarcity. Inflation increases the supply of money, not the supply of goods. The giving away of goods decreases their supply; and if these are *taken* from someone by government, this action decreases the incentive for the production of goods. Loans to enable the buying of goods are not economic, though if the loans be repaid with interest, at or above the market rate, it would be economical for the lender. None of these devices involves frugal management of limited means to deal with the problem of scarcity.

The Development of Economics

Modern (i.e., post-Medieval) economics took shape from proposals for dealing with scarcity. Some of these developments in the sixteenth, seventeenth, and into the eighteenth centuries are known now as mercantilism. Mercantilism was, and is, nationalistic, that is, a proposed economy for dealing with the scarcity which confronts a particular nation. The particular scarcity which mercantilists emphasized was the scarcity of gold, but the value of gold was generally understood to be its virtually universal acceptability as a medium of exchange. At any rate, mercantilists focused attention upon means for increasing the supply of gold within a nation. They thought of one nation's wealth as being got at the expense of other nations and conceived of a variety of devices for getting gold from other nations. Their main invention was the favorable-balance-of-trade idea, by which a nation would sell more goods to a nation than it bought from that nation, the difference being made up by gold. Mercantilists favored manufacturing, for thereby the value of a product would be enhanced before it was sold, and they promoted colonization for the securing of raw materials and markets. Regulatory measures were endorsed as means for enhancing the trade and gold supply of a nation.

Dealing with scarcity was the object of mercantilism, but were such practices economical? It was the great work of the physiocrats and Adam Smith in the latter part of the eighteenth century to show that they were not. These writers took a cosmopolitan or universal view of economics. They were concerned to discover and set forth the natural order for economic behavior. From this broad view, Smith, particularly, demonstrated that true economic behavior is *social*, that when everyone behaves economically, everyone benefits.

In a century beset by world wars—wars rooted mainly in trade conflicts spawned by mercantilism—Smith held that trade is by nature peaceful, that the wealth of a people is not obtained at the expense of other peoples, that when peoples of one country trade with those of another, both benefit. He maintained that when each man pursues his own interest, when exchange is free from arbitrarily imposed obstacles, when each man may buy at the lowest price anywhere in the world and sell to the highest bidder on the world market, when competition is allowed free play, all will benefit. Each man will be able to get the highest price possible for his goods and services and be able to obtain those he wants at the lowest possible price, that is, roughly, at the cost of providing them. There is an invisible hand—an order in the universe—that brings harmony out of the diverse actions of men, if they may act as they choose and are prohibited to use force, fraud, or deception in their dealings with others.

Smith held that government intervention was not necessary to bring about these beneficient results. On the contrary, government intervention is a positive deterrent to economic behavior; it places obstacles in the way of free exchange, promotes uneconomic (viewed socially) behavior, and distorts the market. In short, mercantilist practices are not economic.

Economic thought, after Smith, consisted largely of refinements, extensions, and modifications of positions which he and the physiocrats had set forth. But the philosophical framework within which Smith worked hardly survived the eighteenth century for most thinkers, as we have seen in earlier chapters. The breadth of vision made possible by the cosmopolitanism, universalism, and belief in a natural order within a rational universe gave way to the particularism of romanticism and the numerous abstractions which served as a base for the proliferating ideologies of the nineteenth century. Economics became the "dismal science," the discipline which justified the ways of scarcity and privation to men.

Economists were soon, once again, wrestling with the conundrum which ever and again besets them. The conundrum has had many formulations, but the one which follows may, perhaps, state the essence of them all. If man is confronted with scarcity, if the supply of goods and services is less than the desire for them, it looks as if one man's gain is another man's loss. That is, when one man takes from the limited supply of goods, he has them at the expense of others who might have used them. If this were the case, the quest for goods and services would be a clash or contest between those who had them and those who wanted them for possession, with one side the winner and one the loser. Mercantilists had conceived of such a struggle among nations. Ricardo and Malthus conceived of the matter as a contest between increasing population and the limited means for subsistence. Marx rendered it into a class struggle. The social Darwinists, Spencer and Sumner, saw it as a struggle in which the fit survived.

Concerning Struggle and Scarcity

Economists adopted a variety of postures about the struggle and the scarcity. Ricardo held that that was the way things were and there was nothing much to be done about it (though technological innovations might temporarily ameliorate conditions for workers). Utilitarians held that free exchange and competition were all to the good; though some might get hurt, the greatest good for the greatest number would be achieved. Marx opted for revolution. The Austrians—Menger and Böhm-Bawerk—concluded that everyone benefited from free exchange because wants and values are subjective. The social Darwinists held that it all added up to progress. Utopians, who did not accept scarcity, were searching out the sources of privation in supposed exploitation and envisioning their perfect societies.

The main lines of economic thought in the nineteenth century run from the classicists—Smith and Ricardo—to the utilitarians—Bentham and Mill—to the Austrians. These schools shared the view, more or less, that true economic behavior is that of free men, willingly exchanging goods, making their own calculations, and seeking their own ends. Government intervention was not economic to them; it produced distortions which were antithetical to economic action. Even Karl Marx did not hold much brief for palliative action by governments.

Two points need particular emphasis. Historically, economic thought has been concerned with scarcity, however much the import of this may have been distorted by some thinkers. Nor was this simply an historical accident. The reason for being of economy is scarcity. If there were no scarcity, there would be no justification for economics. There would be no occasion for saving, for careful management, for priorities as to the order of satisfying desires, for choices among goods, or for efficiency. Second, economic thought has been, in the main, noninterventionist. Individual economists have favored this or that interventionist measure—the protective tariff, compulsory workmen's compensation insurance, government inspections—but not on economic grounds (the tariff being a possible exception). If it were economical, for instance, for an employer to take out insurance on his employees, he could be persuaded of this, and compulsion would be irrelevant.

There is no body of thought which demonstrates that it is economical for governments to intervene in the lives of people. There have been numerous claims, of course, that governments could manage businesses more effectively than would private interests, that governments will conserve scarce resources, that government action will render this or that economic benefit. A careful examination will show, I believe, that these are not economic arguments, that they are based not upon the premise of a scarcity of goods and services but an abundance. They are based, in short, upon the premise that economic behavior is unnecessary.

The "Plague of Abundance"

At any rate, interventionist thought has been based upon the view that there exists an abundance of goods and services. The idea that mankind is confronted with a glut of goods and services is not particularly recent. It goes back at least to *The Communist Manifesto* (1848), and possibly before that time. But it has had its particular American articulation. This was provided mainly by that school of "economics" known as the institutionalists. Prominent leaders of this school have been Thorstein Veblen, John R. Commons, Stuart Chase, and, lately, John K. Galbraith.

Their basic position is that conditions have changed, that it was once true, indeed had been from time immemorial, that societies were confronted with scarcity, but that this condition is no longer the case for some societies, notably the United States. Stuart Chase held that the United States reached a condition of abundance in 1902. "Abundance," he said, "is self-defined, and means an economic condition where an abundance of material goods can be produced for the entire population of a given community."[1]

Rexford G. Tugwell, the irrepressible New Dealer, described the change to plenty in this way:

> Our economic course has carried us from the era of economic *development* to an era which confronts us with the necessity for economic *maintenance*. In this period of maintenance, there is no scarcity of production. There is, in fact, a present capacity for more production than is consumable, at least under a system which shortens purchasing power while it is lengthening capacity to produce.[2]

John K. Galbraith, who plays Stuart Chase to post World War II America, describes the development as historical in the following:

> Nearly all [people] throughout all history have been

[1] Quoted in Charles S. Wyand, *The Economics of Consumption* (New York: Macmillan, 1937), p. 54.

[2] Rexford G. Tugwell, *The Battle for Democracy* (New York: Columbia University Press, 1935), p. 7.

very poor. The exception, almost insignificant in the whole span of human existence, has been the last few generations in the small corner of the world populated by Europeans. Here, and especially in the United States, there has been great and quite unprecedented affluence.[3]

Vance Packard, who is to Galbraith as Galbraith is to Veblen and Keynes—that is, derivative—states the development with his usual dramatic flair:

> Man throughout recorded history has struggled—often against appalling odds—to cope with material scarcity. Today, there has been a massive breakthrough. The great challenge in the United States—and soon in Western Europe—is to cope with a threatened overabundance of the staples and amenities and frills of life.[4]

The evidence which purports to support these claims of abundance has run the gamut from Veblen's conspicuous consumption of the leisure class to Packard's charges that industrial waste makers prey upon the gullible public with their shoddy merchandise with its built-in planned obsolescence. The terms which have received the widest acceptance for describing abundance are overproduction, unemployment, surpluses, unused industrial capacity, and underconsumption.

The following is some of the evidence Stuart Chase submitted in 1931:

> American oil wells are capable of producing 5,950,000 barrels a day, against a market demand of 4,000,000 barrels, according to the figures of the Standard Oil Company of New Jersey.[5]

------

[3] John K. Galbraith, *The Affluent Society* (Boston: Houghton Mifflin, 1958), p. 1.

[4] Vance Packard, *The Waste Makers* (New York: David McKay, 1960), p. 7.

[5] Stuart Chase, *The Nemesis of American Business* (New York: Macmillan, 1931), p. 88.

The real problem [in coal] is excess capacity. The mines of the country can produce at least 750,000,000 tons a year, while the market can absorb but 500,000,000 tons.[6]

American shoe factories are equipped to turn out almost 900,000,000 pairs of shoes a year. At present we buy about 300,000,000 pairs—two and one-half pairs per capita. There is admittedly a considerable shortage of shoes [?], but could we wear out, or even amuse ourselves with, five pairs per capita? I doubt it. For myself two pairs a year satisfy both utility and style. Yet if we doubled shoe consumption—gorging the great American foot, as it were—one-third of the present shoe factory equipment would still lie idle.[7]

Jumping now across the economic front to agriculture, we find that the basic problem of the American farmer lies in his "surplus." The government at the present writing has bought and holds in storage millions of bushels of wheat in a heroic and possibly calamitous attempt to keep the surplus from crushing wheat farmers altogether.[8]

One might suppose that these writers would rejoice at the abundance of goods, be glad that an age-old problem has been solved, be jubilant at the prospects of plenty. They might even have been grateful for an economic system that provided them with such an abundance. How good it is, they might have said, to live in America where this has taken place. Of course, they were in the mood to say no such things. Instead, they held that abundance had produced great and difficult problems, problems of a monumental scale that threatened to grow. Poverty has continued to exist alongside abundance, overproduction resulted in waste and profligacy, mechanical production

---

[6] *Ibid.,* p. 89.

[7] *Ibid.,* p. 79.

[8] *Ibid.,* p. 76.

eventuated in technological unemployment, and producers reduced to all sorts of stratagems to dispose of their mounting goods and services.

One writer attempted to account for many of the untoward developments of this century as being a consequence of the efforts of producers to maintain artificial scarcity. The following are methods that he claims have been used to maintain scarcity:

1. *The Destruction of Surpluses by Warfare.* For the *temporary* creation of scarcity, no more effective means has yet been devised than modern warfare. Within a relatively short time it can dissipate industrial surpluses and create an additional demand for goods that taxes productive equipment to capacity. . . .

2. *The Extension of Loans.* With the disappearance of wartime demands, other markets are sought in an effort to avoid an immediate and complete collapse of the industrial structure. . . . The result [after World War I] was a series of . . . loans that by 1929 totaled about $11,023,000,000. . . .

3. *Public Subsidy of the Consumer.* When the process of lending purchasing power to the consumer failed, the Federal government commenced what is now an established practice of *giving* to the indigent funds with which to buy. . . .

4. *The Destruction of Goods and the Curtailment of Output.* Having failed through wars, loans, "gifts," and a variety of other means to make purchasing power keep pace with large-scale production, attempts are now being made to preserve conditions of scarcity by deliberately controlling output so that it does not exceed profitable demand.[9]

Many different specters have been raised over the years which were supposed to have arisen from this overproduction, but none has been more persistent than that of

---

[9] Wyand, *op. cit.,* pp. 44-48.

rising unemployment. Stuart Chase declared, in the early 1930's, that the "current depression will pass." However,

> What threatens to continue unabated, in good times and bad, is technological unemployment with its three faces—the machine, the merger, the stop watch. In four years oil refineries increased output 84 per cent, and laid off 5 per cent of their men while doing it. Tobacco manufacturing output climbed 53 per cent in the same period, with 13 per cent fewer men at the end. This is the trend throughout industry.
>
> It can mean only one thing. An equivalent tonnage of goods can be produced by a declining number of workers, and men must lose their jobs by the thousands— presently by the millions.[10]

This would, according to his analysis, lead to a further increase of surpluses, for there would be less and less income to buy the goods produced.

The System Accused

All those who have written in this vein about abundance have pointed finally to one thing: something wrong in the system itself. Their reasoning is not difficult to follow. Productive power has been developed which can and does produce a glut of goods. All sorts of devices have been got up to dispose of these surpluses. On the other hand, many are in need because it does not require many workers to produce this great bounty. One recent writer has proclaimed that we have been worshiping a false god. He said,

> Some people even seem to think that mass production can cure all the world's economic and social ills. You might almost say that it has become a world mania. Mass production has become our god, our cure-all, our economic savior.[11]

---

[10] Chase, *op. cit.,* pp. 15-16.
[11] Walter Hoving, *The Distribution Revolution* (New York: Ives Washburn, 1960), p. 4.

Writer after writer has proclaimed that the flaw lies in distribution. Stuart Chase put it this way:

> In respect to the whole body of finished goods, it is not so much *overproduction as underconsumption* which is the appalling fact. As a nation we can make more than we can buy back. Save in certain categories, there is a vast and tragic shortage of the goods necessary to maintain a comfortable standard of living. Millions of tons of additional material could be marketed if purchasing power were available. Alas, purchasing power is not available.[12]

Charles Wyand declared,

> More goods are being produced than can be profitably sold. On the other hand, it can be clearly shown that most people are consuming at but a fraction of their potential capacity. . . . As will be shown later, the consumer's buying power cannot absorb all that the nation can produce because (1) incomes are insufficient, (2) too much of the nation's income is saved, and (3) prices are too high.[13]

Horace Kallen said,

> Indeed, at no time in the history of industrial society has the production of the necessities of life been sufficient to meet all needs. It was not need which limited demand. It was price. Prices had so outdistanced wages that wages could not catch up with them.[14]

Those who have written in this vein have not always been quite consistent. On the one hand, they have often indicated that there is an absolute surplus—actually more goods produced than can or will be consumed. On the other hand, and in certain moods, they hold that the problem is

---

[12] Chase, *op. cit.*, p. 78.

[13] Wyand, *op. cit.*, p. 40.

[14] Horace M. Kallen, *The Decline and Rise of the Consumer* (New York: D. Appleton-Century, 1936), p. 404.

only one of maldistribution. Then, too, some writers have focused upon the wastefulness of private enterprise and have advocated the conservation of scarce resources. In recent years, many of those who have dealt with such matters have professed great concern for "economic growth." It would, therefore, be a misconstruction of what has been going on to deal with all of it in connection with scarcity.

Governmental Intervention Rationalized

What all these positions share—whether it be a concern with overproduction, underconsumption, maldistribution, wastefulness, or economic growth—is the view that government must intervene in one way or another to correct the situation. They hold that the "system" produces these unwanted consequences and that collective action must be taken to set it straight.

Simon Patten, an early advocate of the notion that a surplus exists and a teacher of Rexford G. Tugwell, advocated the absorption of the surplus by taxation. He declared that taxation should "be placed not on particular forms of prosperity, but on general prosperity. The State should not try to hunt up the individual who profits by each of the improvements it makes, but should make taxation a reduction of the general surplus of society." His justification of this was that "we can conceive of the State as a factor in production, and hence entitled to a share of the undistributed produce of industry. It has helped to promote general prosperity, and can demand a part of the surplus of society along with landlords, employers, capitalists and laborers."[15]

John R. Commons, an early and late reformer, called

---

[15] Simon N. Patten, *Essays in Economic Theory*, Rexford G. Tugwell, ed. (New York: Alfred A. Knopf, 1924), p. 98.

in 1893 for a guaranteed right to employment in order to take care of the "surplus" of laborers:

> The right to employment when enforced would have the effect of guaranteeing to every worker, even the lowest, a share of the total income in excess of his minimum of subsistence. It would give steady work through the year, which would increase the wages of the lowest labourers by 30% to 50%. And by overcoming the chronic excess of labourers beyond the opportunities for employment, it would raise the marginal utility of the marginal labourers, thus raising the wages of all.[16]

So it has gone through the years: the apostles of surplus, overproduction, technological unemployment (surplus workers), underconsumption, and maldistribution have been proposing some variety of reform or intervention. Stuart Chase proclaimed that the situation called for detailed planning:

> In my judgment the only final way out lies through planned production. We have to scrap a large fraction of *laissez-faire,* and deliberately orient productive capacity to consumption goods. . . .
>
> For America, industrial co-ordination must probably take the form of a drastic revision of the anti-trust laws; an alliance between industry, trade association, and government to control investment (i.e., plant capacity) on the one hand, and to guard against unwarranted monopoly prices on the other; a universal system of minimum wages and guaranteed hours of labor to frighten off fly-by-night entrepreneurs and to stimulate purchasing power; and finally . . ., the setting up of a National Planning Board as a fact gatherer and in turn an advisor . . . on every major economic undertaking in accordance with a master blueprint.[17]

---

[16] John R. Commons, *The Distribution of Wealth* (New York: Reprints of Economic Classics, 1963), pp. 84-85.

[17] Chase, *op. cit.,* pp. 95-97.

Rexford G. Tugwell said,

> Let me summarize: In this era of our economic existence, I believe it is manifest that a public interest . . . commands the protection, the maintenance, the conservation, of our industrial faculties against the destructive forces of the unrestrained competition. . . . For today and for tomorrow our problem is that of our national economic maintenance for the public welfare by governmental intervention. . . .[18]

Charles Wyand held that—

> The gross effect of these trends is to offer American business the choice of some sort of private control of business practice or of growing governmental interference to prevent the complete collapse of the capitalistic economy.[19]

The emphasis has shifted somewhat over the years but not the goal of government control and direction. The problem, according to John K. Galbraith, is one of private affluence and public penury. There needs to be a great deal more spending in the governmental realm. Following his lead, Vance Packard emphasized the desirability of spending for education, government provided recreation facilities, support of research for the desalinization of water, and so forth.

The claims of abundance, surplus, and underconsumption are but a prelude, then, to the calls for positive government action. The arguments move, gradually and subtly or swiftly, from economics to the political arena. Their import can now be spelled out. If the problem were one of production, which it would be if there remained the fundamental difficulty posed by scarcity, it would be a matter

[18] Tugwell, *op. cit.*, p. 9.
[19] Wyand, *op. cit.*, p. 73.

for economics. To deal with scarcity, there needs to be frugal management, saving, investment, balanced budgets, calculations as to the best means to use to get the greatest return from materials, and determinations as to how to produce the most goods with the least expenditure of energy. But if the situation were reversed, if abundance had replaced scarcity, economic behavior would no longer be in order. It might be helpful to spend more than was taken in, to employ more workers than the task at hand required, to use more materials than would be called for by the undertaking. To be economical, at any rate, would be anachronistic.

Economics as a Tool for Reform

Most important, economic analysis has long shown conclusively that individuals and private companies have the incentives when they may exchange freely to deal as effectively as can be done with general scarcity. But the case might be quite different if abundance were the problem. This is the character of the arguments which have been recapitulated above. When the problem becomes one of distribution, it then becomes feasible to argue that governments can intervene for ameliorative purposes. In short, it might be admitted that force would be a poor way to achieve production, but the same would not necessarily go for distribution. Governments can redistribute; they can take goods from some and give them to others; they can spend, expropriate, set aside lands and resources, confiscate, and even waste rather effectively. These are tasks which governments alone, because of their monopoly of the use of force, would be suited to perform, if anybody had to perform such tasks.

The United States government has indeed been engaging in such practices for a good many years, assisted on occasion by local and state governments. The methods for doing these things are many and varied. They run the gamut from low interest rates for those in favored categories to the confiscatory taxation of the wealthy, from the subsidizing of some kinds of production to the limitation of other kinds, from minimum wages to maximum prices, from public welfare to social security, from financing low-rent housing to taxing high-rise apartments, and from the extension of power to organized labor to the intimate regulation of business activity. These are not economic actions; they are, instead, political. They have to do with power and its use. They have to do with artificially creating shortages, with driving prices above or below the market price, with the allocation of manpower according to political considerations, with arbitrary conservation and profligate spending. Even "surpluses" can be created—that is, goods priced higher than anyone can or will pay for them—by the use of force.

This shift from economics to politics is mirrored in the activities of many of those who now bear the name of economist. A popular news magazine noted this change recently. It said, "In the palaces and Parliaments of a hundred countries, economists are increasingly called upon to build, revive, or draw together national economies. Their home is no longer the ivory tower, and their profession is no longer the 'gloomy science' but a romantic and rewarding wielding of power." Moreover, "the Presidents and Ministers are receptive to the advice. . . . Several economists have risen to head governments, including West Germany's Ludwig Erhard, Portugal's Antonio Salazar, and Bolivia's Victor Paz Estenssoro. Others, such as Britain's Harold Wilson, are hopefully planning their own takeover [since achieved in his case]."[20] In America, many econo-

---

[20] *Time* (June 26, 1964), p. 86.

mists have become well-known names in government circles over the years: Rexford G. Tugwell, Walter Heller,
John K. Galbraith, among others. Below this exalted rank,
hundreds more toil away in the numerous government
departments which lay seige to economy in the land.

There has, then, been a flight from economics, a flight
from economics as a discipline for study and exposition
to "economics" as a tool for social reform, a flight from
economics to politics. This has been, also, a flight from
reality. This is because scarcity is still with us, and
may be expected to remain. Scarcity arises from the nature
of the universe and of man. Man wants a great variety
of commodities and attentions. The want of them makes
them economic goods and services. In order for these goods
and services to be provided, someone has to labor, to use
resources, to defer the gratification of wants. Labor and
materials are in limited supply (always); deferment requires discipline; wants are unlimited by these or any
other physical considerations. Hence, scarcity is an enduring fact of life.

Production is not something that is solved, once and for
all. Goods must continue to be produced, else the supply
that exists will be exhausted. Continued production requires the making of economic decisions—of decisions as
to which materials in short supply and how many men in
the limited labor pool and how much capital from the small
store of it to employ to make what goods that will be in
greatest demand.

Distribution is not something separable from production,
not, that is, if production is to be maintained. Distribution
—that is, exchange—is the great spur to production; it
is the close relation between efforts and rewards that in-
duces individuals to apply their energies economically to
production. Surpluses do not indicate abundance; they

rather indicate misallocation of materials, poor judgment, false signals in the economy, price rigidities, and/or the use of force to bring these about.

Scarcity remains. There is no better testimony to this fact than the desperate efforts of socialists to increase productivity, to achieve, as they say, "economic growth." But even these efforts are misunderstood by contemporary "distributionist economists." One writer notes that the Soviet Union has been using all sorts of devices to spur production. "But, nowhere in his talks did Khrushchev say anything about distribution. As a matter of fact he didn't seem to be aware of this side of the economic picture at all. He seemed to think production is the alpha and omega of the economic system."[21]

The view that America is now saddled with problems of abundance has been used to justify intervention, but the roots of economic misunderstanding are even deeper than this. There is a whole body of pseudo-economic literature devoted to attempts to demonstrate that economic behavior results in contradictions that can only be resolved by government intervention. These arguments deserve some examination.

---

[21] Hoving, *op. cit.*, p. 4.

19

Meliorist Economics

THE FLIGHT FROM ECONOMICS PREPARED THE WAY FOR government intervention in what would otherwise be economic matters. It involved, primarily, claims that an abundance of goods and services existed, either actually or potentially. If this were so, it would be possible for government to intervene and redistribute these, for force can be used to confiscate and dispose of property. But such claims would not provide justification for action. Even the existence of abundance does not indicate that redistribution is in order. However, along with the flight from economics has gone the development of a pseudo-economics, an "economics" which purports to show that free economic activity leads to contradictions, that to remove these contradictions government action is necessary, and that certain kinds of actions can be taken which will have the desired effect. Such pseudo-economic theories are here called meliorist economics.

It should be noted, however, that the phrase, "meliorist economics," is used for historical reasons and consistency, not because of its descriptive accuracy or aptness. Throughout this work, meliorism refers to the view that government intervention can improve conditions for people. Meliorist economics is an "economics" which purports to justify government intervention in an economy and show how it can be done so as to improve the material well-being of people generally. This latter usage of the term—to modify economics—is not commonly employed, if it has ever been used in this way before. It is, however, consistent with the practice in this work of referring to reformism in general as meliorism.

The term, "meliorism," was adopted by some reformers within the context of controversies of the latter part of the nineteenth century. Most of the influential economists and social thinkers of the nineteenth century had held that government intervention would produce evils rather than cure them. Karl Marx, along with revolutionary socialists in general, held roughly the same position, though for different reasons. In addition to these views about an ameliorative use of government, social Darwinists held that men could not alter the course of evolutionary development, and that government intervention would fail in any attempt to tamper with evolution. Meliorism, running counter to all these views, insisted that government could be used to improve conditions.

Justifications of Theft and Slavery

In this context it is quite correct to refer to proponents of government intervention as meliorists. In like manner, it is proper to refer to theories in an economic vein along these lines as meliorist economics. It should be made clear, however, that in essence such economics is *not* ameliorative, nor is it in essence economics. Instead, it consists of theoretical and ideological justifications for using the power of government to take from some and give to others. Understood rightly, it consists of more or less subtle attempts to legalize theft.

A little basic economics should make this clear. Economics has to do with increasing the supply of goods or services with the smallest expenditure of materials and energy. For an individual—and economic action is, in the final analysis, the action of an individual or a group of individuals—economics is of importance to him to the extent that he wishes to conserve his supply of materials and energy and increase his supply of goods and services.

There are two ways for an individual to augment the goods and services at his disposal. (1) He can produce or provide them for himself. (2) He can acquire them from others. Again, there are two ways for an individual to acquire them from others. (a) He can acquire them by exchange (which would include gifts, though what is exchanged may be different in character from what is obtained). Or (b), he can take them from someone else who possesses them. This latter method is the one that is the chief concern of meliorist economists.

Everyone understands that when one individual uses force or fraud to take goods from another, theft is involved. When an individual uses force to make another serve him, it is called slavery. But it is not generally understood or accepted that when meliorist economics is applied in society, theft and slavery are entailed.

In the main, this lack of understanding can be attributed to the indirectness, the subtlety, and the sophistry of the methods of meliorist economics. Men are led to believe that public approval somehow changes the character of an action, that confiscation of goods by publicly elected officials is not theft, that the democratic process can be used to legitimize acts which are in themselves illegitimate. Men do not readily understand that the protective tariff is, in effect, the taking of wealth from the consumer for the supposed benefit of the producer, that antitrust suits are subtle assaults upon property, that inflation is a surreptitious theft of money from those who have it or have it owed to them, that compulsory unionization legalizes the taking of money from some by others, that minimum wages and maximum hours are attempts to take from some what is rightfully theirs and give it to others, that to take wealth from some portion of the population and bestow it upon some other portion under the guise of welfare is not even a very subtle form of thievery.

The story thus far, in this work, has been an attempt mainly to explain how men's minds were prepared to accept such things without recognizing them. Men have been taught to take their eyes away from the nature of things and to focus upon the purported object or end for which an act has been performed. They have been taught that it is the motive that counts, not the consequences of the act. They have been taught that morals—and even the language used to describe them—are relative to a given society. If this were so, only that which the generality of men understood to be theft would be theft; only that which was recognized as slavery would be slavery. If the majority voted for a measure, or for those who proposed a measure, this would be indicative of its conformity to morality. After all, one may argue from such premises, whatever the majority accepts as right is *ipso facto* right.

One Man's Gain is Another's Loss

Morality aside, and speaking strictly in terms of what may be *economical for an individual*, robbery could be quite economical. By stealing, an individual can greatly augment the supply of goods and services available to him with only a very little expenditure of energy and materials. A bank robber may spend half an hour using a twenty-dollar gun and enrich himself, say, to the extent of $20,000. Of course, such usage is an abuse and perversion of the conventional term "economy." Economics, as it comes to us from the classicists, is a social study, not an antisocial one. It has to do with what may be economical not only for an individual but for all other men as well. The bank robber increases his supply of goods and services at the expense of those of other men. Moreover, he may actually reduce the general supply by the threat he poses to trade and the loss of incentive men have to produce when they are uncertain that they will be able to keep the rewards of their labor. For these reasons, theft has not been considered economical. Of course, in most societies such penalties have usually been attached to the practice as to make it uneconomical.

The point is important, however, for understanding what happens when meliorist economics is applied within a society. Individuals do not cease, so far as their understanding goes and as a rule, to behave economically in their own affairs. Indeed, a new prospect for "economic" behavior is opened up, for certain kinds of theft are legalized. Men may benefit at the expense of others with impunity in certain definite areas. That such behavior is uneconomic socially, plus being immoral, will not hinder a great many men in their conduct, for what they are doing may well be socially approved.

An example from the contemporary scene of behavior that is "economic" for the individual at the expense of others may clarify the point. Suppose one is a cotton farmer. The price of cotton is held higher than it would otherwise be by a subsidy. The subsidy is paid by tax monies, at least temporarily. There is a "surplus"—that is, more than can be sold at this artificially high price—of cotton. The farmer will likely make his decision as to whether to grow cotton or not in terms of its profitability when the subsidy is added to the market price. It would be economic for him to do so, although socially the effect would be to add only to the "surplus" and the general tax burden. His profit would be got at the expense of others.

The system which results from the application of meliorist economics is one in which men are pitted against men and groups against groups for the spoils made available by redistribution. There has been a concerted effort in the United States to move this contest into the political arena and to get men to accept peacefully the decisions made there. The art of politics becomes the art of guessing rightly about which group to appease at what moment in order to keep the uneasy peace and maintain political power. The portion of spoils to be handed out to any given group must be continually adjusted to take into account both the temper of the group involved and its leverage in maintaining a majority for the politician and party in power. The story of such maneuvering is largely the story of politics in America in the twentieth century.

Meliorist economics is the body of pseudo-economic theory which purports to justify such a system and provides the politician with the methods for establishing and maintaining it. The true nature of these activities is largely concealed behind a cover of words which not only obscures what is going on but reduces discussion of economic matters to high-flown gibberish. The gibberish is then ascribed to the intricate complexities of our times. The general flight from reality prepared the way for the wide acceptance of such obfuscations, and socialists added confusion to nineteenth century economic thought by turning the traditional economic concepts to their ends.

All Schemes Rest on Monopoly

A casual examination of meliorist economics might lead to the conclusion that there are a great diversity of economic conceptions involved. Indeed, names have been given to a number of schools of economics: e.g., socialist, historical, revisionist, Marxist, institutionalist, Keynesian, and so forth. But most, or all, of these schools have a common denominator; they have a common conception from which they start or with which they end. Of course, they share the conception that the "system"—i.e., capitalism—has internal contradictions which lead to dire consequences. But back of this is a key conception which purportedly accounts for these contradictions. The key conception is *monopoly*. In the later part of the nineteenth and in the early twentieth century, reformers saw monopoly under every bed, as it were. There were transportation monopolies, industrial monopolies, land monopolies, money monopolies, and trade monopolies. The formulation of these conceptions ranged from Karl Marx's view that the private ownership of the means of production led inevitably to a class monopoly of production to John Maynard Keynes' subtle notion that profit taking and saving led to shortages of investment money which, in turn, produced depression. However remote these ideas may appear to be from it, they are rooted in a conception of monopoly, and amelioration is to be achieved by breaking up the monopoly.

Monopoly is a very slippery word; therefore, it must be handled with care. It is derived from the Greek, and means, etymologically, the exclusive right of sale. However, it had a much narrower connotation than this in earlier conventional English usage. An article in the *Encyclopaedia Britannica* says, "The term monopoly, in its early usage, was applied to grants from the Crown, to a favourite or as a reward for good service, of the exclusive right to manufacture or sell particular classes of goods." One *American College Dictionary* indicates that this has now become its secondary meaning. In this sense, a monopoly is "an exclusive privilege to carry on a traffic or service, granted by a sovereign, state, etc." An unabridged dictionary calls this an artificial monopoly, which it defines as "an exclusive right granted by a government for the exploitation of anything."

Odium was first attached to this kind of monopoly. But even this development has a history. Initially, in the sixteenth and seventeenth centuries, odium was assigned mainly to the arbitrary grant of monopolies by the monarch. There was an attempt to remove this by taking the power of granting monopolies away from the Crown and vesting it in Parliament. Americans and Englishmen generally accepted the propriety of legislatures granting monopolies in the seventeenth and for much of the eighteenth century. However, by the time of the War for Independence there was considerable resistance to all such monopolies. The resistance continued to mount in America, and by the middle of the nineteenth century, monopolies were among the most generally despised of all human inventions.

A Perverted Terminology

It was at this juncture that socialists began to becloud the issue with their confusions. They expropriated the odium attached to government-granted monopolies and applied it to monopoly in general, in the etymological sense of the word. It is easy to see how the term could be ambiguously used to bring all sorts of things under condemnation. By the original definition of monopoly—the exclusive right of sale—all private property is a monopoly of its owner. In this sense, every man who owns anything, whether it be a factory, a house, a barn, land, an automobile, or a pocket knife, is a monopolist. Every free man is a monopolist, for he has the exclusive right to sell his service. Indeed, it is this right, and this monopolistic condition, which separates free men from slaves.

Socialists have been bent, of course, upon breaking up monopolies, or, more clearly, abolishing private property. But they were notoriously unsuccessful in selling this idea to the generality of men in their early attempts. Most men were not particularly taken with the notion of giving up their private property; and when they had the opportunity to vote upon the matter, they turned down such schemes unceremoniously. Socialists generally found it advantageous to narrow down their assaults upon property to certain kinds, to use "monopoly" in a more specialized sense, and thus to divide the populace on the question of property. At any rate, gradualists have not usually attacked property directly; they have, instead, attacked what they have called monopoly.

A new definition of monopoly was promulgated in the latter part of the nineteenth century. It has since become a part of our language and serves as a lens through which most people see the matter. The *Encyclopaedia Britannica* says, "In its modern usage the term monopoly is applied to the advantage accruing to any undertaking or associated group of undertakings which has the power, however acquired, of fixing the price of its goods or services in the knowledge that those who need them cannot get them in adequate measure elsewhere." One dictionary gives the following as the first meaning of monopoly: "exclusive control of a commodity or service in a particular market, or a control that makes possible the manipulation of prices."

By these definitions, the existence of a monopoly appears to hinge on two things: that there be but one effective seller of a commodity or service in a given market, and that this will enable him to fix or manipulate the price. (For purposes of discussion, the vagueness of such phrases as "commodity or service," "particular market," and "manipulation of prices" in this context may be ignored.)

If such a condition were to exist, it probably could be recognized. If it be considered reprehensible, if it be a matter for legal action, the most fruitful approach for dealing with it would be to seek out its sources.

Two Types of Monopoly: Governmental or Private

There are, in reality, only two sources of such monopolies: government grant or establishment, and private ownership. Other sources are sometimes named, but upon careful examination it can be shown that they do not meet the above requirements or do not exist. Some writers refer to an efficiency monopoly. This is a case where there is only one supplier of a good or service, so that it meets one half of the requirements for a monopoly. But it is a condition of its continued existence that it does not manipulate prices to any significant degree. If it raises prices appreciably, other suppliers can enter the market successfully.

The other type of monopoly frequently referred to is a natural monopoly. The phrase itself is ambiguous. One dictionary defines a natural monopoly as "a monopoly arising from the possession of a part of the earth's surface, having a natural resource or resources." But this is indistinct from a definition of private property in land. More commonly, a natural monopoly is understood to be one in which by nature of things there can be only one supplier of a good or service in a particular market. It is often alleged that the provision of telephone service in a particular locale is a natural monopoly. In the first place, however, "service" is ambiguous in this usage. Is the service the providing of a telephone or of communication? If it is communication, telephone service has no monopoly. One may communicate by mail, by telegraph, by radio, or go in person. But even if the uniqueness of the telephone as a means of communication be taken to signify that it constitutes a separate service, its actual monopoly status is not natural. It rests upon two foundations: government franchise and private property. These are the twin sources of all monopoly.

It is not clear, however, that private property meets all the requirements to be classed as a monopoly by the contemporary usage of the word. Etymologically, private property is a monopoly, for it is the essence of private property that the owner has the exclusive right to sell it. But in modern usage private property is not a monopoly. No man, or group of men, *owns* all of a commodity or service which can be sold in a particular area. No man or group of men does or can own all the means of communication, of transportation, of serving in a community unless all men are his slaves, and that could only exist by the exercise of government power. By the very nature of things, no man can own all of a particular commodity and manipulate prices at the same time. Price is something that can only be determined after the sale of articles. Once an article has been sold, the original seller no longer has a monopoly. It is true that a man might have a monopoly of the sale of a commodity in that no one else would be permitted to sell it, but that would be a matter of law and government prescription.

It follows, then, that the modern usage of monopoly only *appears* to differ from earlier usage. The reprehensible characteristics of monopoly—that is, the exclusive control of a commodity or service which enables one to fix or manipulate prices—apply only to something that has been granted, established, or prescribed by government. Anyone who doubts this should examine carefully into the sources of the ability of any seller of goods or services to fix their price. He should trace out the lines that lead from the seller to the government and find what it is that enables the seller to fix his price. The government action may be very subtle, as in the case of a protective tariff, or it may be very plain, as in the case of minimum wages or rate regulation. But it is always there.

An Assault upon Property

Nonetheless, meliorist economists have quite often referred to what can happen when men use private property to produce goods and from which to provide services as monopoly. Usually, only that seller who has garnered a substantial portion of the market is referred to as a monopolist, or as being "monopolistic." To break up such "monopolies," the meliorist proposes that they be divested of some portion of their property, that the rights of property be circumscribed, and/or that the government regulate the use of the property. Thus, the attack upon monopoly becomes an assault upon property, though not all property immediately comes under the gun.

The amazing feature of this is that such action usually produces the substantive evil it is supposed to prevent. The evil of monopoly is the possibility it affords for fixing and manipulating prices so as to "charge what the traffic will bear." The regulation of "monopolies" eventuates in the fixing and manipulating of prices *by government*. For example, in the latter part of the nineteenth century, railroads were pictured as giant monopolies gorging themselves on a defenseless public. In order to regulate them effectively, politicians were finally convinced that they must establish rates. The government then began to fix and manipulate prices, that is, to impose the conditions of monopoly upon both sellers and buyers. Whether these rates were as high as the traffic would bear or not, the indications are that they have frequently been more than much of the traffic would bear, for railroads have lost much of their custom. In recent years, railroad managers have fought an uphill battle to get at least some of their rates lowered.

Governments cannot intervene to prevent monopoly; when they intervene, they create monopoly, or the effects of it. It is the failure to understand, accept, or admit this that constitutes, in considerable part, the flight from reality of meliorist economists.

Viewed as a school of socialism, and that is what it is, meliorism can be defined in yet another way. It is the view that the instruments of government which have been inherited in the political system can be turned to the purpose of wresting economic power from the hands of those who possess it (the monopolists) and placing it in the hands of the "people." Meliorism is the face that gradualist or evolutionary socialism has worn in America, though it has usually been called liberalism in the twentieth century.

Its opposite in the socialist camp is Marxian (or revolutionary, or communist) socialism. Marx appears to have believed at the time of the promulgation of *The Communist Manifesto* (1848) that the regular instruments of government, in the right hands, could be used to bring about socialism gradually. But after the abortive Revolutions of 1848 he turned toward the view that the system must be destroyed first, that government was an instrument of capitalists, that they would never tolerate its use to undermine their system of exploitation (as he described it).

On the other hand, meliorists have held that violent revolution is unnecessary, that the desired course of change will occur peacefully, gradually, and in an evolutionary manner. Most have held that this process of change can be consciously directed; but they have generally insisted, too, that for it to work it must be in keeping with evolutionary trends. Meliorist economics has been concerned with how to use the instruments of government to bring the economy into line with the course of evolution and/or produce the desired changes.

Some Leading Meliorists

There is a huge body of literature that could be classified as meliorist economics. Undoubtedly, it would take a fair sized building to house the volumes that could be assembled to make a library of it. Even a list of the names of the more influential of such writers upon American thought is rather formidable in length. It would include Francis Amasa Walker, Simon N. Patten, Henry George, John R. Commons, E. R. A. Seligman, Richard T. Ely, Thorstein Veblen, John Maurice Clark, Paul H. Douglas, John Maynard Keynes, Stuart Chase, Adolph A. Berle, Gardiner C. Means, Wesley C. Mitchell, Rexford G. Tugwell, Sumner H. Slichter, John K. Galbraith, Paul A. Samuelson, and Seymour E. Harris, among others.

These and other such writers have not always called what they were writing about monopoly. Some have, and some have not. They have called by a great variety of names the ill that is supposed to beset America: they have called it overproduction, underconsumption, absentee ownership, technological unemployment, finance capitalism, oligopoly, maldistribution, economic royalism, underinvestment, imperfect competition, industrial wastemaking, unearned increment, social surplus, industrial depression, recession, the end of the frontier, a mature economy, corporate domination, and economic disequilibrium. But when the tangle of rhetoric has been unwoven, when the tree of meliorism has been surveyed as a whole, when the branches have been traced back to the trunk, when the trunk has been followed to the root, it becomes clear that meliorist economics is largely rooted in the conception of monopoly.

This can be examined from several angles. It can be shown by examining the thought of meliorist economics. The classic case of a thinker proceeding from the concept of monopoly to a meliorist position is that of Henry George, and he was also one of the first to have any considerable impact.

George's thought proceeded along the following lines. In the first place, he believed that industrial progress was resulting in increasing poverty. The cause of this, he held, was that individuals were deriving profits which should accrue to society. These profits came as a result of the private ownership of land. Land, he reasoned, does not naturally belong to any of us; it was something that was here primevally, and here for all men to use. But some have acquired exclusive possession of it, by whatever means, and employ it to their advantage at the expense of the well-being of all. They take away from society the return from the employment of land, and they keep lands out of use for speculative purposes, thus depriving men of the right to put the lands to economic use. (One of his underlying premises is that lands are not being economically exploited.)

He proposed that the problem could be solved by government intervention, that the government be financed by a single tax, that the tax should take all that accrues to a man from the land itself, as opposed to that which is a product of the labor of the landholder. Not only that, but the tax should fall on unused lands as well. He thought that this would result in the opening up of these lands to economic use and the amelioration of the material conditions of men generally. In short, George's diagnosis of the cause of the ill was land monopoly, his prescription was government intervention by way of the single tax, his prognosis was a general improvement in the well-being of the populace.

If we ignore the difficulty of calculating what part of a man's return can be attributed to his labor and what to his land, a difficulty somewhat akin to the one faced by Jonathan Swift's scientist who was attempting to extract sunbeams from cucumbers, and assume that the differential could be calculated, it still does not follow that economic results would be obtained. With the imposition of the single tax, all advantage to holding title to land would disappear. Not only that, but it would be disadvantageous to hold title to unused land. It stands to reason that if the owner of unused lands could have employed them to his profit before the imposition of the tax he would have done so. The tax would detract from, not add to, his incentives to use the lands productively. The chances are good that the lands would soon be offered at public auction to satisfy the tax claims against them. But that there would be buyers is most unlikely. The risks of holding title to land, even that which at the moment would be productive, would be considerable, and the advantage none. In consequence, all land might be expected to come eventually into the hands of the government. That governments can or will employ lands economically is something of which past experience offers no assurance. The method of meliorist economics is epitomized in the thought of Henry George: the location of the flaw in the system, the proposal of government intervention, the promise of amelioration, the assault upon property, the eventuation, if put into practice, of a giant overweening monopoly.

Henry George showed the way. Many reformers read and were influenced by him. In general, though, they abandoned the specifics of his analysis and prescription while keeping the abstract of the method. Thorstein Veblen was much more influential in specifics. In the main, his was an adaptation of the Marxian analysis to an evolutionary framework; he no longer perceived any necessity for violent revolution. He was the early leading exponent of the institutionalist school, which has been the most virulent branch of meliorism in America. To Veblen, economic activity takes place within, can be understood in terms of, is a reflection of, and is driven by institutional arrangements. Institutions are a product of a long, and largely unconscious, evolutionary growth. They are undergoing continual change, and the task of men is to adjust their practice to the course of historical development. Veblen was the precocious product of that view of reality as consisting of change, society, and psyche, a contemporary of Lester Frank Ward and John Dewey, and an applier of their shared notions to economics.

For a good many years, mainly in the first quarter of the twentieth century, Veblen turned all the acid contained in the English language, both received and invented, to the task of satirizing the economic system. The system was a fit subject for satire, if Veblen's analysis was correct. It was shot through with anachronisms. The major anachronism was the profit of capitalists. These got the profits of production and distribution but no longer contributed to it. The business of production and distribution had been engrossed by corporations, almost exclusively. These, in turn, were managed by specialists who were technologists.

The day had arrived when the capitalists could have been dispensed with and the businesses run for the many rather than for the few, but capitalists continued to receive their ill-gotten gains as a result of the outmoded institutions which prevailed. To put it bluntly, the institutions of private property enabled capitalists to hang on to their "pecuniary gains" which resulted from government protection of what amounted to a monopolistic position. Actually, the corporation was not private property at all; it was a public creation, which, if men were consistent, would be used for the benefit of the public. This would happen, Veblen thought, when the technologists took over entirely and the stockholders were cut away. Veblen did not claim to know how this would come about; all that he could say for sure was that the course of economic evolution had just about reached the point where it would most certainly occur.

Disciples and followers of Veblen were not slow to find means to advance the public takeover. Meliorist economics then branches out into the particular analyses of the assorted ills that are supposed to arise from an economy based upon private profit—of the exploitation of workers, of sweatshops, of depression, of declining farm prices, of inevitable increases in farm tenancy, of wastefulness of natural resources, and so on—and the numerous proposals for amelioration: the establishment of minimum wages, maximum hours, stockmarket regulation, corporate tax, organized labor, and so forth. In short, means are advanced for taking away from owners of property the control of it and a large portion of the profits from it.

One other such analysis may be given as an example. Wesley C. Mitchell was mainly influenced by Veblen. He turned his attention to business cycles, and wrote extensively about them from 1913 into the 1930's. He held that business cycles, at least modern ones, were a phenomenon of an economy based upon profit. He analyzed the business cycle and described its various phases, starting at the depth of depression. What spurred the economy, he thought, was growth in population, depletion of products, and increasing demand, plus new investment. Investment led to profits, and the possibility of profits led to optimism and increasing investment. Prosperity could not be maintained indefinitely, however, because other things did not keep pace with investment and because technological innovation produced disequilibrium. Wages did not rise as fast as production; technology produced unemployment both directly and indirectly because some producers would be stuck with old equipment. Profits would fall off; overproduction might result; distributors would have large inventories; demand would decline; investment would decrease; depression would come again. In the main, he proposed that government should intervene in such ways as manipulating the money supply so as to maintain prosperity.

While this analysis does not appear to hinge upon monopoly, a more careful statement of the theory which would support it would indicate that profits are a corollary of private property and that the basic flaw in the system is the uncoordinated management of the economy that results from the dispersion of property. He proposed (or predicted) increasing governmental planning to maintain an equilibrium. In short, he advocated the circumscription and regulation of private property so as to maintain prosperity.

The Pattern of Legislation Aimed to Curb Monopoly

Legislation over the years spawned by meliorist economics may demonstrate even more clearly that it was aimed at breaking up monopolies. The Interstate Commerce Act was designed to prevent the supposedly harmful effects of railroad monopoly of transportation. The various antitrust acts were attempts to circumscribe monopolistic activities. The Federal Reserve System was supposed to break up the Wall Street money monopoly. Minimum wages were supposed to circumvent the harmful effects of the monopoly of employment activities which employers are supposed to have. Federal provision of electrical power was supposed to provide a yardstick for determining what proper competitive prices of electricity should be. Government supported loans at low interest rates are supposed to remove the harmful effects of private banking. So it has gone, from activity to activity and from industry to industry.

This supposed assault upon monopoly, though it was justified under many guises, has been, in fact, an assault upon private property. It has taken away, or severely circumscribed, the rights that belong to private ownership of property. It has brought more and more activities under the surveillance and direction of government. It has introduced the harmful effects of monopoly into all areas of life. Government agencies now fix and manipulate prices of all sorts of things, from wages to rail rates. Theft has been legalized, for the rights of property have been taken without compensation, and monopoly pervades American society.

BOOK THREE:

The Political Flight

20

Divide and Conquer

Iᴅᴇᴀs ʜᴀᴠᴇ ᴄᴏɴꜱᴇQᴜᴇɴᴄᴇꜱ, ꜱᴀɪᴅ Rɪᴄʜᴀʀᴅ Wᴇᴀᴠᴇʀ. Hᴇ
wrote a book on the subject, mainly to demonstrate that
ideas which entered the stream of thought centuries ago
have continued to inform our thought and unfold in the
directions implicit in them. (Perhaps he also demonstrated
in yet another way, how the sins of the fathers are visited
upon the children to the seventh generation, or beyond.)
Ideas have consequences in two realms. Ideas which serve
as basic assumptions (often unconsciously held and un-
examined) have consequences in the realm of ordinary
beliefs and thoughts. When applied, ideas also result in
acts, which have consequences. This can be stated as a
proposition: Ideas lead to acts which have consequences.

This latter formulation facilitates a most important distinction. Our ideas may become more or less determinative in the area of thought and belief, and thus determine
our actions. But ideas do *not* determine the consequences
of acts. The consequences of acts follow, of necessity, from
the nature of the acts. This is so because the universe is
ordered in a certain way; it is so ordered that the consequences appropriate to the act follow from it. Ideas may
be inaccurate, invalid, or bear no relation to reality. It is
possible to act on the basis of such ideas. But action, any
action, brings the one who acts into the orbit of reality.
What follows is governed neither by his will, his beliefs,
nor his claims about it. A man may, for example, believe

that he is on the first floor of a building when he is actually on the twelfth floor. If a fire breaks out and he attempts to jump to safety from the window, he will fall twelve stories, probably to his death, just as surely as if he had known he was on the twelfth floor.

It is a measure of the extent of the general confusion of our age that so obvious a truth would need spelling out. It is generally accepted, at least among intellectuals, that ideas have consequences; but it is not usually admitted that acts have consequences which bear no necessary relation to the ideas and beliefs or motives which prompted them. If this were well known and admitted, there probably would have been no occasion for undertaking the work in hand; for this work is an account of men under the sway of an illusion, who are on a flight from reality.

The flight, however, has been in the realm of ideas. Once the ideas have been applied, a fateful junction with reality has been made; the consequences that have followed have been quite real, and they have been those that follow from such actions. The matter is more complicated than this sounds, however. There is a sense, also, in which the consequences have followed from the ideas—not from the claims about them, the hopes for them, or the illusions about them, but from the nature of the ideas themselves. Ideas, too, have the consequences appropriate to them when they are applied.

The misunderstanding of reformist intellectuals extends not only to the nature of the universe but also to the nature of ideas. Ideas must be about reality, else, when applied, they will produce not what is claimed and hoped for them but what must follow from their character. The inner contradictions of meliorism have borne their bitter fruit in actuality. Ideas which result in acts have consequences appropriate both to the ideas and to the acts.

Applying the Ideas

This work, thus far, has dealt mainly with the development of reformist ideas and their propagation. That is only part of the story. The ideas have been applied, and this application has had consequences. In many ways, the story of the application and consequences is more important than an account of the development of ideas. At any rate, intellectual history by itself is incomplete and misleading; it needs to be joined to actuality by an account of what happens when ideas are brought to bear on reality. To do this, the first step is to deal with the application, and the second is to treat of the consequences.

Meliorism is the gradualist way to utopia. To accomplish utopia, society must be transformed. Meliorism is the method for gradually transforming society by the use of government power and force. It has been the perennial claim of meliorists that they believed in and were using democratic methods for transforming society.

There were tremendous obstacles in the way of translating meliorist ideas into action and none more formidable than those involved in attempting to justify the use of force to transform society in the name of democracy. The democratic use of force to transform society is such a basic contradiction that it should be rejected *prima facie* as preposterous. It has all the logic of a man's holding a gun to *his head* to force himself to do something. If those who make up a society want to change their ways of doing things, what is to keep them from it? They can only be prevented by force from making the changes they desire; and if government has a monopoly of force, the only obstacle to such changes would be government. But, in this case, all that would be needed would be to remove the governmentally enforced rigidity. There would be no call for the use of force to accomplish the transformation. For a society to be transformed democratically by the use of force would have to mean that the members of a society would be using or sanctioning the use of force on themselves to transform themselves. This is so unlikely that it will hardly be believed until the matter has been carefully examined.

The Beginnings of Society

The examination should begin by getting clearly in mind what society is and by making a careful distinction between society and government. "Society is produced by our wants," Thomas Paine said, "and government by our wickedness; the former promotes our happiness *positively* by uniting our affections, the latter *negatively* by restraining our vices." To make clear the natural origin and felicitousness of society, Paine imagined what might happen to people newly arrived in some land, under no compulsion but that of their own needs:

> In this state of natural liberty, society will be their first thought. A thousand motives will excite them thereto, the strength of one man is so unequal to his wants, and his mind so unfitted for perpetual solitude, that he is soon obliged to seek assistance and relief of another, who in his turn requires the same.[1]

John C. Calhoun made a similar observation a few years later:

> In considering this, I assume as an incontestable fact that man is so constituted as to be a social being. His inclinations and wants, physical and moral, irresistibly impel him to associate with his kind; and he has, accordingly, never been found, in any age or country, in any state other than the social. In no other, indeed, could he exist, and in no other—were it possible for him to

---

[1] Gerald N. Grob and Robert N. Beck, eds., *American Ideas*, I (New York: Free Press of Glencoe, 1963), 190-91.

exist—could he attain to a full development of his moral and intellectual faculties or raise himself, in the scale of being, much above the level of brute creation.[2]

Society, then, is that which results from the needs of men to commune, to exchange, to specialize, to be nurtured, to learn, to express, to be solaced, to associate in common undertakings, to work, to play, to give, and to receive. A society is any community of men who share a preponderance of means—language, customs, habits, traditions, procedures, and beliefs—which facilitate such interchange and communion. Certain practices are anathema to society as well as being harmful to individuals, such as fraud, deception, violence, and thievery.

Government is that agency of a community which has a monopoly of the use of force for the legitimate purpose of keeping the peace by administering justice and deterring or punishing those who would do harm to individuals and disrupt the harmonious relations necessary to society (that is, to the peaceful association of men). As Calhoun said, "It follows, then, that man is so constituted that government is necessary to the existence of society, and society to his existence and the perfection of his faculties."[3]

Those who speak of transforming society must mean the changing of the means generally employed in a society to facilitate interchange and communion. That is, they must mean to change the language, customs, habits, traditions, procedures, and/or beliefs, for there is nothing else to be changed.

Now these things do change, usually very slowly and over a long period of time. For example, language does change; new words are added and old words dropped, pronunciation subtly altered, and even the modes of expres-

---

[2] *Ibid.*, p. 431.   [3] *Ibid.*, p. 432.

sion varied. In the absence of force, it may be assumed that changes in language occur in accord with other changes in the ways of people in a society and in keeping with what is acceptable to the generality of people or those who are looked to for standards.

In like manner, changes may occur in habits, customs, traditions, and procedures. It should be noted, however, that any drastic change in any or all of these will disrupt rather than facilitate social relations, will produce confusion and disorder rather than harmony. For example, if words are suddenly employed in unconventional ways, by decree, as it were, communication will be crippled, and uncertainty will prevail.

If the generality of people want to change their ways of doing things, there is nothing to prevent their doing so. There can be no occasion for the use of force (i.e., government) to produce the change on the grounds that it is what the people want. If they wanted it, they would have only to make the change. Actually, such evidence as I am familiar with would indicate that people do not ordinarily seek change, at least not most people. They may want to change others, but in their own affairs they cling tenaciously to the ways with which they are familiar. This is as it should be, for it means that such changes as are made will be limited, be accepted piece by piece, and will not be disruptive of human relations which make for society. Generally, only such changes will be accepted as can be fitted into the familiar pattern of one's life and social relations.

The Injection of Force

Force, aimed at transforming society, does, in fact, tend to destroy society. It introduces violence into the delicate framework of human relations; it produces resentment and resistance, and, at best, reluctant compliance. Men cannot be made to commune with one another; they can be forced to go through the motions of doing so. Society flees compulsion; it is formed once again in the interstices of the areas of the application of force. As these are closed up, society moves into the black market.

Examples of these developments are numerous in the contemporary world. Compulsory efforts at racial integration have resulted in the movement of people into the suburbs. Compulsory integration of recreational establishments have resulted in burgeoning private clubs. If a language is proscribed, people will speak it surreptitiously. If the sale of alcoholic beverages is prohibited, people will turn to bootleggers. If men cannot exchange goods on mutually acceptable terms, because the law forbids it, they will do so illegally in black markets.

It is doubtful that society ever has been or can be destroyed, so long as men exist. So deep is the need for meaningful and fruitful relationships, for those that arise willingly out of men's desire to participate in them, that when society is driven from the public domain it will be formed once again in the byways and closets which men seek out and find.

It is unlikely that a people would invite such hardship upon themselves. So unlikely is it that attempts to transform society by force prior to the twentieth century have been made in two ways: by conquest and by revolution.

There have been a number of instances in history of conquerors attempting some degree of transformation in society. Before the Modern Era these usually had as their object the consolidation of rule and control by the conqueror. An example of this would be the changes made in England after the Norman Conquest. After William, Duke of Normandy, defeated Harold Godwin at the Battle of Hastings in 1066, he imposed his own system of feudalism upon England. He parceled out the lands to his warriors, making his lieutenants the great tenants-in-chief of the realm. He provided that in cases of subinfeudination the primary allegiance of all vassals would be to him and only secondarily to their particular overlord. Castles, the impregnable fortresses of the Middle Ages, could only be built when he licensed them. The Church was brought securely under William's control.

It is doubtful that William "transformed society" in England; rather, he changed the political organization so that the main lines of power led to and came from him. In general, local custom and tradition continued to hold sway, hardly altered by his innovations. He did authorize a census of the land, the results of which were compiled in the Domesday Book, but even this was met with a great deal of complaint and grumbling.

A somewhat more thorough effort at social transformation, after conquest, was made in the United States after the Civil War. Crusty Thaddeus Stevens proclaimed, from his pinnacle of power in the Congress, "The future conditions of the conquered power depends on the will of the conqueror." Congress proceeded with a right good will to attempt to reconstruct the South. By constitutional amendments slavery was abolished, prohibitions made against payment for slaves and the payment of the Confederate war debt, and restrictions placed on state activity. The South was occupied by military forces, part of the population disfranchised, others enfranchised, and local governmental power fell into the hands of Carpetbaggers, Scalawags, and newly freed Negroes. These attempted to use the force of law, assisted and enforced by Federal troops, to transform the South. The South was changed, too, but not in accord with the vision of reconstructionists. The whites regained political power in the course of time, effectively disfranchised the Negroes, and new laws and practices were adopted in the light of altered conditions. Society lived on in the interstices of political power and, as force receded, regained sway in the lives of men.

Revolution is only a more subtle form of conquest, not an entirely different approach to social transformation. It differs from the conventional idea of conquest in that those who would reconstruct the society are not foreigners but come from among those whose lives they would change. (Even this distinction has begun to break down in the communist revolution of World War II and after.) Nonetheless, it is a kind of conquest, as all historical instances indicate.

Initially, there may be an attempt to make the changes by legislatures, though the members of these shortly cease to stand for election, if they ever did. Military forces are employed in subduing the population. In short order, all power gravitates into the hands of a single man—to Oliver Cromwell, to Napoleon Bonaparte, to Nicolai Lenin, to Mao tse Tung, and so forth—and he uses it to impose his will upon the populace. The differences between William of Normandy and Joseph Stalin are the differences made possible by technology and in aims. They were both conquerors.

"Democratic" Force

A new phenomenon has occurred in the twentieth century: the concerted effort to transform society by force with popular consent. The truly amazing feature of this is that it apparently is being done. Elections are still held, devices for divining the popular will employed, and social reconstruction proceeding apace. Certainly, a great deal of ingenuity has gone into bringing about this state of affairs.

As I have said, the use of the government to transform society by popular consent means that the populace must sanction the use of force upon itself to make it change its ways. It means, too, that men must support measures which decrease the control of their own affairs, that they must give their approval to the reduction of their liberties. They must assent to the reduction of the avenues open to their voluntary endeavor. They must sanction the use of force in ever larger areas (for the transformation is to be achieved gradually) of their lives and the shoving of society into such corners as remain.

An example of how efforts at social transformation by force lead to just such consequences can be given from contemporary developments. One of the bonds that linked most Americans together in society has been religion. More specifically, almost all Americans have a Judeo-Christian background, and for most of them it is Christian. This bond was strengthened by the fact that force was removed from religion early in the history of the Republic, and men were able to live in peace with those of different sects, denominations, and churches while sharing many religious concerns and beliefs with one another. Communities frequently were sufficiently homogeneous in religious background to observe religious rituals in public affairs without giving offense to members of the community.

Eventually, though, the passion for social transformation was introduced into the schools. Attendance at schools was compelled, and schools were financed by tax monies. So long as this was done locally, conflicts about religious observance were minimal. But American society could not be transformed to the ideological prescription if local variation were permitted. Eventually, the governmental unit with power over all America must take over the direction and control of the public schools.

At this level, religious differences are magnified, and are a potential source of perpetual conflict as well as an obstacle to uniform social transformation. Religion must be driven from the schools; even voluntary practices cannot survive the uniform application of force in an area. There is a logic to recent Supreme Court decisions, however illogical they may appear from a strict construction of the Constitution.

Men have not *knowingly* consented to the use of force upon themselves to have their ways of life changed and their liberties circumscribed and reduced. It is conceivable that men, somewhere at some time, may have done or will do so. In some few instances, regarding particulars, they have probably done so in America. But as to an over-all effort at social transformation, which has been going on, Americans have not given their approval to it. Before any such undertaking occurred, the government of America was taken from popular control. More precisely, the control of the United States government has been and is being taken bit by bit from the American people. There has been a rough correlation between the extent of social transformation and the decline of popular control.

The greatest irony of all, perhaps, is that this has gone on in the name of democracy, that is, in the name of government by the people. This development has been advanced subtly, and it must be described in detail before it can be understood or should be accepted.

Certain developments in ideas prepared the way for this flight from "democracy." They have already been presented and need only to be summarized here. Democracy was changed from a means to an end. As an end, it could serve as the object for doing things that could not be done in a "democratic" manner.

A most subtle intellectual device for taking attention

away from the choice to be made has been for reformers to proclaim that whatever they wanted done had become inevitable as a result of trends and developments in history. Obviously, if it is inevitable there is no choice to be made, though one may go through the silly motion of ratifying the "inevitable" trend at the polls by voting for it. (Of course, there have been "die-hards" who have had the temerity to oppose the "inevitable.") At least, one will have voted; and that is, after all, all that matters! More subtly, men were prepared for the turning over of their affairs to supposed experts and authorities by scientism. There was yet another idea—the theory of classes and class struggle —which played a large part in the flight from popular government, but it can be brought up again in connection with the first major step in cutting society apart.

There should be no doubt, however, that majorities frequently have voted for the advocates of melioristic programs. At a casual glance, it looks as if the changes have been made with popular approval. When I say that they have not, I mean that men have not generally known what they were voting for. They have listened to the claims of politicians, not examined the nature of the actions proposed nor the substance of acts passed by legislatures.

Probably, not one person in ten thousand has read any considerable portion of the major acts passed by Congress in the last fifty years. Of those who have, a much smaller number can have understood much about them. As to the consequences of these acts, no man could, in a lifetime of study, perceive more than the outlines of them. It has been beyond the abilities of the electorate to give their approval to what has been done. At best, men have voted in favor of those who made certain claims, not for what was actually done.

Even so, electoral approval has meant more than this

would suggest. The claims often reveal a part of the truth about the nature of what is to be done. It is unlikely that men will vote to have their ways of life changed, but they will vote for changing others. They will vote for those who promise to shackle railroad monopolies, break up the Wall Street money monopoly, make businessmen follow fair trade practices, curb the economic royalists, and handcuff predatory activity. Northerners will vote to make Southerners toe the line on the racial issue. Negroes will vote to make white men behave more congenially toward them. Farmers will vote for forcing industrialists to give them their "fair share" of the national wealth. The aged will vote to have the young taxed to support them. Parents can be attracted by the notion of having those without children assist in educating theirs. There is something irresistibly attractive to most people about others being penalized and oneself benefited.

Class Legislation

Divide and Conquer—that has been the method employed to bring about social transformation. Divide the population into classes: into capitalist and laborer, into farmer and industrialist, into white collar and blue collar, into urban and rural, into Negro and white, into old and young, into Protestant and Catholic. Sow seeds of discord throughout society. Tell the laborer he is being exploited by the capitalist. Tell the Westerner he is being taken advantage of by the Easterner. Tell the farmer he is the backbone of the nation but is having the marrow sucked out of the bone by miserly advocates of the gold standard. Tell Negroes they are being exploited by landlords turned slumlords.

Promise to change all this by forthcoming legislation: by the free coinage of silver, by antitrust acts, by creating a super banking system, by providing low interest long-term loans, by regulating the stock exchange, and so on. When the old demons—Wall Street, capitalists, millionaires —have been controlled or subdued, forge the classes into electoral majorities by making war on abstractions, such as depressions and poverty. Such has been the history of gaining the semblance of popular approval for the effort at political transformation of society in recent decades.

The conquest has been much more subtle. There are many facets to it; for all those actions taken in the supposed interest of some group or class have had consequences. Some of these consequences will be explored at other points in the story. Here, however, the conquest will be examined only for its impact upon men as individuals and upon society, and the import of these developments upon popular government.

First, to the extent that a man has become class conscious, to the extent that he assumes the role that is imputed to him, to that same extent he has ceased to be a whole man. A man may be a worker, any sort of worker, and also be in favor of giving an honest day's work. He cannot, however, belong to the "laboring class" and insist upon giving a *quid pro quo* for his wages. As a "laborer," he must realize that management is out to do him in, overwork him, replace him, cheat him, in a word, exploit him. He must, therefore, insist upon doing as little as possible, resist additional duties, oppose the introduction of machinery, cling tenaciously to every prerogative and position ever created, though there may no longer be any purpose for it. If he belongs to the managerial class, he must see himself in opposition to the "laborers," though he may mute this because it may be advantageous to pose as the friend of labor. A man may be a Negro and oppose switchblade knives, but he cannot be a "Negro," a member of that newly arrived class, and openly oppose switchblade knives, because these are supposed to be symbolically associated with Negroes by white men.

Numerous other examples could be given, but perhaps it is unnecessary. Those who think in terms of class in the contemporary class struggle framework cannot act as whole men. Theirs is not the full-throated voice of man; it is a pipsqueak because part of him is cut off from the rest of him. A man cannot vote the interests of "labor" and vote his whole interests as a man. A man may be not only a worker in a factory but also a husband, a father, a son, a deacon in his church, a Mason, a golfer, a property owner, a debtor, a creditor, a consumer, a seller, a hunter, an army veteran, plus all those tangibles and intangibles which make him the unique individual that he is. His interests are too much those of all other men to be expressed by any single facet of them called "labor." No majority of votes, however large, made up of those who have supposedly voted their class interests can indicate popular approval. It can only mean that a large number of people have voted some small portion of themselves, misled into thinking that they were voting for that which was in their interest.

The impact upon society is equally devastating. Those who have divided the American people into classes have not only set each man who accepts this against himself but also set men against men and groups against groups. They have broken down the lines of communication which link men together in society. Political force that was supposed to transform society has, instead, cut society apart. The politicalizing of life tends to make all groups into pressure groups, absorb the energy that is put into them into seeking favors from government. Those who seek meaningful social life must do so increasingly outside the ambit of organizations.

Yet society is transformed; it is rendered impotent. That is, those who would defend the language, customs, traditions, procedures, and beliefs which make society possible, who would speak in the name of virtue and morality, are drowned out in the cacophony of voices defending one special interest or another. The conquest is of men and society. Of the conquerors, it may be said here that they have great power for their reward. But this was ever the object of conquerors!

Of course, there were other obstacles in the way of those who would use the power of government to transform society. The United States Constitution was probably the most important one. It was so drawn, according to James Madison, as to make exceedingly difficult the concert of special interests which might crowd out the general welfare. We will examine next the flight from the Constitution which made it possible to divide and conquer the American people.

21

The Flight from the Constitution

THE CONSTITUTION OF THE UNITED STATES WAS THE major obstacle to the use of the government to reconstruct American society. Social reconstruction by government, if it could be done, would require the concentration of power in a single government, the central direction of the exercise of that power, and a concerted effort over an extended period of time. The latter would be a requirement if it were to be done gradually, and it should be clear that this was the method generally approved by American reformers. Ushering in utopia by government action would require not only an initial control over the lives of Americans but also a continuing control such as to make continuing popular decisions impractical, undesirable, and disruptive of the whole course of development.

The Constitution was carefully drawn so as to make such uses of the government which it authorized exceedingly difficult, if not impossible. The Founders did not have in mind preventing meliorism (or socialism), of course, for they had never heard of it, though they were familiar with mercantilistic approaches to amelioration. They were concerned with protecting the liberty of individuals and preventing the government from becoming tyrannical. Any provisions that tend to accomplish this object will, at the same time, place obstacles in the way of using the government for social reconstruction. Tyranny is made possible

411

by concentrated and unchecked power, by the very conditions which are necessary for social reconstruction.

Factions and Pressure Groups

The Founders were not familiar with meliorism but they were acquainted with factions, interest groups, and parties. They were aware, by way of history, of the damage done to republics, to popular governments, and to liberty by men joined together in factions and using political power to achieve their aims. In short, they were conscious of the dangers of faction and party. James Madison provided an acute analysis of the sources and dangers of factions in the *Federalist* number 10. He first defined the term:

> By a faction I understand a number of citizens, whether amounting to a majority or minority of the whole, who are united and actuated by some common impulse of passion, or of interest, adverse to the rights of other citizens, or to the permanent and aggregate interests of the community.[1]

He explained that this tendency of men to group as factions arises from human fallibility and liberty. The partiality of men's vision coupled with self-love inclines them to pursue what they think is for their own well-being, though it be at the expense of others.

> The latent causes of faction are thus sown in the nature of man; and we see them everywhere brought into different degrees of activity, according to the different circumstances of civil society. . . . So strong is this propensity of mankind to fall into mutual animosities that where no substantial occasion presents itself the most frivolous and fanciful distinctions have been suffi-

---

[1] James Madison, Alexander Hamilton, and John Jay, *The Federalist Papers* (New Rochelle, N. Y.: Arlington House), p. 78.

cient to kindle their unfriendly passions and excite their most violent conflicts. . . . Those who hold and those who are without property have ever formed distinct interests in society. Those who are creditors, and those who are debtors, fall under a like discrimination. A landed interest, a manufacturing interest, a mercantile interest, a moneyed interest, with many lesser interests, grow up of necessity in civilized nations. . . .[2]

The main purpose of Madison's essay was to refute those who held that a confederated (or federal) republic was inappropriate as a form of government for America, since the population was dispersed over a vast area. On the contrary, he held, this was the most propitious situation for such a government. Factions had destroyed small republics in the course of history. Pure (or direct) democracy had given too great an opportunity for the majority to tyrannize over the minority, whereas in America, the indirectness of representation and the dispersion of the population would make it most difficult for factions to use the government for partisan purposes.

Indeed, the United States Constitution did place formidable obstacles in the way of any interest group which wanted to use government for its ends. Not only is the population dispersed over a country of broad extent but also any potential faction or interest group may be expected to be spread throughout the country. The manner of election of representatives established by the original Constitution made it difficult for any faction to bring its weight to bear in concert upon the government. Only one body of the Federal government—the House of Representatives—was originally chosen directly by the electorate, Provisions were made for Representatives to be selected by voters within states, usually by districts. The electors of the

---

[2] *Ibid.*, p. 79.

Senate came from within even smaller districts, for the Senate was to be chosen by state legislatures. The electors of the President were chosen by states, and could be selected by whatever electorate the states might decide upon.

The difficulties of factions were compounded by dispersing the powers of government between the general (Federal) government and states, and by separating the Federal government into three branches. For action to be taken by the Federal government both houses of the Congress must act by majorities, the President give his assent, and the courts enforce it. If any bill fails to get a majority in either house, it does not become a law. That is to say, either house may prevent legislation from being passed. If the President vetoes a measure, it has to be passed by two-thirds of those present and voting of both houses. If the courts will not enforce an act, it is of no effect at law. In short, it takes the concurrence of both houses of Congress and to considerable degree all branches of government for government to act, but it requires only one house to prevent legislation and any branch of government has considerable power to forestall it.

Constitutional Curbs

The Constitution limits the government both substantively and in the procedures it requires for changing it. The powers which the Federal government may exercise are specifically granted in the Constitution. It is prohibited to exercise certain powers, i.e., the passing of ex post facto laws, the restriction of free speech, the taking of property without just compensation, and so forth. All powers not granted to the Federal government by the Constitution are reserved to the states or to the people.

To make the limitation upon the government as plain as possible, the Ninth Amendment says, "The enumeration in the Constitution of certain rights shall not be construed to deny or disparage others retained by the people." The Tenth says, "The powers not delegated to the United States by the Constitution, nor prohibited by it to the States, are reserved to the States respectively, or to the people."

Moreover, the procedures prescribed for amendment are such as to require overwhelming approval throughout the country for changes to be made in the basic instrument of government. The ordinary route of amendment is for both houses of Congress to pass a proposed change by majorities of two-thirds or more. The measure is then submitted to state legislatures, or conventions within states. When three-fourths of the states indicate their approval, the measure becomes a part of the Constitution.

The purpose of these complex checks upon the Federal government (along generally, with similar checks upon state governments) should be abundantly clear. They were aimed to prevent the use of the government by faction or party for the special ends of interest groups, to protect minorities from abuse by majorities, to keep government action to that which would be in the general interest, and to assure that such action as was taken would have behind it a broad consensus. To make this emphatic, the original Constitution requires that all taxes, duties, imposts, and excises be levied "for the common defense and general welfare of the United States. . . ." In short, moneys should only be appropriated for the well-being of everyone.

These provisions were, of course, only writings on pieces of paper in 1789. They had no force of their own, no power to make anyone adhere to them, no inherent strength to make anyone observe them. They might have become dead letters in short order, as so many constitutions have in later times. Instead, they were given vitality and life by men who found in their attachment to the Constitution means of achieving goals which they sought and retaining the fruits of victories they had won. For those who sought to forge a Union from distinct and disparate states, the Constitution offered them their best hope. For those who valued protection from an overweening and arbitrary government, the Constitution was their shelter. Nor were these disparate ends; union and liberty were reconciled for many men by the Constitution. The Constitution was the primal contract of the American peoples—the union of peoples by states established by it, the powers of the general government stemming from it, the protections against arbitrary government provided in it.

The Constitution did more than this: it provided a symbol and source of continuity to a people who had dispensed with monarchy, who had cast off the hereditary means of continuity, who sought government by law not by men. At the hands of great jurists—John Marshall, Roger Taney, and others—it became the fundamental law by which all other law must be tested, the body of law to which all must submit when they operated within its jurisdiction. It was no longer a mere piece of paper; it was that to which judges deferred when they applied the law, that to which Congress and the President looked for authority, that in terms of which the power of government could be brought to bear upon individuals.

The point is this. The Constitution provided diverse modes of election for those who should hold office under it, separated powers within the government, limited the powers to certain specified objects, and provided protections for the rights of individuals. It provided protections for minorities and made it most difficult for factions to gain control of the government. These provisions gained great force by the sanctity men came to attach to the Constitution. The words became flesh, as it were, as courts deferred to them, as legislators heeded them, as executives based their actions upon them.

Yet, for a good many years now, the government of these United States has been embarked on a program of social transformation—on and off, but more and more. The assent to these efforts at social reconstruction has been obtained mainly by appeals to factions and interest groups. The art of politics has become largely the art of achieving majorities by gaining support from a sufficient number of factions. The reverse of what Madison predicted has occurred; he held that the mode of election of representatives and of the exercise of power would make it extremely difficult, if not impossible, for the government to fall into the hands of factions. The electorate was so dispersed that factions would be prevented from bringing their weight to bear as a unit upon the government. Instead, the country is today divided into factions and interest groups which wield great influence upon the government and promote the concentration of power in government. This concentrated power is then used in programs of experimentation at social reconstruction.

There has been a flight from the Constitution. It has not been by constitutional amendment, though one or two amendments have facilitated the flight; for there are constitutional means for amending the Constitution. In any case, the Constitution has been little changed from the original, with one exception, in regard to the selection of representatives. The flight from the Constitution has been accomplished without altering the verbal content of the document generally: it has been done by extraconstitutional developments, by interpretation, by the assumption of powers not granted, by the gaining of powers by one branch at the expense of another, and by allowing some safeguards to atrophy or be altered.

Some Extraconstitutional Developments

Some early extraconstitutional developments set the stage for the flight from the Constitution, though in themselves they may have been innocent enough. The Constitution provides that the President shall be chosen by an electoral college. Each state has as many electors as it has Senators and Representatives in the Congress. They are chosen in the manner directed by state legislatures. The assumption was that electors would be chosen because of their eminence within their states and that they would select a President without reference to anything other than their own choice. The original Constitution provided that each elector should vote for two persons. The person receiving the highest number of these votes, provided it constituted a majority, would become President; the one receiving the next highest would be Vice-President. In case no candidate got a majority, the election would revert to the House of Representatives, where each state would have one vote. Initially, state legislatures often chose electors.

One extraconstitutional development was the growth of political parties. Some of the early leaders, notably George Washington, hoped that political parties would not develop in America. It was a vain hope. The outlines of parties began to form over the very question of the ratification of the Constitution. Within a few years they had taken definite shape under the leadership of Alexander Hamilton and Thomas Jefferson. The Constitution has no reference to such organizations; they are given no role to play. But Alexander Hamilton was a man with a vision, a vision of a unified people in a nation made great by the vitality and extent of its commerce and manufacturing. He proposed to attain these objects by an energetic use of the

Federal government. Jefferson welded together a party to oppose much of this governmental activity and intervention, and in defense of a strict construction of the Constitution. By 1800, political parties had assumed much of the extraconstitutional role they have continued to play in our history. It has been a fateful role, for it enables factions to determine policy, insofar as political parties determine policy, across the lines of electoral districts.

Parties early gained sway in the electoral college, i.e., electors were chosen on a party basis. But the constitutional mode for the voting of electors tended to thwart this. If all of a party's electors voted for the same men for President and Vice-President, there would be a tie between these two men, and the election would revert to the House of Representatives. Indeed, this happened in 1800 and might have been expected to happen regularly thereafter. Instead, the Twelfth Amendment was ratified in 1804; it provided that each elector should have one vote for President and one vote for Vice-President. Thus, the way was prepared for party determination of candidates and for electors to become mere figureheads for their parties.

Additionally, states decided for a whole slate of electors. When, as happened shortly, the electors were popularly chosen, all the votes of a state were cast for the party's electors receiving a majority of the votes of the citizenry. Most of the electors might have been chosen in congressional districts, the remaining two in state-wide elections, thus dispersing the vote. This was not done. By having all of them chosen by a state-wide majority the way was opened to the forging of majorities by appeal to state-wide factions or interest groups. Political parties provided the instrument for factional use at the national level.

It would be a mistake, however, to make much of these early developments. They provided a potentiality for the factional use of government and for the concentration of power. The Federal government was used for interest groups in the nineteenth century on occasion, most notably in the case of the protective tariff. But there were still many obstacles to concerted party efforts to carry out programs. Most of these developments had to do with the choice of a President. Members of Congress were still chosen in the way originally prescribed.

Nominally, congressmen adopted some party label, but there were few effective devices for enforcing party discipline. A congressman could vote for a program advanced by his party or not, as he chose, and only those within his district could discipline him. Even if one who had voted against most of the planks of his party's platform should be defeated in his district, it would be by no means clear that his failure to serve as a party man had led to his defeat. The President had little authority over congressmen; the Founders had tried, with considerable success, to make it so. Each branch was to be independent of the others. Moreover, the Constitution, as it was observed, placed great substantive limits upon what could be done by government, in any case. Many other changes had to be made before the government could be used for a sustained effort at social transformation.

Reform by Amendment

Three other constitutional amendments deserve mention. The Fourteenth Amendment, declared ratified in 1868, made all those born within the United States citizens of the United States. Also, it extended in other ways the authority of the Federal government. It prohibited the states to take life, liberty, or property without due process of law. Moreover, the amendment was rather vaguely worded, and this ambiguity has been exploited and amplified by the Supreme Court as it has used it as a basis for the extension of the sway of the general government. The Sixteenth Amendment, which authorizes direct taxes without reference to population, enabled the Federal government to enact an income tax, thus greatly increasing the revenue available to it.

But for the empowerment of factions, the Seventeenth Amendment was probably the most important of all. It was ratified in 1913, in the same year as the Sixteenth, and it provided for the direct election of Senators. Thereafter, Senators were to be elected by state-wide popular votes. Factions and interest groups could play roles in these elections now that had formerly been denied to them. A pivotal minority could provide the necessary votes for a majority. An interest group with large numbers in it could virtually dictate the choice of a party candidate in an election. This result has been most noticeable in states which have several important minority groups, such as organized labor and racial minorities.

Most of the changes and accretions of power, however, have been accomplished without benefit of constitutional amendment. One of the most effective devices for evading the constitutional separation of powers and enabling the Federal government to exercise greatly expanded powers has been the so-called independent commission, e.g., the Interstate Commerce Commission, National Labor Relations Board, and Federal Communications Commission. They have played a very important role in the attempts at social transformation. The intricate regulation which reformers have sought could hardly be encompassed in general legislation. The separation of powers made it very difficult to take action. The executive branch might apply legislation in ways not contemplated; the courts could, as they did frequently for many years, nullify the action as a violation of due process, or some other constitutional protection. The independent commissions, however, frequently combined all these functions—legislative, executive, and judicial. Though their powers derive from Congress, they are nonetheless real.

Growth of Presidential Power

The change in the role of the President, particularly in constructing legislation, too, has been done without formal constitutional alteration. The President's formal legislative powers are mainly negative. He may veto bills that come before him. Except in foreign affairs, this is the extent of the grant of powers over legislation to him. (He is, of course, charged with faithfully executing the laws.) Strong Presidents in the nineteenth century were frequently men distinguished for their vetoes. Andrew Jackson and Grover Cleveland come readily to mind. But by the early twentieth century, as some Presidents became enthusiastic about meliorism, they began to perceive possibilities for the chief executive to take over much more of the leadership and initiative in legislation. Theodore Roosevelt showed the way to such leadership, but it was Woodrow Wilson who formulated the theory of presidential predominance in the government.

In his early writings, Wilson indicated his regret that the President was "merely an administrator." On one occasion, he wrote:

> If you would have the present error of our system in a word, it is this, that Congress is the motive power in the government and yet has in it nowhere any representative of the nation as a whole. Our Executive, on the other hand, is national: at any rate may be made so, and yet has no longer any place of guidance in our system. It represents no constituency, but the whole

people, and yet, though it alone is national, it has no originative voice in domestic national policy.[3]

By the early twentieth century, Wilson had seen the way to change this situation. Since the President is the leader of his party, he may become the leader of the nation, or at least he

> . . . has it in his choice to be. . . . His is the only national voice in affairs. Let him once win the admiration and confidence of the country, and no other single force can withstand him, no combination of forces will easily overpower him. . . . If he rightly interpret the national thought and boldly insist upon it, he is irresistible; and the country never feels the zest of action so much as when its President is of such insight and calibre. Its instinct is for unified action, and it craves a single leader.[4]

Some of the devices by which the President's powers were expanded were inherent in the office, or so the proponents of presidential power have argued. The President is charged by the Constitution with notifying each Congress of the State of the Union. He is also authorized to recommend to them "such Measures as he shall judge necessary and expedient. . . ." He is commander-in-chief of the armed forces. He can make treaties, by and with the advice and consent of the Senate. His role in foreign affairs is, by the nature of these provisions, an eminent one. Wilson noted that when foreign affairs are foremost in national concern, the President's stature is apt to increase and his

---

[3] Quoted in A. J. Wann, "The Development of Woodrow Wilson's Theory of the Presidency: Continuity and Change," *The Philosophy and Policies of Woodrow Wilson,* Earl Latham, ed. (Chicago: University of Chicago Press, 1958), p. 58.

[4] Quoted in *Ibid.,* p. 61.

role expand. As commander-in-chief, the President is in a position of leadership in making war.

It is worth noting that the same Presidents who have been most determinedly devoted to melioristic reform have also been those who have gotten us most deeply embroiled in foreign affairs which usually led to war, that is, Presidents Theodore Roosevelt, Woodrow Wilson, Franklin Roosevelt, Harry Truman, John Kennedy, and Lyndon Johnson. Nor is the connection entirely accidental. Embroilment in foreign affairs not only increases the role of the President in decision-making but it is more than likely to involve the United States in such wars as occur. Moreover, twentieth century wars have been leading occasions for the introduction of reformist innovations, regulations, and restrictions, and these can be, and have been, blamed upon the exigencies of war.

This is not to say that Presidents have involved the United States in war in order to advance reform programs. If such a thing had occurred, it would probably be forever beyond the reach of historical proof.[5] Since we lack such proof, the matter can be sufficiently explained in this way. Presidents with a penchant for intervention can most readily exercise it in foreign affairs, for the bulk of their interventionist powers lie in that realm. Intervention is likely to lead to war. Once the country is involved in war, the President can use it as an occasion and opportunity for domestic intervention. The penchant to intervene,

---

[5] Witness, for example, the spate of books during and after World War II attempting to prove that Roosevelt deliberately provoked the attack on Pearl Harbor. Yet, they prove only that he *might* have done so, that the policies he followed did little to inhibit a sneak attack. The chances are good that nothing more than this will ever be proved, for hidden motives are involved.

which is probably rooted in human nature in the will to power, is, of course, nurtured and provided with intellectualist justifications in meliorist ideologies.

The President's powers have been increased in a number of other ways. The incidental authorization in the Constitution for the President to recommend measures to Congress has served as a base for Presidents to take the initiative in legislation. Presidents in the nineteenth century did not utilize this much for promoting particular acts of legislation.

There were many reasons for this. The main one is that nineteenth century Presidents were not committed to extensive reforms. They did not conceive it to be their mission to transform American society. Had they thought otherwise, however, there were good and sufficient reasons for them to abstain from legislative leadership. The President's primary task is administrative, the execution of the laws. If he becomes involved in the making of particular laws, he may take positions which will unfit him for executing them, particularly if he has vigorously opposed measures that are subsequently passed over his veto. Congress might well resent presidential tampering with its prerogatives. The President's prestige would be at stake in the measures he promoted.[6] Moreover, he does not have sufficient leverage over Congress to get his measures enacted. Its members are chosen independently of him.

Most of these objections and difficulties have, of course, been overcome or shunted aside in the twentieth century, for Presidents have taken over legislative leadership. Woodrow Wilson was the first to do so on a large scale, though

---

[6] In parliamentary systems, of course, the Prime Minister does take such leadership. But if he is defeated on an issue he considers crucial, he may resign or be forced to do so. No such alternative exists for a President.

Theodore Roosevelt had pointed the way. Wilson ran on the basis of a program called the New Freedom, and, once inaugurated, he proceeded to get the program through Congress. Since that time, Presidents have gone much farther in assuming legislative responsibilities. This reached a peak in two years: 1933 and 1965. In 1933 many of the bills which were passed by Congress were actually drawn by men in the executive department, sent to Congress, and, in the case of some of them, passed without benefit of committee examination. By 1965, Congress had come to accept the presidential initiatives as standard procedure. The traditional roles of the two branches had been reversed; Congress could exercise what amounted to a veto on bills proposed by the executive, but the initiative had passed to the President.

The difficulties of doing this were overcome in various ways. In the first place, Presidents did become reformers. It became customary for presidential candidates, at least Democratic ones, to set forth a program of changes which they expected to institute if elected. These programs have often been given names, as New Freedom, New Deal, Great Society, and so forth. Not only have presidential candidates run on these, but congressional candidates as well. Once elected, a President is then assumed to be committed to rendering these into bills which he is to push through Congress.

Secondly, the prestige of the office of President has been built up, particularly in wartime. That of Congress has suffered by comparison. When Congress has failed to pass presidential bills, it has been labeled obstructionist, and has suffered from both subtle and not so subtle vilifications by columnists and assorted publicists. In short, Presidents—with assistance from their numerous helpers in the media of communication—have found ways to advance particular proposals without losing face if they fail. Instead, Congress is supposed to lose face by failing to pass them.

Third, Presidents have found ways to bring sufficient congressmen to heel to forge majorities for much of their legislation. In the main, these consist of patronage, spoils, and pork barrel. Congressmen are brought around by promises of government projects to be located in their districts, getting their men appointed to office, a new dam, a new post office building, a new Federal office building, a defense plant, a government contract, and so on, *ad nauseam*.

On the face of it, it is difficult to imagine a more ironic development than this latter one. To Congress belongs the power of appropriation, as well as the initiation of acts. Yet, congressmen truckle to the President to get a portion of the largess they have voted to distribute. There is an explanation for this, however, and it will get us to the nub of the matter. A congressman is one man among many men. Theoretically, his vote counts for no more than any other, and in the course of a few years of legislating, his district should come out on a par with all other districts in getting Federal largess. Of course, not all men are equally influential in Congress; some have important seats on crucial committees, others not. Such a congressman can parlay his influence in Congress into sizeable gains for his district by also serving the President faithfully. Presidential discretion in handing out benefits greatly augments what a congressman could get on his own.

These are but accommodations, however, by which some congressmen get their quid pro quo for yielding up their legislative prerogatives. The prerogatives had to be yielded up as Congress gave its assent to the building of an ever vaster Federal establishment. The fact is that it is no longer practicable for Congress to devise a budget, or, what amounts to the same thing, initiate appropriations. Congress cannot oversee the vast Federal establishment effectively; it cannot devise the intricate regulations and restrictions which now govern the lives of Americans. It cannot do the work which a huge Federal bureaucracy now performs, nor could any other legislative body.

Overriding the Constitution

The flight from the Constitution does not consist simply of the power which factions can now exercise, of the concentration of power, or of shifts in the relative weight of the branches of government. It stems from the overriding of the substantive limitations upon the powers of the Federal government. In short, much of the huge Federal establishment has been built by the exercise of powers that were not granted in the Constitution. Most of the regulations, restrictions, expenditures (excepting for defense) and far-flung activities were not authorized by the Constitution. Nor have they been authorized by amendments. Instead, they have been acquired by reading into the Constitution what is not there, and promulgating mystifications about what is there.

Those seeking a scapegoat to blame for the flight from the Constitution may find it convenient to place the burden of responsibility upon the Supreme Court. Yet such an historical interpretation would be a gross injustice to many of the men who have made up that august body. It is true that the majority of the Court have now joined the flight from the Constitution, may even be in the forefront of it, but this is a recent development. The members of all branches of the government are charged with observing the Constitution, the members of Congress and the President no less than the courts. A majority of either house of the

Congress can just as surely nullify a bill on the grounds of its unconstitutionality—by refusing to pass it—as the Supreme Court can nullify an act of Congress—by refusing to enforce it. The President can veto a bill on the grounds of its unconstitutionality. It could still be passed over his veto, but this would be no reason for a President to fail to do his duty by the Constitution. It is true that the Supreme Court has the last say, but to the extent that the flight from the Constitution has been by the regular legislative route, the courts have only concurred in flights already made by other branches.

Moreover, the Supreme Court held out much longer against the general flight from the Constitution than did any other branch. Initially, it greatly circumscribed the activities of the Interstate Commerce Commission, made of limited effect for a number of years that strange piece of legislation known as the Sherman Antitrust Act, only very reluctantly accepted the privileged status of organized labor. It did not readily concur in the piecemeal absorption of property rights by government in regulatory measures. The Federal courts held out for four years or more against the drastic measures of the New Deal after the Congress had become a rubber stamp for executive measures. It nullified the central acts of the early New Deal when it invalidated the N.R.A. and A.A.A.

But there are limits to what can be expected of men, and those limits apply to justices of the Supreme Court as well as other men. For years before 1937, a literary assault upon the Constitution had been going on. Writers had proclaimed that the Constitution was itself a class document, that it had been drawn by well-to-do merchants and planters to serve their interests. It was outmoded, others said, perhaps well enough suited to an agrarian society but hardly fit for an industrial one. New times re-

quire new measures, other men proclaimed. A new outlook had been developed; in terms of it government was
supposed to act in accord with the needs of the moment,
not in accord with some "ossified" eighteenth century
"piece of paper." In theory, the Court's position is secure;
in practice, it is not certain how long it can hold out
against the combined Congress and President. The men
who make up these branches are popularly elected. They
are the voice of the people, so the argument ran. Could
nine men withstand the wrath of a nation, prevented from
going in the direction it wanted to go? The Court might
have held out with impunity. At any rate, it did not. After
1937, it capitulated, for whatever reasons, following Roosevelt's ill-fated Court Reorganization Bill (popularly known
as his "Court Packing Scheme"). Since that time it has
only rarely called a halt to some particular reconstructionist activity.

The above is to set the record straight. The role of the
Court in defense of the Constitution when the other
branches were irresponsibly evading its limitations has
gone unsung. The point needed to be made, too, that,
legends to the contrary notwithstanding, the Court is not
the sole keeper of the Constitution. This is a solemn responsibility enjoined upon those who serve in all branches
of the government. The courts have, however, played an
increasing role in the flight from the Constitution, and
that story needs to be told also.

It is hardly conceivable that a people would grant the
power to a government of their own making to make over
their lives. Only confusion could produce the notion that
it would be desirable or necessary to grant such powers
to government. If a people wish to alter the character of
their lives and their ways of doing things, there is no need
for government to effect the changes; the people can

make them on their own. Of course, a majority might grant powers to its government to make a minority conform to its will. But any thoughtful majority would wish to circumscribe these powers, for majorities change in their constituency, and a man who is today the member of a majority may tomorrow find himself in a minority.

At any rate, the Constitution of these United States did not authorize the government it provided for to engage in social reconstruction. Moreover, many protections were written for minorities against their subjection to some temporary majority. Yet, for a good many years now, the government of these United States has been engaged in various projects of social reconstruction. Each of these is a flight from the Constitution. But before detailing these flights and explaining how they have been made, let us examine a single instance.

Brown vs. Board of Education

On May 31, 1955, there went out a decree from the Supreme Court at Washington in the District of Columbia based upon a prior declaration by that body of "the fundamental principle that racial discrimination in public education is unconstitutional. . .—All provisions of federal, state or local law requiring or permitting such discrimination must yield to this principle. . . ." This decree ordered subordinate courts to comply in these words:

> The Courts will require—a prompt and reasonable start toward full compliance—and enter such orders and decrees—as are necessary and proper to admit to public schools on a socially non-discriminating basis with all deliberate speed the parties to these cases. . . .

This decree had the purpose of implementing the ruling of the Supreme Court in *Brown* vs. *Board of Education of*

Topeka, et al, which had declared segregated schools unconstitutional in 1954.

A great concert of spokesmen in the media of communication proclaimed that the decision and the subsequent
decree was the Law of the Land. Many vocal elements in
the United States subscribed to the notion, or presumption, that those who did not rush to comply with the Court's
proclamation were defying the law. The import of what
they were saying was this: Those who continued to maintain segregated schools supported by taxes were outlaws.

Such was not the case (and is not the case). Nothing is
more firmly established in the American system of juris-
prudence than that the courts apply the law to particular
cases. If this decision was law for anyone, it was law only
for the defendants in the case (i.e., the Board of Education
of Topeka, and so forth). It would become law for others
only when rulings had been made upon cases brought before courts.

Critics of the decision have charged that the Court was
legislating. Defenders of the decision have, by implication,
claimed that the Court has legislated. When they say that
the decision is the Law of the Land, they must be saying
that the court legislated, for they do not charge that it was
the Law of the Land before 1954. The words of the decision suggest that the Court was trying to legislate, or, at
the least, give this character to its pronouncements, for
it did speak to the general situation, though its order did
and could apply only to those defendants before it.

The Brown case is of particular interest because it is a
dramatic illustration of two intertwined trends involved
in the flight from the Constitution. In the first place, it was
an attempt to make over or reconstruct society. One writer
focuses upon this character of the decision as well as emphasizing the departure from earlier practice as follows:

The Segregation decisions had a social consequence of a vastly different order. They called for a rewriting of state and federal legislation relating to public education. When to the Segregation decisions are added the later judicial acts extending the new constitutional regime to other places of public assembly, one must acknowledge that judicial orders have required a basic revision of social structure and a root change in human relationships. The Supreme Court did not order Alabama and Mississippi and South Carolina to forget about an innovation in public policy and continue life as they had lived it before the promulgation of that innovation; the Court ordered people in those and other states to fashion legislation of a kind that they had never had on their statute books and to institute some social relationships that had never prevailed in those places.[7]

Second, the Court used established judicial procedures to carry out unjudicial action. This gave the act its semblance of legality and claim to be obeyed. But it did not alter the fundamental innovation involved nor departure from judicial functions.

The two judicial instruments used were judicial review and the court order. The so-called power of judicial review is based upon the view that in applying the law the courts must decide which law applies to a particular case. If there are two laws in conflict, the court must choose which one is applicable, and in so doing it makes of the other a nullity. Two sorts of conflict have arisen: one, a conflict between an act of the legislature and a provision of the Constitution; the other, a conflict between Federal legislation and that of the states.

Since *Marbury* vs. *Madison*, the rule has held that an act of legislature in conflict with the Constitution will not be applied by the courts. Such an act is usually said to be

---

[7] Charles S. Hyneman, *The Supreme Court on Trial* (New York: Atherton Press, 1963), p. 199.

unconstitutional. It is also held that a state act in conflict with a Federal act, when the Congress was acting within its constitutional powers, will not be applied. Claims have arisen over the years that the courts were actually making law when they interpreted the Constitution and the laws. But in the above examples, at least, the courts would not be making laws; they would only be deciding between laws as to which to apply.

The Brown decision was peculiar in many ways. The usual route to the testing of a law is to violate it, be found guilty by the appropriate court, and appeal the decision on the grounds of the unconstitutionality of the law. The Brown decision did not arise in this way, though it could have. Two ways to test the segregation laws come to mind. One would be for the parents of a child to refuse to send him to a segregated school. If the state in which this occurred had compulsory attendance laws, the parents might then be prosecuted for failing to require the child to attend. The particular law being challenged would be the compulsory attendance law, but perhaps the courts might decide upon the constitutionality of segregation in connection with it.

The other way to test the constitutionality of segregation would be for a school official to enroll, say, a Negro child in a white school, or vice versa. If he were then brought to court for his act, a perfect test case would be available for the constitutionality of the laws requiring segregation.

In both imaginary cases, the court could have ruled the acts unconstitutional. That is, the court could have held that an act compelling students to attend segregated schools was in violation of the Constitution (or even, that compulsory school attendance was). And, it could have held, in the second case, that the requirement that schools be segregated was unconstitutional. In either case, the

decision of the court would have been negative, and the
initiative for taking action would have remained with the
states and communities. In these cases, the Court would
not have been making law, though it would have reversed
its former position as to what was law.

But the approach to the courts was not made in the
usual way. Plaintiffs in these cases asked for *court orders*
requiring the admission of the pupils in question to all-
white schools. That is, they asked for orders compelling
integration. The court order is a well established instrument of the courts. There is a considerable array of instances in which they may be issued. Roughly, though,
they are of two kinds: those issued prior to adjudication,
and those issued to effect a judgment arrived at in regular
court proceedings. The first usually is of the nature of an
injunction, prohibiting or estopping some action which,
if it is as alleged, will result in irreparable damage if allowed to continue until a case can be decided in court.
Decisions themselves may result in court orders; if so, they
would be of the second kind.

It is remarkable that these cases should ever have come
before the Supreme Court. There was no alleged conflict
between Federal and state statutes. There was no standing
law (that is, legislative enactment) compelling integration upon which a court order might issue. Moreover,
courts (including the Supreme Court) had held on many
occasions that segregation, *per se,* did not violate the
"equal protection of the law" clause of the Fourteenth
Amendment. The ruling principle in such a case might
be expected to be *stare decisis* (to let the decision stand).
In short, there was no law, either statute or constitutional,
upon which a court order might be issued.

Before the Supreme Court could issue the orders that it
did and remand the cases to the lower courts for particular

orders, it found it necessary to establish at least the semblance of such law by constitutional reinterpretation. That is, it reversed earlier decisions. Theoretically, it might have done so by declaring that it would not enforce laws requiring segregation in the schools, though it had no case directly challenging these before it. If it had done so, however, its ruling on the cases before it would, of necessity, have been to deny the suits. The Court was asked to rule not that segregation was unconstitutional but that for the plaintiffs to receive equal protection of the laws integration must be *required* in public schools.

Compulsory Integration

Compulsory integration is the key phrase for understanding the import of the Brown decision. The distinction between declaring segregation to be unconstitutional in the public schools and the compelling of integration may appear to be a distinction without a difference. It is not; it makes all the difference in the world. If the Court had ruled that segregation was unconstitutional, the decision would undoubtedly have been subject to much controversy. It would, nonetheless, have been, in the common parlance, the Law of the Land. That is, the courts would not enforce segregation laws by assessing penalties against violators. In the normal course of events, no such cases would come before the courts. Everyone might know that such laws were of no effect. Ruling in this way, the Supreme Court has an inherent power to say what is the law in these United States. It is a negative power; it nullifies but does not create.

Compulsory integration is another matter altogether. It is not law at all. It lacks the predictability which is an essential requirement of law, about which more anon. There are no minimum nor maximum penalties fixed for violators. There is no provision for trial by jury of offenders, which, if the decisions were law, would be in conflict with the Sixth Amendment to the Constitution. There is no description of the circumstances under which integration must occur, no exclusion of those in which it is not required. The effecting of the decisions is to be done in such a manner as to evade the requirements that due process of law be observed.

"Due process of law" is often treated as if it were a mystery, to be divined, if at all, by those deeply immured in the intricacies of the law. For some of the finer points, this may be so. But much of the outline of the requirements of due process of law is spelled out unmistakably in the Fourth through the Eighth Amendments to the Constitution. For example, the Fifth Amendment says, "No person shall be held to answer for a capital, or otherwise infamous crime, unless on a presentment or indictment of a Grand Jury. . . ." The Sixth says, "In all criminal prosecutions, the accused shall enjoy the right to a speedy and public trial, by an impartial jury of the State and district wherein the crime shall have been committed. . . ." The Seventh says, "In Suits at common law, where the value in controversy shall exceed twenty dollars, the right of trial by jury shall be preserved. . . ." Any law which did not allow or provide for these processes would, itself, be in violation of the Constitution. The Brown decision, and those subsequent to it, allowed for no such processes; contempt proceedings before a judge only were to be the methods of enforcement.

More needs to be said under the heading of predictability. The Brown decision, for all its firmness of tone, did not settle the question as to what is the law. It only raised a host of questions. Let us note some of them. Must a school admit a child of the Negro race when he applies

without regard to where he resides? Does the ruling apply
with equal validity to Indians, for instance? Must a school
district integrate its schools in the absence of the desire
for such integration from any of its constituency? May a
pupil be compelled to attend an integrated school? When
is a school integrated? Must a school have some kind of
balance among the races in its pupil make-up? Must Negroes be imported or white people exported in order to
achieve integration? Any court worth its salt confronted
with the Brown decision under the guise of law would, of
necessity, rule that it was no law.

The Brown decision, and those subsequent to it, was not
judicial legislation; it was judicial compulsion. There was,
and is, no law requiring integrated schools. There have
been a large number of court orders compelling integration in particular instances. They are compulsions, however, without the sanction of law—in the absence of standing law. They are assertions of the will of the courts, or
of the Supreme Court, hence, arbitrary, violative of constitutional rights, and putative usurpations of powers be-
longing to legislatures or to the people.

Those who believe that the Brown decision was nonetheless proper may defend their position by holding that the
integration of the schools could not otherwise have been
obtained, that there would have been insufficient states to
approve a constitutional amendment for it to be adopted,
that Congressional action would have been forestalled by
a filibuster, that grand juries in some parts of the country
would not indict offenders, that trial juries would not con-
vict. All of this is another way of saying that the Constitution does not contemplate the use of the government to
make over the lives of Americans, that it provides for a
government answerable to the people, that the taking of
life, liberty, and property are powers residing finally in

juries selected from among those in the communities where the act is done. In short, Americans did not contract away the power to alter and determine what their lives would be. Such attempts can be made only by flights from the Constitution.

Other Unconstitutional Actions

The above is, of course, only one among many flights from the Constitution in the last eighty years. It is particularly significant because it shows how a nonelective branch of the government claims power for itself to alter society. But all branches of the United States government may and have taken part in action unauthorized by the Constitution. The following are some examples of such actions:

1. Passage of antitrust acts.
2. Authorizing the Interstate Commerce Commission to set rates.
3. Establishing of the Federal Reserve System.
4. The passage of a graduated income tax.
5. The construction of steam generators by the Tennessee Valley Authority.
6. The subsidizing of agricultural prices.
7. The restricting of crop acreages.
8. The subsidizing of interest rates.
9. The establishing of minimum wages and maximum hours.
10. The operating of Social Security.
11. The sponsoring of co-operatives.
12. The giving of Federal aid to education.
13. The providing of low rent housing.
14. The making of loans to other nations.
15. The forbidding of child labor.
16. The arbitration of labor disputes.
17. The controlling of prices.

These and many other actions have been done by the government of the United States. They are nowhere authorized in the Constitution. The legislative powers are enumerated in Article I, and not one of the above is mentioned nor, for that matter, clearly implied in the powers granted. Some will imagine, for example, that a graduated income tax is authorized by the Sixteenth Amendment. It is not. The Amendment reads, "The Congress shall have power to lay and collect taxes on incomes from whatever source derived, without apportionment among the several States, and without regard to any census or enumeration."

True, a graduated tax is not forbidden; but, then, neither is it authorized. Moreover, since the prevailing practice in America was for taxes to be uniform, no presumption existed that this authorized graduation. On the contrary, the supposition would be that income tax rates would be uniform.[8] Any court eager to insure the equal protection of the laws to the citizenry might refuse to enforce the graduated feature of the income tax on the grounds that by its workings Americans are not equally protected from the confiscation of their property.

My point, however, is that the Constitution does not authorize a graduated income tax. Nor does it authorize a host of other actions taken with the purpose of making over American society. The Constitution posed both formal and substantive obstacles to the partisan use of government for such unlimited ends. Some account has been made of how the formal obstacles have been largely overcome. The formal obstacles were the separation of powers within the Federal government, the dispersion of powers among the Federal and state governments, the differing composition of the electorate for various elective offices, and the division of the country into relatively small elec-

---

[8] See Thomas J. Norton, *Undermining the Constitution* (New York: Devin-Adair, 1951), pp. 60-63.

toral districts. The major devices by which these have been overcome have been the development of political parties, the direct election of Senators, the establishment of "independent" boards and commissions which tend to combine powers otherwise separate, the taking of initiative for legislation by the President, and the engaging of the Supreme Court in pseudo-legislative pronouncements.

The substantive obstacles in the Constitution consist mainly of the enumeration of powers granted and reservation of those not granted to the states or to the people, procedural restrictions, and enumerated prohibitions against certain actions. Many of these have been evaded, reconstrued, or ignored, so as to allow the Federal government to act in ways not authorized.

The Commerce Clause

Probably the one provision of the Constitution that has been stretched to the greatest extent to empower the Federal government to act upon Americans has been the interstate commerce clause. Article I, Section 8, gives Congress the power "to regulate Commerce . . . among the several States. . . ." Of this power, along with that of regulating commerce with foreign nations and with the Indians, one writer says: "This grant of authority is in the simplest of words, yet these words have unfolded into a body of propositions and explanations that constitute at least one-half of the constitutional doctrine pronounced by the Supreme Court."[9]

The first thing to be noted about this power is that it is a general and exclusive grant of it to the Federal government, and that the power so granted is vague and imprecise. Chief Justice John Marshall set forth in outline (in

---

[9] Hyneman, *op. cit.*, p. 141.

Gibbons vs. *Ogden*, 1824) the broad expanse of this power. He said, in part, "Commerce, undoubtedly, is traffic, but it is something more,—it is intercourse. It describes the commercial intercourse between nations, and parts of nations, in all its branches, and is regulated by prescribing rules for carrying on that intercourse." Of the power granted, he said: "This power, like all others vested in congress, is complete in itself, may be exercised to its utmost extent, and acknowledges no limitations other than are prescribed in the constitution."[10]

For about one hundred years, from some time after 1824 through 1936, the courts occupied themselves with delimiting and prescribing the extent of these powers. The Supreme Court distinguished between interstate and intrastate commerce, between trade and manufacturing, between that which has a direct effect on commerce and that which does not. Typical of such decisions was that of *United States* vs. *E. C. Knight Company* (1895). This case, testing the constitutionality of the Sherman Antitrust Act, involved the question of whether or not the power over commerce gave Congress the power to control monopolies in manufacturing. While the court did not hold the Sherman Act unconstitutional, it did hold that it did not extend to monopolies in manufacturing. Chief Justice Fuller reasoned in the following way:

Doubtless the power to control the manufacture of a given thing involves in a certain sense the control of its disposition, but this is a secondary and not the primary sense; and although the exercise of that power may result in bringing the operation of commerce into play, it does not control it, and affects it only incidentally and indirectly. . . . The power to regulate commerce is the

[10] Henry S. Commager, ed., *Documents of American History* I (New York: Appleton-Century-Crofts, 1962, 7th ed.), 239-40.

power to prescribe the rule by which commerce shall be governed, and is a power independent of the power to suppress monopoly. . . .[11]

One of the last decisions to attempt to maintain such distinctions and limitations on the Federal power was *Schechter Poultry Corp.* vs. *United States* (1935). The tendency of this decision was to invalidate the National Recovery Act (1933). It was also one of the last decisions to affirm that the Constitution imposes limits upon the Federal government regardless of the conditions which may prevail. Chief Justice Hughes said, in part:

Extraordinary conditions do not create or enlarge constitutional power. The Constitution established a national government with powers deemed to be adequate, as they have proved to be both in war and peace, but these powers of the national government are limited by the constitutional grants. Those who act under these grants are not at liberty to transcend the imposed limits because they believe that more or different power is necessary. Such assertions of extra-constitutional authority were anticipated and precluded by the explicit terms of the Tenth Amendment. . . .[12]

He then concluded for the majority of the Court:

We are of the opinion that the attempt through the provisions of the Code to fix the hours and wages of employees of defendants in their intrastate business was not a valid exercise of federal power.
On both the grounds we have discussed, the attempted delegation of legislative power, and the attempted regulation of intrastate transactions which affect interstate commerce only indirecly, we hold the code provisions here in question to be invalid. . . .[13]

From this point on, though, the obstacles to the use of

---

[11] *Ibid.*, I, 618-19.
[12] *Ibid.*, II, 280.   [13] *Ibid.*, 283.

power over interstate commerce to regulate a multitude of business activities began to be removed. The Federal courts had never exercised much restraint over state regulation of industry and commerce (about which, more later), but now they began to reduce the restraints on Congressional power. A turning point can be seen in *NLRB* vs. *Jones & Laughlin Steel Corp.* (1937). Chief Justice Hughes came as close as a judge is apt to do to reversing his earlier opinion in this one. He said,

> We do not find it necessary to determine whether these features of defendant's business dispose of the asserted analogy to the "stream of commerce" cases. The instances in which that metaphor has been used are but particular, and not exclusive. . . . The congressional authority to protect interstate commerce from burdens and obstructions is not limited to transactions which can be deemed to be an essential part of a "flow" of interstate or foreign commerce.[14]

Thereafter, all sorts of legislation has been validated under this clause, as, for example, child labor laws, social security, minimum wages, maximum hours, and so forth. By 1953, a student of constitutional interpretation, William W. Crosskey, could conclude that the whole panoply of distinctions and restrictions upon the Federal government in the regulation of economic affairs had been in error. Correctly construed, he said, the powers granted are plenary: "The national government shall have power to regulate the gainful business, commerce, and industry of the American people."[15] The Congress, the President, and the courts have increasingly operated upon such a premise.

But let us examine some of the implications of this

---

[14] Charles Fairman, *American Constitutional Decisions* (New York: Holt, 1952, rev. ed.), p. 220.

[15] Quoted in Hyneman, *op. cit.*, p. 149.

doctrine. Such an examination will lead us to other flights from the Constitution. If Congress may regulate all gainful business, what is to keep it, for example, from regulating newspapers? Might it not enact legislation to the effect that no newspaper may be sold in any state other than the one in which it is published? Might it not prohibit the dissemination of religious information?

But, it may be objected, these acts would be in violation of freedom of the press and of religion. So they would; Congress is prohibited from making such legislation by the First Amendment. The power of regulating interstate commerce is limited by the Constitution. One writer notes that there are four limitations upon this regulatory power in the original Constitution, relating to "importation of slaves and migrations of other persons into a state, imposition of taxes on imports and exports, and discrimination against one state in favor of another in ocean shipping.[16]

Much more to the point, however, are the limitations in amendments. Not only are religion and the press protected by amendment, but life, liberty, and property are as well. The Fifth Amendment prescribes that "no person . . . shall be deprived of life, liberty, or property, without due process of law. . . ." The courts assumed that this restriction did not apply to state governments, but the Fourteenth Amendment made such an extension explicit: "nor shall any State deprive any person of life, liberty, or property, without due process of law. . . ."

Life, liberty, and property are in a slightly different category from speech, the press, and religion. The Constitution contemplates occasions where the former may be taken away; whereas the latter are absolutely protected from Congressional intervention. But life, liberty, and prop-

---

[16] *Ibid.*, p. 141.

erty are only taken by due process of law. It should be clear that these provisions have the purpose of limiting government action. It should be clear, also, that the regulation of interstate commerce may affect property. (It may also affect liberty, and perhaps life, but let the consideration be restricted here to property.) The Constitution provides for two occasions for the taking of property: by taxation and (by implication) by the right of eminent domain. The taxing power is limited by the requirement that taxes be for the common defense and general welfare, and that some of them be uniform throughout the United States. The power of eminent domain may only be exercised when private property is taken for public use and just compensation is paid.

Any taking of property other than by taxation or eminent domain by the Federal government would be unauthorized. Any regulation which had the effect of taking property, or some portion of it, would have to follow established procedures, namely, those for levying and collecting taxes or those for condemning property. Otherwise, it would be unconstitutional because it did not observe due process of law.

My point is that the power to regulate commerce among the states has been used so as to take property. Take a simple case, the establishment of minimum wages. Whatever wages an employer paid, under this enactment, above what he otherwise would have paid would be property taken from him by the working of the law. It would be property taken not as taxes nor for which he had received compensation. Such confiscation would be unauthorized and in violation of the due process clauses of the Constitution. This would appear to apply as well to state action as to that of the Federal government.

A nice distinction occurs at this point. The regulation of

interstate commerce does not usually result in taking *all* of the property in question. It only takes some portion of it or some traditional (or natural) rights to its use. It limits the right to buy and sell, to transport goods, to hire and fire, to contract, and so forth. It is an eminently effective device for taking property bit by bit and piece by piece. The gradual thrust to socialism has no more appropriate Fabian method in its arsenal.

Changing "Due Process"

While Congress and Presidents have been employing these methods ever more effectively, the courts have been weaving a fabric of opinions which enable them to evade responsibility for negating such action. The courts never did much, though they did some, to protect property from states under the Fourteenth Amendment. Early and late, they reduced this protection by declaring that states had an inherent power, which they had never yielded up, to exercise the police power to protect the health, safety, and morals of their citizenry. No mention is made of this in the United States Constitution, and no exceptions for it are to be found in the Fourteenth Amendment.

As far as "due process" is concerned, the Supreme Court has, as regards property, reduced this to something that the courts can determine without reference to any objective standard. For example, Justice Roberts ruled for a majority of the Court in *Nebbia* vs. *New York* (1934) that "the guaranty of due process, as has often been held, demands only that the law shall not be unreasonable, arbitrary or capricious, and that the means selected shall have a real and substantial relation to the object sought to be attained. . . . The reports of our decisions abound with cases in which the citizens, individual or corporate, has vainly invoked the Fourteenth Amendment in resistance to

necessary and appropriate exertion of the police power. . . ."[17] There is in none of this language any reference
to anything objective to which the courts must bow in
making their decisions.

Other lines than these have been followed to override the
constitutional limitations on the use of governmental power. The general welfare clause has been interpreted as if
it were a grant of power.[18] Courts have ruled, in effect,
that there is a presumption in favor of the constitutionality
of an act of Congress, thus tacitly placing the burden of
proof on anyone who claims that it is not constitutional.
Courts have turned limitations upon governments into requirements that governments provide some service. Examples of this can be found in such rulings as that states
must provide counsel for those criminally charged and who
are unable to afford it, that "civil rights" demonstrators
must be permitted to use the highways of a state, and so
on. In effect, the courts create "rights" (more precisely,
privileges) by their decisions while they take away constitutional rights.

Advanced Decay

Whatever evidence and analysis should be summoned
to support the judgment, there should be no doubt that a
general flight from the Constitution has taken place. The
obstacles in the way of using government to make over
Americans have been, to a large extent, overcome, so far
as the Constitution is concerned. The Presidents have
taken over much, or most, of the initiative for legislation.
The courts have made decrees that have no basis other

---

[17] Commager, *op. cit,* II, 300.

[18] See, for example, Justice Cardozo's opinion in *Helvering et al.* vs. *Davis* (1937).

than their wills. Many of those in Congress think of the Supreme Court as the only limitation on their actions, and the Court, as has been shown, is ill disposed to limit. The formal limitations upon the political activities of factions have been mainly overcome.

The balance of powers within the government has been upset, as Presidents and courts have gained power. Much of the power of the Federal government now resides in the least representative branches. The courts are not popularly elected, and the members can be removed from office only by difficult impeachment proceedings. This was not to be feared so long as courts applied the standing law, but as they have begun to innovate, the matter has changed. They are usurping powers that belong to the people. The dispersion of powers among the Federal and state governments has been greatly altered as more and more power has been centralized in the Federal government. Departures from the basic and fundamental law of the land— the Constitution—signal lawlessness in high places. If the Supreme Court may interpret at will, what is to keep each man from doing so?

There is an answer to the last question. The answer is that he is kept from doing so by superior force. Force is being introduced into every area of life, but not by regular means. It is done increasingly pursuant to decrees and proclamations. In short, the power of government is being used to make over Americans, not by consent for that would hardly be given, but arbitrarily and capriciously. We are on a flight from the reality of our political foundations which evinces itself in a flight from the Constitution.

22

Political Experimentation:

THE FOUR-YEAR PLANS

I stand for the square deal. But when I say that I am for the square deal, I mean not merely that I stand for fair play under the present rules of the game, but that I stand for having those rules changed so as to work for a more substantial equality. . . .
THEODORE ROOSEVELT, 1910

And the day is at hand when it shall be realized on this consecrated soil,—a New Freedom,—a Liberty widened and deepened to match the broadened life of man in modern America. . . . —WOODROW WILSON, 1912

I pledge you, I pledge myself, to a new deal for the American people. —FRANKLIN D. ROOSEVELT, 1932

I hope for cooperation from farmers, from labor, and from business. Every segment of our population and every individual has a right to expect from our Government a fair deal.
—HARRY TRUMAN, 1949

. . . So that, although the United States is an old country— at least its Government is old as governments now go today— nevertheless I thought we were moving into a new period, and the new frontier phrase expressed that hope.
—JOHN F. KENNEDY, 1961

Building the Great Society will require a major effort on the part of every Federal agency in two directions:—First, formulating imaginative new ideas and programs; and—Second, carrying out hard-hitting, tough-minded reforms in existing programs. —LYNDON B. JOHNSON, 1964

THE FUNDAMENTAL SHIFTS, CHANGES, AND DIRECTION OF American government in the twentieth century have not been generally clearly outlined in historical accounts. The shift of the office of President from primary concern with execution of the laws to legislative innovation, the yielding up of legislative initiative by Congress, the subtle intellectual impetus to shift the American respect for the Constitution to adulation of the decisions (or at least acceptance of them) of the Supreme Court, the change of government from protector of rights to granter of privileges, have not been much emphasized by those charged with keeping the record straight. Superficial continuities have been allowed to obscure fundamental changes.

Of course, historians have noted the appearance of the Square Deal, New Nationalism, New Freedom, New Deal(s), Fair Deal, New Frontier, and Great Society. These names have often been used as convenient pegs from which to hang the assorted information and developments associated with presidential administrations. But the phenomenon itself—and what it may signify that a line of Presidents should get up a program, name it, attempt to embody it in legislation, and have it associated with them— has not been much attended to. There is in these things a new form of presidential activity, something that had not occurred in the nineteenth century. As a form, its appearance symbolizes the taking over of leadership in the Federal government by Presidents; but much more than this is involved.

Similarities with Five-Year Plans

No one, to my knowledge, has pointed to the analogy between the Square Deal, New Freedom, New Deal(s), Fair Deal, New Frontier, and Great Society on the one hand and the five-year plans of the Soviet Union on the other. Yet, there is an analogy that warrants examination, and the reference to the American programs as four- (or eight-) year plans is used to call attention to it. Such an examination will be useful in revealing the character of much that has been happening in America.

There are many differences of detail between the Soviet five-year plans and the American four- (or eight-) year plans. The five-year plans are not coterminous with some electoral period. They are not identified with the whole administration of some Soviet premier. The leaders of the Soviet Union are openly committed to the achievement of socialism, those of the United States are not. Moreover, the communists avow the revolutionary character of their way to socialism, and Americans have adopted no such way. The five-year plans are broad and comprehensive blueprints for social and economic reconstruction. Joseph Stalin said of the first five-year plan, begun in 1928:

> The fundamental task of the Five-Year Plan was, in converting the U.S.S.R. into an industrial country, fully to eliminate the capitalist elements, to widen the front of Socialist forms of economy, and to create the economic base for the abolition of classes in the U.S.S.R., for the construction of Socialist society. . . .
> The fundamental task of the Five-Year Plan was to transfer small and scattered agriculture to the lines of large-scale collective farming, so as to ensure the economic base for Socialism in the rural districts and thus to eliminate the possibility of the restoration of capitalism in the U.S.S.R.[1]

By comparison with such boldness, the American four-year plans appear timid and pale. Moreover, the American four-year plans began before the Russian ones, though the point is of no importance as to any fundamental similarities. There are many other differences, but let them all be

---

[1] Richard Powers, ed., *Readings in European Civilization since 1500* (Boston: Houghton Mifflin, 1961), pp. 632-33.

summed up by this observation: In detail, the Soviet plans differ in every respect from American ones.

But analogy deals with essences, not with differences of detail. There is an essential difference between the Soviet way to socialism and the American one. It has been alluded to above. The Russian Communists have pursued a direct revolutionary approach to socialism. American meliorists have pursued an indirect evolutionary approach to socialism. Communists have proceeded by destroying the old order as completely as they could and erecting a new one in its stead. Meliorists have attempted to operate within the framework of the old order, to keep as much of its superficies and forms as possible, and to turn the received instruments of power to the task of gradual social and economic reconstruction. The five-year plans are Soviet programs in the revolutionary road to socialism; the four-year plans are American programs in the gradualist route to socialism. They are both instruments of national planning by central authority; they employ a quite different assortment of paraphernalia; they differ as to methods; they have the same goal in view.

The four-year plans are really devices for using the Presidency for social reconstruction. The kind of planning which will move a country toward the goal of socialism must be centrally directed. Policy making, legislating, and execution must be coordinated. Congress can pass laws, but it cannot execute them. Moreover, left to their own devices the members of Congress are not apt to thrust the country in any consistent direction. Power is dispersed among the many members. They represent a great diversity of interests throughout the country. Legislation that originates in Congress is usually subjected to numerous compromises before it is enacted, compromises that turn it to ends not originally conceived or that vitiate its impact.

The very division of Congress into two houses makes it virtually impossible for any leadership that arises in one of the houses to have any influence or control over the other. The Presidency is the only office established by the Constitution that could provide such central direction. The four-year plans are means for giving Presidents apparent electoral authorization for taking over in legislative innovation.

Presidents did not concoct such programs in the nineteenth century. They usually were satisfied to restrict their endeavors to the more modest activities of administering the laws. Presidents did sometimes emerge as strong leaders, but this leadership was either exercised in war and foreign affairs, where the President has great constitutional authority, or in the form of a restraining hand upon Congress. Excepting for Lincoln, the man who stood out as the most vigorous leader in the nineteenth century was Andrew Jackson. He summed up his policy in this way: "The Federal Constitution must be obeyed, state rights preserved, our national debt must be paid, direct taxes and loans avoided, and the Federal Union preserved. These are the objects I have in view, and regardless of all consequences, will carry them into effect."[2] Presidents did, of course, sometimes press for some innovation and some particular line of legislation in the nineteenth century, but none of them advanced any four-year plans.

Theodore Roosevelt

The twentieth century was hardly under way, however, before a man came to power who would give shape and

---

[2] Quoted in Samuel E. Morison and Henry S. Commager, *The Growth of the American Republic,* I (New York: Oxford University Press, 1942, 3rd ed.), 472.

form to the new method. The four-year plan does not appear to have come by way of any advance calculation. Theodore Roosevelt forged its outlines during nearly eight years in the Presidency. But Roosevelt did not come to the Presidency, initially, on his own. Lore has it that "Boss" Tom Platt got him nominated to the Vice-Presidency in 1900 to get him out of New York.[3] President McKinley was assassinated in 1901, however, and Roosevelt succeeded to the Presidency. The phrase, "square deal," was used by Roosevelt in the campaign of 1904 to describe his actions in the coal strike of 1902. He wanted both labor and capital to get a square deal, he said.[4] The phrase caught on and has since been used by historians as a vague label for Roosevelt's administration.

The phrase, "square deal," did not fall into a historical vacuum, nor was it uttered by a nonentity. The stage had been set by the development of ideas for the phrase to connote and evoke a particular vision. If the view had been accepted that Americans were generally getting a square deal, the phrase could hardly have meant anything more than that in a particular instance the President had sought to see that justice was done. Once it was done in this case, there would have been no occasion for the phrase to have any continued vitality. But it was uttered at a time when a great clamor was arising against conditions as they were, and the cry was for changes that would bring about social justice.

The Progressive Movement was underway. Back of it lay more than a quarter-century of writing and agitation by social theorists, reformers, utopians, and social reconstructers. These ideas and visions were moving from the pe-

---

[3] George E. Mowry, *The Era of Theodore Roosevelt—1900-1912* (New York: Harper, 1958), pp. 108-09.

[4] *Ibid.*, p. 139.

riphery of American society, where they had been uttered
by men and women outside the pale of respectability,
toward the center where they would be taken up by more
respectable and restrained spokesmen.

Muckrakers, novelists, social analysts, professed socialists, and others were presenting a most unpleasant picture
of America. Things were not as they should be, they said.
Great concentrations of wealth threatened the Republic
with rule by a plutocracy. The influence of John D. Rocke-
feller, Marcus A. Hanna, and J. P. Morgan, among others,
resulted in the use of political power to strange ends. At
any rate, economic "power" was outmatching and overaw-
ing political power, so the story went. A beef trust gouged
consumers with high prices and fed them unclean meat.
City governments were corrupt, the cities themselves
gorged with immigrants from a swelling tide living in
slums, and alcohol addiction and prostitution growing
apace.

Behind all this criticism of externals lay a call for fundamental social reconstruction. Social gospelers were preach-
ing the coming of the Kingdom, progressive educationists
working for the transformation of the school, and assorted intellectuals delineating the transmuted shape of
things to come. Talk of a square deal in this intellectual
setting evoked visions of a crusade to remake America;
the seeds of reform contained in a simple phrase fell upon
fertile ground.

The phrase picked up meaning and gained currency,
too, from the vitality and zeal of the man who uttered it.
Theodore Roosevelt was a man of action. Before coming
to the Presidency, he had engaged in a great variety of
activities. By turn, he was state legislator, member of the
Civil Service Commission, head of a police board, Assist-
ant Secretary of the Navy, governor of New York, rancher,

historian, biographer, Roughrider, and huntsman. As President, he was soon in the thick of all manner of affairs, domestic and foreign: arbitrating a labor dispute, trust busting, settling international disputes, intervening in Caribbean countries, and conserving natural resources. Roosevelt's conception of the role of the Presidency was a lofty and extensive one. "He believed that, acting in the public interest, he could do whatever was not expressly prohibited by the Constitution or the laws."[5] His views of the duties of the office were comprehensive:

> The President did not confine himself to political matters. He saw nothing incongruous in using his great prestige to urge the reform of English spelling, or to pillory the "nature fakers" who wrote stories humanizing animals. He delivered exhortations on the necessity for women in the upper classes to bear more children and for everyone to live strenuously according to his creed of "Muscular Christianity."[6]

Along with being a man of action he was also a superb publicist. He had that quality known as charisma, an attractiveness and charm which helped him to surround his actions with an aura of rightness—even righteousness, for he was a moralist. The place of his administration in history needed a unique phrase to identify it. That it was the Square Deal may have been an accident, but the times and the man united in such a way as to make it virtually necessary.

Theodore Roosevelt was a reformer, a meliorist. He was the first man to occupy the Presidency who could be so identified. Some historians question how deeply he was

---

[5] Dumas Malone and Basil Rauch, *Empire for Liberty*, II (New York: Appleton-Century-Crofts, 1960), 217.

[6] *Ibid.*, p. 218.

committed to reform, or, at any rate, to social transformation. Perhaps he was only an opportunist, they say, and
in this they are echoing the sentiments of some of his contemporaries. He has even been called a conservative.[7] This
latter claim stems, in part, from the fact that he steered
a course between calling for reform and making compli-
mentary remarks about businessmen.[8] Whatever the motives may have been behind his straddling of the fence on
occasion, they served the practical political object of making reform respectable by dissociating it from out-and-out
radicalism.

At any rate, Theodore Roosevelt was a reformer. Of that,
there should be no doubt. He had been a reformer, of sorts,
as governor of New York. He had no sooner succeeded to
the Presidency before this vein began to be exposed at
that level. Roosevelt pressed to extend the powers of the
Interstate Commerce Commission, had his Attorney General begin a rigorous enforcement of the Sherman Antitrust
Act, and in general began to adopt a reformist tone. After
his election to the Presidency in 1904, when he could hold
the office in his own right, he became more strident in his
reformism. As one historian says:

> His message to Congress in December, 1904, was sig-
> nificantly without most of the equivocations of the past.
> Over half the document was given over to proposals for
> new economic and social legislation.[9]

---

[7] See, for example, Daniel Aaron, *Men of Good Hope* (New
York: Oxford University Press, 1951), pp. 246-52.

[8] There is also a tendency among "liberal" historians to
classify meliorist politicians generally as conservatives, presumably because they do not press for violent revolution. Also,
these historians have created, or perpetuated, a myth that if
reforms had not been made, a revolution would have occurred.

[9] Mowry, *op. cit.*, p. 197.

He called for the Federal government to pass an employer's liability act for its employees and those of contractors employed by the government. There were requests for such things as requiring the use of safety devices on railroads, regulation of hours of labor of railroad workers, giving the Interstate Commerce Commission power to establish rail rates, establishing a Bureau of Corporations to license interstate business, the instituting of numerous reforms in the District of Columbia, and so forth. Some of these were made into law, and other reforms were instigated during his second administration.

By 1908, most of the ingredients of the four-year plan had been exemplified by Roosevelt. It remained now only for them to be used by others and made into a regular way of doing things. In 1912, the four-year plan as a campaign device was taken up by two candidates: Theodore Roosevelt and Woodrow Wilson. They called their plans the New Nationalism and the New Freedom. Significantly, these were alternative plans to the revolutionary proposals of the Socialist party, led by Eugene Debs. The Socialists had been gaining a following rapidly in recent elections. The four-year plan began its career of draining away the appeal from those who called themselves socialists.

Main Features of the Plans

Before recounting the story of the four-year plans, however, it will be useful to describe their main features. First of all, it is worth noting that they were taken up by the Democrats and have, since the time of Theodore Roosevelt, been exclusively employed by that party. There was a considerable contingent of reformers in the Republican party between the Civil War and World War I. In the early twentieth century, there was a lively meliorist wing of the party, called the Progressives. But Theodore Roosevelt drew many of these away in 1912 when he ran on the Bull Moose ticket. Since that time, meliorists have never dominated the Republican party, if they ever did. By contrast, the Democratic party had stuck fairly close to its Jefferson-Jackson heritage in the nineteenth century. It began its turn toward meliorism with the campaign of William Jennings Bryan in 1896. Woodrow Wilson and Franklin D. Roosevelt fixed it on this path in the twentieth century. Much of the impulse for the gradualist movement toward socialism has come from the Democratic party, and the particular infusions of energy toward this end have come from a succession of four-year plans.

Several features of the four-year plan can be described by showing its relation to the political party. A political party may be the lengthened shadow of a man, of Thomas Jefferson or of Abraham Lincoln, for instance. At its inception, a political party may even be the political instrument of an individual, as the Jeffersonian Republican party was for its founder. But political parties quickly have become institutions themselves in our history. They are organizations, having continuing existence (beyond the life or time of those who founded them), are devices for winning elections at various levels, have a widespread membership which participates in the choice of candidates, and are labels with which a succession of politicians can identify and be identified. In an important sense, political parties are impersonal and nonideological. A great variety of individuals find political shelter within their folds. Issues come and go, but parties continue as they shift from this position to that.

By contrast, a four-year plan is not the *lengthened* shadow of a man; it is the *shadow* cast by a particular man who has come to the Presidency. It is the personal instrument of a President. Political parties may be said to be democratic, or at least federal, in character. Their widespread membership plays a part in determining their stand on issues. Platforms are drawn by committees. A Senator or Representative may, so far as his district goes, have as much to say about what the party stands for as does the President.

With four-year plans, it is not so. They are centristic and autocratic. They are devices which can be and have been used to bridge the gap, politically, of the separation of powers. Through a four-year plan, a President can identify the whole governmental program with himself. He can make the other branches of the government more or less adjuncts to his administration. To the extent that a President can bring off the *coup* that is implicit in the four-year plan, he can centralize power and use the whole government as if it were an extension of himself. That concentrated power which is necessary to governmentally directed social transformation is made available by the four-year plan.

Four-year plans appear, also, to have subsumed much of the role which third parties played in the meliorist movement at its outset. No new major political party has emerged in America since 1860. It would have been logical for a socialist party, by whatever name, to have come to majority status in the United States in the twentieth century, in view of the course of developments, as the Labour party did in England. The original impetus to socialism came from third parties in America in the late nineteenth and early twentieth centuries, from the Greenback-Labor party, Populist party, and Bull Moose (or Progressive) party. But since the 1920's, third parties have either been ephemeral or have had little appeal.

Two things happened. Such socialism as appealed to any considerable portion of the electorate was advanced by one or both of the major parties. And the impulse for a new surge toward socialization was embodied in the four-year plans. Third parties with a penchant for socialism had their issues taken away from them as soon as the issues attained popularity, and were much more attractively packaged by the regular organizations and presidential candidates for them.

Appeals to Americanism

The names given to the four-year plans are interesting and revealing in themselves. Rhetorically, they evoke American values and even American experience. Three of them—Square Deal, New Deal, and Fair Deal—call up an image of sporting behavior and appear to derive from card-playing terminology. Perhaps the references to games of chance are unintended—though the pragmatic stance is that all human action is a kind of chance taking, and the proponents of these programs are often called pragmatists. But the appeals to fair play are surely intentional. Americans are much addicted to sports and, in that connection, are committed to the virtue of fair play. (It was the Beards, Charles and Mary, I think, who observed that the one thing Americans would not tolerate in the twentieth century was crooked officials in their athletic contests.)

The New Freedom called up one of the basic values for Americans, for they have understood that one of the distinctive features of the American system has been the extent of freedom it provided. The New Frontier evoked memories of an earlier American experience. The only phrase that appears not to have any American context is the Great Society. Perhaps the utopian vision is now sufficiently a part of the mental baggage of Americans that it is politically feasible to appeal to it directly.

At any rate, those terms which do rely on American

values for their appeal place them in a new framework. The call was for a *new* freedom, a *new* deal, and a *new* frontier, for a *square* deal, and a *fair* deal. The phrases take established values and use them as the basis for the building of a new order. The battle cries of socialist rhetoric—class struggle, vanguard of the elite, the rise of the masses, the dictatorship of the proletariat—are foreign and repulsive to the American ear. By contrast, the rhetoric of the four-year plans is familiar, nonradical in sound, and brings to mind pleasing associations. The territory into which Fabian methods take us is strange, but the markers along the way are familiar.

Finally, the four-year plans are means for translating meliorist ideology into political action. They are devices for linking ideas (or visions) to power. The connection is made by a single man, the President of the United States. His personal historian has said of John F. Kennedy that "he was intensely committed to a vision of America and the world, and committed with equal intensity to the use of reason and power to achieve that vision." He desired "to bring the world of power and the world of ideas together in alliance. . . ."[10] If so, his outlook and aims were perfectly suited to the role of being President by the requirements of the four-year plan.

The Role of the Intellectuals

Another way of saying the above is that the four-year plans have been the creations of intellectuals under the sway of ideologies. This accounts for the increasing role played by intellectuals in twentieth century governmental undertakings. A President may be both an intellectual and

---

[10] Arthur M. Schlesinger, Jr., *A Thousand Days* (Boston: Houghton Mifflin, 1965), pp. 108-09.

a man of action. Theodore Roosevelt was, and just as he may be credited with founding the four-year plan so may he be described as the prototype for the kind of man it ideally requires. Theodore Roosevelt was probably more the man of action than the intellectual, though he had ideas enough, while Woodrow Wilson was more the intellectual than the man of action. Both of them, however, combined both traits in sufficient degree to translate ideology into action with only a minimum of help from specialists so far as the formulation of programs was concerned. Their successors in the line of four-year planning were not so adequately equipped. The tendency from Franklin D. Roosevelt on has been for Presidents to gather about them a corps of intellectuals—a brain trust—to provide the ideas and render them into programs.[11]

There were premonitions of things to come, however, in the planning of the first Roosevelt and Wilson. One writer holds that Brooks Adams was the formulator of the basic ideas which Roosevelt advanced. "Had Roosevelt followed his counsels," he says, "(as he sometimes did, for Roosevelt instinctively agreed with Adams on some issues even though he prudently rejected Adam's [sic] suggestions when the times called for compromise), he might have become an even greater and perhaps more sinister figure."[12] There has been considerable debate among historians as to the extent of the influence of Herbert Croly's *Promise of*

---

[11] The prototype for the "brain trust" may have been provided by Andrew Jackson who had an assortment of budding intellectuals in his "Kitchen Cabinet." There was an important difference, however, for his advisers were liberals of the nineteenth century variety who did not go in much for government intervention.

[12] Aaron, *op. cit.*, p. 252.

American Life upon Roosevelt's New Nationalism idea.[13] Be that as it may, Roosevelt was undoubtedly influenced by the intellectual currents of his day. His programs were his, however, not those of some coterie of intellectuals.

Wilson was, if anything, more the intellectual than Roosevelt. Despite, or perhaps because of, this, he appears to have relied more extensively upon intellectuals than did Roosevelt. The man closest to Wilson was Colonel Edward M. House. He was most influential upon Wilson. One writer says, "Nearly all accounts agree that Colonel House dominated the decisions on appointments. Wilson frankly didn't want to be bothered."[14] Colonel House's credentials as an intellectual may not be particularly impressive, but they are sufficient to show that he was under the sway of a vision that was the fruit of ideas.

Before he rose to the eminence of presidential adviser, he wrote and caused to be published a utopian novel, *Philip Dru, Administrator*. It is about a man who establishes a dictatorship in America and brings about sweeping reforms. Among these reforms were a graduated income tax, compulsory incorporation act, flexible currency system, an old age pension and labor insurance, a cooperative marketing system, Federal employment bureau, and so forth.

As one account of this utopian novel observes: "This fantasy could be laughed off as the curious dream of Colonel House were it not that so many of these reforms strikingly resemble what the Wilson, and later the New

---

[13] For contrasting assessments, see Eric F. Goldman, *Rendezvous with Destiny* (New York: Vintage Books, 1956), p. 159, and Charles Forcey, *The Crossroads of Liberalism* (New York: Oxford University Press, 1961), pp. 127-30.

[14] Horace Coon, *Triumph of the Eggheads* (New York: Random House, 1955), p. 87.

Deal, administrations either accomplished or proposed."[15] The ideas are not original, but this advocate of them had the ear of a President. Louis D. Brandeis was another intellectual who had a great deal of influence on Wilson.[16] There were others, such as George L. Record, George Creel, and Bernard Baruch.

But the practice of assembling a host of intellectuals around the President to provide the ideas and programs to translate four-year plans into action was really established by Franklin D. Roosevelt. Harry Hopkins played Colonel House to Roosevelt, and Felix Frankfurter was his Brandeis. But below these in the hierarchy of influence came a horde of others: Averell Harriman, Francis Biddle, George Peek, Henry Wallace, Samuel Rosenman, Harry Dexter White, Robert E. Sherwood, and so on. Of those who came, a historian has said that "the common bond which held them together . . . was that they were at home in the world of ideas. They were accustomed to analysis and dialectic. . . . They were . . . generalists, capable of bringing logic to bear on any social problem."[17] In short, they were intellectuals with visions of a transformed America and ideas about how to bring it about.

Each administration since has had its complement of intellectuals serving as ghost writers, special assistants, economic advisers, board members, and members of the middling rank of division heads within established departments. The assembling of intellectuals in Washington

---

[15] *Ibid.*, p. 86.

[16] See *ibid.*, pp. 14-15, 90; Charles A. Madison, *Leaders and Liberals in the Twentieth Century* (New York: Frederick Ungar, 1961), pp. 200-01.

[17] Arthur M. Schlesinger, Jr., *The Coming of the New Deal* (Boston: Houghton Mifflin, 1958), p. 18.

reached a new peak during the Kennedy Administration, when the President bade fair to take a goodly portion of the prestigious men from some major universities. Among the more famous gathered were Theodore Sorensen, McGeorge Bundy, Arthur Schlesinger, Jr., Walt W. Rostow, David Bell, and Walter Heller.[18] Truman, Eisenhower, and Johnson were less at home with university men, but they, too, had their intellectuals.

These intellectuals are the American equivalent, in socialist terminology, of the "vanguard of the elite." They have moved into the centers of power by providing the ideas and programs of meliorism. They bring ideology into the political market place, help to make it attractive, and thrust political action in the direction implicit in their assumptions. The fateful connection between utopian visions, the new reality, the new creativity, and meliorist economics on the one hand and political action on the other is made by the intellectuals in the four-year plans.

---

[18] Lester Tanzer, ed., *The Kennedy Circle* (Washington: Luce, 1961), *passim.*

23

The Pen *and* the Sword

It has been said that the pen is mightier than the sword. The phrase is poetic; it calls attention to a paradox. Taken literally, the statement is not true, of course. A swordsman pitted against a penman might be expected to make quick work of him. Obviously, the phrase is not meant to evoke the vision of any such contest when it is employed. It is meant, instead, to call attention to the sway of ideas in the affairs of the world, a sway more complete and determinative even than that of the sword.

However this may be, there should be no doubt that the pen and the sword together are invincible. That is the situation which confronts us today. The flight from reality has culminated in the linking of the pen and the sword. The Commander-in-Chief of the armed forces of the United States with his brain trust signalizes the union.

The direction in which we are impelled by the combined force of pen and sword should not be in doubt. Earl Browder, former head of the Communist party of the United States—but unrepentant socialist—has lately described the tendency felicitously:

> America is getting socialism on the installment plan through the programs of the welfare state. There is more real socialism in the United States today than there is in the Soviet Union.
>
> Americans may not be willing to vote for a program under the name of "socialism," but put it under another

468

party label—whether liberal Republican or Democrat—
and they're by and large in favor of the idea. . . .

We have no real socialist party, no socialist ideology,
but we have a large—and growing—degree of what 50
years ago would have been recognized as socialism.[1]

Some of Browder's points may be debatable, such as that
there is more socialism in America than in the Soviet
Union, or that we have no socialist ideology; but his main
contention—that the United States has been moving gradually toward socialism—should be beyond dispute. The evidence for this is mountainous. It can be seen in the spreading government intervention in the economy, in the increasing control of the economy, in the numerous welfare
programs, and in the amazing array of governmental activities and programs. The question for the historian should
be not whether we have been moving toward what was
once billed as socialism but rather how has this development come about. In the absence of a victorious Socialist
party, without political leaders who profess the socialist
ideology, in a situation in which most of the populace has
never consciously accepted socialism, how has America
proceeded to the point that an old communist can proclaim we are achieving socialism?

To Meet Changed Circumstances

Though few American historians would be as blunt as
Earl Browder, there is a conventional explanation of the
phenomena to which he refers. Indeed, in the interview
cited above. Browder alluded to and used the conventional
explanation. He said, "We got it . . . merely in the piling
up if [sic] single decisions under the pressures of need and
crisis."[2] In greater detail, the explanation would go some-

---

[1] Quoted in Pittsburgh *Press* (June 19, 1966), sec. I, p. 11.
[2] *Ibid.*

thing like this: In consequence of industrialization, the mechanization of agriculture, urbanization, and the transportation revolution came depressions, concentrations of wealth, the dependency of the worker, declining opportunity, "monopolies," and spreading poverty. Government had to intervene to bring justice to the people in view of these changing circumstances. Politicians, operating pragmatically, have tried first this, then that, to come up with programs which would work. They have been moved not by ideology but by the pressure of circumstances.

The generality of men do not question familiar explanations; they do not even analyze them. In order for an explanation to become familiar it need only have been repeated enough times. This has occurred regarding the justification of reform on the grounds of changing circumstances. It has been drummed into our ears for decades now. It sounds right to us. The rhetoric by which it is expressed has etched grooves in our minds which allow each additional statement of it to be taken in without causing pain. The point approaches where it is hardly more apt to be challenged than was the view that the earth was flat seven hundred years ago. Yet, it is an explanation that does not explain when put to the test.

Some of the reformist surges have come at times of general prosperity. The Progressive movement, in the early twentieth century, came at a time of the greatest prosperity America had known. The Kennedy and Johnson programs were introduced at times billed as ones of unprecedented prosperity. The rationale changes with the times, not the programs or direction. If it is a period of depression, the programs are described as remedies for depression. If it is a period of prosperity, they may be justified on the grounds that poverty is inexcusable in a land of plenty.

Nor does the pragmatic claim stand up under analysis. If the reformers were pragmatists, they should be concerned with whether their programs work or not. On the contrary, they cling to them, once established, and press for the enactment of others of like nature. If workability were the test, the farm programs should have been scrapped long ago. They were supposed to rescue the small farmer and benefit agriculture generally. On the contrary, the number of farmers has decreased from 1930 to the present, and the brunt of this has been borne by small farmers. Large farmers generally have become more wealthy; and we have all paid for this continuing experiment with higher prices for certain products and with higher taxes as well.

Various programs, such as housing projects, were supposed to reduce delinquency, yet crime mounts in America. Americans were supposed to be helped by government programs to become independent, but dependency on government increases apace. Antitrust legislation was supposed to prevent the fixing of prices, yet prices in numerous instances are set by government decree and union monopolies. Far from working as intended, the programs often have produced results the opposite of those desired. If their proponents were pragmatists, they long since should have abandoned many of the programs which they still cherish.

Though a much more thorough analysis of the explanation by circumstances and comparison of it with the evidence would be valuable, it is not necessary. An explanation is satisfactory to the extent that it accounts for all of the relevant phenomena. This one does not, and it must be discarded as inadequate. Not only are there too many loose ends, but it does not even come to grips with the process of historical change.

The Conspiracy Theory

Another explanation has gained some following, though not generally in academic circles. It is that the trend to socialism is a product of a conspiracy, or of conspiracies. Such an explanation is particularly appealing because, if true, it would account for the fact that we have moved toward socialism without those responsible for it ever announcing it as the goal. The plausibility of this explanation is increased by the existence of a communist conspiracy, by a magnetic field surrounding it into which sympathizers are drawn, and by the affinity which many reformers have had for communists. Its attraction is probably greatly enhanced by the obvious solution it offers: expose the conspiracy or conspiracies, imprison the malefactors, throw the scoundrels out, and get on with the business at hand.

The exposé occupies a position today in the Conservative movement similar to the place it had for Progressives at the beginning of the century. Books gain considerable currency that deal with Red spies at the United Nations, that rehash the story of the fall of Nationalist China, that tell again the story of Pearl Harbor, and so on. Much of their appeal is but testimony to the frailty of human nature, to the preference of men for reading something that will make their blood boil rather than help to make their minds work. Even so, if the present Conservative movement should emerge victorious politically, some part of its rise probably could be attributed to the exposés. Moreover, some of these have made valuable contributions to our understanding of what has happened.

Nonetheless, the exposés are largely offshoots of the conspiracy theory, so far as they offer any general explanation of what has happened. They deal with events which are only the flotsam and jetsam of the major developments of our time. They are of the surface of the waters on which we ride, not of the undertow which pulls us in the particular direction. The conspiracy theory may account for a particular *coup d' état,* for this or that hidden manipulation, for some particular bit of espionage, for the introduction of some unfortunate phrase in a document, and so on. But it does not tell us what made the conspirators become what they are. Moreover, it does not account for the millions, perhaps billions, of people in the world who are drawn to support what is being done, or what they think is being done.

Victims of Illusion

We are the victims, not of conspiracy, but of illusion. Even the conspiracies are largely sustained by the illusion. The illusion is that men are, or can be, gods, that they can by taking thought reconstruct human nature, that they can create a world of their own devising, that decision-making can be separated from power, that tension and stress can be removed from the world, that reward can be separated from effort, that all-embracing governments can bring peace, that people can be treated as things and retain their dignity, that men will cease to pursue their own interests when the social system is changed, that evil is the product of circumstances and not of men, that consequences are determined by motives rather than by the nature of the acts, that the nature of acts is altered by the number of people who participate in them, that the nature of man is plastic, and that the universe is malleable.

The heart of the illusion is in the view that the meaning of life is to be found in participation in the political process through which utopia is to be achieved by continuing social reconstruction. According to this view, men find their fulfillment in voting, in collective activity, in group projects, in civic undertakings, and in extending these methods as widely and universally as possible. This ethos goes by the name of democracy. It provides the rationale for the progressive politicalizing of life, for the interpenetration of all human activity with force.

The transcendent rituals of this pseudo-religion are group discussion and voting. Its end is a heaven-on-earth utopia which is to be achieved by social transformation. Its chief virtue is action, social action, action to produce the desired changes according to the modes of the rituals. Anything that is not politicalized is an affront to the adherents of this ethos. They talk continually of peace, but they foment strife because they continually intrude in the affairs of other men. They arouse the vague and restless discontents which are a part of the human condition and attempt to harness these for the purposes of social reconstruction.

The burden of this work has been to show that men have succumbed to illusion by a flight from reality. This flight from reality has had a long and checkered career. It began at a level remote from the lives of most people, on the philosophical plane. Philosophers began to break the connection between cause and effect, between the evidence of the senses and logic, between the metaphysical and the physical realms, between ideas and reality. After Immanuel Kant, if there was a duality to reality—if there was body and soul, heaven and earth, physical and metaphysical, temporal and eternal, and so forth—the two realms were so disjoined from one another as to make them distinct and unrelated orders of being. The pure reason cannot arrive at validatable propositions; the practical reason can establish facts, but these fall far short of the truth for which man yearns.

Kant had, in effect, demolished the connections which

enabled philosophers to provide a unified account of all the levels of reality. Philosophy gave way to ideology, and "isms" multiplied as thinkers attempted to account for all of reality by some piece from the wreckage of philosophy. Perhaps no better description can be given of ideology than that it is an attempt to account for the whole of reality by some abstraction of a fragment of it.

Social Idealism

Many ideologies emerged in the nineteenth century, but two of them were basic to the particular direction of the flight from reality: idealism and materialism. Dualism did not disappear; it tended to survive in the more or less independent development of idealism and materialism. Idea and matter remained, and thinkers labored to bring them together into some kind of synthesis. The work of G. W. F. Hegel was central to the development of thought. He held that idea became actuality in the historical process. All of reality was reduced to the historical plane where its being consists of its becoming. The purpose of life becomes the rendering of the ideal into the actual. Here is the tap root of the meliorist and revolutionary roads to socialism.

There was no longer any fixed and enduring reality for most thinkers, only an historical process of change. Some followed Hegel in holding that ideas can be used to shape actuality from matter (though Hegel did not think much of matter); others followed Marx in holding that there is a dialectic of matter and that ideas are really a product of this. To the materialists, all things are determined by the fluctuations of matter; to the idealists, all things are a product of ideas. Both of these notions went into the stream of thought picked up by American meliorists, have been strangely combined and eclectically used.

At any rate, idealism provided the mental framework

for the construction of utopias, while materialism gave substance. For many, the utopian vision served as the idea which they would make an actuality. The utopian idea was not new to the nineteenth century; it had been around for some time. But men had treated such ideas largely as playthings of the imagination, ridiculous because unattainable, undesirable even if attainable because they do not take into account the character of life on this earth.

The atmosphere began to change in the nineteenth century. Not only were more utopian novels written but also they began to get a wider acceptance. For some at least, utopia began to seem both possible and desirable. Many had lost their certainty of a metaphysical and enduring order which would make them impossible. The declining vitality of belief in life after death opened up the possibility that Heaven would have to be on this earth.

Even so, most men have not consciously accepted the notion that utopia actually could be achieved. Any man of common sense can find numerous flaws in any particular version of utopia. Probably, most men will never accept the notion that utopia actually can be attained. They can, however, be convinced that conditions can be improved. This has been the method of the meliorists in America. Behind the thrust of meliorist effort lies the utopian vision, which is itself the impelling dream of socialism, but the programs which are supposed to lead to it are billed neither as socialism nor utopianism in America. They are only called improvements. Not all of them would produce utopia, but each of them might result in some improvement, so men have been led to believe.

There is a fragment of truth in the conception of translating ideas into actuality, a most interesting and important fragment of truth. Men do translate ideas into actualities, not perfectly but sufficiently well for us to recognize that it happens. A boy has a dream, a vision, an idea of what he will become when he is a man. If he plans well, if his idea is viable, if he works hard at it, the man he will become will bear some relationship to his dream.

Ideals, too, have played an invaluable role in the lives of men. The world would be immeasurably poorer, indeed an intolerable place, if individuals did not seek truth, strive to act justly, and yearn for the good. The Revelation by Jesus Christ of what is good in the sight of God contains the highest ideals for Christians. Each man who labors to order his actions to accord with ideals is, in a sense, translating idea into actuality.

In many ways, both mundane and sublime, men labor to translate ideas into actuality. The farmer who raises a crop translates his ideas about the employment of his land, labor, and capital into the actuality of produce. The man who builds a factory starts with a conception of it, even a dream, just as does the builder of a house. An artist who paints a picture begins with an idea; so does a novelist, a composer, an architect, and a cook. The inventor begins with a conception of a device that does not exist but which he believes can be produced by combining certain materials and principles. If his idea is valid, and if he knows how to apply it, an invention can result. Indeed, translating ideas into actuality plays a most important part in our lives. That this can be done is such an important fragment of truth that men might be expected to want to apply it universally.

Let us return to the process of invention. Inventors have supplied us with an amazing array of conveniences and technology in the last hundred years. In no other area of human activity has the process of translating ideas into actuality been so dramatically demonstrated. We have come to associate this process of technological develop-

ment with progress, and the word "progress" has for us
the attraction derived from the association. Meliorists were
able to capitalize on this association and claim that they
were using the method in a new area. Both Lester Frank
Ward and John Dewey talked of "social invention." The
pseudo philosophy of pragmatism, with its emphasis upon
experimentation, is largely built upon an abstraction from
the process of invention. Reformists were going to produce
the marvels in society that mechanical invention had done
for technology. Their innovations would constitute progress
in the social realm just as invention does in the realm of
technology. Hence, those who were opposed to the political
innovation and intervention which resulted would be described as antiprogressive and reactionary.

There is a major difference, however, between mechanical invention and "social invention." The mechanic works
with *things*. He shapes them in such ways that they do
his bidding. He becomes master of them. By contrast, the
"social inventor" deals with *people*. They have hopes, plans,
and wills of their own. Otherwise, the analogy with mechanical invention holds. The "social inventor" attempts to
shape people so that they will do his bidding (though this
is supposed to be for their own good). He becomes their
master to the extent that he gains political power over
them. That is, to the extent that the "social inventor" (or
social planner as he has come more commonly to be
called) succeeds in his efforts, men lose control of their
own affairs. The association with what men have thought
of as progress is a bogus one, though it does become progressively tyrannical.

Translating Idea into Actuality

The flight from reality has had many facets. Some of
them have been described in earlier chapters. My point,

however, is that the flight from reality took place in the realm of ideas and was a product of what are called intellectuals. Many ideologies have provided grist for the mills of American reformers or meliorists, but the central idea is the translation of a vision, a vision of utopia, into actuality by the use of political power. It is a perversion of idealism, an extension of it into unwarranted areas.

For an individual to have an ideal which he wishes to translate into the actuality of himself is healthy on the whole. But for a man to have an ideal for what others should become is likely to make him a nuisance at the best and a tyrant at the worst. When he uses force to make others over, he certainly becomes a tyrant.

The idea of transformed men and society was projected as utopia. It was taken up by American thinkers, read into an evolutionary framework, and methods were devised for a gradual movement toward its fulfillment. The ideologies were subsumed into mythologies which bent those who accepted them toward programs of amelioration and reform. These reformist ideas were intermingled with religion by the social gospelers and injected into educational theory and practice by progressive educationists. They were propagated in the media of communication. Earl Browder would have been correct if he had said that most Americans have no conscious socialist ideology; they have, instead, a mythology which carries in it an implicit socialist ideology.

The method of translating these ideas into actuality is epitomized and concentrated in the presidential four-year plans—the Square Deal, New Freedom, New Deal, Fair Deal, New Frontier, and Great Society. The pen has been linked with the sword in these plans. As was shown above, intellectuals provided the ideas. It will be enough now to indicate briefly that Presidents put them into effect.

Most of these Presidents have not frankly avowed their

aim to reconstruct society. However, occasionally it has come out, as in the following declaration by Woodrow Wilson:

> We stand in the presence of a revolution—not a bloody revolution; America is not given to the spilling of blood—but a silent revolution. . . .
> We are upon the eve of a great reconstruction. It calls for creative statesmanship as no age has done since that great age in which we set up the government under which we live, that government which was the admiration of the world until it suffered wrongs to grow up under it which have made many of our compatriots question the freedom of our institutions and preach revolution against them. I do not fear revolution. . . . Revolution will come in peaceful guise. . . . Some radical changes we must make in our law and practice. Some reconstructions we must push forward, for which a new age and new circumstances impose upon us. But we can do it all in calm and sober fashion, like statesmen and patriots.[3]

In milder language, Franklin D. Roosevelt made a similar proclamation:

> At the same time we have recognized the necessity of reform and reconstruction—reform because much of our trouble today and in the past few years has been due to a lack of understanding of the elementary principles of justice and fairness by those in whom leadership in business and finance was placed—reconstruction because new conditions in our economic life as well as old but neglected conditions had to be corrected.[4]

As a general rule, however, Presidents with four-year

---

[3] Woodrow Wilson, *The New Freedom,* William E. Leuchtenberg, intro. (Englewood Cliffs, N. J.: Prentice-Hall, 1961), p. 32.

[4] Franklin D. Roosevelt, *Nothing to Fear,* Ben D. Zevin, ed. (New York: Popular Library, 1961), p. 50.

plans have not emphasized the revolutionary character of what they were proposing. On the contrary, they have made as little of the innovation as possible and have tried to maintain that what they were doing was somehow profoundly in keeping with true American tradition and purpose. For example, when Theodore Roosevelt called for out-and-out regulation and supervision of American corporations in 1905, he described the program as in keeping with the American past. He said, in part:

> This is only in form an innovation. In substance it is merely a restoration; for from the earliest time such regulation of industrial activities has been recognized in the action of the law-making bodies; and all that I propose is to meet the changed conditions in such a manner as will prevent the commonwealth abdicating the power it has always possessed not only in this country but also in England before and since this country became a separate nation.[5]

The second Roosevelt was even more masterful in describing his alterations as if they were entirely constructive in character. On one occasion, he likened them to the way an architect can renovate a building, joining the new to the old so felicitously that the whole will retain its integrity. The following references were to a renovation of the White House that was going on:

> If I were to listen to the arguments of some prophets of calamity who are talking these days, I should hesitate to make these alterations. I should fear that while I am away for a few weeks the architects might build some strange new Gothic tower or a factory building or perhaps a replica of the Kremlin or of the Postdam Palace. But I have no such fears. The architects and builders are men of common sense and of artistic American

---

[5] Marvin E. Meyers, *et al.*, eds., *Sources of the American Republic*, II (Chicago: Scott, Foresman, 1961), 105.

tastes. They know that the principles of harmony and of necessity itself require that the building of the new structure shall blend with the essential lines of the old. It is this combination of the old and the new that marks orderly peaceful progress, not only in building buildings but in building government itself.[6]

The above is, of course, the rhetoric of gradualism. It is the beguiling language which has concealed the thrust of the sword into virtually every area of American life. The sword is an apt symbol for the use of government power. The first penetration of the flesh by a sharp sword will hardly be noticed. It is a mark of the ingenuity of American gradualists that they are able to appeal to the fact of the lack of pain caused by their programs at first as an argument for extending them. The argument goes something like this, figuratively: the sword is already in; the first thrust did not hurt much; there can, therefore, be no objection to driving it further in. It is not even much of an innovation to drive the sword deeper once it has been introduced into the body.

The Process of Intervention

Rhetoric aside, however, this is how the application of meliorism has resulted in extending force into more and more of American life. Step by step the control, regulation, and intervention has mounted. It began mildly enough in the early twentieth century. At first, it involved only such things as regulating interstate transportation, a pure food and drug law, a meat inspection act, the establishment of a postal savings system, the interstate transportation of females for immoral purposes, and the bringing of telephones and pipelines under government regulation. It proceeded to the passage of a minimal graduated income

---

[6] Roosevelt, *op. cit.*, pp. 53-54.

tax, to the setting up of the Federal Reserve System, to the establishment of rules for dealing with railroad labor, to the exemption of organized labor from antitrust legislation, and to special rules for the directors of large corporations.

Leaving out of account the war years of World War I, the speed of intervention mounted precipitately in the 1930's. Farm prices were subsidized, crops restricted, the stock exchange regulated, labor unions empowered, a government arbitration board created, the income and inheritance tax raised, minimum wages and maximum hours established, loans to farmers provided, Federal aid for slum clearance authorized, vast relief programs undertaken, and so on.

Since World War II, the pace of intervention has been maintained. Social security has been extended to ever larger portions of the population, labor unions regulated in new ways, Federal aid to education extended, conscription extended into peacetime, relief programs of various sorts continued, disaster relief inaugurated, vast programs of urban renewal started, world-wide embroilment by foreign aid begun, and so on.

The above only scratches the surface of the total regulation, control, and intervention by governments in America. There are, in addition to the above, many Federal laws not alluded to, the rules and regulations propounded by boards and commissions, and the fantastic variety of state and local laws, rules, and decrees. To these should be added an increasing number of judicial decrees which are given the force of law.

Depending upon the circumstances and locale, in some instances, an American cannot decide how much he will plant, how he will build, what interest he will charge, what he will buy, to whom he will sell, whom he will serve, what price he will charge, how much education his children will have, what school they will attend, what he shall say (on radio and television), what causes he will support, what size container he shall use, what medication his family shall receive, what business he will enter (since there are government monopolies in certain enterprises), whom he will hire, whom he will fire, with whom he will negotiate, whether he will go out of or remain in business, whether he will contribute to funds for his old age or not, what kind of records he will keep, what he will pay to those he employs, what books his children will be exposed to, and much more besides. The amount determined by the exercise of political power increases and those things left to individual choice decline.

The sword is now deep in the body. However slowly it has entered and however gradual the thrusts, it must eventually reach the vital organs. That this has already occurred and is occurring is indicated by the loss of liberty, the destruction of money by inflation, a mounting and unpaid national debt, rising costs, increasing relief rolls, inflexibilities and rigidities, and spreading lawlessness.

The Reality of Power and Privilege

It is not illusion alone that sustains the movement toward socialism, however. Some men may have succumbed to the illusion that the politicalizing of life is desirable. There may be those, even a great number, who believe that the melioristic programs of politicians are advanced for altruistic reasons. Some portion of the populace may believe that the meaning of life is to be found in democratic participation. Certainly, there are ideologues who are committed to socialism and are utterly blind to the consequences of the efforts in that direction. But behind the façade of altruism, beyond the cloud cover of rhetoric, there is a solid reality which sustains even the flight from reality. It is the reality of government favors and the enticements of political power and prestige.

Men do not readily succumb to illusion in matters close to them with which they are familiar. They follow their own interests, narrowly or broadly conceived or misconceived. Pen and sword are linked together in a web of self-interest that extends outward from the centers of power in America to embrace almost everyone who has some special prerogative, franchise, benefit, exemption, concession, or office derived from government. These are too numerous even to summarize here, but they include such diverse favors as welfare checks, government contracts, radio and television franchises, oil depletion allowances, F. H. A. requirements for escrow balances, loans, subsidies, building projects hoped for, military establishments in the vicinity, and so on through an almost endless array of special privileges.

Virtually every American has been drawn into the orbit of dependency upon government, willingly or not, and to a greater or lesser extent. It may be an illusion to believe that each of us can benefit from the largess taken from all of us, but it becomes increasingly difficult, if not impossible, for an individual to calculate whether his benefits exceed his costs or not. Since they do not know the answer to this multi-billion-dollar question, men fear to disturb the status quo of benefits.

At the apex of this structure of power and privilege is an elite of politicians, intellectuals, labor leaders, scientists, military men, and assorted leaders of specially privileged minority groups. At the pinnacle is the President and those who enjoy his favor. Here, the benefits are such as would dazzle and tempt a saint. There are the obvious perquisites of office, of course: the black limousines, the jet planes, the helicopters, the Marine band, the medical care at Walter Reed Hospital, the admiring crowds, and the fawning assistants. Some of these might be found, even if there were no welfare state, no movement toward socialism, and no spreading assertion of government power.

But the pushers of the pen have provided the wielders of the sword with a rationale and justification of their position that places them above mere mortals. They have set forth an ethos supporting the concentration and exercise of power which makes of those who wield it virtual gods. As more and more of American life is politicalized, the stock of the politician rises in direct ratio. As more and more of our actions are politically directed, the importance of the politician increases. As decisions over their lives are taken from individuals and made political, the politician who makes the decision rises in his own estimation and that of his fellows. As the political mode of doing things—that is, voting, debating, legislating, negotiating— is made the ideal for all activity (such procedures being called democratic in the contemporary argot), the man who has politics as his profession can believe that his is the most meaningful of lives.

My point is that meliorist intellectuals have shown politicians the way to enhance their prestige and increase their power. They have led them to believe that they can control the economy, increase purchasing power, rehabilitate cities, rescue farmers, promote learning and the arts, integrate the races, abolish poverty, produce plenty, develop undeveloped nations, remove fear and want, provide medical care, and give security to a whole people. Politicians have not been slow to claim the credit for anything desirable that is accomplished. If the "national income" increases, it must surely be the result of political effort. If unemployment decreases, the party in power must have provided the jobs. The following pronouncement by President Johnson is typical of such claims:

> We have come far in the past few years. Since January 1961 [the date of inauguration of John F. Kennedy, by which we are to understand that what has been done can be credited to the Democrats] our gross national product has risen 22 percent, industrial production is up 25 percent, the unemployment rate is down 24 percent, disposable personal income is up 18 percent, wages and salaries are up 19 percent, and corporate profits are up 45 percent.[7]

Presidents have claimed credit for virtually everything now but the weather, and they are working on controlling that.

There has been an attempt to give the electorate a sense of participation in the heady experience of exercising power. The instrument by which this is supposed to be accomplished is voting. According to the lore of our time, when a man votes, he is making the ultimate decisions, is causing the whole paraphernalia of government to dance to his tune. Whatever action government takes is his action; whatever good is accomplished is done by him; whatever power is exercised is his power. Through the mystique of the ballot box, the mighty are supposed to be brought low and made to answer to the will of the voter.

Voting is important; it can be used to hold politicians in check, to control, to some extent, the exercise of power, and to short-circuit the surge to power of government agents. But voting does not work this way when it becomes an instrument in the gradual movement toward socialism. The voter does not increase his power by voting

---

[7] *Public Papers of the Presidents of the United States, Lyndon B. Johnson, 1963-64,* I (Washington: Government Printing Office, 1965), 777.

for more government intervention; he decreases it. It is an illusion that an increase in government power over the lives of the citizenry is an increase of the power of the individual voter. The man who votes for more government intervention is voting for diminishing his control of his own affairs. It is a sorry swap to trade the very real control which a man may have over his life for the illusory control this is supposed to give him over the lives of others. He who does this is exchanging his heritage for a mess of pottage. He exalts the politician and debases himself.

A Vested Interest in Promoting Socialism

Politicians have acquired a vested interest in moving the United States toward socialism. Not only does it provide them with prestige and power, but it helps them get elected to office. Politicians run for office on the basis of benefits, favors, subsidies, exemptions, grants, and so forth which they did or will provide for the electorate. Notice how this impels us toward more and more governmental activity, for the man who would continue to be elected should promise ever greater benefits to his constituency. Most men have long since forgotten how to run for office without buying votes with money to be taken directly from the taxpayers, or indirectly by way of inflation.

There is a sense in which meliorist politicians may be described as pragmatists, though not in the way we have been led to believe. The workability or success of a plan or undertaking is relative to the goal for which it has been adopted. The stated goal of the various meliorist programs is the improvement of the lot of the people. If this had been the goal of the farm program, for instance, it has not "worked." Instead, farmers have left the farms in ever larger numbers; the marginal farmers were progressively impoverished and those with large holdings and considerable capital enriched. The generality of the population have paid for this by taxation and higher prices for farm products.

If, however, the objects of the farm program (and other such programs) were socialization and/or political power, it has worked. More and more of the decisions about the utilization of farm land are politically ("socially") determined, and those who have supported the farm programs have quite often been elected and re-elected to office. The same is true for many other interventionist programs. In short, the programs do "work" in moving America toward socialism and in maintaining or increasing the political power of those who advance them. In this sense, they are pragmatic, and those who advocate them are pragmatists.

Those who provide the justification for Leviathan have their reward, too. A select few are able to move into the circle of the President himself. One intellectual who did— Arthur M. Schlesinger, Jr.—has described the rewards dramatically: "One could not deny a sense of New Frontier autointoxication; one felt it oneself. The pleasures of power, so long untasted, were now being happily devoured —the chauffeur-driven limousines, the special telephones, the top secret documents, the personal aides, the meetings in the Cabinet Room, the calls from the President."[8]

There are other rewards of a more tangible nature. Schlesinger wrote a best-selling book which was an account of the Kennedy days when he was close to the President. It won a Pulitzer prize. Nor did the rewards end with the period of residence in the White House. Since leaving Washington, Schlesinger has "signed a contract for the $100,000 Albert Schweitzer chair in humanities at City

---

[8] *A Thousand Days* (Boston: Houghton Mifflin, 1965), p. 213.

University of New York."[9] The rewards are not so great for the generality of intellectuals, of course, but those who support Leviathan are more apt to find their talents rewarded than those who do not.

The Illusions of Power

Yet the reality of power and privilege is based on illusion, too. It is an illusion that the wielding of the sword can produce prosperity. The actions of Presidents Kennedy and Johnson did not really increase the gross national product by 22 per cent, or industrial production by 25 per cent, or reduce unemployment by 24 per cent, and so on. They could, of course, have used political power to inflate the currency to the extent that these statistics would be accurate in monetary terms, and that unemployment could have been reduced because workers formerly priced out of the market could now be afforded. But any solid gains that occurred would have been the result of the efforts of those who actually produced the goods or hired the workers. If this were not true, we could all quit work and let Presidents provide for us by waving the magic wand.

The most profound illusion of all is that men can escape the consequences of their acts. Jesus said that "all who take the sword will perish by the sword." There are different levels upon which Scripture should be interpreted, but this one seems to apply, too, to what actually happens in history. From 1865 to the present, four Presidents have been assassinated, and attempts have been made on the lives of others. In the twentieth century, Presidents have been placed under heavier and heavier guard. They are now preceded by a host of government agents on their visits

---

[9] Geoffrey Gould, "College Profs Earning Better Pay Every Year," Pittsburgh *Post-Gazette* (July 4, 1966), sec. II, p. 32.

anywhere, agents who strive to make sure no dangerous characters shall get a vantage point from which to attack the President. There is an obvious explanation for this increasing danger of assassination. It is the increasing power of the President. To the extent that the President symbolizes the government, to the extent that he is responsible for government action, to that same extent does his position become more perilous for him. In short, the increasing power and prestige of his office exposes him the more to an assassin's bullet. When he becomes the wielder of the sword, he becomes subject to perishing by the sword.

The nation that takes the sword may be expected to perish by it also. This can occur in numerous ways, or combinations of them. Most obviously, a nation may be defeated by some foreign power. But this is most apt to occur after death has already begun. It may perish by the corruption that attends reliance upon the loot brought in by wielding the sword. It may succumb by the route of the runaway inflation which follows prolonged political manipulation of the money supply. It may be weakened gradually by the loss of incentive to produce that attends the ever larger amounts taken from producers by taxation. It may fall finally as a result of the inflexibilities and rigidities introduced by government intervention which eventually make it impossible to adjust to changed conditions. Any or all of these, or others unnamed, may cause a nation to perish.

But let us return to the particular once more to exemplify the destination of those on the flight from reality. What of the intellectuals who have engineered the journey? What is their fate? What are the ineluctable consequences of their act? They have moved the pen into the orbit of the sword; in a sense, they, too, have taken the sword.

The pen is only mightier than the sword so long as it is independent of the sword. Once it comes into the orbit of the sword, it comes under its sway. Those who push the pen must serve those who wield the sword. They must become the adjuncts of those who have political power, or give up their influence. It depends upon the circumstances whether they will literally perish or not. For those interested, there is an object lesson in what happened to communist intellectuals in the Soviet Union. They either knuckled down to the political power or were silenced. What is going on in the United States is much more subtle today. More and more research and teaching are becoming dependent upon government bounty. Already the path to preferment—to research grants, to positions in great universities, to book publication, and so forth—is virtually closed to those who will not pay their tribute to Caesar in the form of fulsome praise for Leviathan.

The pen is mightier than the sword when it is moved to express truth; it is but an adjunct of the sword when it can only be effectively used in praise of the state. Free speech and press may never be forbidden in America, but the time approaches swiftly when there will be no organizations which are independent of government support and whose leaders will dare to risk the consequences of biting the hand that feeds them by succoring those who dissent from official positions. When this occurs, tyranny may have come, but there will be no effective voices to say it nay. Those who take the sword perish by it.

24

The Return to Reality

THE AMERICAN REPUBLIC IS IN CRISIS TODAY. IT IS NOT a momentary crisis, such as may be denominated, for example, the Suez Crisis. Such crises are only temporary, and they suggest only that some particular decision must be made. By contrast, the crisis of the Republic has been building for many years, is not restricted to some aspect of the affairs of the country, and cannot be brought to an end by some palliative. There is, of course, a surrounding world crisis, and the United States has been drawn into the vortex of that. It is a crisis which afflicts a whole civilization, to define its scope. This crisis is a direct product of the flight from reality.

The last of the above chapters was written more than two years ago. In that interval, the outward signs of an inner deep-running crisis have mounted and become nearly all-pervasive. The crime rate in the United States has soared, as it has been reported annually, but one suspects that it soars almost daily. The violence in the streets has become more strident, if that is possible. Another Kennedy has been assassinated. A murderer's bullet has claimed the life of Martin Luther King. The President is fearful any longer to announce his itinerary before he makes his journeys. Violent assaults have interrupted education at once-great institutions of learning. Political bodies are continually disrupted by unruly demonstrators and protestors. War has continued in Vietnam without visible result. A Generation Gap separates the young from the mature, according to interpreters of such things; a Credibility Gap separates the governed from the governors; and a Decorum Gap certainly separates the militant from the rest of the citizenry.

That many American cities are today imperiled there can be no reasonable doubt. Not only are they the prime targets for destruction wrought by rioters, but they are sitting ducks for every disruptive element. Cities are the marvels of our civilization with their tightly packed population, great and diverse productivity, infinitely complex grids of transportation and communication networks. But they are entirely dependent upon the smooth functioning of the delicate mechanism by which inflow and outgo of goods and services is maintained: upon incoming gas, electricity, coal, raw materials, foodstuffs, component parts, messages, and so forth; upon police, firemen, water and sewage and sanitation services; upon the markets in the surrounding hinterland and around the world who employ them. If all rail and truck services were halted for any considerable length of time, life would become unsupportable in a large city. Even the stoppage of garbage removal for a brief period can pose major problems. Labor unions pose continual threats to cities, and organization has spread rapidly in recent years to police, firemen, sanitation workers, teachers, and medical personnel. Laws forbidding strikes or injunctions to halt them can have no effect if and when the officers of the law will not enforce them.

An endemic monetary crisis afflicts the Western world, coming to dramatic climaxes from time to time. The most dramatic aspect of this, as publicly presented, is the particular crisis that grips the leaders of a country when they are faced with the prospect of official devaluation. But these are only the surface indicators of a much more fundamental set of difficulties that arise from inflationary manipulation of currencies. Most directly, the requirement to devalue means that a government did not and will not live within its means. This profligate behavior is financed by a subtle form of taxation—expansion of the money supply. In consequence of the increase of the domestic supply of money, exports are overpriced and imports underpriced. The result: an imbalance of trade in goods and services and the pressure on the supply of whatever money remains acceptable in international exchanges.

It may be easy to delude oneself into supposing that all this is a matter of concern only for international bankers. After all, they are about the only ones who are conversant with the internal workings of it. But such is not the case. Its effects extend to the length and breadth of each and every society which is afflicted by inflation. Nineteenth century thinkers used to say that ours was a contract society. They meant that all sorts of relations are defined by arrangements entered into by individual choice—contracts. In point of fact, every society, insofar as it allows for the operation of the wills of people, is a contract society. What distinguished modern Western civilization was the expression of contracts in, or the possibility of reducing them to, monetary terms. This greatly increased the range of choices for human action, provided almost unlimited modes for satisfying the terms of contracts, and freed men from the brute necessities of personal servitude. But contracts reducible to monetary terms are only valid so long as the money supply remains relatively stable.

Government manipulation of the money supply tampers with all human relations expressed in contracts of any very long duration. Prolonged manipulation of the money supply tends not only to destroy the value of the money but also to undermine the very foundations of society. Fraud enters into every kind of relationship. This is so because promises to pay in the future are only partially fulfilled. Debts—or some portion of them—are repudiated by substantial increases of the money supply. Contracts become regressively perilous instruments to use. Stratagems are adopted to compensate for the fluctuations in the value of money—as, for example, charging much higher interest than the legal interest rate by such devices as increasing the price of the good or service when payment is deferred. As inflation continues, promises to pay lose their value even as one holds them. The lines of communication by which we express our intent toward one another are blocked—that is, by way of money in contracts; suspicion replaces confidence; a man's word is no longer his bond, for it is as worthless as the paper his currency is printed upon. This last is only finally true, of course, at the end, but it tends to become true with each new manipulation of the money supply.

American society is sick, so say certain pundits in our time. The statement is true enough, though not in the way that is meant. American society is sick in the way that a man is sick whose oxygen supply to the brain has been dangerously diluted. One of the main sources of that dilution is the increase of the money supply—the dilution of its strength. Society has been made nearly impotent because its members are increasingly ineffective in expressing their wills by way of contracts.

The loss of vitality in contracts is apparent in many areas: rampant divorce indicates the deterioration of the marriage contract; student rebellions violate the tacit contracts between them and their institutions; rent strikes violate contracts between tenants and landlords; tax evasion violates the contract between government and citizen;

increase of crime signifies the violation of the contract between individuals and society; industrial strikes violate contracts between employee and employer. Violence at any level signifies the abandonment of the contractual mode and the resort to force. The "sickness" of which the pundits speak is in the initiators of violence, but society is incapacitated—sick, in normal usage—thereby.

I have dwelt upon the monetary crisis above for several reasons. In the first place, it gives a sort of mechanical clue to what has happened. To a considerable extent, the assault upon the value of money can be calculated. The more the supply is increased, the less its value. In the second place, money is the essential medium by which the contracts which knit a society together are expressed. Thirdly, the role of government in the manipulation is so obvious here. Government is, indeed, the instrument which has been used to dilute the value, to vitiate contracts, and to introduce widespread fraud in contracts. Government not only increases the money supply but also requires that it be the medium by tender laws. And fourthly, the manipulation of the money supply shows the crucial link between the flight from reality and socialism. The flight from reality occurred via the illusion that prosperity could be produced by increasing the money supply. The thrust to socialism has been mightily advanced by the surreptitious taxation involved in inflation and the subsequent redistribution. The body charged with keeping the peace has introduced fraud into the very fabric of society.

The Violation of Contracts

The crisis of the American Republic is, from one angle, the dissolving of the bonds of society resulting from the violation of contracts. The most fundamental contract of the American Republic is the Constitution. The Constitution is the law for American governments. To the extent that governments have violated this law, and it is great and increasing, to that same extent has the basic contract between the American people and their governments been invalidated.

Underlying this political contract is an even more fundamental contract, one upon which all societies as such are based, whether or not they have a written constitution. Traditionally, it has been called the social contract. It is that tacit, essential, and necessary agreement which binds man to man, members of a family to one another, members of communities together, binds generation to generation, binds people to government and government to people. It is everyman's tacit agreement not to use violence to get his way, to leave others to the enjoyment of the fruits of their labor, not to trespass upon the property of others, to fulfill the terms of his individually entered into agreements, to honor his parents, to succor his children, to keep his word, to meet his obligations—to family, to community, to country, to keep all treaties, and to observe the amenities of his culture. The social contract embraces, too, the obligation of the citizen to support the government —with a portion of his means and, if need be, even his life—which protects him and his in the enjoyment of his life.

Society can, of course, endure violations of the social contract so long as they remain exceptions. It can even endure some generalized violations of the contract, else we should have to conclude from history that there have been no societies. But it cannot endure these when they become pervasive, when all relations are vitiated by fraud, and when force has been universalized. Universalized fraud is but a subtle mode of universalized violence, and such violence will not lurk for long beneath the surface.

The crisis of the American Republic is, from another angle, the threatened dissolution of society by fraud and other less subtle devices of violence. We have examined the fraud practiced by inflation. It is but one of many. It is commonplace today that the promises and platforms of politicians are empty promises. When they promise to provide their goodies without additional taxes, what man can believe them? Promises to stay out of foreign wars by Presidents at election time have at least twice been casually ignored. More generally, the debt of the United States constitutes a promise to pay, yet no fund exists for its retirement. The massive promises of the government by way of Social Security rest only on the government's future potential for taxation. The bonds of the United States are worth less at maturity than they were at the time of purchase, because of inflation, at least some of the time.

But these are, in a sense, at the surface of the pervasive fraud. What is fraud? It is the result of varying from the truth. It is prevarication—the successful telling of a lie—in essence. But what if there is no truth? Then all statements purporting to be true are fraudulent. Or again, there is no fraud because there is no truth. That is not quite the guise in which the matter presents itself. On the one hand, we have been brought along on the flight from reality by the claims that there are no fixed realities. On the other, there is a body of thought that says that truth is relative to the person who sees it. This position is generally known as relativism. In essence, though, this is the position that there is no public truth. Fraud is surely licensed by such a position. To the extent that this doctrine has been spread, to the extent that its implications have begun to be realized, to that same extent fraud has become prevalent.

No contractual society can exist without public truth.

Contracts are only enforceable to the extent that the words in them have fixed meanings. Any contract may be readily evaded if one may put whatever meaning to it that suits him. Indeed, this destroys the whole purpose of a contract, for it involves commitments which will occasion inconvenience to the parties. One's word can only be his bond when that word given has conveyed a proposition accurately to someone else. Historians have sometimes made fun with Calvin Coolidge's statements vis a vis the European war debts of World War I to the United States: "They hired the money, didn't they?" And he was saying: "They should pay it back." The humor should escape all honest men. Nations should not commit themselves to debts, and then claim that they should not have to pay them back. At any rate, contracts depend for their validity upon public truth.

In another way, the assault upon the bonds of society has gone on by way of the introduction of force into area after area of life. The family ties have been loosened by government intervention: compulsory school attendance, compulsory Social Security, taxation at such levels that many have difficulties meeting their family obligations. The so-called Generation Gap has been and is fostered by government. Young people are virtually forced into "peer group" surroundings by governmental school policies. They are freed from dependence on family by government scholarship programs. Government aid to the aged relieves the young of their responsibilities for their parents and grandparents. Aid to dependent children, so-called, frees women from dependence upon men. Communities lose their vitality as responsibility for looking after and caring for the indigents among them has been assumed by impersonal government agencies. At the deepest levels, the relations among men lose their free and voluntary character as government prescribes more and more about what their character shall be.

The American Crisis

The crisis of the American Republic, then, is the threatened dissolution of the bonds of society. The violence, the disorder, the crime, the divorce, the juvenile delinquency, the riots, the strikes, the disruptive demonstrations, are the outward signs of the progress of an inward dissolution. Underlying these is the disintegration of the free individual contractual society. The American crisis is part of a world crisis—the crisis of a civilization disintegrating because its modes of relating man to man and community to community have been undermined. Disillusion and delusion are rampant. The disillusion is with the modes of operation which are still half-way preserved in our institutions, with freely entered contracts, with marriage, with voluntary churches, with communities, with so-called bourgeois society, with international treaties, with nation-states, with law courts, and so on.

These cannot work, of course, as they are increasingly hampered by the intervention of force which has come to prevail. The delusion is that larger measures of force—by demonstrations, by riots, by the compulsive state—can bring accord. No wonder that crime increases, when men have been taught by generations of intellectuals that private property is *theft,* that one has a right to a "decent" living, that it is proper to take from those who have and distribute to those who have not, that freedom is the absence of responsibility, that entrepreneurs are sophisticated robbers, that wealthy nations should redistribute their wealth to poor nations, and so on. Those who turn to overt violence are taking to heart the lessons they have been taught. If the state may use violence for such ends, why may not individuals and groups? They are cutting out the middle man. All of this, again, is grist for the mills of communists, who may and do use such disorders to advance their ends.

Neither society nor civilization can survive without viable and enforceable contracts. Indeed, society itself depends at its most rudimentary level upon defined relationships which are, in effect, contracts. Society is that setting within which men exchange, converse, commune, succor, and benefit from the presence of one another. All of history testifies that men will serve and/or be served by one another. The modes for this are four: (1) by contracts expressed in terms of money or in kind; (2) by service contracts, which is serfdom; (3) by out-and-out slavery; (4) by combinations of these.

The assault upon the money and the increasing use of force, then, is taking us down the road to serfdom, as Frederick von Hayek called it some years ago. Serfdom in our age is most readily recognized as statism. It is the compulsory service of the state. It can be seen most directly in communist lands, where the inhabitants have been reduced to minions of the state on state-owned farms, in state-owned factories, in the state-maintained universities, and so on. But it proceeds apace in other lands and in the United States. Compulsory service of the state is most obvious in compulsory military service, but this is probably minor in comparison with the other compulsions. Servitude is advanced subtly but surely by the manipulation of the currency (by which we can be induced to use our money in ways sought by the powers that be), by the higher and higher taxes which take more and more of our lives to pay, and by the controls by which we keep formal title to our property but its use is prescribed by government.

But to call it statism-as-serfdom does not fully reveal its character. The "state" is an abstraction of an instrument, that instrument which is charged with the power to use force. The underlying reality of the state is the men who control and operate it. On its human side, statism is bureaucracy in the twentieth century, the rule by bureaucrats. The new serfdom is the serving of the bureaucracy by the populace. The measure of its spread is the increase in numbers and powers of bureaucrats. They are the ones who assert their wills over us: by way of vaguely worded laws, by means of the "executive power," and by turning the constabulary into instruments of their will. Actually, the police have been by no means subdued by the bureaucracy in America yet. To a considerable extent that is what is at issue today in the contest with the police, and the cries of "police brutality." The police still attempt to perform much of their traditional function of protecting life and property. When they have been made instruments of the will of the bureaucracy, all protests against them will be silenced. It is more likely, however, that the bureaucracy will be subdued by the police, and that both police and bureaucrats will enter their own serfdom to some concentrated power. That is what has happened in communist lands. Those who put their faith in law and order, then, will find themselves hoist by their own petard.

Such is the nature of the crisis. It is the result of a prolonged flight from reality. It is a deep crisis which will not be removed by palliatives. Yet it will be alleviated sooner or later, for anarchy will not prevail, nor can men withdraw into shells and sever all relations with one another. Serfdom can be universalized, or free contracts and the cash nexus may be restored. That is the choice, but it must be made clear that each of these courses entails unpleasantness. Utopia is nowhere, but those who pursue it end up somewhere. That the somewhere is serfdom, the records of this century bear profound witness. What of the other possibility?

The first thing to be said is this: Anyone who approaches the topic of the good society should do so in deepest humility. We have had far too many prescriptions for the good society in our era. That, indeed, is the root of our sickness. It is not for writers or intellectuals to prescribe the lineaments of society, to tell us what shape human relations shall take, to lay down the manner in which we shall be educated, how we shall earn our living, what distribution of goods and services is meet, how we shall be transported, what our morals shall be, how we shall conduct our private affairs. None of us is called to so exalted a task, and none but a dictator would presume to attempt it. None of us is equipped to construct a viable society, and when we attempt it we achieve not society but tyranny.

But there is something to be said on this head, nonetheless.

The beginning should be very basic. It is true, no doubt, that in a profound sense man is a pilgrim and stranger on this frequently hostile planet. That is, spiritually man is a pilgrim and a stranger, and ever has been. His spirit would soar and rise up to the heavens. He would commune with God. Man's spirit would confront directly the spirits of other men, rather than always be hidden behind the layers of flesh, convention, and outward forms. He would walk ever in green pastures, move to the chords of music purified of earthly dross, be caught up in the glow of love, see only beauty, hear only truth, feel always exalted. The spirit of man is, at its best and ideally, alien to the body which encloses it and the planet which provides its environment.

That is, however, only half the truth. For man is also

made of flesh and bones, and his flesh is flesh of this earth, his bones bone of its bone. As flesh and blood, man is bound by the laws governing matter, dealing with elements that are only partially plastic, and placed in company with other flesh and blood beings with wills and desires of their own, to his discomfiture quite often. He is a little lower than the angels, according to a traditional formulation; or, as Franz Winkler so felicitously stated it in the title of a book: *Man: The Bridge Between Two Worlds*. The two worlds are, for our purposes, the world of the spirit and the world of the flesh.

Man has attempted in our time to end the alienation of the spirit *by his own efforts*. Prometheus Unbound has grasped for the fire of the gods. Christianity teaches that God alone can end the alienation of the spirit, that he alone can reach through to link spirit with spirit, and that he has done so within time. But man has attempted to reverse the revealed Order and bring Heaven to earth by his own will. Man, however, is linked to the flesh; he is earthbound. By such efforts, he only succeeds in degrading the spirit, in enthralling the spirit and further encumbering the flesh—in short, he succeeds only in bringing tyranny.

Return to Reason

The mediating faculty between flesh and spirit is reason. Reason is that power given to man whereby he can discern the order of things, find his particular place among them, and leave room for the proper operation of both flesh and spirit. It was the deactivation of reason by which the flight from reality was begun. The return to reality in a way to safeguard freely entered and accepted contracts involves a return to reason.

But to return to reason we must first be able to recognize it. That is not as easy as one might suppose. Every party claims that its members are reasonable. Yet this cannot be. Thinkers once used a phrase which describes the reason we seek; they called it right reason. That there is right reason assumes that there is also wrong reason. Investigation confirms this conclusion. Indeed, there are many varieties of wrong reason. It probably is not necessary, if it could be done, to delineate all the varieties. Truth is one, but error is manifold.

But examples may help in showing what is not right reason. Right reason is not simply a familiar thought which one has become accustomed to accepting. It is not a groove worn in the mind by the repetition of an idea so that when one encounters it again there is no resistance to it. For example, we are all familiar with labor unions and their activities. They are both familiar and unquestionably accepted by many. But this does not make them or their activities reasonable. Right reason is not simply logic. Reason may be logical, but logic can be used to arrive at quite unreasonable conclusions. Right reason is not abtract reason, or the product of it. Right reason is not simply inductive reasoning, for though this is a method which may be validly used in reasoning, it does not comprehend all of right reason.

It is not so easy, however, to define right reason. We get an inkling of what it is from the following quotation from the Roman philosopher Cicero. Cicero is here discussing natural law, but he uses the phrase in question interestingly:

> True law is *right reason conformable to nature,* universal, unchangeable, eternal, whose commands urge us to duty, and whose prohibitions restrain us from evil. . . . This law cannot be contradicted by any other law, and is not liable to derogation or abrogation. Neither the senate nor the people can give us any dispensation for

not obeying this universal law of justice. . . . It is not one thing at Rome, and another at Athens; one thing today, and another tomorrow; but in all times and nations this universal law must for ever reign, eternal and imperishable. It is the sovereign master and emperor of all beings. God himself is its author, its promulgator, its enforcer, and he who does not obey it flies from himself, and does violence to the very nature of man.

Thereby hangs the tale, for the flight from reality is the flying of man from himself, and the end product is the violence done to his nature.

But the immediate task here is to delineate right reason. Right reason, we gather, is conformable to nature. This is a very helpful clue. Right reason is thought in accord with the nature of the mind. More, right reason is reason with a built-in content. The mind does not operate in a void; it has a conception of the way things are. Modern thought got hung up over the question of how the mind gets this conception. The Platonists have held that it is innate. John Locke broke radically with this view to hold that the conception of the way things are comes to us from the senses. Let us admit that we do not know how we know what we know, and rather affirm that we do indeed know what we know. However acquired, then, right reason has content which consists of the conception of the way things are. It should be kept in mind, too, that man has made great progress in our era in discovering and utilizing the particulars of the way things are. He has gone most drastically astray when he has tried to change them.

Reason does proceed by analysis. It takes things apart, seeking for the underlying structure of reality, for the basic forms which give shape to things, for essences or the ways in which things are essentially the same, for the laws which undergird the universe. Right reason, however, does not mistake the parts for the whole, does not identify that which it has learned by analysis and abstraction with the whole of reality, knows that the skeleton which its methods disclose is not the full-fleshed creature. In short, right reason neither becomes enamored of fixed ideas nor spins out its own versions of reality from abstractions—i.e., ideologizes. Right reason, then, uses the methods of reason for gaining that knowledge appropriate to them, but does not proceed to the abuses of abstract rationalism. Right reason is not, of course, the possession of some of us as opposed to the rest of us. It is the potential of every man capable of reason, a potential within the nature of mind, the potential of using reason rightfully.

Reason, rightly used, does not intrude upon the realm of the spirit. It does not deny mystery, nor conclude that by its discoveries mystery has been dispelled. Reason enables us, by disclosing the order governing things, to order our affairs so as to allow men to care for the needs of the flesh and leave room for the things of the spirit. It provides that knowledge by which public affairs can be managed so that they leave a private realm for individual growth and fulfillment. It shows us the proper sphere of government, that which is in keeping with its nature and that which takes into account the nature of man and of society. Reason chastens the spirit when it would use force to achieve its ends, rightly distinguishing between, for example, government favors and charity. It rightly reveals to us that power must be limited that the spirit may have full play. Moreover, it sets the stage for us to achieve our spiritual growth by way of earthly undertakings, not destroying, as socialism does, the spiritual value of work and industry by taking from us choices and decisions.

The return to reality requires, then, a return to reason, if that return is to include liberty and a free contractual society. The flight from reality was made when logic was cut loose from content, when abstractions were used to construct their own realities, when the spirit was denied, when the flesh was denied, when their separate existences were fused in thought so as to allow neither room to operate. The tyrannies of our age proceed from the fusion and confusion. The meaninglessness which pervades men's outlook arises from the denial of the spirit; just as physical hunger proceeds from the denial of the claims of the flesh in refusing to men the fruits of their labor. Reason distinguishes the two spheres and would allow men freedom to operate in each.

An Earlier Crisis

The return to reality for Americans requires the attending to the crisis of the Republic. This is not the first crisis of such dimensions, and there are in some other crises and the way they were handled some guidelines for us. Perhaps the crisis which is most nearly analogous to ours today in our history occurred in the 1780's. John Fiske called it *The Critical Period of American History.* Recent historians have accused him of exaggeration, but the evidence still points to a crisis, and most of the leading thinkers of the day—such men as James Madison, Alexander Hamilton, John Adams, Gouverneur Morris, Robert Morris, Benjamin Franklin—declared that one existed.

Among the more pressing and distressing problems were these: a huge debt left over from the War for Independence and no fund for its retirement, the credit of the government under Congress prostrate, lack of respect from foreign powers—the British would not evacuate posts in the old Northwest; the Spanish were stirring up Indian troubles and would not agree on boundaries or the vital navigation of the Mississippi; the British West Indies were closed to American trade—, dissension among the states, and disorders within the states. Monetary troubles posed the most immediate threats. Undoubtedly, the domestic and foreign disrespect for the government under Congress was heightened by the fact that it had virtually repudiated the Continental currency a few years before and could not now meet the interest payments on the debt. Within some of the states, too, monetary troubles led to disorder. In several states, the legislatures had knuckled under to demands for inflation, for the issuance of paper money, and for tender laws to make the inhabitants use it. Rhode Island was notorious for such fiscal shenanigans, but some of the others were little better. In Massachusetts, the legislature refused either to issue paper money or to relieve debtors of the obligation to pay their debts. Groups of armed men refused to allow courts to sit in some places. An army of discontents was assembled—Daniel Shays being one of the leaders—, and an outright rebellion followed. Above all else, these people wanted paper money issued. They were generally ignorant men; even if there had been such sophistries as those of John Maynard Keynes available to provide a rationale for paper money, they would not have read them. They just wanted easy money and relief from their debts.

Though this rebellion was put down, the threats to American society ran deep. Within a few years, though they could not have known it at the time, a world war would break out—the wars of the French Revolution and Napoleon—and their safety would be threatened for many years.

Delegates from twelve states met in Philadelphia in 1787 to wrestle with these problems and try to find a way out of them. A "more perfect union," they judged, was needed, and to bring that about an energetic government with powers to tax and with sanctions to use on the citizenry. The states must be made stable and be restrained. The licentious portion of the citizenry must be denied so much direct influence on government. Debts must be paid, and the credit of the United States established. Laws must be enforced, and means established for doing so.

Here is not the place to recount how the Constitution provided for all this in detail. Suffice it to say, that the states were restrained by denying them certain powers, such as that of emitting bills of credit, i.e., issuing paper money, or making anything but gold or silver legal tender. Though there were many who opposed such action, the debt was declared to be valid. And Alexander Hamilton and his successors in the Treasury labored to see it funded and eventually retired. States were prohibited from invalidating private contracts. Both the states and the United States government were limited by the Constitution and the Bill of Rights. In the ensuing years, Presidents followed a resolute course in world affairs, maintaining an independent posture. Whatever hardships were entailed, the debt was paid (finally retired under Andrew Jackson), and America began to be respected around the world.

The crisis in our day does not stem, of course, from government without sufficient power. In part, it does stem from a lack of will to use that power effectively: to follow an independent course in the world, to protect American citizens abroad, to hold other nations to their contracts— i.e., treaties—to fund the debt, to balance the budget, and to enforce the laws with an even hand. Indeed, much of the crisis has arisen because of over-expanded and unrestrained governmental power. (In this, there *is* an analogy with the state governments of the 1780's.) There are many people in America today who would and do use the government to achieve their illegitimate ends by force. In the main, though, government has been unleashed, and the citizenry restrained. Government engages in so many activities that it is no longer much devoted to protecting life and property. Government attempts to do all things, and it ceases to do well at all even those things which it is suited to doing.

Toward Ending Today's Crisis

The crisis of the Republic can be ended, if at all, in much the same way as it was in the 1780's and shortly thereafter: that is, by restraining the powers of all governments, by resolutely enforcing the laws, by denying to factions the power of government for partisan ends, by balancing the budget, by beginning to retire the debt, by stabilizing the currency, by securing property, by freeing the citizenry to pursue their own ends. Men are truly interdependent, and when they are protected from violence and permitted to pursue their own ends, they will work out ingenious ways to foster good relations with one another. The bonds of society will be reknit, they will provide for themselves with freely entered contracts.

But all this will remain only a pipe dream so long as the deepest sources of disorder are not reached and considerably changed. Only that political action which reflects the will of men who have that integrity which proceeds from an inward order can be effective in restoring an outward order. The disorders of our day spring from disorders in the souls of men. Only men who have found some inward peace can make peace at large.

There is a clue for the cure of much of this in a certain passage in the Bible. The following is from Micah (RSV):

> For out of Zion shall go forth the law,
>   and the word of the Lord from
>   Jerusalem.

> He shall judge between many peoples,
>   and shall decide for strong nations
>   afar off;
> and they shall beat their swords into plowshares,
>   and their spears into pruning hooks;
> nation shall not lift up sword against
>   nation, neither shall they learn
>   war any more.

That much is familiar and has served as texts and the basis of song on many occasions. What immediately follows may not be so well known:

> but they shall sit every man under
>   his vine and under his fig tree,
>   and none shall make them afraid. . . .

To say that every man shall sit under his vine and under his fig tree, to couple this with plowshares and pruning hooks, is a way of saying, I think, that every man should tend to his own plot of land. Or, we shall have peace when each man tends his own plot. There is great wisdom for us in this. The flight from reality has taken us into a way of thinking which justifies every man trying to tend every other man's plot of land. The sword has been taken to force people to do what others think they should. Meddlesomeness, busybodiness, do-goodism have been linked with the sword to produce the turmoil of our times.

There is guidance, too, as to the meaning of life in these passages. It is not in the restless efforts to make the world over, not in political adventures to solve problems, not in the making of collective decisions about all that concerns us, not in embroilment in the affairs of others, not in living the lives of others, that we can find meaning and fulfillment. The restless quest for power is not assuaged by the acquisition of power; the appetite is only whetted for more. The meaning of life is not to be found in the use of force to translate ideas into actualities. It is not in the assertion of our wills over others that we grow and attain maturity. We are disordered when we think so; and when we act upon such premises we extend our inward disorder into the world about us.

Such meaning as there is to life on this earth is found in tending our own plot of ground, in tasting the fruits of our own labors, in developing our own skills and perceptions, in sharing with others freely, in doing that which is appropriate to our talents, in striving to fulfill our ideals for ourselves, in the pleasure of a job well done, in the company of friends we have chosen and who have chosen us, in bringing up our own children, in short, in sitting under our own vine and fig tree.

It is so, says the Prophet, "for the mouth of the Lord of hosts has spoken." Each of us makes his own return to reality when he concludes with the poet:

In His will is our peace.

25

The Bent to Destruction

THE LORELEI IS A ROCK WITH AN UNUSUAL ECHO, IN THE Rhine River near St. Goar. There is an old legend surrounding the sounds emitted from this rock: the Song of the Lorelei. The legend is to the effect that a maiden who had been betrayed by a faithless lover threw herself into the river. She was turned into a siren, and her song has since that time lured fishermen to their destruction against the rock. There is a connection between this tale and the myth of Holda, the queen of the elves. The man who beholds Holda loses sight of reason. If he listens to her, he is compelled to wander with her forever.

This legend provides a kind of parable for our era. And it is appropriate, at the last, to turn to story, legend, and myth. Rational analysis of the data of history can provide us with a great deal of information and explanation about *how* we came to be where we are at present. Yet, reason and evidence are inadequate to the task; at least, the facts which this writer has in hand and his reason are inadequate to the task of describing the movement toward the triumph of reformism in America. Much as has been told, there is more that has not, or has been touched upon only lightly. Many aspects of the development and spread of ideas and methods of reform have not been described. Yet, the time has come to bring the story to an end. This

requires a summary that will hold the movement up whole
and grasp its character. We still want to know *why* reformers have been so determinedly attached to their effort,
even in the face of the near obvious contradictions involved. For grasping things whole, reason is the wrong
instrument. It proceeds by taking things apart, not by
wholes. The nearest man comes to talking about things
whole is by way of parable, story, poem, legend, and
myth. Men have ever had a penchant for these tools of
simplicity by which to see things whole, even though such
accounts lack precision.

The Vision of Utopia

The song of the siren, the lure which has led reformers
on and the lure they have held out to others, has been the
vision of the good society they would create for the future.
It has been a vision of peace, plenty, and progress, of a
time when all struggle and tension would be removed
from this world, when felicity and goodness would reign
without end. The vision, fabricated by utopians, embedded
in an historical eschatology by ideologues, rendered into
a kind of idealism by philosophers, described in glowing
terms for the vulgar by politicians, finally has become a
mirage which men see just before their eyes. The vision
has such powers of attraction that before it men do indeed
lose sight of reason and wander hither and yon over the
face of the earth seeking devices to fulfill it.

The rock upon which the reformers are continually ship-
wrecked is, above all, human nature and the nature of the
universe. The projections from the rock may be described
in many ways, however. They are the attempts to apply
force to the accomplishment of ends which can only be
achieved by willing consent. They are the tendencies to
concentrate power and to leave it unchecked in the hands

of men. They are the treatment of men as if they were things.

But why, it may be asked, if the boats launched by reformers are one after another and time and again foundering upon the same rock, are markers not placed around the rock and why do not pilots take care to avoid it? We know, of course, from earlier exposition that reformers have cut themselves off from their experience; they have deactivated history. But the answer runs deeper than this. The answer will not be believed at first, for it appears incredible. The reformers will the destruction: part of it intentionally, part of it unintentionally through the methods that they employ.

Civilized Inhibitions and the Urge to Destroy

The reformist effort does founder upon the rock of human nature, but that is only part of the story. Reformism appeals to something deep and enduring in human nature. Reformism appeals to the desire to destroy, the desire to build or reconstruct, and the will to power. The story of the flight from reality has been told largely in terms of the vision of a reconstructed society which has lured men on. Destruction, however, is what we encounter when we follow the trail left by reformers. In the wake of reformers we find customs and traditions trampled upon, sacred beliefs gutted and lifeless, institutions toppled, constitutions rifled, the wreck and ruin of economies, and the lives of peoples in disarray because of the dissolution of moral codes.

These things are justified in the ethos of the reformer, for the destruction is claimed to be the necessary clearing away of the rubble that must precede the reconstruction. That they are destroying when they claim to be building also is not clear to them. My point here is that destruction is not simply a device for getting rid of the old, not merely an unintended consequence of the methods employed and the ends sought, but part and parcel of the appeal of the reformist effort.

I suspect that each of us has within his breast a desire to wreck, to plunder, to lay waste, to make havoc—in a word, to destroy. It may be tamed by civilization, be held in abeyance by the threat of punishment, be inactivated by the Grace of God, but it is nonetheless there. Some find innocuous ways for it to come out. They follow the fire trucks to the scene of the fire to watch the building burn. They line the highway in the vicinity of a collision of automobiles in order to view the wreckage. They stand on the sidewalks and peer up at the work of men who have been employed to wreck old buildings. Other men find more subtle ways to express their urge to destroy. They defame men, denigrate conventions, make wisecracks, write satires, hold up to scorn, sneer at, and make fun of things held sacred by others. When civilizing inhibitions are removed, the bent to destruction in men comes out ever more violently, as those who have participated in wars may testify.

Reformism (and its more lethal companion, revolution) focuses attention upon and sanctions destruction in an area that is particularly rewarding for the release of the bent to destruction. It sanctions an assault upon civilization itself. Every person of any spirit and initiative must have felt the galling burden of customs, of traditions, of rules, of regulations, of the mysterious imperatives of an adult world when he was growing up. Many surely have resented the restrictions that private property represents, the limitations that the rights of others impose upon them, the hardness of the discipline imposed upon them by having to learn the structure of the language, the workings of mathematics, and the lessons of history. Any healthy child surely can think of more exciting things to do than sit in a church or a schoolroom. The young child knows only the order that is exemplified and imposed upon him by adults. This order will seem arbitrary and capricious to him quite often; he would not be equipped to understand it if it were explained to him, and the adults who accept the order often have not thought it out themselves. The child does not even know his own nature, much less that of the universe; instead, he feels his impulses strongly and hardly understands why he cannot follow their promptings.

The resentment of and resistance to the restraints of civilization usually reaches its peak in adolescence when the youth is being pressed into the role of manhood. He must learn to subdue his impulses himself, must undergo the disciplinary rigors of learning to do some job, must prepare himself for the responsibilities that attend being an adult. Ahead of him looms the routine and order into which the lives of men must fall if they are to be effective.

The reformer (or revolutionary, as the case may be) offers a most attractive alternative to this prosaic ordering of one's life. He holds out the prospect of casting off the galling restrictions, leaving behind the authority of the past, having done with that which hampers and restrains the full and free development of personality. He offers a license to the adolescent—and some of the adolescent remains in men—to lash out and destroy the appurtenances of civilization which have so often set unwanted bounds to his activities. More, when he has destroyed the old, he can build a new society in keeping with his wishes. Thus does the reformer conjure up a prospect that appeals both to the delinquent and the constructive in us. There has developed a mental outlook which, when accepted, perpetuates this moment of adolescence throughout life and within which the vision of the reformer appears attainable.

Turgenev Points the Problem

The bent to destruction of reformist intellectuals was pinned down and imaginatively portrayed by Russian novelists in the latter part of the nineteenth century. It is ironic, in view of later developments, that it should have been Russians who saw with such luminous clarity the nature of the ill that was even then becoming epidemic among intellectuals. The bent to destruction reaches its *intellectual* epitome in a nonphilosophy called nihilism. Ivan Turgenev laid bare this particular viewpoint in 1862 in the novel, *Fathers and Children* (also called, sometimes, *Fathers and Sons*). It is a novel of ideas, but it is not simply a novel of ideas. Turgenev tells an engrossing story with characters who come alive on the pages of the novel.

The novelist takes for his theme a universal condition: the differences between the older and younger generations and the conflicts that arise from them. But it is particularized as to time, place, and people. The setting is in the provinces of Russia, and the time is past the mid-point of the nineteenth century. The parents are landlords and would-be liberals of the nineteenth century variety. They would have their sons believe that they believe in and practice the new ways. Both fathers involved are eager to hold on to the affections of their sons, anxious to please them, and cautious about doing or saying anything that might alienate them. Yet they are men of tradition, also; their liberalism has not cut them off from their past. It has only made them uncertain about taking a stand against any change or any new viewpoint.

The sons are home for the summer from college. There are two families involved in the story, the Kirsanovs and Bazarovs. Young Kirsanov has just graduated from college. Bazarov is a young physician who has not yet completed his work at the university. Bazarov is the nihilist, and, when the story begins, Kirsanov is his worshipful disciple. Bazarov is a veritable bull in the delicate china shop of human relations. He proudly proclaims in the presence of the elder Kirsanovs that he is a nihilist, or rather young Kirsanov does for him.

> "A nihilist," said Nikolai Petrovich [Kirsanov, the father]. "That comes from the Latin *nihil, nothing,* as far as I can judge; the word must mean a man who . . . recognizes nothing?"
>
> "Say—who respects nothing," interposed Pavel Petrovich [Kirsanov, an uncle] and lowered his knife with the butter on it.
>
> "Who regards everything from the critical point of view," said Arkady [young Kirsanov].
>
> "Isn't that exactly the same thing?" asked Pavel Petrovich.
>
> "No, it's not the same thing. A nihilist is a person who does not bow down to any authority, who does not accept any principle on faith, however much that principle may be revered."[1]

Bazarov takes up the delineation of his view a little farther on in the story.

> "A decent chemist is twenty times more useful than any poet," interrupted Bazarov.
>
> "Oh, indeed!" remarked Pavel Petrovich. . . . "So you don't acknowledge art?"
>
> "The art of making money or of advertising pills!" cried Bazarov, with a contemptuous laugh.
>
> "Ah, just so; you like joking, I see. So you reject all that. Very well. So you believe in science only?"
>
> "I have already explained to you that I don't believe in anything; and what is science—science in the ab-

---

[1] Ivan Turgenev, *Fathers and Children,* intro. Ernest J. Simmons (New York: Rinehart & Co., 1948), p. 24.

stract? There are sciences, as there are trades and professions, but abstract science just doesn't exist."[2]

Elsewhere, Bazarov explains his position more fully.

"We act by virtue of what we recognize as useful," went on Bazarov. "At present the most useful thing is denial, so we deny—"
"Everything?"
"Everything."
"What? Not only art, poetry . . . but . . . the thought is appalling. . . ."
"Everything," repeated Bazarov with indescribable composure. . . .
"But allow me," began Nikolai Petrovich. "You deny everything, or to put it more precisely, you destroy everything . . . But one must construct, too, you know."
"That is not our business . . . we must first clear the ground."[3]

We learn eventually, however, that nihilism does have a function; it is preparing the way for reform. This time the conversation is between Bazarov and a woman. Bazarov has been maintaining that all people are essentially alike, that significant differences are the product of disease or poor education. He continues:

". . . We know more or less what causes physical ailments; but moral diseases are caused by bad education, by all the rubbish with which people's heads are stuffed from childhood onwards, in short, by the disordered state of society. Reform society, and there will be no diseases. . . ."
"And you suppose," said Anna Sergeyevna, "that when society is reformed there will be no longer any stupid or wicked people?"
"At any rate, in a properly organized society it will

---

[2] *Ibid.*, p. 28.
[3] *Ibid.*, p. 56.

make no difference whether a man is stupid or clever, bad or good."

"Yes, I understand. They will all have the same spleen."

"Exactly, madam."[4]

Bazarov's stance is that of a god. He views all beings as objects. Even human beings are objects to be studied and discerned just as all other objects. The differences between men and frogs are unessential to him. He makes this clear in a conversation with peasants while he is hunting frogs for his experiments.

"What do you want frogs for, sir?" asked one of the boys.

"I'll tell you what for," answered Bazarov . . .; "I shall cut the frog open to see what goes on inside him, and then, as you and I are much the same as frogs except that we walk on legs, I shall learn what is going on inside us as well."[5]

Bazarov makes it clear in other connections that this is to be taken literally. What goes on inside people is either physical or it is of the nature of illusion. Faith is an illusion. Principles are only illusions. Even the sentiment of love is an illusion; it is all a matter of sex, which is all a matter of physiology. It follows from this that human beings are to be studied, manipulated, and made to conform to the correct pattern as are other things. Such are the premises from which melioristic reform (as well as revolution) must proceed. Sociology is the instrument for studying the ills of society and correcting them just as medicine is that for studying the body (though Bazarov does not say so). The god-like stance of Bazarov, the clinical attitude, the lack of emotion, the treating of all beings

---

[4] *Ibid.*, p. 95.
[5] *Ibid.*, p. 21.

as objects, the absence of all values (except for the ultimate one of a reconstructed society), the use of nature in
the existential sense as a model, are the appropriate tools
for the social reformer.

But Bazarov was not a god, any more than other men
are. Arkady Kirsanov assured Bazarov's father that his
son would be a great man some day. Not in medicine, most
likely, but in some broader field where his talents would
have full play. Perhaps in government service, who knows?
None of this was to be. Even before the end, there are
many intimations that Bazarov is only a man, culture
bound and limited, moved by those passions that spring
from the deeper nature of man, living in a universe that
is not fundamentally altered by genius and talent. Although
his ideas would place him above such things, Bazarov
fought a duel with Arkady Kirsanov's uncle. Nor did he
evade the fate of most humans; he fell in love, blindly, ir-
rationally, and passionately. Even in his relations with his
parents, he showed more sensitivity than his ideas would
warrant. To the extent that he falls short of living up to
his ideas he becomes understandable and almost a character with whom we can sympathize.

Bazarov dies at the end of the book. He dies young, even
in that same fateful summer away from the university.
The cause and manner of his death are prosaic enough. He
has assisted a physician in performing an autopsy on a
typhus case. In so doing, he cut himself, and the medical
instruments were filthy enough if they had not been employed on the matter in hand. In consequence, he gets
blood poisoning and dies. There is nothing out of the ordinary in all this. After all, Bazarov was a physician, a
man of medicine, a student, and might be expected to
avail himself of any opportunity to advance his skill. He
had not, as he explains, had an occasion to open up a man

before. Yet all of these details are joined to the main theme and bring it to its appropriate conclusion. There is no civilized act that more aptly demonstrates the treatment of the human body as an object than the performing of an autopsy. There is no more common instance nor better illustration of human weakness than of a man cutting himself with a sharp instrument. The god-like Bazarov had succumbed to this weakness in the very area of his specialization. Nature makes no exceptions even for a Bazarov; germs enter a cut in his flesh and blood poisoning follows its course in him as for other men.

The skill of physicians cannot aid him in the end. He does receive solace in his last waking moments from the one he has loved, for she has come to be with him. The concluding conversation leaves little doubt of the author's point. Bazarov is speaking:

> "Ah, Anna Sergeyevna, let's speak the truth. It's all over with me. I've fallen under the wheel. . . ."
>
> ". . . You see, what a hideous spectacle, a worm, half-crushed, but writhing still. Of course I also thought, I'll break down so many things, I won't die, why should I? There are problems for me to solve, and I'm a giant! And now the only problem of this giant is how to die decently, though that too makes no difference to anyone. . . ."

And, at last,

> "Good-by," he said with sudden force, and his eyes flashed with a parting gleam. "Good-by . . . Listen . . . you know I never kissed you then. . . . Breathe on the dying lamp and let it go out."
>
> Anna Sergeyevna touched his forehead with her lips.
>
> "Enough," he murmured, and fell back on the pillow. "And now . . . darkness. . . ."[6]

The giant had fallen; the god was dead.

---

[6] *Ibid.*, pp. 225-26.

"Crime and Punishment"

Fyodor Dostoevsky, another and more famous Russian novelist, illustrated the destructiveness and futility of the reformer in another way. He probably wrote more novels exploring the psyche of the reformer and revolutionary than has any other writer. But the particular novel to which I would refer is *Crime and Punishment*. The main character of the story is a student (or a former student, for he had dropped out of school) by the name of Raskolnikov. One of the main ideas which the novel explores is the possibility of doing good by first doing evil. (This is surely the central ethical problem for social reformers and revolutionaries, however much it may be obscured by subtleties.) The story, of course, is about a murder and a murderer; the murderer is Raskolnikov.

In the course of the novel, he murders an old woman, a pawnbroker. But before this occurs, while the idea is just taking shape in his mind, he overhears a student and a young officer discussing the justice of the murder of this old woman. They talk about how wealthy she is, how she gives her patrons only a small portion of the value of their articles, and how she sells them for many times what she has paid for them. Not only that but she has a half-sister, a much younger woman, who lives with her and whom she treats like a servant. Not only does the half-sister work for the old pawnbroker but she cooks, washes, sews, and serves as a charwoman for her. The pawnbroker already has made a will; its contents are known to the half-sister, who virtually has been disinherited. The bulk of the woman's wealth is to go to a monastery to pay the monks to pray for her. All of this prompts the student to remark that he "could kill that damned old woman and make off with her money, I assure you, without the faintest conscience-prick."

They then discuss the matter more seriously.

"Listen, I want to ask you a serious question," the student said hotly. "I was joking of course, but look here; on one side we have a stupid, senseless, worthless, spiteful, ailing, horrid old woman, not simply useless but doing actual mischief, who has not an idea what she is living for herself, and who will die in a day or two in any case. . . .

"Well, listen then. On the other side, fresh young lives thrown away for want of help and by thousands, on every side! A hundred thousand good deeds could be done and helped, on that old woman's money which will be buried in a monastery! Hundreds, thousands perhaps, might be set on the right path; dozens of families saved from destitution, from ruin, from vice, from the Lock hospitals—and all with her money. Kill her, take her money and with the help of it devote oneself to the service of humanity and the good of all. What do you think, would not one tiny crime be wiped out by thousands of good deeds? For one life thousands would be saved from corruption and decay. One death, and a hundred lives in exchange—it's simple arithmetic! Besides, what value has the life of that sickly, stupid, ill-natured old woman in the balance of existence! No more than the life of a louse, of a black beetle, less in fact because the old woman is doing harm. She is wearing out the lives ⌐f others. . . ."[7]

The officer agrees that the woman does not deserve to live, but, then, he announces, somewhat ambiguously, that her living is a matter of nature, that, in effect, there is nothing to be done about it. The student will take no such answer. He says,

"Oh, well, brother, but we have to correct and direct nature, and, but for that, we should drown in an ocean of prejudice. . . ."

---

[7] Fyodor Dostoevsky, *Crime and Punishment*, Constance Garnett, trans. (New York: Modern Library, no date), pp. 66-67.

The officer has had enough of abstractions and so he puts the obvious question:

> "You are talking and speechifying away, but tell me, would you kill the old woman *yourself*?"
> "Of course not! I was only arguing the justice of it. . . ."[8]

The student is the perfect example of the reformist intellectual. He would not personally steal and kill; he would not use terror and violence to effect his ends. But if it were done, he could see the justice of it.

Raskolnikov, who had listened to this talk with mounting excitement, lacked the intellectual's schizophrenic capacity to objectify a situation in such a way as to make evil appear good and then to deny that it is good and proper when applied to the private and personal level. Raskolnikov was on the verge of insanity, if not actually insane, but his was the insanity of subjectivism. The student was talking about what has come to be called social justice. His was that particular moral obtuseness, endemic in our era, that cannot or will not see that the moral character of an action is unaltered by raising it from an individual to a collective level. Raskolnikov, on the other hand, has the medically detectable variety of insanity; he has drawn so deeply within himself that the question posed can only be personal and individual. The student proposes that individual morality does not apply to social questions. Raskolnikov places himself outside morality, beyond good and evil, as Nietzsche phrased this position. The officer dismisses the question with the sane and common sense observation, "But I think, if you would not do it yourself, there's no justice about it." There is, in short, no essential difference between murder done by an individual acting

---

[8] *Ibid.,* p. 67.

on his own and murder done in the name of society. From this point of view, Raskolnikov's case becomes a test case for the social question as well as the individual one.

Raskolnikov does not commit murder for some great social end. It is not quite clear why he does it. He is in straitened circumstances; he long since has ceased paying his rent; he eats only occasionally; he has dropped out of school. His sister, as he sees it, is about to sacrifice herself for him by marrying a man who is well off. He could use the money that might be obtained by robbing the old pawnbroker.

At any rate, he does the deed, not a nice, hygienic, technologically proficient murder, but done in the most horrid manner imaginable, botched as might be expected of an amateur. The author spares the reader none of the gory details. If they attended to details, he thinks, there is no He attempts to rob her, but while he is about the task the half-sister, Lizavetta, comes in, and he kills her, too, by splitting her head. He gets away with a few trinkets of little value, and these he does not use.

Raskolnikov has imagined that he will commit the perfect murder. He knows, as any reader of detective stories knows, that murderers are trapped by not attending to details. If they attended to details, he thinks, there is no reason why they should not get away with murder. He theorizes that they do not attend to these matters properly because their reason is eclipsed at the time they commit the crime. But Raskolnikov is committing no crime, or so he thinks. Therefore, he can be in full possession of his faculties.

It is not neglected details, however, that bring Raskolnikov to the bar of justice. He is agitated and careless enough. Probably Sherlock Holmes would have had more than enough trivia to solve the crime. But the policeman who finally gets Raskolnikov is no Sherlock Holmes. He is a student of the human heart and psyche. He knows that the penalties for crime are not just something artificially contrived by society, that man has within his nature a need to pay these penalties. The criminal has by his act cut himself off from his humanity, from humanity, and from God. He cannot rest, at least Raskolnikov cannot, until he has confessed, repented, made retribution, and found atonement. Raskolnikov had committed a *crime*. He came to know that, and as he did he came to know the rightness of *punishment* also. No man is beyond good and evil; his very humanity is to be found in a life bounded by these poles. If he were continuing the story, the author says at the end, it would be "the story of the gradual renewal of a man, the story of his gradual regeneration, of his passing from one world into another, of his initiation into a new unknown life." It would, we gather, be the story of a man living in the consciousness of morality.

There is further interpretation to be made of this story, however. We are led to believe that we are dealing not only with the question of whether crime pays for an individual but whether it pays for larger social units. Of course, Dostoevsky might have put in the conversation between the student and the officer only as a piece of motivation for the actions of his main character. Had this been the only novel ever written by Dostoevsky, such an explanation might be acceptable. The conversation did motivate Raskolnikov. But Dostoevsky wrote other novels. We can know from some of them, at least, that the casuistry of reformist intellectuals was one of his main themes and a great concern of his work. It is much more plausible, then, as I have suggested, that Raskolnikov's story was a test case for the social question.

There seems to be a major flaw in the story, however, if

it is to be taken as a test case. The student had suggested that it would be a justified action to kill the old woman. But Lizavetta was portrayed as the innocent victim of the pawnbroker's grasping meanness. It was her treatment of Lizavetta as much as or more than anything else that made her unworthy to live. Yet Raskolnikov killed the half-sister as well as the old woman. This act is plausible enough if we are dealing only with a murder by a man. If such a murder actually had taken place, it would have been quite possible for the innocent sister to have walked in and been slain also.

But in the novel, Dostoevsky seems to have altered the happenings so much that they can no longer be applicable to the social question. The student had proposed no justification for killing Lizavetta. She was one of those who would, at least in theory, be aided by the murder. Why did not Dostoevsky so tell his story that it could be interpreted in such a way as to answer the social question?

My point is that he did. However he arrived at the conclusion, the author must have felt or known that the sister had to be killed also. The student had set forth only half of his proposition. He only held that the killing of the old pawnbroker could be justified. But the interior logic of his position leads to a question which few social reformers and revolutionaries have been willing to face, for when they do the inherent despotism of their position is revealed: namely, could the killing of those who are supposed to be helped be justified?

The Remaking of Man

Let us examine the inherent logic of the position of the social reconstructionist. The student in the novel said that nature must be changed and directed. This is the necessary position of both the meliorist and revolutionary. Taking men as they are and the situation as it is, the reforms cannot be made. Men must be remade; conditions must be changed. Choice must be taken away from men, for this leads to the conditions that are deplored, even to the existence of pawnbrokers. The initiative must be taken away from men. They must be deprived of their powers to do good and evil. The social planner must plan and direct things so that men will behave in the desired way to produce the desired ends. In brief, men as we know them must be destroyed; they must be deprived of their humanity. Men must be treated as objects or things, to be manipulated at the will of the planner. In a word, and speaking figuratively now, they must be killed.

The reformer no more divests men of their humanity, however, than Raskolnikov effectively robbed the old pawnbroker. He does cut himself off from his own humanity. By treating men as things, he wounds himself deeply. Reformist intellectuals have dreamed, above all, of ending their own alienation, of building a world in which they would be at home. Yet their approach to this by way of social reconstruction only increases the alienation, whether they are aware of it or not.

The prophetic warnings of the Russian novelists were not heeded. Much of history since their time has been the coming to pass of the consequences of ideas which they foresaw. Their beloved Russia has been a principal theater for such a blood bath. The point is that the reformists have a twofold impact: the old way must be destroyed—that is one; and the other is that even when they attempt to build, they destroy instead.

Destruction need not be so obvious as it has been in communist lands. It need not be as open as the starvings and killings in the Russian and Chinese revolutions. It need not be so blatant as the firing squads of Castro's Cuba.

It is not even necessary that the destruction be so clear-cut as the destruction of crops and animals during the New Deal. Indeed, the gradualist approach to socialism followed in the United States, and in some countries of Europe, is largely distinguished by the subtle manner in which its destruction is wrought: by the piecemeal undermining of incentives, by the gradual removal of the acquired learning of the race from education, by the step-by-step usurpation of property rights, by the partial reversal of the teachings of traditional religion, by the slow but sure deactivation of society, and so on. The attempts to build a new order are equally destructive, for they are carried out by an aggressive use of force which can only be destructive. The destruction is of competition, of private initiative, of the inherited certainties, of the security of the currency, and of liberty.

Only by .Love

Before quitting this theme, there is something else to be learned from the Russians. Neither Dostoevsky nor Turgenev wrote of reformers and revolutionaries simply to hold them up to scorn or to turn them into objects of hatred. They are men, too, not things, as we can learn from the pages of the novels. The Song of the Lorelei leads men to their destruction, but those most completely destroyed are the reformers themselves. Their great need is to be reclaimed for and take their place within humanity once more. And that can be done, if at all, only by love. Turgenev pointed the way in the heart-rending final passage of *Fathers and Children*. Bazarov's old parents loved him dearly and could not forget him.

> Often from the near-by village two frail old people come to visit it [the tomb of Bazarov]—a husband and a wife. Supporting one another, they walk with heavy

steps; they go up to the iron railing, fall on their knees and weep long and bitterly, and gaze intently at the silent stone under which their son lies buried; they exchange a few words, wipe away the dust from the stone or tidy up some branches of a fir tree, then start to pray again and cannot tear themselves away from that place where they seem to be nearer to their son, to their memories of him. . . . Can it be that their prayers and their tears are fruitless? Can it be that love, sacred devoted love, is not all powerful? Oh, no! However passionate, sinful or rebellious the heart hidden in the tomb, the flowers growing over it peep at us serenely with their innocent eyes; they tell us not only of eternal peace, of that great peace of "indifferent" nature; they tell us also of eternal reconciliation and of life without end.[9]

There is a final clue for us in this poignant description of parental love. Though the author does not point it out, the ultimate flaw in the reformist position is that it stems from a defect of love. The defect lies in the inability of the reformer to accept and love fallen man, and to stand in awe before a cross-grained universe wherein he may be redeemed.

There is a peculiarity of parental love. Most of us have noted it at one time or another. It is that extra love and devotion which parents frequently give to a child that is defective in some way, mental or physical. It is as if they would make up for the flaw, which somehow they suspect stems from them, by an outpouring of devotion over the years. By so doing, they come as close as man can do to revealing the kind of love which God has for flawed man.

The reformers may indeed be concerned, but they cannot truly love in the way that they try—that is their defect. They cannot love man as he is. They cannot accept the

---

[9] Turgenev, *op. cit.*, pp. 232-33.

universe for what it is. They would replace the Creation of God with human invention; they would change all things to conform with their wishes. But love does not require the transformation of its object; instead, it offers itself in sacrifice to make up for the defect in the loved one. The flight from reality ultimately is the result of mistaking the wish to assert one's will over man and the universe for concern, of confusing pride with love. Efforts springing from this confusion destroy. In reality, love transfigures the lover, and the loved one is accepted as he is, being changed only insofar as the power of attractive example will have that result. Concern must be subjected to the purifying fire of love before it can be constructively expressed. Only then does constructive effort replace destructive.

Index

537

Government (Cont.)
  majority and minority, 415, 431
  money supply, 23, 494, 502, 510
  monopoly, 105, 318, 377, 381, 386, 390
  nationalism, 198
  nature of, 49
  planning, 104, 249, 310, 335, 345, 453, 532
  power, 11, 136, 240, 329, 342, 485, 489
  privileges, 229, 326
  reconstruction, 480
  republican, 198, 222, 238, 413, 459, 493
  role of, 241, 270, 308
  socialistic. *See* Socialism
  sovereignty, 341
  spending, 367
  statism, 502
  subsidies, 311, 321, 327, 343, 362
  taxation, 243, 352, 365, 386
  totalitarian, 5, 89
  welfare program, 338
Gradualism, 202, 397, 482
Great Depression, 310
Great society, 205, 450, 462, 479
Groves, Ernest R., 281

Hamilton, Alexander, 207, 412n, 418, 509, 511
Hanna, Marcus A., 456
Harding, Harold F., 180n
Harriman, Averell, 466
Harrington, James, 76
Harris, Seymour E., 385
Hayek, Friedrich von, 502
Hegel, G. W. F., 70, 145, 280, 301, 475
Heller, Walter, 370, 467
Henry, Patrick, 219
Henry, Robert S., 327, 328n
Heraclitus, 39, 70
Herder, Johann Gottfried, 145
Herron, George D., 263, 267, 271, 273

Hertzler, Joyce C., 73n, 77n, 87n
Historicism, 145
History
  deactivation of, 133-52
  guide for, 146
  ideology in, 297, 395, 463, 468
  "liberal," 458n
  mythology and, 297, 479, 515
  personification, 162
  reforms and, 148, 206
  tool for change, 155
  writing, 306
Holmes, Oliver Wendell, Jr., 155
Hoover, Herbert, 309, 346
Hopkins, Charles H., 264n
Hopkins, Harry, 466
Hospitals, 87
House, Edward M., 465, 466
Hoving, Walter, 364, 371n
Howe, Frederick C., 250n
Howells, William D., 102
Hughes, Charles E., 443, 444
Hughes, H. Stuart, 153
Human nature, 49, 54, 66, 106, 110, 258, 473
Humanitarianism, 26, 176
Hume, David, 55, 56, 68, 134
Hunter, Robert, 319
Hyneman, Charles S., 433n, 441n, 444n

Ideology, 297-330, 395, 463, 468
Illusions, democratic, 214-33, 473
Images and myths, 303
Imagination, 68
Income, 315, 486
Individualism, 98, 110, 307, 408
Industrial Revolution, 266, 315
Industrialism
  control of, 366
  disaster of, 266, 315
  inequalities in, 254